"The wonderful gastronomical in equal measure. Selections from Brillat-Savarin, Alexandre Dumas (père) and an especially welcome translation from the pioneering journalism of Grimod de la Reynière represent the French. But the big surprise lies across the Channel. Denise Gigante makes a truly original contribution with her promotion of English gastronomers such as Launcelot Sturgeon, Dick Humelbergius Secundus, and The Alderman (all pseudonyms), Charles Lamb and Thackeray. Successors to the French, the English gastronomers come into their own as descendants of the Enlightenment writers on taste. The perceptive introduction to the anthology with its connections to literary and philosophical concerns, the useful presentation and thorough notes to each selection, the contemporary illustrations—and of the course the delicious texts themselves—make *Gusto* a succulent feast for twenty-first century diners and readers alike."

—**Priscilla Parkhurst Ferguson**, author of *Accounting for Taste*

"Informative and witty, these essays demonstrate the application of science, philosophy, and medicine to the developing culture of gastronomy. Denise Gigante has assembled the writings of the founders of modern ideas about eating, taste, and manners, framing robust selections with illuminating and authoritative scholarship."

—**Carolyn Korsmeyer**, author of *Making Sense of Taste*

GUSTO

ESSENTIAL WRITINGS IN
NINETEENTH-CENTURY GASTRONOMY

Edited and with an introduction by

Denise Gigante

With a Foreword by Harold Bloom

Routledge
Taylor & Francis Group
New York   London

Published in 2005 by
Routledge
Taylor & Francis Group
711 Third Avenue
New York, NY 10017

Published in Great Britain by
Routledge
Taylor & Francis Group
2 Park Square
Milton Park, Abingdon
Oxon OX14 4RN

International Standard Book Number-10: 0-415-97092-X (Hardcover) 0-415-97093-8 (Softcover)
International Standard Book Number-13: 978-0-415-97092-1 (Hardcover) 978-0-415-97093-8 (Softcover)
Library of Congress Card Number 2005006001

Library of Congress Cataloging-in-Publication Data

Gusto : essential writings in nineteenth-century gastronomy / edited with an introduction by Denise
 Gigante ; with translations of Grimod de la Reynière's Almanach des Gourmands and Manuel
 des Amphitryons by Michael Garval.
  p. cm.
 ISBN 0-415-97092-X (hardback : alk. paper) --- ISBN 0-415-97093-8 (pbk. : alk. paper)
 1. Gastronomy-History--19th century. 2. Cookery, French-History--19th century. 3. Cookery,
 English-History--19th century. I. Gigante, Denise, 1965- II. Garval, Michael D., 1963- Manuel des
 Amphitryons.

TX637.G85 2005
641'.01'3--dc22   2005006001

Taylor & Francis Group
is the Academic Division of T&F Informa plc.

Visit the Taylor & Francis Web site at
http://www.taylorandfrancis.com

and the Routledge Web site at
http://www.routledge-ny.com

For my parents

Contents

Illustrations

Acknowledgments

Many thanks to Mike Garval, whose work on Alexandre Grimod de la Reynière originally inspired this anthology and whose translations included here will provide many hours of delectation.

The Stanford University Libraries were both generous and helpful. I am particularly grateful to Sarah Sussman, Curator of the French and Italian Collections, John Mustain and Polly Armstrong in Special Collections, and Mary-Louise Munill in the Department of Interlibrary Loan. In addition, I thank the Stanford Humanities Center, the Department of English and School of Humanities and Sciences at Stanford for financial support.

Several research assistants, especially Jenny Kim, Elizabeth Ridgeway, and Devon Sherman, but also Amalia McGibbon, Yvonne Toepfer, Johanna Winant, and Jesse Zuba made the anthology possible, and a number of readers, including Carolyn and George Collier, Erik Gray, Christine Guth, and Christopher Rovee offered helpful comments on the manuscript. I also wish to acknowledge useful discussions of the material by the members of the North American Society for the Study of Romanticism who participated in my gastronomy workshop in Colorado in 2004, the English graduate students at the University of California at Irvine, the Food Studies Seminar at the University of California at Davis, and the 2003–04 fellows and staff of the Stanford Humanities Center.

Finally, thanks are due to Harold Bloom, for kindly offering to contribute a foreword to this volume, and to Bill Germano at Routledge, who saw the whole thing from a loose collection of ingredients to a more seasoned production with intelligence and flair.

Foreword

HAROLD BLOOM

Gusto in art is power or passion defining any object.— It is not so difficult to explain this term in what relates to expression (of which it may be said to be the highest degree) as in what relates to things without expression, to the natural appearances of objects, as mere colour or form. In one sense, however, there is hardly any object entirely devoid of expression, without some character of power belonging to it, some precise association with pleasure or pain: and it is in giving this truth of character from the truth of feeling, whether in the highest or the lowest degree, but always in the highest degree of which the subject is capable, that gusto consists.

William Hazlitt in his "On Gusto" (*The Examiner*, May 26, 1816) is concerned with defining his favorite critical term in regard to Titian and Shakespeare, and not to gastronomy. Denise Gigante in her marvelous *Taste: A Literary History* (New Haven and London, 2005) brings together aesthetics and appetite by employing gusto as a metaphor for taste, in Hazlitt's wake.

"Gusto" once meant any strong preference, for anything or anyone, but in general usage it tends now to mean any enthusiastic enjoyment performed with zest: speaking, playing, eating and drinking, or whatever. Gigante wisely wishes to restore the word to its High Romantic eminence, perhaps best represented by the celebration of the human senses and the human seasons in the poetry of John Keats.

My own favorite Romantic poet remains Shelley, who sustained himself on uncooked fruits and vegetables, distilled water, and recurrent love affairs not altogether Platonic. Shelley's one deviation from vegetarianism came in the autumn of 1815, when the twenty-three year old lyrical genius composed

Alastor, or the Spirit of Solitude, his first truly great poem. He wrote fearing imminent death from tuberculosis (which in fact he did not have) and recovered his health from being fed a momentary diet of "well-peppered mutton chops" by his genial friend, the comic novelist Thomas Love Peacock. The ex-pirate Trelawny, who worshipped Shelley and rather disliked Byron (with whom he went off to fight for the freedom of Greece), tells us that the noble lord went beyond their mutual friend Shelley in matters gustatory:

> He would exist on biscuits and soda-water for days together, then, to allay the eternal hunger gnawing at his vitals, he would make up a horrid mess of cold potatoes, rice, fish, or greens, deluged in vinegar, and gobble it up like a famished dog. On either of these unsavory dishes, with a biscuit and a glass or two of Rhine wine, he cared not how sour, he called feasting sumptuously. Upon my observing he might as well have fresh fish and vegetables, instead of stale, he laughed and answered:
>
> "I have an advantage over you, I have no palate; one thing is as good as another to me."
>
> The pangs of hunger which travellers and shipwrecked mariners have described were nothing to what he suffered; their privations were temporary, his were for life, and more unendurable, as he was in the midst of abundance.

Gigante's *Gusto* makes the leap from Romantics poetical to Romantics pragmatic, from Shelley and Byron to Grimod and Brillat-Savarin. This vaulting from the Sublime to the stomach is subtly seasoned by the presences in *Gusto* of Charles Lamb, William Makepeace Thackeray, and Alexandre Dumas. They assure that this anthology mixes the gastronomic with the literary.

It fascinates me that Gigante verges upon creating a new genre in *Gusto*: call it the Romanticism of the restaurant-bookstores, which increasingly surrounds us. Here again, William Hazlitt is her critical precursor. In his beautiful essay, "On Going A Journey," he celebrates the creative solitude of the road:

> In general, a good thing spoils out-of-door prospects: it should be reserved for Table-talk. L[amb] is for this reason, I take it, the worst company in the world out of doors; because he is the best within. I grant, there is one subject on which it is pleasant to talk on a journey; and that is, what one shall have for supper when we get to our inn at night. The open air improves this sort of conversation or friendly altercation, by setting a keener edge on appetite. Every mile of the road heightens the flavour of the viands we expect at the end of it. How fine it is to enter some old town, walled and turreted, just at approach of night-

fall, or to come to some straggling village, with the lights streaming through the surrounding gloom; and then, after inquiring for the best entertainment that the place affords, to "take one's ease at one's inn"! These eventful moments in our lives' history are too precious, too full of solid, heart-felt happiness to be frittered and dribbled away in imperfect sympathy. I would have them all to myself, and drink them to the last drop: they will do to talk of or to write about afterwards. What a delicate speculation it is, after drinking whole goblets of tea—

"The cups that cheer, but not inebriate," and letting the fumes ascend into the brain, to sit considering what we shall have for supper—eggs and a rasher, a rabbit smothered in onions, or an excellent veal-cutlet! Sancho in such a situation once fixed upon cow-heel; and his choice, though he could not help it, is not to be disparaged. Then, in the intervals of pictured scenery and Shandean contemplation, to catch the preparation and the stir in the kitchen [getting ready for the gentleman in the parlour].

The innocence of this mingling of reading and eating is antithetical to the negative aspect of combining literature and gastronomy, the gusto of cannibalism, which seems to demand a comic totality, from Ovid to Evelyn Waugh. Gigante is splendid on the Miltonic trope of "mortal taste," and there are excellent books on the subject by Maggie Kilgour and Claude Rawson. The cannibal feast in Byron's *Don Juan* is commended by Gigante for its "utter tastefulness." One thinks of W. S. Gilbert's "The Yarn of the Nancy Bell" and Thackeray's "The Three Sailors" as only a touch less Swiftean than Byron. But as I sample the delights of Gigante's anthology, some of which border upon sado-masochism (as she knows), I find myself wishing that Grimod and Brillat-Savarin could have read Mark Twain's sketch, "Cannibalism in the Cars," where we are told of some two dozen travelers stranded by heavy snows when their St. Louis to Chicago train breaks down in December, 1853. They are nowhere, and after a week's starvation they elect some of their number for breakfast, lunch, and dinner. Only a few other moments in American literature are as delicious as the remembrances of Twain's narrator after ending a week's hunger:

> "We improvised tables by propping up the backs of car-seats, and sat down with hearts full of gratitude to the finest supper that had blessed our vision for seven torturing days. How changed we were from what we had been a few short hours before! Hopeless, sad-eyed misery, hunger, feverish anxiety, desperation, then—thankfulness, serenity, joy too deep for utterance now. That I know was the cheeriest hour of my eventful life. The wind howled, and blew the snow wildly about our prison-house, but they were powerless to distress us any more. I liked

Harris. He might have been better done, perhaps, but I am free to say that no man ever agreed with me better than Harris, or afforded me so large a degree of satisfaction. Messick was very well, though rather high-flavored, but for genuine nutritiousness and delicacy of fiber, give me Harris. Messick had his good points—I will not attempt to deny it, nor do I wish to do it—but he was no more fitted for breakfast than a mummy would be, sir—not a bit. Lean?—why, bless me!—and tough? Ah, he was very tough! You could not imagine it—you could never imagine anything like it."

That is gusto, at its most exuberant. I think Mark Twain would have been honored to be quoted at the conclusion of a Foreword to Gigante's essential anthology.

Introduction

DENISE GIGANTE

It formerly was considered well-bred to affect a certain indifference for the fare before you; but fashion has acquired more candour; and there is now no road to the reputation of a man of ton, so sure as that of descanting learnedly on the composition of every dish.

—Launcelot Sturgeon[1]

Today, we tend to associate gastronomy with a popular food culture that expresses its standards and principles by way of gourmet magazines and journalism. But the first gastronomers of modern Europe considered themselves to be doing more than catering to consumerism through restaurant reviews and other periodical writing about food. Modern gastronomy developed as an expansion of the eighteenth-century discourse of aesthetic taste, a cultural field opening onto the material pleasures of appetite. As such, it offered a radical rethinking of the fundamental condition necessary for aesthetic experience, namely the disinterested attitude. As the British gastronomer Launcelot Sturgeon suggests above, by the nineteenth century, to show an indifference toward food was no longer the best way to distinguish oneself as a person of taste. The idea of aesthetic disinterestedness (a condition of personal objectivity from which to practice the aesthetic art of judgment, or a knowing discrimination among the arts) gave way at this time to a new imperative to show *interest* in all matters gastronomical. The French connoisseur Jean-Anthelme Brillat-Savarin claimed that a lack of interest in food was evidence not of aesthetic disinterestedness, but of "culpable indifference."[2] This book represents the literary genre of gastronomy as it announced itself at the turn of the nineteenth century: a serious philosophical effort, expressed in a lively tongue-in-cheek manner, to define a new cultural arena for the practice of aesthetics—one with a substantial moral and epistemological component.

The transformation in taste that took place in Britain and France at this time can be traced in the main to the events of the French Revolution. These had dramatic effects, not only on existing political structures but on the social codes governing conviviality. The most elite chefs and pastry cooks, trained in the luxurious kitchens of the French aristocracy, found themselves suddenly dispossessed once the nobility fled France for their lives (or lost them on the scaffold). Released from the private into the public sphere, these talented culinary professionals helped foster a new and complex world of discretionary dining in the form of the restaurant. Unlike previous eating establishments, such as the early modern table d'hôte or the English inn, where groups would gather for a meal prepared in advance by a host, the restaurant provided diners with a chance to express their individual tastes by choosing from an assortment of dishes presented on the menu. Originally a term meaning slender or small, the *menu* made its appearance in the first French restaurants as a work that was daunting, even epic, in scope. Diners suddenly found themselves challenged to demonstrate their culinary literacy and savoir faire before all the *haute ton* of Europe.

By disseminating upper-class cuisine and etiquette to an enlarged, bour-geois clientele, gastronomers in part helped to maintain the elitist social codes of the ancien régime. Yet, the very publication of these taste rules performed a democratizing function, giving the nouveaux riches access to a previously exclusive sphere of cultural distinction and the cultural tools necessary to distinguish themselves within it. Gastronomers stressed, time and again, that the art of good living (*bonne chère*) could not be bought. It had to be earned through painstaking study and experience. One needed to be able to afford the meal, to be sure, but restaurants enabled more people to dine in a manner they could never have done in their own homes. With this increased consumer power, came the social responsibility to comprehend, and express oneself eloquently upon, the pleasures of the table.

As the public exercise of taste became literalized in this way, social hier-archies became more subtle and unspoken, stratifying the growing band of financially empowered consumers through the performance of gastronomical expertise. The culinary capital of the world at this time was Paris, but as large numbers of professional French chefs emigrated to London, establishing new spaces for discretionary dining in taverns, clubs, and hotels, its influ-ence spread. Taste professionals in the two cosmopolitan hubs of Europe, postrevolutionary Paris and early Regency London, transformed the very concept of aesthetic taste from a disinterested appreciation for the fine arts to a set of material practices for consumers seeking cultural distinction.

Gastronomers guided this transition through a new literary genre of writing about food, formerly the poor cousin of the arts.

Like its best practitioners, gastronomy was generically omnivorous, swallowing a wide variety of literary forms into itself. One finds, for example, gourmand maxims and reflections, gourmand meditations, gourmand geographies and travel narratives, fictional and nonfictional epistolary exchange between epicures, as well as poems, dialogues, satires, and parables on the gastronomical model. Together, though little known today, they comprise a distinct genre that is witty and eclectic, but with the philosophical prowess to treat food as a matter for serious thought and analysis. This anthology brings together for the first time the major gastronomical writers of nineteenth-century Britain and France. It includes representative selections of the two founding fathers of French gastronomy, Alexandre Balthazar Laurent Grimod de la Reynière and Jean-Anthelme Brillat-Savarin, along with their British successors, including William Kitchiner, Launcelot Sturgeon, and Dick Humelbergius Secundus. The book you are holding therefore is not just another food history, etiquette manual, recipe book, or metropolitan restaurant guide (although these modes are vitally implicated too). Instead it makes available the most vibrant and theoretically resonant writings on the arts and pleasures of the table from nineteenth-century Britain and France. Assembled in this manner, and augmented with copious biographical and bibliographical notes, they reveal much about the original culture and theory of modern gastronomy.

Premier Service: The Gastronomic Philosopher

The Enlightenment obsession with the concept of taste was the motivation behind the first forms of gastronomical writing in French and English. The so-called Man of Taste was a "rational epicure," no mere unthinking eater or glutton driven by physical compulsion. Whereas choice played no role for the traditional glutton, unable or unwilling to reason upon his alimentary intake, the early nineteenth-century gourmand was a "sagacious *Gourmand*" whose very sagacity was founded on the etymological connotations of taste as knowing (*sapere*, taste in Latin, means knowing).[3] "However extravagant, and whimsical the rational pleasures of the table may appear to a sober and sensible mind," wrote one gastronome in 1821, "we must, in justice to epicures, cursorily observe, that there exists a material difference between a *gourmand*, or epicure, and a *glutton*."[4] So too, the Latin gastronomical poem, *Tabella Cibaria; The Bill of Fare* (1820) by Ange Denis Macquin, is careful to explain that whereas the glutton shamefully "lays aside nearly all that relates to the rational pleasure of creating or stimulating an appetite by the excellent quality of the cates [provisions], and looks merely to quantity," the gourmand "seeks for peculiar delicacy and distinct flavour in the various dishes presented to the judgment and enjoyment of his discerning palate."[5] Just as the eighteenth-century Man of Taste had sought to distinguish nicely between different qualities of beauty, gastronomers emphasized empirical exactitude and objective discernment in parsing the different flavors of food.

While in ancient times Plato had metaphorically tied the stomach down in the lower body as an unruly beast, modern gastronomers considered it a vital participant in aesthetic activity. For if cookery were to come into its own as a legitimate member of the arts, an audience needed to be trained in the capacity to appreciate this culinary artistry. The nineteenth-century Man of Taste worked hard to refine his appetite as well as his palate, to maintain them always on the edge of provocation, alert to surrounding possibilities for "rational pleasure." Infusing the classical trio of the beautiful, the true, and the good with new gusto, Romantic gastronomers thus involved appetite in aesthetics.[6] In fact, they identified three separate categories of appetite: a basic hunger for food, a desire aroused by the presentation of an appetizing dish, and an appetite stimulated by all the arts of cookery when our hunger has already been satisfied.[7] The first class of appetite (raw hunger) was of little interest to aesthetic taste theorists or to gastronomers. The second was relevant insofar as it involved the pleasures of the imagination in sensory experience.[8] Principally, however, gastronomers were concerned with the third, artificial or cultivated type of appetite, at the furthest remove from need. This allegedly required the greatest sensibility and promised the most lively play of the senses in relation to the mind.

Taken seriously as an object of taste, food, like other objects of art promised an occasion for judgment and the exercise of the higher mental faculties. Grimod de la Reynière thus spoke of syrups "considérés philosophiquement," just as his British successor Launcelot Sturgeon wrote "On Mustard, Philosophically Considered."[9] Stressing the importance of mental application on the part of the consumer, Grimod redefines the gourmand for the nineteenth-century, postrevolutionary era as follows:

> The gourmand is not only he who eats with profundity, that is, with reflection and sensuality; he who never leaves anything behind on his plate nor in his glass; he who never afflicts his host (Amphitryon) with a refusal, nor his neighbor by an excess of sobriety: rather, he should join to the most hearty appetite that jovial humor without which most festivals are nothing but a sad hecatomb; always ready with repartee he should keep up a continual activity of the senses which nature has given him; finally, his memory should be replete with anecdotes, amusing stories and histories, which he should deliver in the interval between courses, and in the interstices of the meal, so that even the most sedate and sober participants will pardon his appetite.[10]

This definition contributes to the idea of the Romantic gourmand as a revitalized Man of Taste, self-consciously seeking the mental pleasures of the imagination with physical gusto. According to Grimod, the gourmand "eats with profundity, that is, with reflection and sensibility," activities both essential to the aesthetic art of judgment. Turning food over in one's mouth as an object of appreciation and analysis, however, does not preclude corporeal pleasure. The gastronomer is no glutton, but he leaves nothing behind on his plate or in his glass, and he "never afflicts his host with a refusal, nor his neighbor with an excess of sobriety." Despite the emphasis on wine connoisseurship in gourmet circles today, wine and other spirituous liquors came second to food in nineteenth-century gastronomy. Intoxication was thought to dull the sensibility and lessen the capacity to exercise discernment. Gourmands therefore heeded the maxim that a man who knows how to live well eats and drinks little at table ("Un homme qui sait vivre mange peu et boit peu à sa table").[11] The gourmand must labor to "keep up a continual activity of the senses which nature has given him," preserving his appetite for dinner, the most important event of the day. Modern gastronomy rises or falls by moderation, and all writers in this tradition insist on temperance as a key to good taste.

Crucial to the gastronomer's stance as postrevolutionary Man of Taste was his capacity for eloquent self-expression. One needed not merely to grasp the rational principles upon which one's pleasure was based, but to discourse gracefully upon them. This gastronomical imperative for self-expression spilled over from the Enlightenment arena of belletristic, philosophical disputation into the more everyday art of table talk, a complementary activity to gastronomy. One of the most gifted table talkers of eighteenth-century England was Dr. Samuel Johnson, whose thoughts on eating have been handed down to posterity by his friend James Boswell. Boswell furiously scribbled down the well-turned phrases of Dr. Johnson, whom he portrays as a gastronomer *avant le lettre*, discoursing on the affairs of the stomach as if they were an urgent philosophical matter ("stomachical metaphysics," as one nineteenth-century gastronomer put it).[12] "Some people," declared Johnson in an oft repeated flourish, "have a foolish way of not minding, or pretending not to mind, what they eat. For my part, I mind my belly very studiously, and very carefully; for I look upon it, that he who does not mind his belly will hardly mind anything else."[13]

Johnson preferred dining out to dining at home, where there was bound to be some repetition in the dishes served harmful to that lively activity of the senses which Grimod identifies as a precondition for *gourmandise*. "I," Johnson bragged, "who live at a variety of good tables, am a much better judge of cookery, than any person who has a very tolerable cook, but lives much at home; for his palate is gradually adapted to the taste of his cook; whereas... in trying by a wider range, I can more exquisitely judge."[14] Boswell informs us that Johnson would look down on invitations to dinners that might have been fit for consumption, but not for the mental reflection necessary for gastronomical appreciation of the meal. Above all, Johnson preferred the tavern, where he could choose food adapted to his taste and express his pleasure or displeasure at will. He believed that it was possible to reason intelligently about the pleasures of eating, and perhaps, had he not exhausted himself with compiling the first dictionary of the English language, he might have written "a better book of cookery than has ever yet been written." According to him, "it should be a book upon philosophical principles."[15]

The typically eighteenth-century concern with "philosophical principles" so prevalent in gastronomical writing of the postrevolutionary era traces back to the most knotty point in Enlightenment taste theory: the fact that individual taste, while subjective, must be regulated by certain universal laws. As the philosopher Edmund Burke remarked in 1759, "if Taste has no fixed principles, if the imagination is not affected according to some invariable and certain laws...it must be judged an useless, if not an absurd undertaking, to lay down rules for caprice, and to set up for a legislator of whims and fancies."[16] Similarly, if one aspired to the "rational enjoyment" that modern gastronomers were after it was necessary to discipline one's palate according to principles. Without principles to guide pleasure, the age-old maxim that there can be no disputing about taste (*de gustibus non est disputandum*) must hold, cutting off the possibility for rational deliberation. The Romantic essayist Charles Lamb, taking up this call to discern the "philosophical principles" of food, announced his desire to seek a "rationale of sauces, or theory of mixed flavours" in order to understand, for instance, "why the French bean sympathizes with the flesh of deer" or why loin of pork "abhorreth" butter.[17] His playful use of the eighteenth-century discourses of taste and sympathy characterizes gastronomical writing in both French and English.

A genre in which not only the combination of ingredients, but the social combination of guests, or *convives,* and the arrangement and sequence of courses all provided matter for philosophical disputation, however, posed a radical challenge to the age-old hierarchy of the arts, based on that of the senses. Joseph Addison, a founding father of Enlightenment aesthetics, may have compared the literary critic to a tea connoisseur in his 1711 *Spectator* essay "On Taste," but he was principally concerned with the mental appreciation of beauty.[18] Poetry, music, painting, and the plastic arts were all experienced through the "higher" cognitive senses of sight and hearing, and neither he nor his contemporaries would have taken seriously, as matter for discussion, those pleasures perceived through the "lower" physical senses of taste and smell. By contrast, gastronomers sought to elevate to philosophical respectability the visceral region of the mouth, that "crimson chamber, where sits the discriminating judge, the human tongue."[19] For these writers, the "lower" senses of taste and smell *could* be subject to the same regulating principles of consciousness and morality as other, more supposedly reflective sensations.

Despite the reasoning of Aristotle, who held that pleasure was not the purpose of art and that the products of the cook could have nothing to do with the more lofty affairs of aesthetic judgment, cuisine became a legitimate category of the arts in the Romantic period, if not an epicenter and source of epistemological inquiry. Straddling the arts and the sciences (chemistry and physiology, among others), modern aesthetics, founded on the concept of taste, entailed pleasure right from the start. From the Romantic Carême's elaborate architectural patisseries, to the enormous sculpted pâtés by the celebrated restaurateurs, the brothers Véry, the kitchen became (in the words of one British gastronomer in 1814) the "source of all the arts."[20] Eugène Briffault points out in *Paris à Table* (1846) that to make a good dessert, one must be not only a good confectioner, but a talented decorator, painter, architect, sculptor, and florist as well.[21] Far from considering the cook a mechanic, Grimod de la Reynière and his fellow gourmands compared the leading chefs of their day to Raphael, Michelangelo, and Rubens.[22] Echoing this triumvirate, the Victorian food historian Abraham Hayward would classify culinary artistry into the Classic and the Romantic schools, headed by Antonin Beauvilliers and Antonin Carême, respectively.[23]

To gulp one's food without deliberating its merits was now to disqualify oneself from the standard of taste. As the British gastronomer William Kitchiner put it, "The sagacious *Gourmand* is ever mindful of his motto—'Masticate, Denticate, Chump, Grind, and Swallow.'"[24] Kitchiner himself claims to have tested all the recipes in his best-selling cookbook, *The Cook's Oracle*, on a "COMMITTEE OF TASTE (composed of thorough-bred *Grands Gourmands* of the first magnitude)." This committee "during their arduous progress of proving the respective Recipes," he assures us, "were so truly philosophically and disinterestedly regardless of the wear and tear of teeth and stomach, that their Labour—appeared a Pleasure to them."[25] Kitchiner was also a physician, and he calculated with admirable precision the number of bites per minute that it would take to achieve the greatest pleasure in consuming different foods. "From 30 to 40 (according to the tenderness of the meat) has been calculated as the mean number of Munches, that solid meat requires, to prepare it for its journey down *the Red Lane*," he instructs us, though "less will be sufficient for tender, delicate, and easily digestible white meats." The gastronomical quest to comprehend the most minute principles of pleasure amounted to an epistemology with the rigor of science. The "sagacious *Gourmand*" would of course prefer his own experiments "and not waste his precious moments in useless Jaw-work, or invite an Indigestion by neglecting *Mastication*."[26] With an emphasis on objectivity, scientific principles, and procedure, gastronomy legitimized not only the cook, but the consumer as a modern Man of Taste.

Kitchiner's "Committee of Taste" was based on the French model of Grimod de la Reynière's famous Jury des Dégustateurs, which deliberated in bureaucratic fashion the respective merits of the best culinary products in Paris. Because the judgments of the Tasting Jury could not be ascribed to any single individual, they laid a claim to objectivity and universality, asking to be taken as the aesthetic standard of a group of ideal critics: the fantasy of Enlightenment taste theory come true. In his 1759 essay on taste, the Enlightenment philosopher David Hume identified five qualities of the ideal critic that would allow him to contribute his vote to the "joint verdict" of the standard of taste: "Strong sense, united to delicate sentiment, improved by practice, perfected by comparison, and cleared of all prejudice."[27] For the Romantic gourmand, these translate into (1) "a capacious stomach"; (2) "an insatiate appetite"; (3) "a delicate susceptibility in the organs of degustation, which enables him to appreciate the true relish of each ingredient in the most compound ragoût, and to detect the slightest aberration of the cook; added to" (4) "a profound acquaintance with the rules of art in all the most approved schools of cookery," and (5) "an enlightened judgment on their several merits, matured by long and sedulous experience."[28] Here, the standard of taste becomes embodied in the gourmands of the tasting jury. The stomach serves as partner to the palate, and it is "the happy combination of both these enviable qualities that constitutes that truly estimable character, the real epicure."[29]

The frontispiece to the third year of Grimod de la Reynière's *Almanach des gourmands* (1806) depicts a grand session of his Tasting Jury, *Séance d'un jury des gourmands dégustateurs* (fig. 1).[30] In this image eight gastronomical "professors" occupy themselves with different taste objects (labeled *légitimations*) that have been submitted for accreditation and honorable mention in the *Almanach*. Just as physicians in the eighteenth century were designated "Faculty," and booksellers "the Trade," counselors of law formed the "Profession" from which these gourmands take their cue.[31] Grimod points out in his discussion of this image (see appendix B) the profound reflection legible in their faces that characterizes all gourmands in the exercise of their functions. At a separate table from the jury sits a scribe, who takes down the verbal deliberations leading up to each judgment of taste. This record is then transmitted to the Secretary, who reads from it at the head of the table, until the President finally gives voice to the collective. What we witness here for the first time in the cultural history of taste is the subjection of those most seemingly subjective pleasures (chemical sensations registered by the tongue) to the same rigorous, deliberative procedures as aesthetic judgments of taste, with their insistence on universal principles.

3ème Année.

Séance d'un Jury de Gourmands dégustateurs.

Dunant del.   Grimod de la Reynière inv.   Maradan sculp.

Figure 1 *A Jury of Gourmand Tasters in Session (Séance d'un Jury de Gourmands dégustateurs)*, from Grimod de la Reynière, *Gourmand's Almanac* (Vol. 3, 1806). See Appendix B, p. 284.

For the premier gourmands of Grimod's Tasting Jury, "the result of the changes of *gourmandise* is much more important to the happiness of man in society than that of social, administrative, or judiciary changes."[32] This Jury was modeled on his luncheon clubs of the 1780s, which had been devoted to the discussion of literature and drama.[33] It included delegates from different social spheres, among them lawyers, actresses (as unvoting sister members), and men of letters united in the quest for critical consensus. The jury's weekly sessions (séances) were modeled on official state sessions and commonly lasted four to five hours, testifying to the mental application necessary to the task of gustatory discernment. As the bureaucratic apparatus of government was adapted to aesthetics in this way, the diligent records of taste experiments performed by seasoned gourmands formed the stuff of gastronomical almanacs, periodicals, and treatises. And because the titles the tasting jury bestowed seemed to have little relation to those earned in other realms, it offered a convenient fiction for a powerful cultural élite, pointing the way toward the best commercial purveyors of taste.[34]

Second Service: The Culture of Gastronomy

The birth of the restaurant as a public scene of discretionary dining after the French Revolution was a distinct phenomenon from the coffeehouse culture that had shaped the intellectual life of Enlightenment Europe. The cafés, which first opened in Paris in the 1670s and in London by the end of the 1680s, had attracted wits, scribblers, and politicians, who mingled with members of the growing bourgeoisie (financiers, bankers, lawyers) over stimulating cups of coffee.[35] Exchanging information and conversation, they contributed to the formation of what the historian Jürgen Habermas has called the bourgeois public sphere, a spoken and written forum of public discourse that we now associate with the media.[36] The central difference between the Enlightenment café or coffeehouse and the restaurant, which became popular roughly a century later, is that the former venue did not feature food as its primary concern. While refreshments or pastries could be served in cafés, and even more substantial victuals in some of the English coffeehouses, food was not an item to draw attention, much less appreciation. As topics of conversation, politics and art were privileged, though this all changed once the restaurant, spurred by talented French chefs, encouraged the arts of gastronomy. With the more abstract mental appreciation of beauty brought down to the material pleasures of the table, more consumers found themselves seeking cultural distinction through their palates.

The restaurant also differed from the English inn or French table d'hôte, which had served as public eating places from medieval times. Although the inn was more of an alimentary institution than the coffeehouse, providing hospitality to those staying on its premises, it did not offer a variable menu to suit individual taste. At the inn as at the table d'hôte, the meal was generally served at a common table, and the bill of fare was little more than a list of the dishes served along with their cost.[37] Such meals were not discriminatory affairs, and the diner was not there principally for the sake of the food. Those who were, treated it more as a necessity than an objet d'art. Similarly, the French table d'hôte, which existed in London from the late sixteenth century, provided a catered dinner at a fixed time of day.[38] The price of the meal was prefixed, suited to a regular clientele made up mainly of workers from the neighborhood and locals who came for the company. The cook-caterers (or *traiteurs*) who ran these public eateries in prerevolutionary France and in England served the meal as a communal affair, employing large serving dishes from which diners helped themselves. As a result, those nearest the food had the advantage, and quantity was privileged over quality, the pleasures of a satiated belly prevailing over the refinements of a sensitive palate.[39]

Perhaps closest in approximation to the revolutionary French restaurant were the taverns of later eighteenth-century London. Under the Restoration rule of Charles II, every tavern had had its own table d'hôte and this had gradually become a place for men to gather, order a meal, and drink wine rather than beer (served at alehouses or pubs). Johnson, as mentioned above, praised the tavern as a place where he could pay for his meal, relax, and think of his own pleasure, criticizing the food when necessary.[40] Cooks at the leading London taverns by the end of the century took special pride in their food, and like the finest chefs employed by the court, often published their recipes in books. English taverns served French dishes along with more traditional British fare, and to boost their clientele and reputation they often employed French chefs. From a similar but opposite perspective, Antoine Beauvilliers, who opened the first French restaurant to great acclaim in Paris in 1782 (alternately 1786, the precise date is unclear), named it "La Grande Taverne de Londres." Despite the loose association between restaurants and taverns, the former were far more ambitious in their culinary ambitions and often dizzying in the range of dishes they featured on their menus. They were also more aesthetically attuned to the accompanying pleasures of the table, from décor to the quality of service.

Whereas the word tavern derives from the Latin *taberna* (a public shop or shack constructed from wooden boards), the term restaurant has its origins in food. Originally a soup or broth, the *restaurant* (restorative) was distilled from choice meats, fresh vegetables, and other healthy ingredients. Most nineteenth-century gastronomers were familiar with the story of the French boulanger Champ d'Oiseaux, which in 1756 offered these "restaurants" under a sign in Latin proclaiming: "Venite ad me, omnes qui stomacho laboratis, et ego vos restaurabo" (Come to me all ye whose stomach "labors," and I will restore you). Rebecca Spang has shown how these delicate broths, constituting the first restaurant food, intersected with the eighteenth-century cult of sensibility, which privileged an ideal of delicacy, both of body and of mind, in her excellent book, *The Invention of the Restaurant*. A delicate taste was a central aspect of this fashion. Sensibility in this manner enabled the restaurant to emerge as the thinking man's tavern—and potentially the woman's too, insofar as women found it acceptable to dine in these new Parisian establishments.[41] Unlike other forms of public eateries, the early restaurants catered to individual preference by introducing the novelty of separate tables within a single dining space. Personal taste and the public performance of choice operated together under a general standard of taste established by the chef. Accordingly , the restaurant gave physical form to the tension between private choice and universal standards that had marked eighteenth-century aesthetics. Respecting the cultural ideals of taste and sensibility, this new institution allowed intellectual, reflective pleasure to retain ideological precedence over bodily enjoyment.

While some scholars of late have wanted to downplay the influence of the French Revolution on the rise of the restaurant on the grounds that the trend began earlier, there is little doubt that in its modern manifestation the restaurant is a result of revolution. Once the political events of the 1790s released the most talented chefs from aristocratic patronage into the open market of Paris, they set up as restaurateurs in abandoned hotels or in the arcade of the Palais Royale. With the French aristocrats having escaped to other cities in Europe, they found themselves catering to a new bourgeois clientele, the nouveaux riches. The restaurateur Beauvilliers, for example, prior to opening the Grande Taverne de Londres, had been pastry chef to the Count of Provence and to the corpulent younger brother to Louis XVI, afterward Louis XVIII. In addition, the revolution attracted large numbers of provincial deputies to Paris who took their meals in these new public spaces.[42] Brillat-Savarin, a provincial lawyer from the town of Belley, joined their ranks and wrote his best-selling *Physiologie du goût* (1826) as a record of his gastronomical experiences. Soon, with professionally trained chefs putting the best products of their artistry on the open market, the restaurant rose to heights of sophistication.

Briffault remarked in 1846 that whereas in the seventeenth and eighteenth centuries France had been known for its literature, in the nineteenth century it was known for its cuisine.[43] As French food and dining practices spread into Britain and America, they gave traditional cookery new verve. The most influential British cookbooks of the eighteenth century had been written by women, who emphasized domesticity and economy, but their professional male counterparts, the chefs and *cordon-bleus* of France, did not let themselves be regulated by cost. Hannah Glasse's *The Art of Cookery Made Plain and Easy* (1747), a leading English cookbook, reveals its cultural bias in its economical approach to both food and language directed against what was perceived as French frippery. Mrs. Glasse (whom several contemporaries, including Dr. Johnson, assumed to be one Dr. John Hill) prided herself on her solid common sense, ostentatiously refusing to write "in the high, polite stile" and scolding English readers for their French pretensions: "one might have a genteel entertainment for the price of the sauce one dish comes to. But if gentleman will have *French* cooks, they must pay for *French* tricks.... So much is the blind folly of this age, that they would rather be imposed on by a *French* booby, than give encouragement to a good *English* cook!"[44] What Glasse denounced in the eighteenth century as luxury and extravagance would become the rage by the 1830s in Britain. By 1890, there were more than five thousand French chefs employed in London, leading the fine arts of cookery.[45]

The glory years of restaurant dining in Paris peaked between 1815 and 1830, when menus expanded like the novel to grandiose dimensions. Foreign travelers to France were often overwhelmed by the culinary variety offered in restaurants. They found that it was not enough simply to enter the privileged space of a grand dining room: once inside, the diner had to perform *savoir-vivre*, or to behave in the manner of a food connoisseur with an experiential body of knowledge about gustatory taste practice. Although the British war with France from 1793 had made trade and travel problematic, immediately following Napoleon's defeat at Waterloo in 1815 gastronomy took off in Britain.[46] To qualify as a person of taste, one now needed to know what dishes were best put together, in which order, and which wines and desserts should accompany them. This was often no easy task, and new taste professionals inspired by Grimod de la Reynière and his fellow gourmands emerged to instruct the public in the art of *bonne chère*.

In the preface to the first volume of his *Almanach des gourmands* (1803), Grimod acknowledged gastronomy to be a mode of bourgeois consumerism:

In a necessary follow-up to the Revolution, a turn-about put fortunes into new hands and the mind of all these *nouveaux riches* turned especially toward purely animal pleasures. It was believed that they would be rendered service by being offered a reliable guide to the most solid part of their dearest pleasures. The heart of most wealthy Parisians had suddenly been transformed into a gullet; their emotions are nothing more than sensations, and their desires, appetites. They are properly served by being given in several pages, in the guise of good food, the means of getting the best for their appetites and money.[47]

As the rebel son of aristocratic parents, Grimod expresses nostalgia for a world in which the arts flourished and belles lettres were taken seriously by persons of power. But by their very nature, his restaurant reviews and other gastronomical writings participated in a democratization of taste by publicizing the codes of good living. Along with his more forward-looking, bourgeois follower Brillat-Savarin, he instructed the socially mobile how to ape aristocratic tastes, while simultaneously disseminating knowledge that would undermine the formerly exclusive status of that taste. The restaurant represented a new order in which the poor could be on a par with the rich, so long as they could pay the bill (*carte à payer* or *l'addition*). Seated at a leading restaurant, with aesthetic pleasure apportioned in the form of the meal, anyone could demand the treatment of a prince.

The English Prince Regent, George Augustus Frederick of Hanover, later George IV, scored his own coup after Waterloo by hiring Carême, head of the Romantic school of cookery. By January of 1817, Carême was preparing hundred-dish dinners for the Prince and his guests at Brighton, transforming the royal summer seat into an international resort and introducing the nation to cutting-edge French cuisine. The "King's Kitchen" at the Brighton Pavilion rapidly became the most technologically advanced kitchen in Europe, at a cost of £6,000 on trimmings alone. Its elaborate confectionery consisted of three separate rooms devoted to the preparation of desserts, plus an additional two for the construction of pastries. From the ice of the adjacent ice room, drawn from a detached icehouse, a steady flow of sorbets and ice cream passed through the alimentary architecture of the prince's pleasure palace to his own ever-ready palate. France thus sparked a culinary revolution in Britain, where new institutions, including dining clubs and restaurants, emerged to meet the lifestyle and tastes of the rising middle classes.[48] George himself joined the exclusive "Sublime Society of Beef-steaks," which like virtually every other dining club in England boasted a French chef.

Once the Parisian high style of dining swept over London, the British middle classes abandoned the pub. The pub resembled the tavern insofar as its primary commercial function was not board but provisions, though it served beer rather than wine. The more exclusive gentlemen's clubs took its place, for as Amy Trubek explains, "as the social personas of the non-aristocratic residents of London became increasingly differentiated, there was something insufficient about the open milieu of the coffeehouse"—or pub or tavern.[49] With more people seeking social distinction through food, the very language of dining turned French. In his 1877 *Book of the Table*, Eneas Sweetland Dallas condemned "the ignorant importation of French names" that many had come to equate with "that peculiar condition known as Acquired taste."[50] While early in the nineteenth century, only a few homes and private clubs in London could afford to serve French haute cuisine, by midcentury it was assumed that to acquire taste was to acquire French eating habits. French restaurateurs for their part considered themselves missionaries of civilization, spreading ideals of cultured taste and acquired appetite beyond the borders of France. And because every art has its critic, they were assisted in this project by gastronomical litterateurs.

One turn-of-the-century Englishman, recollecting his travels through France in the years 1802 to 1805, remarked that Grimod's *Almanach des gourmands* "embraces one branch of luxury, but a branch particularly cultivated by the new rich; whose cellars and larders are far better replenished than their libraries. This taste has become so general, that many booksellers have become *traiteurs*, and find the corporeal food far more profitable than the mental."[51] Despite its bid for aesthetic autonomy, the gastronomical devotion to its "one branch of luxury" was always implicated in other currents of thought and activity (economic, political, and cultural). Restaurants provided effective spaces for individual and group interventions into political life, and one reason given for the development of the restaurant in the first place was the urban influx of undomiciled legislators who needed to take their meals in public spaces.

Napoleon, at the height of his empire, was no gastronome, but he recognized the power of the table as an engine of state. He would frequently send diplomats and dignitaries to dine with his arch-chancellor Jean-Jacques Cambacérès (1753–1824), dismissing them from state affairs with the auspicious, "Go and dine with Cambacérès."[52] Cambacérès for a while employed Carême as his chef, and he was regularly accompanied at his table by the Marquis d'Aigrefeuille, reputedly the most gifted gourmet of the era. An anecdote circulates about a certain Genevan trout served by Cambacérès, which cost the Imperial Cour de Comptes 300 francs, suggesting the degree to which Napoleon would go to avoid all "vexatious economy in matters pertaining to his chancellor's table."[53] For this shrewd politician, cuisine was an instrument of state, and by this means, as Jean-Robert Pitte observes, "French *haute cuisine* remained very tied to the exercise of political power, just as it had under the *ancien régime*."[54]

In addition to the sumptuous table of Cambacérès, Napoleon profited from the exquisite taste of his Minister of Foreign Affairs, Charles-Maurice de Talleyrand-Périgord (1754–1838). Carême singles Talleyrand out from his many prestigious employers (including Cambacérès, the English Prince Regent, Czar Alexander I, and the English émigré Baron de Rothschild) as the gourmand for whom he had the most esteem.[55] Talleyrand held a daily conference with his chief officers of the kitchen. At this meeting the assembled artists of his staff would submit their culinary proposals for the evening's meal.[56] Often this involved exquisite taste tests, with Talleyrand sampling particular ingredients and sauces, conferring on their merits, and pronouncing his final judgment. All provinces of France were tributaries to this important event of Prince Talleyrand's busy day. After these weighty deliberations, he would return to the affairs of government, having cleansed his palate with bread and water—and so, it would seem, his mind for further intellection.

The arts and pleasures of the table had always involved a political dimension as a social force of community, but nineteenth-century gastronomers literalized this tradition. Grimod considered it "the linchpin of political, literary, financial, and commercial matters," observing that "Promotions, academic successes, business dealings, negotiations all take place at the dining table, or at least get started there."[57] Grimod's British imitator, Dick Humelbergius Secundus, observed similarly in 1834 "that the table is the only chain which connects every branch of society."[58] Gastronomy, as a cultural-material expansion of the philosophy of taste, takes into account this aspect of commensality: it reveals the social nature of the *sensus communis*, or aesthetic community united through shared ideals of pleasure. Enlightenment taste theorists had been concerned with rational deliberation regarding matters of beauty, though they were content to leave individuals to their private gustatory taste preferences. Gastronomers, by contrast, applied the same imperative for social consensus to food as an artistic medium.

Of course, juries of taste were supposed to involve "free choice" on the part of consumers unable to imagine that their desire could be compelled. Based on the Civil Code established in France in 1804, Grimod proposed in the fifth volume of his *Almanach des gourmands* (1807) that an analogous "Code of gourmand etiquette would be a necessary work of equality; but who would be charged with drawing it up, and above all executing it on a day to day basis? The Gourmand Empire is a completely voluntary republic in which coercion is banished and persuasion governs."[59] Aesthetic taste could not be forced, but it could be "cultured" or trained, as experts continue to argue today. As the new taste professionals of nineteenth-century Europe, gastronomers helped to transform the urban topography of France and Britain into a matrix of flavors predicated on cosmopolitanism and burgeoning consumer capitalism. They provided a way of discussing the politics of culture and the culture surrounding politics at a time when political tensions were high, paranoia rife, and ideas of social change dangerous.

Dessert: Gastronomy as a Literary Genre

As the founding text of *littérature gourmande*, Grimod de la Reynière's *Almanach des gourmands* was modeled on the *Almanach royal*, published in Paris during the eighteenth century to provide information about bureaucrats and other state officials. Spang has shown how "the first restaurateurs were venal office holders deeply implicated in the growth of urban commercialism" and demonstrates how this consumer almanac of late eighteenth-century France figured into the circulation, communication, and commerce that fueled the rise of the restaurant.[60] Compared to the French entrepreneur, Mathurin Roze de Chantoiseau, who produced an *Almanach général* in 1769 (a version of the *Almanach royal* for the commercial sector), Grimod focused far more intensely on the literary nature of his project to shape the taste of the nation. Romantic gastronomical literature was encyclopedic in its impulse to assemble a wide range of generic models into a delightful "dinner of fragments."[61] This included not only the typical writerly modes of gastronomy—food histories and etymologies, recipes, menus, restaurant reviews, guides to table etiquette—but other "nutritive varieties," such as gastronomical travel narratives, gourmand aphorisms, philosophical meditations, dramatic sketches, dialogues, dedications, calendars, charades, geographies, reveries, logogriphes (puns), and poetical enigmas.

The first gastronomical essay of note in English, *The School for Good Living* (1814), refers to Grimod de la Reynière's *Almanach* as a way to judge "the merit and legitimacy of every piece destined to appear on the alimentary stage. There, the patents of preference are granted, the stars of culinary honor distributed."[62] In this language one can hear echoes of the dramatic review, with which Grimod began his literary career, developing the restaurant review and food journalism more generally upon it.[63] Grimod also had a flair for the dramatic, staging elaborate dining spectacles at his parents' hotel on the Champs Elysée with the help of Marie Antoinette's acting instructor and emphasizing performativity in all aspects of the meal. "All the world of London sighs for the establishment of a similar tribunal," sighed the anonymous author of *The School for Good Living*, and merely three years later, Kitchiner responded with his "'COMMITTEE OF TASTE' (composed of thoroughbred GRANDS GOURMANDS of the first magnitude)."[64] Kitchiner's work appeared to great acclaim in London in 1817, comparing favorably in popularity (as contemporaries noticed) to the works of literary celebrities like Sir Walter Scott and Lord Byron.

Along with other English Romantic writers, gastronomers considered it their duty to instruct the nation in matters of taste—no small affair if one believed (with William Wordsworth) that "the taste, intellectual Power, and morals of a Country are inseparably linked in mutual dependence."[65] In 1807 Wordsworth expressed his view, shared with Coleridge, "that every great and original writer, in proportion as he is great or original, must create the taste by which he is to be relished."[66] At first glance, it might seem incongruous to consider the gastronomical effort to culture public taste alongside that of more overtly literary ventures. Wordsworth complained in his 1800 Preface to *Lyrical Ballads* of those who confuse gustatory and aesthetic taste and "converse with us gravely about a taste for poetry, as they express it, as if it were a thing as indifferent as a taste for rope-dancing, or Frontiniac or Sherry."[67] The analogy to food or drink could only go so far in eighteenth-century taste theory, and Coleridge would add in a verbal tirade without punctuation, and with a good deal of irony, in 1819: "One man may say I delight in Milton and Shakespeare more than Turtle or Venison another man that is not my case for myself I think a good dish of turtle and a good bottle of port afterwards give me much more delight than I receive from Milton and Shakespeare you must not dispute about tastes."[68] But by this time the fine arts had begun to make space for culinary artistry, and gastronomers *would* argue that gustatory taste also entails cognition.

Just as the Romantic poets sought to descend from the airy castles of eighteenth-century poetic diction and find pleasure in the everyday, gastronomers sought to throw the veil of imagination over lived reality, revitalizing it with artistry and sensibility. The difference is that while it may have been acceptable for poets to discover beauty and sublimity in the minute particulars of nature, the idea of imbuing *food* with these qualities would have struck many English readers as frivolous. From a certain British point of view, the project of identifying the philosophical principles of food was bound up in a French preference for sensuality and luxury. French chefs would boast their ability to distill fifty hams into a single, thimble-sized quintessence, which to a British consumer would look less like skill than waste. Further, the French penchant for fricassees and other culinary embellishments such as sauce, the foundational element of French haute cuisine, appeared merely to mask the true nature of the food . Throughout the eighteenth century, the English had prided themselves on their common sense as a nation of beef-eating, plain speakers with no patience for foreign (particularly French) ostentation.[69] But the literary genre of gastronomy, perhaps recognizing from its very origins this potential for critical rebuff, evolved its own satiric, self-mocking style.

To assume the stance of a gastronomical "professor" descanting learnedly on the pleasures of the table, with sensibility and intellectual acuity, was a slippery means to evade the would-be critic. In his flamboyant performativity, the early nineteenth-century gourmand can be seen as the spiritual twin of the flâneur, or as he was known in England and America, the dandy.[70] The gourmand treated food as a weighty topic for philosophical debate, and the "traditional dandy," as Regina Gagnier writes, "was the first to make dress and fashion the basis of a philosophy, of the only philosophy, in fact, that was consistent with modern, materialist life."[71] Broadly defined, dandies were "opposed to business pursuits or habits, ostentatiously even refusing to wear a watch, and spurning all domestic burdens," as the social historians Leonore Davidoff and Catherine Hall explain, "the antithesis of domesticated masculinity dedicated to business."[72] Gastronomers resembled dandies as countercultural philosophers insofar as they lived to eat, rather than eating to live (in the ascetic manner of Socrates). Whereas bourgeois morality mandated that we eat to gather our energies for work (no matter what kind), gourmands reversed this traditional formula to assert, in the spirit of dandies, that we must work for our own pleasure. Unlike earlier eighteenth-century forms of eating that were coded feminine (in the manner, for example, of Hannah Glasse), nineteenth-century gastronomy was a male-gendered aesthetic and the culinary dandy a distinctly male (if not masculine) figure: a gastronomically revamped Man of Taste. Their writings worked in many ways against the feminized aesthetic of the novel, founded on ideals of bourgeois domesticity.

What was at stake, in both gastronomy and dandyism then, was aestheticism. At a time when the vital energies of society were becoming more explicitly economic in nature, gastronomers (like dandies) insisted on the continuing value of remaining alive to sensation. As Walter Pater would write in 1873, "To burn always with this hard, gem-like flame, to maintain this ecstasy, is success in life."[73] But the paradox, particularly in the cosmopolitan centers of Britain and France, is that as taste became increasingly identified with the materialist sphere of consumerism in its affiliation with food and fashion, "aesthetics" as such was constructed apart from, or even in opposition to, the commercial sphere. Popularizing the aesthetic art of judgment at the same time as they clung nostalgically to its elitist ideals, nineteenth-century gastronomers were perhaps inevitably self-ironizing in tone.

This is not the road gastronomy *had* to take, but it was the road taken by Romantic gastronomers who had their palates educated in the Century of Taste. Their approach differed radically from that of classical gastronomy, which had favored extravagance (as exhibited by imperial Roman banquets with single dishes made from hundreds of peacock brains). Yet, even as they abandoned the ancients as exemplars of taste, they continued to look to the classics for textual authority. Gastronomical writing of the nineteenth century manifested a distinctly antiquarian penchant for lists, extracts, arcana, and anecdotes cobbled together from diverse sources. This genealogical tendency is evident in its erudite histories of the "art of cookery," dating as far back as the first Greek cook of any reputation, Cadmus. The pseudonymous Dick Humelbergius Secundus, self-styled after the sixteenth-century annotator of the Roman cook Apicius, devotes at least half of his *Apician Morsels* (1829) to the cuisine and dining practices of the ancients.

Gastronomy, marked by its obsession with erudition and etymology, is itself a linguistic derivation of the Greek term (γαστηρ) for stomach. Fine distinctions pervaded the compounded language of the genre, as one can see in the following terms defined in a glossary for English readers:

Gastrology	The Science of Eating
Gastronomy	Precepts for Eating
Gastrophilism	The Love of Eating
Gastrophililist	One Who Loves Eating
Gastropolitechnical	The Various Arts for the Gratification of the Belly
Gastrophilanthropic	The Benevolent Purveyor for the Belly of Others.[74]

For the gastronomical writer, as for his readers, the belly is a linguistic epicenter, just as the kitchen is "the prolific fountain whose savoury streams have watered the tree of knowledge, and fed it to luxuriant growth."[75] The characteristically anonymous author of this 1814 text does "not presume to offer to the scholar etymologies or explanations, which to him would be superfluous," assuming a readership not only conversant with the classics but also sympathetically predisposed to an antiquarian, anti-capitalist idiom.

With the novel rapidly becoming the most consumable art form of the nineteenth century, suited to a commercial age in more ways than I can discuss here, antiquarian artistry clung to outmoded objects and forms of expression. This mode included, among others, Scottish border ballads, philosophical reflections, and a certain breed of nationalist tale intersecting with the historical novel. Ian Duncan describes this stylistic approach as "a reaction-formation of the economic modernization of literary production in Great Britain."[76] With their antiquarian passion for authenticating apparatuses and documentary devices, gastronomical texts positioned themselves (somewhat paradoxically) outside mainstream culture. Romantic antiquarians of all stripes were drawn to this precapitalist ideal of culture in which local particularity, myth, and poetry still held sway over the nascent commercial form of the novel. Viewed from this perspective, gastronomers displayed an unexpected affinity with contemporary poets as defenders of the arts and artistry, increasingly defined as aestheticist in the consuming world of nineteenth-century Europe.

Against a "natural" sensibility that would cry out in defense of animals subjected to torture for the sake of human pleasure, gastronomers cultivated a sensibility focused on those same cruelties.[77] Whereas Charles Lamb, in the persona of his "judicious epicure" Elia, debates the benefits of whipping pigs to death in order to tenderize their flesh, his brother John Lamb, a barrister, conformed to the tone of the age in a political pamphlet deploring animal abuse from the perspective of an eel who indignantly objects to the cook who would "stick a fork into his eye, skin him alive, coil him up in a skewer, head and all, so that in the extremest agony he could not move, and forthwith broil him to death."[78] One story preserved in nineteenth-century gastronomical literature recounts how the French chef Louis Eustache Ude, who worked for such illustrious employers as Louis XVI and George IV, was forced to defend his recipe for "matelotte of eels" ("take one or two live eels. Throw them into the fire. As they are twisting about on all sides, lay hold of them with a towel in your hand, and skin them from head to tail…as it is the means of drawing out the oil, which is unpalatable") to an outraged audience.[79] In a note to the seventh edition of *The French Cook* (1822; first pub. 1813), Ude claims that his culinary methods are "entirely devoted to the gratification of [his patrons'] taste, and the preservation of their health," insisting that it is his moral "duty to attend to what is essential to both."[80] In *The Art of Dining* (1835), Hayward praised this emotionally offended chef, asserting that the true gastronome must be "as insensible to suffering as a conqueror."[81] In fact, he argued, Ude might have gone further "and urged not merely that the eel was used to skinning, but gloried in it" and that it would exalt and honor him to practice "the same noble spirit of endurance that has been attributed to the goose" (who gives his liver, abnormally expanded through a process of torture, to the famous foie gras of Strasbourg).[82]

Grimod exhibits a similar sadistic tendency in his writing, disguised as acute sensibility. For Grimod, whose hands had been deformed since birth, the knife was a physical extension of the body and the most beautiful embellishment of the chef: "Le couteau est l'arm du cuisinier, le plus bel ornement de sa personne."[83] In a playful commentary, which Hayward cites, he writes of the martyred Strasbourg goose:

> Crammed with food, deprived of drink, and fixed near a great fire, before which it is nailed by its feet upon a plank, this goose passes, it must be owned, an uncomfortable life. The torment would indeed be altogether intolerable if the idea of the lot which awaits him did not serve as a consolation. But this perspective makes him endure his sufferings with courage; and when he reflects that his liver, bigger than himself, larded with truffles, and clothed in a scientific *pâté*, will, through the instrumentality of M. Corcellet, diffuse all over Europe the glory of his name, he resigns himself to his destiny, and suffers not a tear to flow.

While the sympathetic Man of Feeling would find the plight of this goose insufferable, the gastronomer takes pleasure in such descriptive detail. Evidence of this same aesthetic, which relishes suffering as an appetizing event, extends past Grimod (and his contemporary the Marquis de Sade) to British gastronomy of the 1820s, including Lamb's famous essay on "Roast Pig": "Behold him, while he is doing—it seemeth rather a refreshing warmth, than a scorching heat, that he is so passive to.…To see the extreme sensibility of that tender age, he hath wept out his pretty eyes—radiant jellies—shooting stars."[84] To the Romantic gourmand, the jellies pouring from the young pig's eyes are "radiant" as opposed to vile, a long way from distasteful. Middle-class ideals of moderation and refinement may have upstaged aristocratic excess, but in nineteenth-century gastronomical literature, the concept of "moderation" was far from signifying that avoidance of extremes, or abatement of rigor, synonymous with bourgeois complacency.

Like dandyism, gastronomy entailed a certain a resistance to that self-control and relentless quest after spiritual objectives that had marked eighteenth-century aesthetics. As Stephen Mennell writes, gastronomy shows "a preoccupation with bringing order into the old and reprehensible disorder and superfluity, and a sense of the correct and incorrect, the delicate and the vulgar in the serving of dishes," but the gastronomical code of politeness reinvents the idea of correctness.[85] Whereas traditional conduct books dictated that one "picks not the best, but rather takes the worst out of the Dish, and gets of every thing, unless it be forced upon him, always the most indifferent Share," gastronomers would caution, "let not a mistaken notion of politeness induce you to part with all the choice bits before you help yourself." [86] For true gourmands, such reticence shows a "culpable indifference."

Accordingly, gourmands encouraged punctuality less for the sake of civility than for the sake of the food. Culinary artistry demands precision timing, and while guests were expected to wait patiently for the cook, the cook was never to wait for the guests. Such a precept completely reverses the traditional order of priority governing hierarchical codes of conduct whereby the cook is the anonymous servant of the host. Rather than something to be dispensed with before dining out, gastronomers stressed the value of appetite, the importance of maintaining and pampering, rather than denying, it. Among gourmands, therefore, "instead of the common-place salutation of 'how d'ye do?' the first question should be, 'have you a good appetite to-day?'"[87] The mid-nineteenth shift century from *service à la française* (in which dishes are presented together in a formal, symmetrical arrangement on the table over three courses) to *service à la russe* (in which dishes follow one another in succession) accentuates this newfound respect for the epicure's appetite and ability to "do justice" to a good meal (a phrase much beloved by Dickens). In a changed attitude toward *gourmandise*, meals came to include sorbets or other palate cleansers in the intervals of the service, augmenting the effect of each dish as an individual taste object. Together such practices highlighted the culinary artistry of the chef, now no longer a mere anonymous servant but a professional of some social standing and cultural status.

Gastronomy also challenged existing cultural codes by favoring food over females as aesthetic objects of commodification and consumption. While traditionally polite behavior, as portrayed often in fictional romance, would have the male diner privilege the woman next to him over the food before him, gastronomy mandated that "every one's attention should be entirely given up to what is *on* the table, and not to what *surrounds it*—ladies should not expect particular notice until the dessert is served."[88] If this suggests a lack of gallantry, it is also suggests a textual aesthetic devoted to flavorful, episodic transitions. Unlike the novelistic marriage plot, which drives straight through dinner parties and social gatherings on its way to its romantic telos, weaving courses and conversation into its overarching narrative, the gastronomical text is by nature picaresque, focused on alimentary sequence.

More than mere miscellanies, however, gastronomical writings are anthologistic in the manner that Seth Lerer describes as "volumes guided by a critical intelligence." If the anthologistic impulse is a distinguishing feature of literature made prior to commercial technologies of production, as Lerer argues, gastronomical anthologies also transcend those "largely haphazard or practical assemblies of material" that we can identify as miscellanies."[89] William Hazlitt's conception of modern books as "made-dishes," scrapped together from leftover fare in his 1821 essay "On Reading Old Books," is particularly suited to the genre of Romantic gastronomy as a feast of *rifaccimentos* (leftovers).[90] The typical British gastronomer recognized himself as a "gatherer of other people's stuff—a collector of shreds and patches!" as Humelbergius writes; putting together his dinner of fragments, he demands, "whose are the ingredients, whose the art that deceives the palate and pleases the eye? They are not his own—they nevertheless swallow well, and better than if they had been of his pure invention."[91]

If it is true (as suggested above) that the antiquarian nature of gastronomical writing formally resists commercial ideology, then its generic fragmentation, its unexpected mix of ingredients that somehow add up to a recognizable taste, stakes its claim on the margins of European Romanticism as an alternative to the unified narrative of the novel no less than to the supposedly unified consciousness of the lyric poet. At once suited to, and strangely subversive of, their own materialist tastes, Romantic gastronomers remained one step to the side of mainstream culture, in the manner of their counterparts, the dandies. Espousing a unique brand of aestheticism, they helped to pave a fertile literary path, an idiosyncratic mode of writing that promoted a preference for the unusual—the Indian hen or Corsican blackbird over the common barnyard fowl, ass's ears vinaigrette over the family joint—that became a kind of road not taken for Romanticism. Forgetting its origins, food writing today (overly obsessed with wine and food, perhaps) has lost touch with much of the theory grounding it in these cultural and philosophical concerns.

Notes

1. Launcelot Sturgeon, *Essays, Moral, Philosophical, and Stomachical, on the Important Science of Good-Living*, 2nd ed. (London: G. & W. B. Whittaker, 1823), 41; in this volume, 92.
2. Jean-Anthelme Brillat-Savarin, *Brillat-Savarin's Physiologie du Goût: A Handbook of Gastronomy. New and Complete Translation* (New York: J. W. Boulton, 1884), 198; in this volume, 165.

3. The phrases "rational epicure" and "sagacious gourmand" are used by William Kitchiner, *The Cook's Oracle; Containing Receipts for Plain Cookery, on the Most Economical Plan for Private Families... Being the Result of Actual Experiments Instituted in the Kitchen of William Kitchiner, M.D.* (1817; London: Robert Cadell, 1831), xv; in this volume, 67, 73; cf. 12–15.
4. Fredrick Accum, *Culinary Chemistry, Exhibiting the Scientific Principles of Cookery... with Observations on the Chemical Constitution and Nutritive Qualities of Different Kinds of Food* (London: R. Ackermann, 1821), 17.
5. Ange Denis Macquin, *Tabella Cibaria; The Bill of Fare: A Latin Poem, Implicitly Translated and Fully Explained in Copious and Interesting Notes, Relating To the Pleasures of Gastronomy, and the Mysterious Art of Cookery* (London: Sherwood, Neely, and Jones, 1820), 15. Along similar lines, a group of French chefs recently petitioned the Pope to rename the deadly sin of gluttony, arguing "that the French word for the sin—gourmandise—has changed its meaning over the years and is now used to denote a gourmet, someone who truly appreciates good food and wine, rather than a glutton." Caroline Wyatt, "Gourmands at War with the Deadly Sins," Wednesday, September 24, 2003, BBC News World Edition. http://news.bbc.co.uk/2/hi/europe/3135560.stm.
6. Gusto is a term of Romantic aesthetics used by Lord Byron, Leigh Hunt, John Keats, and others; most fully elaborated by William Hazlitt in his 1816 essay "On Gusto."
7. Humelbergius, this volume, 179–80. Alexandre Dumas, *Dictionary of Cuisine*, ed. Louis Colman from *Le grand dictionnaire de cuisine* (1873; London: Spring Books, 1958), 7–8. Cf, 76n31.
8. The phrase "pleasures of the imagination" derives from Joseph Addison's 1712 series of essays in *The Spectator* of that title (No. 411–21), which were foundational texts for the Enlightenment discourse of aesthetic taste. See Joseph Addison, *The Spectator*, ed. Donald F. Bond, 5 vols. (Oxford: Clarendon Press, 1965), 3: 535–82.
9. Sturgeon's ninth essay, "On Mustard, Philosophically Considered; and on the Use of Garlick as a Perfume" is adapted from Grimod de la Reynière's "De la moutarde et des sirpos, considérés philosophiquement," and his fifth essay, "The Fatal Consequences of Pride Considered in its Effects Upon Dinners" is adapted from Grimod de la Reynière's "Des funestes effets d l'amour propre; considéré dans ses rapports avec la cuisine"; see Alexandre Balthazar Laurent Grimod de la Reynière, *Almanach des gourmands, servant de guide dans les moyens de faire excellent Chère*, 8 vols. (Paris: Maradan, 1803–12), 2: 93–104 and 2: 84–93, respectively.
10. Grimod de la Reynière, *Almanach des gourmands*, 2: vi–vii. Amphitryon, the eponymous character of a comedy by Jean Baptiste Poquelin Moliere, is the foster-father of Hercules who gives a great dinner. In gastronomical discourse of the Romantic era, the term "Amphitryon" becomes a code word for "host" or entertainer.
11. Eugène Briffault, *Paris á table* (Paris: J. Hetzel, 1846), 65.
12. Dick Humelbergius Secundus, *Apician Morsels; or, Tales of the Table, Kitchen, and Larder: With Reflections on the Dietic Productions of Early Writers; on The Customs of the Romans in Eating and Drinking; on Table Ceremonies, and Rules of Conviviality and Good Breeding; with Select Epicurean Precepts, Gourmand Maxims and Medicines, &c. &c.* 2nd ed. (1829; London: Whittaker, Treacer, and Co., 1834), 90–91; in this volume, 180.
13. James Boswell, *Life of Johnson* (London: Oxford University Press, 1953), 756.
14. Ibid., 332.
15. Ibid., 942.
16. Edmund Burke, *A Philosophical Enquiry into the Origin of our Ideas of the Sublime and Beautiful*, ed. James T. Boulton (Notre Dame, IN: University of Notre Dame Press, 1958), 12.
17. Charles and Mary Lamb, *The Works of Charles and Mary Lamb*, ed. E. V. Lucas, 8 vols. (London: Methuen, 1903), 1: 349–50.
18. Addison's "Man of a Fine Taste in Writing" was able to discern "not only the general Beauties and Imperfections of an Author, but discover the several Ways of thinking and expressing himself, which diversify him from all other Authors, with the several Foreign Infusions of Thought and Language, and the particular Authors from whom they were borrowed"; *The Spectator*, 3: 527–28.
19. Accum, *Culinary Chemistry*, 18.
20. *Gastronomy: or, the School for Good Living; A Literary and Historical Essay on the European Kitchen, Beginning with Cadmus the Cook and King, and Concluding with the Union of Cookery and Chymistry*, 2nd ed. (London: Henry Colburn, 1822), 9.
21. Eugène Briffault, *Paris à table*, 88. Cf. this volume, 8.

22. Grimod de la Reynière, *Almanach des gourmands*, 8: 58, in this volume, 38–39.
23. Hayward, *The Art of Dining*, 30.
24. William Kitchiner, *Peptic Precepts, Pointing Out Agreeable and Effectual Methods to Prevent and Relieve Indigestion, and to Regulate and Strengthen the Action of the Stomach and Bowels*, 3rd ed. (London: Printed for Hurst, Robinson, 1822), 265; in this volume, 73.
25. Kitchiner, *Cook's Oracle*, 3–4; in this volume, 61.
26. Kitchiner, *Peptic Precepts*, 263; in this volume, 73.
27. Hume, *Essays*, 241.
28. Sturgeon, *Essays*, 4. It may be worth noting that Sturgeon profers these qualities immediately following an anecdote about Hume; in this volume, 83.
29. Ibid.
30. Michael D. Garval suggests that "the idiosyncratic space of the frontispieces is best understood as that of the gourmand's mind—inwardly turned, fiercely independent and intensely original, yet open to the burgeoning wonders of the gastronomic new world; the site not only of focused observation and reflection, but also of free-ranging imagination and invention"; "Grimod's Gastronomic Vision: The Frontispieces for the *Almanach des Gourmands*," in *Consuming Culture: The Arts of the French Table* (Newark & Melbourne: University of Delaware Press, 2004), 15–33), 20.
31. Johnson disapproved of these designations; Boswell, *Life of Johnson*, 942n.
32. Grimod de la Reynière, *Almanach des gourmands*, 7: 31.
33. Giles MacDonogh, *A Palate in Revolution: Grimod de la Reynière and the Almanach des Gourmands* (London: Robin Clark, 1987).
34. Rebecca L. Spang, *The Invention of the Restaurant: Paris and Modern Gastronomic Culture* (Cambridge, MA: Harvard Univ. Press, 2000), 158.
35. In 1674, a Sicilian named Francesco Capelli (nicknamed Procope) opened the first coffee shop in Paris under the name "Procope Café"; by 1684, the establishment was serving not only coffee and tea, but chocolate, pastry, jams, frozen drinks, and sorbets. By 1721 about three hundred coffeehouses had opened in Paris; and by the end of the century, under the Directory, two thousand. A version of the story is told by a contemporary Englishman traveling in Paris who relates that in 1672 "one Paschal, an Armenian, first opened, at the *Foire St. Germain*, and, afterwards on the *Quai de l'École*, a shop similar to those which he had seen in the Levant, and called his new establishment *café*. Other Levantines followed his example; but to fix the fickle Parisian, required a coffeeroom handsomely decorated. PROCOPE acted on this plan, and his house was successively frequented by Voltaire, Piron, Fontanelle, and St. Foix." *Paris as it Was and As it Is; or A Sketch of the French Capital* (London: printed by and for C. and R. Baldwin, 1803), 159. According to Massimo Montanari, the first London coffeehouse was opened in 1687 by Edward Lloyd and by 1700 roughly three thousand of them were catering to the city's 600,000 inhabitants. *The Culture of Food*, trans. Carl Ipsen (Oxford: Blackwell, 1988), 125.
36. Jürgen Habermas, "Excursus on Leveling the Genre Distinction between Philosophy and Literature," *The Philosophical Discourse of Modernity*, trans. Frederick Lawrence (Cambridge, MA: Harvard University Press, 1987).
37. On the dining practices of the inn, see Amy B. Trubek, *Haute Cuisine: How the French Invented the Culinary Profession* (Philadelphia: University of Pennsylvania Press, 2000), 36–37; also Stephen Mennell, *All Manners of Food: Eating and Taste in England and France from the Middle Ages to the Present*, 2nd ed. (Urbana: University of Illinois Press, 1996), 136.
38. Early tables d'hôte in London are described by John Cordy Jeaffreson, *A Book About the Table*, 2 vols. (London: Hurst and Blackett, 1875), 2: 243–51.
39. See Spang, *Invention of the Restaurant*, esp. 34–63.
40. Boswell, *Life of Johnson*, 694.
41. Ibid., 83.
42. Mennell, *All Manners of Food*, 139.
43. Briffault, *Paris à table*, 149.
44. Hannah Glasse, *The Art of Cookery Made Plain and Easy; which Far Exceeds any Thing of the Kind yet Published*, 3rd ed. (Printed for the Author, a Lady, 1748), iii.
45. Amy C. Trubek, *Haute Cuisine: How the French Invented the Culinary Profession* (Philadelphia: University of Pennsylvania Press, 2000), 47.
46. John Burnett, *Plenty and Want: A Social History of Food in England from 1815 to the Present Day*, 3rd ed. (London: Routledge, 1989), 83.

47. Grimod de la Reynière, *Almanach des gourmands*, 1: i–ii; trans. Michael Garval, "Grimod de la Reynière's *Almanach des gourmands*: Exploring the Gastronomic New World of Postrevolutionary France," in *French Food: On the Table, on the Page, and in French Culture*, ed. Lawrence R. Schehr and Allen S. Weiss (New York: Routledge, 2001), 51–70 (53).

48. Trubek, *Haute cuisine*, 43. There have been various approaches by historians, sociologists, and cultural critics to define the segment of society labeled "middle class," or "middle classes" since this social tier need not be seen as a block, though "by the middle of the nineteenth century, these disparate elements [of the middle class] had been welded together into a powerful unified culture," Leonore Davidoff and Catherine Hall, *Family Fortunes: Men and Women of the English Middle Class, 1780–1850* (Chicago: University of Chicago Press, 1987), 23. While the income bands of the middle ranks could range from as low as £100 per annum to several thousand from 1780 to 1850, generally £200 to £300 per annum would suffice for the average family. John Burnett estimates that in early nineteenth-century Britain, an income of £150 to £350 per annum would secure a family firmly within the middle class, or £250 per annum for a family with three children; *Plenty and Want*, 74–77.

49. Trubek, *Haute cuisine*, 44.

50. Eneas Sweetland Dallas, *Kettner's Book of the Table* (London: Centaur Press Ltd, 1968), 12.

51. J. Pinkerton [John Thompson?], *Recollections of Paris, in the Years 1802-3-4-5*, 2 vols. (London: Longman Hurst Rees and Orme, 1806), 2: 196.

52. Abraham Hayward, *The Art of Dining* (London: John Murray, 1899), 24; also in Briffault, *Paris à table*, 20.

53. Jeaffreson, *A Book About the Table*, 2: 282–83.

54. Jean-Robert Pitte writes in *French Gastronomy: The History and Geography of a Passion*, trans. Jody Gladding (New York: Columbia University Press, 2002), 119.

55. Born in Paris, Edmond de Rothschild (1845–1934) devoted himself instead to art and culture instead of entering the family banking empire.

56. The story is retailed in Jeaffreson, *A Book About the Table*, 2: 287–88 and Briffault, *Paris à Table*, 19.

57. Grimod de la Reynière, *Almanach des gourmands*, 8: 61; in this volume, 40.

58. Humelbergius, *Apician Morsels*, 177.

59. "Un Code de politesse gourmande seroit un ouvrage également nécessaire; mais que se chargera de le rédiger, de le mettre un jour, et surtout de le faire exécuter? L'empire gourmand est une république assez volontaire, contre laquelle les lois coërcitives viendroient échouer, et qui ne peut se gouverner que par la persuasion." Grimod, *Almanach des gourmands*, 5: 173.

60. Spang, *Invention of the Restaurant*, 24.

61. "A dinner of fragments is said often to be the best dinner. So are there few minds but might furnish some instruction and entertainment out of their scraps, their odds and ends of thought." Quoted from Julius Charles Hare's *Guesses at Truth*, "a guidebook to the idioms of early nineteenth-century thought" in Seth Lerer, "*Middlemarch* and Julius Charles Hare," *Neophilologus* 87 (2003): 653–64 (658–69).

62. *Gastronomy: or, the School for Good Living*, 17n.

63. Earlier in his life (his early twenties) he had been a theater critic for the Parisian *Journal des Théâtres*, proclaiming it his mission to "defend taste and truth," and several years later he started his own biweekly breakfast club to debate the merits of contemporary arts and letters. MacDonogh, *A Palate in Revolution*, 12.

64. *Gastronomy: or the School for Good Living*, 17n; Kitchiner, *Cook's Oracle*, 3; in this volume, 61.

65. William Wordsworth, *The Prose Works of William Wordsworth*, ed. W. J. B. Owen and Jane Worthington Smyser, 3 vols. (Oxford: Clarendon Press, 1974), 3: 85.

66. Letter to Lady Beaumont of May 21, 1807; in *The Letters of William and Dorothy Wordsworth: The Middle Years*, ed. Ernest De Selincourt, 2nd ed. Mary Moorman, 2 vols. (Oxford: Clarendon Press, 1967), 2: 150; cf. his essay supplementary to his 1815 *Collected Works in Prose Works*, 3: 80.

67. Wordsworth, *Prose Works*, 1: 139.

68. Samuel Taylor Coleridge, *The Collected Works of Samuel Taylor Coleridge*, gen. ed. Kathleen Coburn, 14 vols. (Princeton: Princeton University Press, 1969-98), 8.2: 668–70.

69. "In England, during the early times, the food served upon the table was simply a gigantic forerunner of the taste of the English at present. They were always a race of meat-eaters. Wild

boars and huge bullocks were roasted whole at their mediæval feasts. An ancient ballad-singer asserted the invincibility of the Britons so long as they were 'fed upon beef,' and according to present appearances their invincibility will not be subverted for a long time to come, if beef is, in reality, the basis of England's strength." Helen S. Conant, "Kitchen and Dining Room," *Harper's New Monthly Magazine* 54 (1876–77), 425.

70. Seth Lerer demonstrates how British lexicographers etymologize this as an American word, American lexicographers a British word, both expressing a certain discomfort with the dandy's otherness. "Hello, Dude: Philology, Performance, and Technology in Mark Twain's Connecticut Yankee," *American Literary History* 15:3 (2003): 471–503 (482–85).

71. Regina Gagnier, *Idylls of the Marketplace: Oscar Wilde and the Victorian Public* (Stanford, CA: Stanford Univ. Press, 1986), 139.

72. Davidoff and Hall, *Family Fortunes*, 21.

73. Walter Pater, *The Renaissance: Studies in Art and Poetry*, ed. Adam Phillips (Oxford: Oxford University Press, 1986), 152.

74. *Gastronomy: or, the School for Good Living*, 19.

75. Ibid., 9

76. Ian Duncan, "Authenticity Effects: The Work of Fiction in Romantic Scotland," *The South Atlantic Quarterly* 102:1 (2003): 93–116 (96).

77. When he wrote to the Romantic man-about-town Henry Crabb-Robinson, for help in getting his brother's pamphlet reviewed, Lamb jokingly suggested that Crabb-Robinson not show it to his landlady, "for I remember she makes excellent Eel soup, and the leading points of the Book are directed against that very process." Lamb, *The Letters*, 3: 41.

78. Quoted in Lamb, *The Letters*, 3: 41n.

79. Quoted in Jeaffreson, *A Book About the Table*, 1: 268.

80. Jeaffreson, *A Book About the Table*, 1: 268. Characteristic satires of M. Ude and his eel include, Thomas Moore, *The Fudges in England; being a Sequel to the "Fudge Family in Paris"* (London: Longman, Rees, Orme, Brown, et al., 1835), 115–16.

81. Quoted in Hayward, *Art of Dining*, 140.

82. Hayward, *Art of Dining*, 141.

83. Grimod de la Reynière, *Almanach des gourmands*, 2: 244, in this volume, 8.

84. Lamb, *Works*, 2: 124.

85. Mennell, *All Manners of Food*, 73.

86. Erasmus Jones, *The Man of Manners; or Plebian Polished*, reprint of the 3rd London edition, 1737 (Sandy Hook, CT: The Hendrickson Group, 1993), 9. Sturgeon, this volume, 94.

87. Humelbergius, *Apician Morsels*, 162; in this volume, 187.

88. Sturgeon, *Essays*, 15; in this volume, 86.

89. Seth Lerer, "Medieval English Literature and the Idea of the Anthology," *Proceedings of the Modern Language Association* 118, no. 5 (2003): 1251–67 (1255).

90. William Hazlitt, *The Complete Works of William Hazlitt*, ed. P. P. Howe, 21 vols. (London: J.M. Dent, 1981), 12: 221.

91. Humelbergius, *Apician Morsels*, 348; in this volume, 201.

1

Alexandre Balthazar Laurent Grimod de la Reynière (1758–1837)

IN ENGLISH TRANSLATION BY MICHAEL GARVAL

Almanach des gourmands, servant de guide dans les moyens de faire excellente chère. Par un vieil amateur [The Gourmand's Almanac; A Guide to the Art of Fine Dining. By an Old Connoisseur] (Paris, 1803–12)

Manuel des Amphitryons [The Host's Manual; Containing, A Treatise on the Dissection of meats at the dining table, a Taxonomy of the Latest Menus for Each Season, and Elements of Gastronomic Etiquette. An Indispensable Work for All Who Are Eager to Dine Well, and to Have Others Dine Well at Their Table] (Paris 1808)

Introduction

Alexandre Balthazar Laurent Grimod de la Reynière was the genius behind the Romantic gastronomical tradition. Though he has been eclipsed by Jean-Anthelme Brillat-Savarin, whose *Physiology of Taste* (1826) recapitulates in a single volume many of Grimod's finest thoughts upon food and good living (*bonne chère*), Grimod's work was enormously influential in nineteenth-century Europe. It was adapted and, in some cases, transported wholesale into English, influencing the development of haute cuisine beyond the borders of France into England and America. In the Paris of his day, Grimod was a minor celebrity, dining with everyone from dignitaries down to actresses (not at this period the cultural elite) and spurring the rise of the restaurant in post-revolutionary France. He was extremely prolific, publishing eight volumes of the *Almanach des gourmands* between 1803 and 1812 (its first volume selling out at 20,000 copies), along with contributions to the monthly *Journal des gourmands et des belles* (1806–07) and a handbook for hosts (*Manuel des amphitryons*) in 1808. While the first and last volume of his *Almanach* have been reprinted (and the rest of it plundered and plagiarized), it has never, except for the odd recipe here and there, been translated into English. This anthology makes available for the first time some of Grimod de la Reynière's most flavorful writing from the *Almanach des gourmands*.

Despite his later rise to gastronomical fame, Grimod had an inauspicious beginning. He was born with hands deformed beyond recognition, one allegedly in the shape of a goose leg, the other in the shape of a claw. His father too was a gastronome, his mother the daughter of the Marquis d'Orgeval, one of the most ancient names in France, dating its nobility back (at least) to the fourteenth century. To avoid family shame from their son's deformity, his parents claimed that he was dropped accidentally in a pigpen where his hands were chewed off by hungry hogs. He was baptized secretly, his godparents the widow of a tailor and an illiterate carpenter, and thus the noble cachet never made it onto his birth certificate—a fact that probably saved his life during the French Revolutionary Terror. His education at first left to servants, he taught himself to write and to draw with mechanically constructed hands, covered always with white gloves.[1] At the age of twenty-one, he began to dine in high Parisian circles, attend the theater, and contribute articles to the *Journal des théâtres*. He joined the illustrious Société des Mercredis, which met every Wednesday from the 1770s through 1812 at prestigious restaurants (Villain and then Le Gacque) to do justice to sumptuous dinners. The club's seventeen members were led by the Marquis d'Aigrefeuille, the most eminent gourmet of the era and dining companion of Napoleon's arch-chancellor, Cambacérès. Grimod's early period of high life in Paris came to an abrupt halt on the first of February 1783, when he hosted a notorious supper at his parents' home, Hôtel de la Reynière, stage-managed by Marie-Antoinette's acting teacher. The meal came at great expense to his absent parents, both financially and in terms of filial mockery, for at the meal he claimed to be descended from pig farmers and grocers on his father's side.

After several more pranks embarrassing his parents, Grimod was incarcerated by a *lettre de cachet* (under which parents of the ancien régime could imprison their children) at the Abbey of Domèvre-sur-Vezouse in Lorraine. During his time at the monastery, he learned much about the art of *gourmandise* and the pleasures of the table from monks who made the most of their grounds, flowing with fresh fish and produce. After two years, he obtained leave to travel to Lyon, the gastronomic capital of southern France, where he established himself as a trader. There, he met Adélaïde Feuchère, who became his mistress for twenty-four years and eventually his wife. Soon his friends and relatives began dying at the guillotine in Paris, and his revolutionary sympathies suffered a severe setback. On February 14, 1794, following the death of his father, he returned to Paris at the height of the Terror to observe firsthand the devastating effects of famine and bloody misrule. Protected by papers that confirmed his ignoble birth and his work as a provincial trader, Grimod regained control of the Hôtel de La Reynière and managed to save his mother from the scaffold. Ironically, he was given a salary by the revolutionaries to maintain his paternal home, which later became (in succession) the Allied residence during the occupation of Paris in the Napoleonic wars, the Imperial Russian Embassy, the seat of the Ottoman Legation, then of several elite clubs, or *Cercles*, and finally of the American Embassy, which had it knocked down and rebuilt to match the building across the street.

The Revolution had abolished the ancien régime system of tables d'hôte, but it encouraged the growth of restaurants, which began cropping up around the Palais Royal to employ the former aristocrats' chefs. In the mid-1790s, Grimod's Société des Dîners du Vaudeville met at the leading Parisian restaurant, Le Rocher de Cancale, and produced the short-lived *Journal des gourmands et des belles*. At this time, he also dined with the Société des Mercredis, the Dîner des Mystificateurs (pranksters), as well as the Société des Gobe-Mouches (Fly-Catchers). But Grimod truly came into his own with the establishment of his Jury Dégustateur (Tasting Jury), his group of select gourmets who met weekly at the Hôtel de la Reynière to sample the finest culinary products of Paris. Their 465 sessions each lasted five hours, from 7:00 p.m. until midnight, and their official judgments were published annually in the *Almanach des gourmands*.

Jean-Baptiste-Joseph Gastaldy (1741–1806), Grimod's favorite gourmand, served as President of the Jury, succeeded by Grimod's cousin, Grimod de Verneuil, a former postal controller and member of the Mutton Leg Club of Caen. The restaurateur M. Chagot served as Vice President, the pastry cook Rouget as chancellor and keeper of the seal. Other members included the writer Marquis de Cussy and the former royal acting instructor, Albouy Dazincourt. Parisian actresses were invited to participate as non-voting sister members. As one might imagine, Grimod's tasting jury sparked a number of spoofs. In the fall of 1804, *L'École des Gourmands* (or School for Gourmands) satirized him as "Gourmandin," a gastronome obsessed with educating his son in the art of *bonne chère*.[2] In 1810, a pair of Vaudevillean song writers caricatured him as "Arlequin Gastronome, ou M. de La Gourmandière," president of the Jury Dégustateur of Lyon. More sarcastically, published under the pseudonym "anti-Grimod," Ducray-Duminil's *Almanach des pauvres diables* contrasted Grimod's Tasting Jury with the widespread situation of starvation in Paris. It was followed by the anonymous *Annales de l'inanition pour servir de pendant à l'almanach des gourmands* (Journal of Starvation Serving as Pendant to the Gourmand's Almanac) of 1808. When Grimod's *Almanach* was suspended in 1812, along with the restaurant furor after Napoleon's retreat from Moscow, a pirated version written by Léonce Thiesse and Horace Raisson, the *Nouvel almanach des gourmands* (1825–27), circulated under the pseudonym A. B. de Périgord.

Grimod sensationally retired from the gastronomical life of Paris in 1812 by hosting a bogus funeral dinner for himself in July of that year. In the hand of his mistress, he invited the leading chefs, restaurateurs, and artists of Paris, who were then surprised when he emerged in the dining room from his coffin. His retreat was a château on the Villiers-sur-Orge, formerly owned by one Antoine d'Aubray, who had been poisoned along with the other male members of his family by his sister, Marie Madeleine, the Marchioness of Brinvilliers (1630–70). (She had been burned at the stake for her trouble.) Grimod had this gothic castle refitted with trap doors and secret exits, and he continued to host memorable dinners for the remaining twenty-five years of his life. Retaining his eccentricity into old age, he took his daily meals with five cats and a pig, whom he served from a silver platter. This talented, iconoclastic diner was always somewhat out of step with his age, clinging to ancien-régime manners and unable to adapt himself to the Romantic school of cookery led by Carême. Yet, in many ways he was ahead of his time. He banished servants and ceremony at the table. He introduced service *à la russe*, in which dishes could be sampled one at a time as individual taste objects, long before Prince Kourakin, Emperor Alexander's envoy in Paris, would introduce guests to the so-called Russian method. This style of dining took hold among the bourgeoisie in the 1870s, and it remains the standard method of service in restaurants today.

For more details of Grimod's colorful life, see Ned Rival's *Grimod de La Reynière: Le gourmand gentilhomme* (Paris, 1983) and Giles Macdonough's *A Palate in Revolution: Grimod de La Reynière's Almanach des Gourmands* (London, 1987)

From *The Gourmand's Almanac* (1803–12)

On Hosts (1805)

"I think the world of people who give dinners," a lady butcher at the market said one day to the author of this Work, whom she took for a caterer. Men of Letters, and especially courtiers in the old days, would say the same about Farmers General,[3] whose table they would populate regularly. A successful man who desires disciples; a poet of merit in search of admirers; the ambitious

Figure 2 *The Library of a Nineteenth-Century Gourmand (Bibliothèque d'un gourmand du 19e Siècle)* from Grimod de la Reynière, *The Gourmand's Almanac* (Vol. 1, 1803). Courtesy of Department of Special Collections, Stanford University Libraries. See Appendix B, p. 284.

sort looking for protectors; the rich man who wants to make an impression; the doctor who wishes to be forgiven his wealth; and finally the minister who would like to be seen as a great man of State, have no surer means of reaching their goal than to give dinners. The table is a hub around which all reputations are formed; it is a theater where there never is a flop; and without a doubt, plays would never fail if, on opening night, their authors could give a dinner in the orchestra.

There is therefore no finer role for a rich man to play in this world than that of Host. But as we shall repeat throughout this Work, money alone does not suffice to have a fine table. While one who spends much may serve miserable fare, another, with mediocre fortune, may give excellent dinners. All depends on the care, knowledge, and studies one has undertaken in all aspects of the art of dining. Like all other callings, that of Host requires an apprenticeship, and it is far easier to acquire an immense fortune quickly than to know how to do it justice. A man who goes from stockbroker's lackey, to cashier, to millionaire speculator on the trading floor, is incapable of governing properly his kitchen and wine cellar. Spending your life rinsing glasses does not make you a wine connoisseur, nor does giving out plates to everyone mean that you know how to organize a good meal.

Within the realm of fine dining, the sudden wealth that has transformed so many man servants into Midases has not advanced the cause of politeness; this has been the case as well in many other professions, for one does not learn to be a Host by starting as a pale imitation.

As this suggests, while this role offers a chance to shine, it is also a difficult one; and, to perform it well one must, in addition to a fine education, have an understanding of human nature as deep as that of fine dining itself. This will strike many people as paradoxical, for one would think that with some money, a good cook, an intelligent maître d'hôtel,[4] and the desire to make a favorable impression, nothing is easier than to keep a fine house and have an excellent table.

How terribly mistaken is such an opinion. First of all, there can be no doubt that a man who himself knows nothing about the great art of fine dining, and is forced to rely on his servants in matters of both kitchen and wine cellar, never eats nor drinks well. The first, indispensable quality of a man anxious to serve food and drink properly, is an extreme delicacy of the palate, which allows the appreciation, in tasting, of a full range of flavors. Beyond this, attention must be paid to an infinite number of details, in order to exercise a necessary vigilance in the choice of provisions, without which one is cheated over and again, and risks financial ruin without ever acquiring a reputation.

It takes long years, unimpeachable relations, boundless activity, and constant watchfulness to cultivate and maintain a good cellar, without which one cannot earn the renown of a true Host. Nine out of ten households in Paris serve bad wine, because this task is left to wine stewards, rascals whose stock comes from wine merchants who are even bigger rascals. There are scarcely two in the entire capital who do not adulterate their wine. They are public poisoners, whom the Police cannot watch too closely. So, if one wants pure, premium quality wines, one absolutely must procure them through honest channels, and even have in each famed vineyard one's own agent of unfailing taste, integrity, and vigilance, for most wine agents in Burgundy, Champagne, and Bordeaux meddle with their wares before offering them for sale. One must take possession of wines as they leave the vat, just as, in days past, one would take possession of a young girl as she left the convent, in order to be more or less sure of having an unsullied wife, though many were still deceived, for nothing is rarer in this world than pure wine, or a young girl's complete innocence.

Human qualities are no less essential for a Host than those we have just mentioned. How indeed should he gather together and match up congenial guests, without unfailing judgment, a fine understanding of human nature, and the sort of worldliness that cannot be acquired from books, yet is so essential for he who wishes to keep a fine house, and prides himself in the success of his table? No matter how excellent the dinner, one cannot eat for five hours straight; alas! mere mortals, feeble creatures are we, and soon reach the limits of our appetite. The most intrepid eater is full by the time he has helped himself to the first two courses, which is when there is felt the need to have a congenial neighbor, and to be able to converse with him, for in many nutritive gatherings, it is impossible to hold a general conversation. But often the guests do not know each other at all; and if the Host, who must know them all, has not taken care to place them appropriately, they shall end up mutually paralyzed. Further on in this Work, under the title *Seating Arrangement*, I shall indicate the means to accomplish this without awkwardness or confusion, and we believe that this essay shall not be without its usefulness for those who wish to use this *Gourmand's Almanac* as a course in all aspects of fine dining.

After this rapid overview of the most essential qualities needed to become a good Host, let us deplore the ingratitude with which, in general, Hosts today are repaid for having done their best to fulfill their duties. Guests often make sport of their Host's vulnerable position; they take pleasure in ridiculing him; they appoint themselves his critics and judges, as if this were a right they had acquired by entering his door; and soon masters will be booed in their own households, just as playwrights are booed regularly by students from the *École Polytechnique* at the *Théâtre Français*.

We cannot find strong enough terms to condemn such disgusting ingratitude. A good dinner is one of life's greatest enjoyments: should one not feel grateful to he who provides it, and who takes such trouble to have us consume his estate? Instead of mocking and abusing him, should we not rather encourage him through fitting praise of what he serves us? Let us pay our share with joyous *bons mots*,[5] cheerful sallies, erotic couplets, witty rejoinders, and amusing but brief stories;[6] and let us keep in mind that, rather than trying to discourage those who pride themselves on feeding us well, we should instead nurture them with our praise. Since the Revolution has so reduced the number of Hosts, we must try to revive the species. In working to assure their glory, we cannot help but increase our own pleasure.

Some Thoughts on Cutlery, as it Relates to Dining (1805)

It is widely held to be true that all of the arts are interconnected, that they overlap, and that they are mutually beneficial; it is a less generally held opinion, but just as true, that cuisine is linked to nearly all branches of human knowledge, by which we mean all the physical sciences, as well as the applied arts, and even those offering only pure enjoyment. Chemistry, painting, sculpture, architecture, geometry, physics, pyrotechnics, all are more or less closely allied with the great art of fine dining; and the artist who, in addition to a profound knowledge of culinary art, possesses a fair smattering of all these sciences, should reap great benefits indeed.

Were it necessary to justify this assertion, we would offer as proof the example of the younger M. Rouget, whose most distinguished education has given him that wealth of knowledge that a young man raised in Paris, and eager to learn, gains from his studies. At age twenty-five, the disastrous repercussions of our Revolution obliged him to seek refuge in his father's hearth where, in less than two years, he became a leading practitioner. The pastry-making art owes him a great deal of the progress it has made, and continues to make each day. His knowledge has bolstered his talent, and helped him simplify many procedures; invent others; and, bring to the art of ornamentation—until now subject only to mindless routine or the vagaries of ignorance—the full integrity of proper design, the full rigor of trigonometric structure. In short, this is doubtless the reason why no one would dare deny the preeminence that Rouget's establishment has achieved, indeed the constant crowd of connoisseurs there offers ever-renewed proof of the same.

But it is not only the arts and sciences that, as we have just mentioned, are more or less closely allied with cuisine; within the trades are an infinite number of related endeavors; and whether one qualifies Cutlery as such or, by virtue of its progress and its challenges, one considers it an art, it is certain that cooking and fine dining could not do without it, and that its perfection contributes conspicuously to their glory.

The knife is the cook's weapon, his finest ornament, the hallmark of his worthiness. A cook without a knife is just a lowly scullery boy, however the

Les audiences d'un Gourmand.

Dunant del.   Grimod de la Reyniere inv.   Mariage Sc.

Figure 3   *A Gourmand's Audiences (Les audiences d'un gourmand)* from Grimod de la Reynière, *The Gourmand's Almanac* (Vol. 2, 1805). Courtesy of Department of Special Collections, Stanford University Libraries. See Appendix B, p. 284.

weapon that he wears on his belt is more for show than for daily use: it is used only on special occasions. It is his small carving knife that he wields throughout the day, for a thousand tasks: this is used to truss chickens, to scale fish, to trim vegetables; it is the draftsman's pencil, the bricklayer's trowel, the upholsterer's hammer. In the hands of a skillful artist, this small, sheathed knife can do anything; it is the universal tool. As for the slicer, it is just as absolute a necessity; the better it is sharpened, the more splendid shall appear a larded fowl, with bacon cubes whose contours are clean and crisp and, as long as the bacon is firm enough, never lose their shape under the larding needle.

Passing from the kitchen to the dining room, we shall complete this proof of the important services that Cutlery renders each day to the art of fine dining.

In France, since the carving of all large cuts of meat is done right at the table, and in front of guests who watch this interesting operation most attentively, it must be done not only with dexterity, but with elegance. Yet how can the Host hope to achieve this, if his large table knife has not been fashioned by the finest craftsmen, nor tempered to withstand every eventuality? Nothing looks more appetizing than a fine piece of boiled meat, and nothing is better when it is tender, but also nothing is harder to cut properly. A steel fork with an ebony handle should be the large knife's constant companion, used to hold the meat in place, in order to facilitate cutting. But this knife should only be used for larger cuts of meat; for carving fowl, one needs a smaller but no less well-sharpened one, with a slim blade that can slip in between the members, and joint them with no trouble at all. Cold pâtés require a third sort of knife, not as long as the first, and narrower than the second, but particularly solid in its construction.

Ham requires exclusive use of a fourth type of knife, which combines the slicer's slimness and the table knife's strength. Finally, stuffed tongue, galantines, saveloys, hard sausages, and mortadellas also demand a tool to be used for them alone, since their glory derives mainly from their crisp contours, and even surface.[7]

But not only the Host, or whoever carves in his place, must be equipped with the right tools; it is essential as well to provide each guest with a proper knife in his table-setting. This is a consideration too often neglected, even in wealthy households, where table knives are often veritable saws, and an otherwise fine dinner remains deficient. It is therefore crucial to choose only the best knives, to maintain them scrupulously, and always to have one or two sharpening steels on hand, to hone the edges. With such precautions, no guest shall appear awkward; each plate shall be filled with pieces carefully divided; more shall be eaten, with greater pleasure and speed; large cuts of meat carved artfully shall reflect favorably on the master of the house, who shall also get more in the bargain, for whatever is cleared away to reappear in other guises shall retain an appealing purity of form.

On Indigestion (1805)

A Gourmand's Almanac would be incomplete if it did not deal at some length with Indigestion, the most common of ailments for Gourmands, and especially inept Gourmands, for those who are truly worthy of the name know how to avoid this or, if they have the misfortune to be afflicted, know how to obtain prompt relief.

Indigestion is the result of the improper breaking down of foodstuffs in the stomach; it is sometimes so marked that the stomach has not the strength to expel these, nor to produce the other symptoms typical of the illness. When this happens, people suddenly fall unconscious, and appear lifeless, as if stricken by apoplexy. One must not be fooled and bleed the patient,[8] for such a mistake would surely kill him, and there are examples of this. Fortunately, such cases are rare: Indigestion is normally accompanied by such tell-tale signs as heaviness in the stomach, heartburn, hiccups, nausea, diarrhea, etc.

At this point, it is necessary to help Nature, by provoking a swift evacuation. The means to achieve this are known, and the results so prompt that when the stomach is freed from its burden, the patient recovers straight off. Even so, he should take care not to overdo it; to return this precious organ to its original state, a day or two of abstention and cleansing with plenty of fluids are needed.

It is often less the quantity than the quality of the foodstuffs that produces the Indigestion. One man may eat ten times more than another without becoming indisposed; yet another may suffer terribly from partaking of a single dish contrary to his constitution. It is up to the Gourmand to know his own stomach, so that he can supply it with compatible foodstuffs. Dairy products, warm pastries, etc., which generally suit women, do not always agree with robust stomachs, that would digest an ox, yet pale before a little bowl of blancmange.[9]

But when, through oft-repeated experiments, one has acquired a perfect understanding of one's constitution, one may follow one's appetite without fear. There is an essential difference between a Gourmand and a voracious eater. He chews more than others, because chewing is a true pleasure for him, and when food lingers on his palate, it gives him profound joy: but chewing is also a first step in the digestive process; the food thus arrives in the esophagus already pulverized, more ready to be broken down and assimilated into our bodies.

It is thus essential to chew long and well; to lessen the impact of hard substances, like pâté crust, ramekins, etc.,[10] by combining them with a good deal of dry bread; to swallow only small mouthfuls; and, to drink in sips. With such precautions—to which there must be added an after-dinner brandy, and another in the middle of the meal, plus coffee and liqueurs—one should but rarely become indisposed, even after the longest and most substantial of dinners.

Moderate exercise (or at least an upright position after the meal) is a very good way to aid and even hasten digestion. Nothing is worse than to bury oneself in an armchair, and especially to slouch after dinner for, by constricting the internal organs, this position necessarily shuts down the digestive process. This is why those who need to write after dining would be well advised to do so standing up, at a lectern-table specially designed for this purpose by Doctor Tronchin, and named after him as well. It is also crucial to keep the stomach warm during this time, and to protect it from cold air, for often a chill suffices to shut down this bodily function in a person with a delicate constitution. In such cases, a sturdy flannel camisole, like that sold at the *Barbe d'or*, n° 39 rue Vivienne, is an excellent preventative measure; but once one has taken to wearing it, it must never be removed.

By observing these precautions, one may eat much, and for a long time, without becoming indisposed; this is what a Gourmand desires above all. Indeed for him, more than for others, an illness that puts him on a light diet for a few days is a truly distressing state of affairs: it's that much precious time stolen from his existence, and what an existence is that of a true Gourmand!—the very image of Mohammed's paradise!

On Gourmands and Gourmandise (1806)

If one were to believe the Dictionary of the Academy,[11] *Gourmand* is a synonym of Glutton and Gobbler, and *Gourmandise* of Gluttony. This definition does not strike us as completely accurate; rather, the epithets Glutton and Gobbler should apply to intemperance and insatiable greed, whereas the term Gourmand has, in recent years, in polite society, gained a far less unfavorable, dare we say noble meaning.

The Gourmand is more than just a creature whom Nature has graced with an excellent stomach and vast appetite; all vigorous men of sound constitution enjoy the same privilege; rather, he also possesses an enlightened sense of taste, the first principle of which lies in an exceptionally delicate palate, developed through extensive experience. All his senses must work in constant concert with that of taste, for he must contemplate his food before it even nears his lips. Suffice it to say that his gaze must be penetrating, his ear alert, his sense of touch keen, and his tongue able. Thus the Gourmand, whom the Academy depicts as a coarse creature, is characterized instead by extreme delicacy; only his health need be robust.

But it would be a mistake to think the Gourmand materialistic and narrow-minded because he pays constant attention, indeed devotes all his senses to every aspect of the art of eating. It seems to us that, quite to the contrary,

4ᵉᵐᵉ Année.

Les méditations d'un Gourmand.

Dunant del.   *A.B.L. Grimod de la Reynière invt.*   *Maradan sc.*

Figure 4 *A Gourmand's Meditations (Les méditations d'un gourmand)* from Grimod de la Reynière, *The Gourmand's Almanac* (Vol. 4, 1807). Courtesy of Department of Special Collections, Stanford University Libraries. See Appendix B, p. 285.

he possesses an unusual ability to make others like him, and even to make temperate sorts forgive rather than envy his superior taste and appetite.

In his *Synonyms*, Abbé Roubaud is less favorably disposed to Gourmands than the Academy.[12] He compares the Gourmand to a Gorger, to a Gobbler, then to a Glutton, and explains the differences. According to him, "the Gourmand likes to eat, and eat well, but eat what he chooses. The Gorger has such a hardy appetite, or rather such a voracious appetite that he crams food into his mouth, and stuffs it all down, filling himself up indiscriminately; he eats for the sake of eating. The Gobbler eats with such greed that he swallows instead of eating, or rather he swallows things whole, as the saying goes; he doesn't chew, he gulps. The Glutton rushes to the table, makes unpleasant noises with his mouth, and eats with such voracity that each bit of food seems to chase the next and soon all before him has disappeared; he swallows things up, or at least one is tempted to say so."

While this definition could no doubt be written more delicately and tastefully, we are in general agreement, and the differences that the Author notes between the four terms he defines are basically true and accurate. But when he wrote this, Gourmands did not yet play the role in society that they do today; they were far from enjoying the status they have now attained; in short, Gourmandise had not yet become a calling.

It began however to be recognized as such at the time of the Encyclopedia,[13] for it is defined there as a *refined* and inordinate love of fine dining. Abbé Roubaud, harsher than the Encyclopedia toward Gourmandise, claims that "it perhaps goes too far, for this description would better fit the vice of the Sweet-tooth, who loves dainty morsels, savors them, and knows all about them." As one can see, his assessment turns on the adjective refined, which the Encyclopedia uses to describe Gourmandise; as for us, we think it most accurate, and would find fault instead with the other one. In fact, the term inordinate would better fit Gluttony than Gourmandise, since the Gourmand is really quite methodical in his tastes.

As far as the term "Sweet-tooth" is concerned, perhaps the sense of the word has changed since the time of Abbé Roubaud—this was not so long ago, however—or perhaps he did not render it with the accuracy that normally characterizes his definitions. It seems to us that it is the Gourmand rather than the Sweet-tooth who loves dainty morsels, savors them, and knows all about them; and, that Sweet-tooth is used in particular for someone with a taste for all sorts of confections, in other words for preparations in which sugar is an essential ingredient, indeed it would be true to say that, at a well-appointed table, the role of the Gourmand ends before dessert, when that of the Sweet-tooth begins.

This proves how difficult it is to be both one and the other—to participate in and to be equally knowledgeable about all the components of a good meal, from soup to coffee. This requires a depth of judgment and universality of taste that few people possess. There are some however who can, in a most distinguished way, play the role of both Gourmand and Sweet-tooth; but it must be said that this is quite rare. The renowned Doctor Gastaldy was one of the few, and took with him to his grave a reputation as one of the top Gourmands and one of the foremost Sweet-tooths in the capital.

We shall doubtless be criticized for having waited so long to ponder the true meaning of the word Gourmand, and to try to clarify the precise idea it embodies. Many readers may contend that this little discussion should have been placed at the beginning of our first volume, and they would not be entirely wrong to say so. But if all we have said about Gourmands in our two preceding volumes has helped to recognize them for what they are, then we no doubt shall be forgiven for having only just now taken the time to craft a definition.

On the Importance of Invitations (1806)

Dining invitations should be taken seriously, and this is a matter that needs to be stressed all the more since many people do not value them as much as they should, indeed as much as they are valued by a man who knows how to live—by a true Gourmand. Perhaps, in treating this matter so lightly, some hosts may be as much in the wrong as many guests. They truly believe that they have done their duty once they have invited guests verbally, following a meal at a third party's household, at a time when the frenzied state of their minds offers little hope of thinking clearly, or even remembering. Now supposing that the recipient of the invitation retains this part of the conversation, shall the Host not regret in the morning that he acted so rashly the night before? that he implored people whom perhaps, deep down, he cares little about? finally, that in the heat of the moment he gave in to a passing inclination, rather than weighing carefully all the ramifications?

On their end, guests who accepted the Invitation as lightly as it was proffered may forget it, or may not believe they have been invited properly, and in either case neglect to go.

The stoves are lit, the spit turns, the table is set, and no one comes. The appointed hour passes in vain, the first courses dry out, the roast burns, and the Host must sit down at the table, either alone, or with the people who interest him the least, for unfortunately they are always the most punctual ones.

Thus is a dinner spoiled, irreparably, and feelings hurt, sometimes for a long while, not to mention the useless expense, and all this because of the little importance both parties attached to the Invitation.

We must therefore come back to what we have said elsewhere about the need to make Invitations in writing, and to treat these as the only valid kind. They should be written in the morning, before breakfast, with calm composure and mature reflection. Indeed this requires a great deal of judgment, for it is almost as important to match up guests well as it is to feed them well. One should see to this several days ahead, include one's address with each of the invitations,[14] send them by reliable means, and request a response; with these precautions one can be nearly certain that nothing shall go amiss.

There are other kinds of Invitations, aside from those for specific days, and we should say a word about them here.

Some are vague, general, always verbal, and valid for any day of the year. A true Gourmand should not take this sort of Invitation seriously, and not let himself be fooled. It is nearly impossible for one man to be in the right state of mind to receive his guests graciously and offer them a fine dinner, every single day of the year. This would require absolute independence, a tremendous fortune, and a perfectly even temperament, three things that are hard to find in one person, and harder yet to reconcile. This kind of invitation is just routine, hollow politeness, and men with a little experience in the ways of the world take no heed, and are never deceived.

Others are valid for a certain day of the week for an entire season, or even the whole year. These deserve to be taken more seriously. If the guest list is limited, one must be conscientious, and let the Host know if a major hindrance makes it impossible to attend, so that he may dispose of your place. These Invitations, which we shall call semi-general, require of the Host less formality than those for specific days; but if the number of guests thus invited is extensive, it becomes cumbersome for him; this is why it is absolutely essential to notify him of any cancellation. Gatherings of this sort have advantages as well as disadvantages, and these are obvious enough for us to refrain from pointing them out here.

Finally, there are *ex abrupto* Invitations, made the same day, following a morning visit. As these are very rarely sincere, one should be very wary about accepting them. But one cannot offer general rules in this respect. All depends on how well one knows the Host, what one knows about his way of entertaining, etc., and only experience can teach this. One must therefore possess a great deal of judgment to know what to do in these circumstances, and readers should therefore remain cautious.

This brief overview of Invitations and their importance should suffice to show just how vast a subject this is; we should therefore be thanked for only having touched upon it here. We shall perhaps return to this another year and, in the meanwhile, would be most grateful for any reflections that this may have inspired, that you would be so kind as to share with us.

Essay on Gourmand Geography (1806)

In a very funny little comedy entitled *The Gourmand's School*, by Messieurs Chazet, Francis, and la Forterelle, which had a successful run at the *Théâtre des Variétés du Palais-Royal* in the summer of 1804, there is an original idea that, in our view, one might use to good advantage.[15] A first-class Gourmand has taken responsibility for his godson's education, and is raising him at his home; he gives him only cookbooks to study, but this is not what is most humorous; rather, he teaches him Geography through gourmandise, which is truly enchanting.

Thus, instead of asking what is the capital of Alsace, he asks him what town is famous for its carp, its salmon, its goose liver pâté, and its crayfish? The young man responds Strasbourg, in fact the only town blessed with all four of these specialties.

If he asks next from what town comes the best duckling, the most tender veal pâté, and the best apple jelly, the name Rouen will of course be on the tip of our pupil's tongue, like that of Verdun if asked where the best sugared almonds are made.

These questions are easy, because they can only apply to a single town, but they could be made much more complicated. If, for example, one asked from whence Paris receives the best oysters, the pupil would think immediately of Dieppe, Cancale, Marrêne [now Marêne], Étretat, and Grandville; it would therefore be necessary to divide up the question, and ask specifically what kind of oysters, such as green, white, fatty, marinated, etc., so that there would be no ambiguity and no misunderstanding.

Thus the town most famous for its partridge terrines would be Nérac; for its duck liver pâté and terrine, Toulouse; for its skylark pâté, Pithiviers; for its lamb and veal tongue, and head cheese, Troyes; for its gingerbread and red pears, Reims; for its olive oil, Aix; for its vinegar, Orléans, etc. But if one asks from whence we in Paris get the best mutton, once again the question is a complicated one, and the pupil hesitates of course between the Ardennes, Cabourg, Beauvais, and the salt-meadows of Normandy. So too for butter, and he would be hard pressed to choose between Isigny, Gournay, and Brittany. In this case, to avoid any ambiguity, one would need to specify the season, whether it is sold in slabs or in baskets, etc.

But things become more complicated still if, for example, we speak of a town famous for its partridge, its wine, and its truffles, but also for the delicacy of its carp and its eel; the sweet bouquet of its grapes, which taste at once of violet, lemon, and orange flower; the creaminess of its small cheeses, comparable to those of Neuchâtel and Viry; and finally, the excellence of its bread which, according to its inhabitants, is alone worthy of a king's table, indeed they prize it so that for them, it is as superior to Parisian bread as manna from heaven was to Egyptian onions, for the children of Israel. Our pupil shall lose himself in this labyrinth of superlative things, some of which may only be enjoyed on site. Here the master must help out and, sharing his expertise, reveal that all these assets belong to Cahors which, if we should believe the native son who provided us this information, must in matters of Gourmandise be one of the most interesting towns in the French Empire.[16]

Such bewildering profusion occurs rarely however, and there are perhaps only two other towns in France that produce as many articles worthy, in all respects, of a gourmand's delectation.

This method of teaching French Geography to children seems to us as simple as it is ingenious; it is all the more likely to make them remember the names of towns and even of the smallest villages, for children are very inclined toward gourmandise, and thus will retain faster the name Sotteville by thinking of its delicious cream, than the names Ivry, Poitiers, or Azincourt, sites famous for memorable battles, but not renowned for any culinary specialties.

Should one wish to train star pupils using this method, one should not limit it to France, but rather apply it to all the towns in Europe, for there are doubtless few that do not enjoy the happy privilege of providing our tables with some more or less famous, more or less sought after specialties. Thus for our pupil, excellent smoked beef shall be synonymous with Hamburg; cod, with Ostende; freshly salted young herring and Holland shall be as one in his memory; at the mere mention of macaroni, he shall chime in "Naples"; or "Constantinople" as soon as he hears talk of smoked tongues; likewise Genoa and crystallized lemon, Bologna and sausage, Zara and maraschino, Florence and chocolate, vermouth and Turin shall in a sense be for him one and the same.

Finally, one could apply this method as well to other parts of the world, thus salep from Persia,[17] wine from the Cape, liqueurs from Martinique, and salt-cod from Newfoundland would teach him to identify Asia, Africa, and America better than accounts written by the cleverest of travelers.

With this new way of considering Geography, this science which before just studied names shall now study things; those who travel to perfect their command of it shall no longer consult each country's scholars, but rather shall seek out its Gourmands and its cooks. They shall visit markets instead of libraries; and be just as eager to bring home the knowledge of a new dish, as they used to be proud to return with a drawing of an ancient monument.

We shall let our readers reflect upon this text, which invites extensive commentary. Perhaps they shall agree that to this knowledge of so many succulent things should be added that of their preparation in each country, so that one would train at once good geographers and skillful cooks, at least in theory. This new breed of savant would spread the science of Gourmandise swiftly, and also enhance French cuisine with the finest stews from all four corners of the globe.

On Porcelain, as it Relates to Dining (1806)

Of all the objects that contribute to decorating the dining table, Porcelain is perhaps the one that delights the eye most pleasingly, because its elegance of form and brilliance of color combine to enchant our vision and rouse our imagination.

When displayed, a table service all in silver, even if it comes from the celebrated workshops of Auguste,[18] or those of Odiot, speaks more eloquently of the Host's great wealth than of his exquisite taste. This sight inspires greed in some, envy in others; it gives rise to thoughts that, to one degree or another, torment the soul.

It makes one groan to see such a great deal of precious metal taken out of circulation. One imagines that, converted to coin, this treasure would revitalize commerce and the arts, but in a sideboard it seems only a fruitless display of wealth.

Yet other considerations join with these to make us look upon this sort of luxury with more astonishment than pleasure. First of all, there is the risk inherent in using any vessel made of metal, which can be dissolved by acid and therefore, at any moment, endanger the health and even the life of those who use it; this quite suffices to temper the admiration that a first glance occasioned. Then there is also the continual fear that must be endured by the owner of such wealth, necessarily more coveted than other sorts because it is displayed more prominently; the suspicions that this fear arouses, even toward the most faithful of servants; the care that a table service like this demands to maintain its full luster, requiring one man devoted solely to this task, who therefore takes the place of a truly useful servant; the oft-exaggerated impression that this gives of the Host's wealth may indeed cause tax collectors to give him all manner of grief, etc., etc.; when one thinks about all this, one is more tempted to pity than to congratulate this slave to misguided splendor, who may well have jeopardized his fortune in order to adorn his sideboard.

This form of opulence should therefore be left to kings, or at most to princes; the private citizen should limit his silver to a good quantity of table settings, and to a few dozen platters (for it is a fact that silver platters represent a true savings for households that entertain often); he shall, as a result, be happier, calmer, less envied, and even his table shall be set more suitably.

He should then procure a selection of the finest Porcelain, not only soup tureens, soup plates, and regular plates, but also ones for hors d'oeuvres and others for dessert, compote dishes, ice buckets, punch bowls and cups, a coffee service and, in a general way, all that is put out on the table, except for platters which, as we have said, should be made of silver, but flat and without trim, so as to be less expensive, easier to maintain, and less dangerous to use.

This kind of splendor shall not arouse envy, and shall please by its very simplicity. It does not hold tremendous amounts of capital hostage, it encourages the artists who work in the production and decoration of Porcelain, and who are not only more numerous but also in many ways more interesting than those who practice silver and gold smithing; finally, it offers proof of the Host's taste. One need only be rich to have a magnificent silver table service, but one must be both rich and a connoisseur to acquire a Porcelain table service that commands our attention, and deserves our admiring gaze.

On Distractions at the Dining Table (1807)

The dining table is the place where it is most important to concentrate, and think about what one is doing, for Distractions here are of great consequence, disturb the proper serving of the meal, and put everyone in a bad mood, particularly the Host for, in the end, they almost always occur at his expense.

Such Distractions are more frequent than one might think. Perhaps a petulant and awkwardly stiff doctor, wishing to serve a lady water, grabs a carafe carelessly, knocks it against a bottle that another careless soul has grabbed for the same purpose, breaks it and in the blink of an eye soaks the tablecloth so that bread, place settings, and plates all swim about as if in a flood.

Or maybe a hapless drinker, who always leaves his glass half full, has it knocked over or knocks it over himself during the course of the meal, so that an embroidered or lace tablecloth is stained indelibly, despite the efforts that other dimwits make to cover it straight off with salt.

Or an inexperienced guest, wishing to carve a cut of meat placed before him, wipes his keenly-honed knife blade side down, thus treating a damask napkin like a barber's towel.

Further down the table, a patriotic author gesticulates with his knife and, while speaking of his dreary works, hacks to pieces a mahogany bottle rest in front of him.

Another guest, whose neighbor is serving him something to drink, lifts his glass abruptly, for fear that it will get overfilled, and in so doing shatters it. At his side is a starry-eyed poet who, wishing to return a porcelain dessert plate that he has just picked up, lets it fall down on its side, and instead of putting back one breaks two.

Someone else, not knowing that coffee, no matter how hot, should always be drunk from the cup, pours it in his saucer, burns himself, and lets it fall; another guest allows himself to place his cup directly on the table, thus leaving a long-lasting stain on the tablecloth; yet another, toasting his friend's health, wants to clink glasses, and in the process breaks both his and his friend's; still another, trying to serve himself some salt, ends up spilling the contents of the saltcellar, to the great despair of the more superstitious guests, etc. etc.[19]

Le premier devoir d'un Amphitrion.

Figure 5 *A Host's First Duty (Le premier devoir d'un Amphitryon)* from Grimod de la Reynière, *The Gourmand's Almanac* (Vol. 5, 1807). Courtesy of Michael Garval. See Appendix B, p. 286.

We would never finish if we tried to list all the Distractions that take place at the dining table, always with more or less unfortunate results and which, in the final analysis, can always be attributed to a lack of vigilance or a lack of manners. Little faux-pas like these are the clearest indicator of insufficient social graces, and end up affecting all of the guests to one degree or another, but of course the Host pays the highest cost. Thus we cannot help but applaud Hosts who expel or even banish those who disturb the peaceful pursuit of Gourmandise, indeed it is by no means an overreaction to deal harshly with such stiff, clumsy clods.[20]

On Gourmands' Visits (1807)

In general, nothing is duller than a Visit for no reason and with no objective. Of all the ways to use or lose one's time, this is certainly the most tedious. It is best left to those who are so inordinately bored with themselves that they seek to mitigate their boredom by sharing it with others; who, under the crushing burden of their own idle uselessness, take their boredom on the road, and go gallivanting about all over the place; who, if the theater cost nothing, would flock there day after day but, as it does not, make up for this by going from house to house to pay what are called Visits; in other words, they lavish compliments, needless repetitions, absurd and inane reflections—in a word, grave trivialities—on all those they meet, most of whom, one must admit, lead more or less the same kind of life.

For a man of wit and understanding, for a true Gourmand, there are but two ways to spend one's afternoons, or rather one's evenings in Paris, for dinners have gotten to be so late at present that one can no longer divide the day between theater and dinner table. One must choose, for it is scarcely possible to go to the theater when even the most modest dinner ends at ten o'clock, at earliest; and, one is obliged to eat some chicken on the run when one wishes to go see either a new play or some other sort of performance. We say on the run because, with just a little business to attend to it is impossible to sit down to eat before four o'clock, and even the most restrained Gourmand, served the most frugal dinner, cannot finish in less than two and a half hours.

Some Visits however are a duty, an obligation in fact, and even a Gourmand cannot forego them, indeed these are called Gourmands' Visits, which consist of *Digestive Visits* and *Appetizing Visits*. We have already said a word about the first kind in the second Year of this Almanac. But as this passage was only twelve lines long, it was in a sense included just as a reminder, and we have always planned to return to this some day, and treat it at greater length. As for the second kind, we have never discussed this before. It is essential however to clarify our Readers' thinking on such an important subject; their ignorance in this respect could have serious consequences, and make them either lose time or appear impolite, both pitfalls that a true Gourmand should seek to avoid.

When one has dined, and dined well in another household, custom demands that, within ten days, one pay one's respects to the Host in person; this is what one calls a Digestive Visit. One must agree that, in this instance, custom coincides with gratitude, indeed with all the true feelings of a noble heart. As no matter in this world is more important than dinner, nothing can rival a first-rate dinner, and even in the eyes of the least thankful man in the world, no gift can compare to this, for it produces the most delectable and longest-lasting pleasure that one may enjoy; it is nearly the only one that one may accept, even from a superior or a stranger, without feeling ashamed; and it is also the only one that does not require reciprocation in kind, for if your means or social conventions[21] do not allow you to return the favor, you can be acquitted with a simple Visit.

We should add that since the Revolution, there are no more social gatherings in Paris, except in houses where people dine; many have taken advantage of this, for a single dinner offers them the opportunity to receive guests on three days, namely that of the meal, that of the Digestive Visit, and that of the Appetizing Visit, which we shall discuss in a moment.

But in order that the guests' polite gesture not be in vain, and that a Visit in person not be reduced to a simple note, we encourage Hosts to indicate a day of the week when one is always sure to find them at home; and, if they do not want to be bound by a set day, it is easy for them to say loud and clear, during the dinner, that they will not go out the following Monday, or Thursday, for example; this is an indirect way of announcing to the guests that their Digestive Visit shall take place on that day, and all who have some social graces shall keep the appointment.

Digestive Visits have moreover been around for a long time, and even been known by the same name. We do not think that this is the case for Appetizing Visits.

About two weeks after the Digestive Visit, one should call on the Host again, and it is essential to do this on a day and at a time when he is sure to be at home. During this second Visit, one should make every effort to ingratiate oneself, and to flatter the Host's pride with the sort of subtle and delicious praise that Gourmands know how to cook up and serve with such flair. One should recall the dinner's most remarkable dishes, the excellent wines, the affable and distinguished way in which the Host officiated, etc., etc. One should weave in gracefully news of the day, provocative and scandalous anecdotes, recent accounts of the literary and theatrical world, the latest epigrams about town and lines from the latest comedies, etc.; in short, one should make every effort to appear entertaining, and should deploy all of one's charm. Often the Host will get swept up in the spirit of the moment and, while seeing you out, will invite you to come again soon; or, the very next day, you may already receive a written invitation. But if more than a week goes by, then your Appetizing Visit has missed its mark; this is quite clear, and there is no need to make a second Visit, which would only seem like a tiresome appeal, and benefit neither your cause nor your reputation. Instead, one should stay calm, and start looking for another Host.

It is rare however for a Host with a fine table and a respectable fortune to not respond to an Appetizing Visit, which offers him the only reliable means to gather a sufficient number of amiable guests for, if the truth must be told, only Gourmands know how to be truly congenial. Fine food and wine are the very wellspring of wit, pleasure, and good cheer. Sober sorts are good for nothing, and should be avoided; lovers are true egotists, who are good only for themselves, and burden polite society with the torments that consume them; dreamy and lacking appetite, they exist only for their mistresses, to whom they should be sent back, and where they should stay from morning until evening to study love, then from evening to morning to practice it, and thus not cast a pall on temples devoted to the gods of the feast and the vine with their pale faces and languorous eyes.

The Gourmand, quite to the contrary, is congenial by nature, indeed his first priority is to ingratiate himself, and he has all that it takes to accomplish this: his playfulness, his sparkling wit, and his infectious cheerfulness make him the life of the party, its very heart and soul. Hosts would be well advised to do whatever they can to assure themselves his company. They shall succeed by managing their kitchen and dining table with the greatest of care and vigilance, for real Gourmands, *true to their calling*, must opt for households that serve the best food and wine.

We hope that this brief overview of Gourmands' Visits will clarify any uncertainty concerning this important subject; and if this essay, by giving Gourmands a clearer idea of their duties, and Hosts of their obligations, leads to more good dinners in our capital, we shall congratulate ourselves for having written it.

On Commitment, Relinquishment, and Dis-Invitation (1807)[22]

Within the realm of Gourmandise, there is no general agreement on several points of decency and politeness, and it is important to arrive at a clearer understanding of these. Throughout the five volumes that now make up this Work we have tried, whenever possible, to weigh in on this subject, but we must admit that until M. Aze's much talked-about Rules have been published, there shall remain significant differences of opinion over what constitutes proper social conduct relative to dining. A Gourmands' Code of Politeness would also be indispensable, but who would want to write it, publish it and,

Figure 6 *A Gourmand's Dreams (Les rêves d'un gourmand)* from Grimod de la Reynière, *The Gourmand's Almanac* (Vol. 6, 1808). Courtesy of Department of Special Collections, Stanford University Libraries. See Appendix B, p. 286.

above all, enforce it? The Empire of gourmandise is a voluntary republic, where coercive laws are doomed to failure, and which can only be governed through persuasion. It is the sole responsibility of Writers dedicated to the literature of Gourmandise to pursue this path from time to time, by venturing carefully considered opinions which, if fortunate enough to take root in a few good minds, may become the basis for a long-awaited charter, without which the great art of fine dining shall never be boiled down to its fundamental principles. We should never lose sight of a goal so crucial to the happiness of humankind.

While waiting for this happy day to dawn, we shall continue our career in the realm of Gourmandise, and try to foster a clearer understanding of these three points, on which there does not yet seem to be enough agreement.

In our third volume, we dealt with the Importance of Invitations and, while much more could be said about such an inherently inexhaustible subject, we believe that we have said as much as is appropriate in a brief Work like this, where there is not room for overly long commentary. We shall therefore discuss Commitment, Relinquishment, and Dis-Invitation. As we have already explained meticulously in a note what we mean by these three terms, we shall not bother to define them again here.

In Paris, all sorts of Commitments are treated much too lightly, resulting in so many bankruptcies, acts of adultery and other infidelities, and ill-attended dinners. We shall only deal here with this last sort of Commitment.

A guest who is invited and accepts the invitation, either formally or by remaining silent for twenty-four hours, should see himself as a soldier under orders, and consider his Commitment as equally sacred; indeed it is even more so, for it was undertaken in complete liberty. Nothing obliges us to accept written invitations, the only valid and binding ones. You have an entire day and night to decide, but once you have said *yes*, you are Committed. This is as sacred a contract as marriage and, in the eyes of a man of honor, even more binding; the duties it involves are so agreeable, moreover, that one is doubly guilty when one tries to renounce or to shirk these.

This last sentence brings us quite naturally to the subject of Relinquishment.

This word has various meanings in our language, but one cannot deny that almost all refer to something more or less shameful. It can refer to a hidden staircase, used only for the purpose of amorous or other secret intrigues, or to escape from one's legitimate creditors, which is scarcely more honorable. One can only Relinquish one's word if one is not true to it; in almost all circumstances, this is an act of patent insincerity. Relinquishing one's obligations means shirking one's duty to fulfill them; letting one's property be seized, making arrangements with one's creditors, pleading for legal delays, these are all forms of Relinquishment, indeed in many cases, Relinquishment is a synonym for failure, and even for bankruptcy.

Within the realm of Gourmandise, to Relinquish one's Commitment means to be untrue to one's word, to disorganize a dinner, to disturb and distress the soul of a true Host, to insult him mortally, and to risk never again being invited by him, for it would require preternatural indulgence on his part to re-invite a rude guest who dared break his Commitment once.

Only the most serious of illnesses, a broken limb, imprisonment, or death may excuse a Relinquishment and make it, if not justified, at least acceptable. But in the first two instances, one must furnish an affidavit, from the doctor or surgeon, certifying the patient's condition; in the third, a certificate of admission should be attached and duly noted; and, in the last, the death certificate should accompany the Relinquishment note, or be sent in its place. Aside from these exceptions, Relinquishment is admissible on no other grounds; and, in addition to the Relinquisher's shame, all Hosts familiar with M. Aze's Rules shall demand that he pay a 500 pound fine within a week, or risk imprisonment. Nothing is more supremely rude, indeed more shameful than a Relinquishment, and the Author of this Work considers it the greatest insult one can inflict on him, and on all those proud to know and uphold the laws governing the Empire of Gourmandise. No, nothing is more offensive than a Relinquishment, except perhaps a Dis-Invitation.

There are two sorts, the general and the individual. They are equally insulting, the sole difference being that in the first case, an entire group is offended, whereas in the second the offense is limited to just one or a few persons.

Nothing in this world can release a Host from his responsibility to give a dinner for which he has sent invitations and received Commitments. Business, pleasure, pressing circumstances, duels, injuries, illness, or death itself cannot absolve him of this sacred duty. Even in the last two instances, the only ones that might be considered true impediments, nothing is absolutely impossible, since nothing prevents one from having the table set in one's bedroom, or from being carried into the dining room; and, in the case of death, heirs inherit the deceased's obligations as well as his privileges, indeed they are required to fulfill the former before enjoying the latter.

A Host who Dis-Invites, should this Host be a woman, a pretty woman, or even a pretty Actress (the *ne plus ultra* of persons from whom one puts up with anything), no matter: this individual shall forever be dishonored in the eyes of all Gourmands. We should agree, in future, to refuse all his (or her) invitations, and not to accept from him so much as a glass of water, even if he had someone like Morillion, Robert, Méot, or Philippe as his cook; and, for the rest of his days, let us condemn him to eat by himself which, for a Host, is a sort of living death.

These are harsh truths, no doubt, but understanding and practicing them forms the very basis of our social order. May they spread throughout society, and forever protect us from Relinquishments and Dis-Invitations for, aside from diets and so-called "friendly dinners," these are the greatest scourges we have to fear in this world!

On *Savoir-Vivre* (1807)

Beaumarchais, that witty and ingenious writer, one of the best comic poets of the late eighteenth century, said somewhere that *savoir-faire* is worth more than *savoir*, or knowledge alone; this is a truth that our Revolution, begun by cultivated people for the benefit of ignorant ones, has made abundantly clear.[23] But he says nothing about *Savoir-Vivre*, which is no less valuable than *savoir-faire*, and which plays a particularly crucial role in dining.

Perhaps the Reader has already guessed that we are not using this phrase in the usual sense, and that we do not mean it here as a synonym of politeness and mastery of social graces. In the great Dictionary of Gourmandise, *Savoir-Vivre* signifies knowing how to eat; and, the man who best knows how to live is he who, like the immortal M. d'Aigrefeuille, knows how to get the very most out of an excellent dinner.

At this point, more than one innocent Reader is likely to exclaim, "But is it so difficult to eat when one sits down at the dining table? Does it not suffice to bring along a big, hearty appetite?"

Certainly not, Monsieur, this does not suffice. For the dining table is a country which, like all others, has its ways and customs, and the Gourmand's Code contains an abundance of rules that one must follow so as to not seem like a savage, but which would lead a reserved gentleman who observed these laws faithfully to die of starvation at a four-course dinner—unless, that is, he possessed a thorough knowledge of *Savoir-Vivre* to help him open his mouth.

We good Parisians must agree however that we are novices in this great art, which most of our compatriots from Provence, the Languedoc, and Gascony have mastered. This can be explained easily. Circumspect and polite to a fault, a Parisian feels bound in a sense by civility and discretion, and remains reserved in many circumstances which a Gascon would know how to handle skillfully. Indeed, a Parisian's inherent caution and timidity can best be observed at the dining table and, in a more general way, in relation to Gourmandise. On the contrary, the Gascon (in Paris this term refers to all Frenchmen born south of the Loire) never lags behind, because he avails himself of a certain boldness, daring, even cheekiness; and, since he usually has mastered the art of doing this playfully, cheerfully, even comically, he possesses as well the means to be forgiven his audacity.

Indeed, such ingenuity is often necessary when dining in France today, for there is a new breed of Host and, either out of pride, or lack of education about and experience in the ways of society, Gentlemen of this sort frequently are not very considerate, and their wives even less so. Perhaps it shall be the wife of a Cabinet Minister who, so unlike the excellent Madame de Beaumarchais,[24] shall let an entire dinner go by without offering a thing to her guests. Here, whole courses shall be taken away untouched, even at the beginning of the meal. There, you shall be served Malaga in liqueur glasses,[25] which do not even allow you to wet your lips. In one household, dinner will be rushed to facilitate the clearing of the table; in another, if you are offered anything, it is done in such a way as to take away your desire, or even your freedom to accept, etc., etc. It is precisely when dining in households like this that it is most essential to know and practice this fine art of Savoir-Vivre, which is the subject of this chapter.

This art is all the more challenging, since one must always navigate between two pitfalls that are hard to avoid. One constantly must walk the fine line between the childish shyness that plagues most Parisians, and the truly cynical cheekiness that characterizes so many a Gascon or Provençal.[26] For in the first case, you are likely to die of hunger; and, in the second, by vexing the Host, you may no longer be invited in future.

How then to strike a balance between these two extremes? This is the challenge for any man who wishes to thrive at the dining table, yet finds himself invited by a Host barely worthy of the name, for true ones anticipate their guests' every wish, and in their homes one needs only one's appetite: unfortunately, such Hosts are quite rare.

In order to thrive in most households today, it is crucial to know how to carve and serve well. This offers a quite natural opportunity to get one's hands on the dish, in which case one would have to be most unskillful not to set aside the best pieces for oneself: all it takes, when carving roasts, is to keep these pieces from being seen, and to conceal these with such dexterity that, in serving oneself last, one may be served best. It is nearly impossible to teach this maneuver in theory, but with a little bit of intelligence, skill, and practice, one can manage quite easily. Just ask M. d'A . . . .

As for smaller dishes, by helping yourself to those in front of you, you in a sense acquire the right to ask for those placed further away; and, if three or four people place themselves well at a large table, and work together, they can manage to eat some of everything, even if the Host offers them nothing.

When the Host has reserved the right to serve roasts or to pour wine himself, it is generally indiscreet to ask for some directly, indeed it reeks of the Gascon and the parasite. Yet there is an art to doing this, in a legitimate, and even a likeable way: all one needs to do is to bring the conversation round to the wine or the dish one desires; or, with clever, subtle, and well-targeted praise, to oblige the Host to offer you some himself. This is when one must enlist intelligence in the service of appetite, and prove that a Gourmand does not lack the one any more than the other.

Precepts alone are inadequate in this realm, and one session at the dining table teaches us more than fifty pages of the most careful analysis. Still, some general rules shall have to suffice here, to wit: at the dining table, a true Gourmand's attention should be focused on what is on it, not dispersed over whatever surrounds it; not only should he not succumb to distractions, but should take advantage of the situation when others do; after having set his heart on whatever appeals most to him in each course (when the fare is so plentiful that it is physically impossible for him to make it *'round* the table, which in truth is rare), he must use all his skill and ingenuity to make this come to his plate or into his glass; adept at flattering the Host, he must also know how to play on the Host's pride for the benefit of the guests; indeed, like a great captain, he must turn every circumstance to his advantage; finally, he must be just as vigilant in avoiding the shyness that can make him a dupe, and the cynicism that can make him odious. By practicing these principles carefully, while taking into account the time, place, and people involved, one may indeed acquire in short order the perfect knowledge of Savoir-Vivre that is so essential to fulfilling one's proper role at the dining table.

On the *Ambigu* (1808)[27]

If we consult the Dictionary of the French Academy to see what this word means in the realm of Gourmandise, we see that an Ambigu is a "sort of meal where meat and fruit are served at the same time, and which partakes of both a collation and a supper."

This definition strikes us as far from complete, and leaves us convinced that the French Academy counts among its members few devotees of Gourmandise, unless one were to offer the excuse that, over time, and with the Revolution, our mores have changed, lending this meal a completely different aspect, indeed making it no longer the same as it was forty years ago.

The very essence of the Ambigu is to bring together all the courses in one, and one can even find in this gathering together the origin of the meal's name, which at first glance would seem to offer a double meaning for, in seeing this combination, one cannot know where one is in the meal—at the appetizers, the roast, the entremets, or the dessert—and one might believe that in clearing away each of these courses, the Maître d'hôtel had forgotten some dishes, out of which this assemblage was formed. It is this ambiguity that gave rise to its name; we even suppose that the principle behind this confusion would first have been the result of chance, then organized in turn with some attention to symmetry; and, as this often facilitates laziness, savings and, in some ways scheduling, it has been adopted even in the most orderly of households.

But, in addition to meat and fruit, entremets, pastries, and all manner of fish are served in an Ambigu. In this respect, the Academy's definition is

Le lever d'un gourmand

Figure 7 *A Gourmand Rising (Le lever d'un gourmand)* from Grimod de la Reynière, *The Gourmand's Almanac* (Vol. 7, 1810). Courtesy of Department of Special Collections, Stanford University Libraries. See Appendix B, p. 287.

incomplete. It lacks precision in saying that the Ambigu partakes of both a collation and a supper, first because we no longer know what a collation is, and secondly because one could just as well say that the Ambigu partakes of both lunch and dinner, since it is more often served at the halfway point between these two meals, than in the evening.

The Ambigu is therefore a meal in which soup is never served, but where all the courses are combined into one, and during which no dish is ever cleared away. Appetizers, center and end pieces, pièces de résistance, hot and cold entremets, roasts, dessert, all is gathered and practically mixed together, which requires a huge table, capable of holding at once what normally would be divided into three courses, and even sometimes into four.

This amalgamation gives rise to several disadvantages worth noting. No doubt the greatest is to eat roasts cold, and entremets virtually frozen. But how to keep these dishes just right when they have to wait their turn for two hours! Supposing that tin balls and bricks would be allowed in an Ambigu, which is scarcely the custom, this would still provide only a partial solution to the problem. This artificial heat dries out entremets instead of keeping them properly. There are even some, like ramekins, soufflés, etc., which need to go straight from the oven or stove to the table, and are only good when served just ready to be eaten; one can see how a two-hour wait would spoil these completely, and turn a delicacy into a disgust.

Another disadvantage of the Ambigu is that it offers the eye a bewildering assortment that curbs the appetite in advance, rather than whetting it. The smells of each course, inhaled separately, stimulate the nose agreeably and, passing through the nasal cavity into the mouth, they arouse in the nerve endings that line the palate those voluptuous sensations that are so pleasant to feel and so hard to describe, and are the sweetest prelude to the most ineffable of joys. When all these smells are combined, this hodgepodge results in a dubious odor, a nauseating mixture more apt to turn the stomach than to delight the mind. So too the colors on a skillful painter's palette, judiciously distributed on the canvas, form enchanting scenes whereas, when mixed together pell-mell they become the very image of chaos.

Because this sort of service is so overwhelming, it throws guests into a quandary that, inevitably, is fatal to their appetite. The act of tasting needs to be methodical and successive in order to be enjoyable, which is what makes serving one dish at a time the best way to stimulate and satisfy the appetite. Thus a Sultan surrounded by fifty odalisques,[28] and not knowing to whom he should throw his handkerchief, feels his desires waning when confronted by such an array of choices that, separately, could not fail but to arouse them; so too a Gourmand feels his appetite faltering at the sight of so many fundamentally different dishes, whose individual appearances and smells such juxtaposition obliterates. Lock away the former in a boudoir, in a tête-à-tête with a fresh-faced, provocative beauty like Mlle. Bourgouin; sit down the latter in front of a delicious dish, which shall be replaced successively by twenty-odd more, and the sacrifices made to the Goddess of Love, and to the God of the Feast, shall be as fervent as they are plentiful, as substantial as they are enjoyable.

This confusion inherent to the Ambigu has yet a thousand more drawbacks. Everyone wants to be served what he wishes, all at once. While one eats cutlets, the other slurps down compote. You see, side by side, plates filled with veal sweetbreads and others with jam; stuffing and marmalade; little pâtés and macaroons; émincés and creams; crayfish and marzipan. This all gets chewed simultaneously; our eyes are revolted by the mixture, our noses afflicted, and our sense of decency offended.

The advantages that might outweigh so many disadvantages are few indeed. They are limited to a certain savings, for by combining four courses into one, there is no need to make each of these as copious. The Host simplifies the serving of the meal, since there is only one course, which is all set out before anyone sits down at the table. Finally, for those who find that too much time is spent at the dining table—since there are some unhappy souls who cannot help being bored here—it has the advantage of being shorter than a regular meal, not only because there is no more pause between the courses, but also because one actually eats less. For, as we have already noted, such an abundance and amalgamation of foods paralyzes rather than stimulates our appetite. The sense of taste, the primary one for any reasonable man, needs to be spurred on by change; it thrives on surprises, and one might say that the stomach's capacity grows with each new arrival at the dining table.

Let us conclude from all this that a Host who wants his guests to eat well, and to do so both leisurely and decently, should never proffer an Ambigu. If this sort of meal is tolerable, it is only so at balls, or parties, where eating well, at one's leisure, and in a refined way, is not the main purpose. Moreover true Gourmands only attend such an affair when they absolutely cannot get out of it.

On Dinners, Blond and Brunette (1808)

Culinary art is a vast, sprawling domain, and any man who sets out to study it seriously, and reflect upon it deeply, shall find that its horizons recede, again and again, before his eyes. This art, which encompasses the three kingdoms of Nature, the four corners of the Earth, all questions of moral philosophy, all societal considerations as well, indeed to which everything connects more or less directly, more or less closely, only seems superficial to those common minds who see in cooking only pots, and in the dishes served only a dinner.

These numerous connections and resemblances, which strike any reflective and contemplative mind, are what make this great art form so truly admirable. Who would think, for example, that between a pretty woman's complexion and the color of a dinner, there might be correlations and analogies that could engender myriad comparisons? Yet nothing is truer. A moment's reflection, and a few lines of discussion shall suffice to prove this.

All complexions can be divided into two categories, namely dark and light, for all shades in between fall under one of these two main headings. It is the same for Dinners, which can thus be called Brown Dinners or Blond Dinners, depending upon which colors prevail at the beginning of the meal. For, in this respect, only the first courses count, just as a woman's face alone determines her coloring.

From the very outset, a man well-versed in gastronomy can classify the dinner he is attending according to its color. A true Gourmand's gaze is so discerning, that a single glance at the table suffices; moreover, this capacity for discernment is linked inextricably to his discriminating sense of taste.

Let us try to define what is meant by a Brown Dinner, and a Blond Dinner, even if common minds do not grasp this, for only a true devotee possesses that insight, that inner feeling—one might call it a seventh sense—which combines whatever is most subtle and diffuse in the other senses, and which enables him to recognize, and above all to feel what for most men shall always remain an incomprehensible puzzle.

Let us thus imagine a first course in which all or at least most dishes would be in the form of ragouts, which necessarily are dark in color—like, for example, stews, roux-based compotes, hashes, stewed turnips, hot pots, and a hundred other such items, which belong more to popular cooking than to *haute cuisine*. Our observer shall decide if it is a Brown Dinner, and therefore of an inferior sort, for it should be noted that all brown dishes are much easier to make than others, because nothing is simpler than to cover up one's mistakes with them, just as a painter can do so much more readily within the darker tones of his composition, than within the lighter ones.

If, on the contrary, he sees that this first course is made up of those dainty and subtle dishes whose color comes closer to white than to any other—like Béchamels, quenelles, chicken fricassees, cucumber émincés, chicken *à la reine*, sautés *au suprême*,[29] braised veal garnished with cockscombs, and a multitude of other such complex and difficult dishes, whose names we cannot recall for the moment, but which are composed of the most refined fish, the most tender meats, and most delicate fowl—he shall decide that this deserves, indisputably, to be called a Blond Dinner; that it must have been imagined and executed by a first-rate artist; and, that it ranks at the top in any hierarchy of fine fare.

Virtually the same is true of women's complexions. With but a few exceptions, light coloring indicates distinguished ancestry; a subtle mind; and soft, delicate skin (as sensitive to darkness as to light, which is why connoisseurs value this especially among feminine charms); moreover, it usually betokens sweetness, as well as all the other qualities most appreciated in the fairer sex. A blond seems to ask for your heart humbly; a brunette tries to steal it. And it is always preferable to be given requests, rather than orders.

However accurate this comparison may be, it nonetheless is certain that a Blond Dinner is absolutely superior in every way to a Brown Dinner. All cooks can make the latter reasonably well, without much trouble, but only first-rate artists like Réchaud, Morillon, Véry, Robert, Balaine, etc., can rise to the heights of the former. Q.E.D.[30]

On *Pièces de Résistance* (1810)[31]

If we wanted to continue a comparison that we tried to establish in our earlier volumes, it would not be hard to point out some further parallels here between the different parts of a festive meal, and those that help to make a palace, or any other opulent structure, either useful or decorative. We could demonstrate, for example, the many similarities between *Pièces de résistance*, placed on the table as luxury goods, which no one touches out of consideration for the Host, indeed which seem to satisfy our eyes at our appetite's expense, and official rooms where no one lives, furniture meant only for show; in short, all those monumental trifles conceived in pomp, to impress others and not to be of any use to them. But this comparison would take us too far: perhaps there would not even be general agreement on its accuracy, and many might only see here one of those forced analogies, where a penchant for paradox takes precedence over clear thinking. We prefer to focus on our subject, and only consider *Pièces de résistance* in relation to dining.

In general, the term *Pièces de résistance* designates the kind of dish that absolutely does not belong to the category of Appetizers, nor to that of Roasts, nor yet to that of Entremets; and they are often confused, wrongly, with large spit-roasted appetizers, *relevés*, end pieces, and center pieces. Strictly speaking, in a large meal, *Pièces de résistance* accompany the roast, and are placed at the two ends or four corners of the table, depending on whether this is a single or double roast because, in the latter case, a pâté is normally used as the centerpiece. *Pièces de résistance* most often stand alone, in other words they are the only one of a kind on their serving platter. Thus there could be a terrine from Nérac, a goose-liver pâté from Strasbourg, a truffled galantine, a skylark pâté from Pithiviers, a baba, a Rhine carp *au bleu*, a Strasbourg trout, elaborately-decorated hare brawn, a *gâteau de Compiègne*, a macaroni *timballe*, a cheese brioche, a large iced cake, a croquembouche, a sponge cake, a potato soufflé, a millefeuille, a *gâteau à la Périgord*, a *flan à la Maréchale*, etc., etc. But sometimes the *Pièce de résistance* is made up of a combination of things: for example, a *buisson* in which crayfish from

Strasbourg, shrimp, lobster, and ramekins are gathered together artfully, to form a coherent whole.

The first salient characteristic of *Pièces de résistance* is their size, because they are intended to occupy a significant place on the table; and the second is their dryness, because the hallmark of a *Pièce de résistance* is to be served dry and without sauce (not even served on the side). This latter particularity should enable us to distinguish them from *relevés* and end pieces, which often are only large appetizers served out of order.

As this definition suggests, *Pièces de résistance* never arrive until after the first course (upon which completely unspoiled appetites have been exerted, sometimes even with the voracity exemplified, fifty-two times per year, by the famed Wednesday Society); they are moreover subordinate to the roast; and, since they impress the guests with their size, and their grand and majestic air, they rarely are touched. It would take a substantial army of seasoned and insatiable eaters to decide to lay siege to such fortresses, which always stand in the second and sometimes in the third place within the meal. Indeed most of them are taken away without sustaining the slightest damage (except in the case of flans, ramekins, or soufflés, which must be eaten hot). They can thus be brought out on display again at another festive dinner, and only reach the end of their existence at a later, informal lunch, where all is for eating, and nothing just for show.

On Gastronomic Changes (1810)

It would perhaps not be hard for us to demonstrate that Gastronomic Changes have a far greater effect on the happiness of men's lives in society than civil, administrative, or judicial ones; and this assertion, which at first glance seems a strange paradox, should quickly become an undeniable truth, if only one took the trouble to think about it. Indeed, when a Cabinet Minister replaces another, the odds are a thousand to one that the same thinking shall inform the workings of the ministry, or the daily work in its offices, and that the directives given to all second-tier employees shall remain the same. These fine machines are organized in such a way that they will always continue to spin on their axis at uniform speed, no matter what driving force governs them.

When someone in the public trust, like a Notary, sells his practice,[32] the Public neither benefits nor suffers from this: one would not expect the legal documents produced to be any the less well-crafted than before, particularly if this new Notary is M. Viault, who has succeeded M. Thion de la Chaume, who replaced M. Belurgey, who was preceded by M. Fourcault de Pavant, all men of worth and integrity. The fine qualities of such a practice carry on indefinitely, and the newcomer makes it his duty, indeed prides himself on

Le plus mortel ennemi du diner.

Figure 8   *Dinner's Most Mortal Enemy (Le plus mortel ennemi du dîner)* from Grimod de la Reynière, *Gourmand's Almanac* (Vol. 8, 1812). Courtesy of Department of Special Collections, Stanford University Libraries. See Appendix B, p. 288.

following in his predecessor's footsteps, convinced that this is the safest way to take his place.

About the same is true, but in a different sense, concerning Changes of Prosecutor, or of Bailiff: the querulous, contentious, plundering spirit that reigns in these dens of Discord gets perpetuated from generation to generation, and from office-holder to office-holder, whether these are called prosecutors or attorneys, and plaintiffs shall not be better served nor less robbed if this Prosecutor or that Bailiff is named Paul, Jacques, or Nicolas. Most of these gentlemen have long since parted ways with kindness and honesty. A decent Prosecutor, like a humane and upright Bailiff, is a virtual freak of nature—indeed, in all times, and all places, a veritable phoenix.

We could push this comparison further, but what we have just said should suffice to prove that Changes of this sort matter fairly little to the Public, since only people, and not things change.

The same is not true of Gastronomic Changes; on the contrary, they have a most striking effect on the realm of Gourmandise, both in theory and in practice.

We had proof of this assertion when the elder Robert left his establishment in the hands of his brother, in order to oversee the kitchen of a Prince, become King since. As a result of this one Change, the finest restaurant in Paris was transformed, in less than a month, into a fancified greasy spoon,[33] which soon had to be closed, because the place was so often empty. It even was impossible to find a purchaser.

On the Progress of Culinary Art
in the Nineteenth Century (1812)

In one of our earlier volumes (2), we dealt with Progress in the art of baking, and believe to have demonstrated, through the current state of pastry-making in France, that in the past twenty years this progress has not only been undeniable, but also so swift that during these two decades, this art has advanced more than it did during the preceding century. We said a word about the reasons for this improvement, and think that we have even convinced those most incredulous souls, the *laudatores temporis acti* who believe that all is in decline,[34] just because they are, and think that nothing today could be made any better than it was in their youth.

We would like to speak here about Progress made in Culinary Art over the past fifteen years or so, and we are not unaware that many will beg to differ when we affirm that, while less marked than in pastry-making, this progress is undeniable all the same. It is true, and we must agree, that there are no practitioners today who can rival Réchaud, Morillion, or Robert, who so distinguished themselves in their art toward the end of the last century and who, like Raphael, Michelangelo, and Rubens, founded three major Schools in the art of fine dining.

But if the many pupils trained by these great masters have not yet reached the height of renown attained by their illustrious teachers, this by no means undermines our assertion. Instead of three first-rate cooks, there is now a multitude of very skillful ones, themselves able to train excellent pupils, and who have in a sense disseminated the lofty knowledge once limited to a small circle of initiates. Ultimately a branch of applied chemistry, moreover, Culinary Art has benefitted from the progress of Chemistry itself, and one might say that it has its own Fourcroys, just as it has its own Vauquelins and Chaptals.[35]

Reductions and sautés are operations based on the highest principles of Chemistry, and alone suffice to demonstrate the advancement of human knowledge, indeed to prove how much Culinary Art today, while simpler and healthier, is however more sophisticated and profounder than that of our ancestors.

Far more varied than before, this art has also been enhanced, over the past twenty years, by more than sixty preparations unknown to our fathers. Finally, not satisfied with the discoveries that their genius and study of the more abstract sciences have achieved on a national level, our great artists have not hesitated to explore foreign lands, and to draw upon the Culinary Art of an entire Continent, while simply correcting, and adjusting for our taste the dishes brought back from their journeys. This has resulted in an immeasurable increase in the number, and in the very nature of our pleasures.

Along similar lines, Hosts have come to consider the dining table a serious matter. Their work with their cook has become almost as important as that of Princes with their Ministers: no longer is the planning of a Menu left to blind routine or subject to shameful penny-pinching. Contemporary Hosts, who needed both to establish their reputation and to prepare their dining table, realized that since the one was inseparable from the other, it was essential to give first priority to all aspects of the great art of fine dining.

From whence the primary importance that chefs have acquired. No longer simple cooks, they have become true artists and, in the process, have gained more respect and better wages than even the greatest maîtres d'hôtel in the past.

Furthermore, guests have become more refined in their taste and, in becoming more enlightened, have become more demanding. Taking but one meal nowadays, they have wanted it to be excellent, indeed to offer both the delicacy that once characterized supper, and the greater solidity that was the hallmark of dinner. Thus, through an ingenious combination, as pleasing as it is sophisticated, our contemporary artists have brought together in one meal all the advantages that used to be found in two.

Might we be allowed to add, without being accused of ridiculous pride, that our Work may not be altogether unrelated to the Progress of this art? Since the Gourmand's *Almanac* first appeared (in 1803), it has become customary for people to study, and to deepen their knowledge of the great Art of dining. *Hunger,* which can be appeased indiscriminately and is therefore fatal to Art, has been left to common folk, whereas appetite has been prized because it must be stimulated through artistry. Dinner has come to be seen as more than appetizers, a roast, and some entremets, and he who prepares it as more than a simple cook—indeed, the importance now accorded his work has given rise to an all-important competitive spirit, truly the mother of all inventions.

The Host is no longer seen as a sort of automaton, only too happy to squander his estate feeding a few clever souls; he has come to be considered a man of understanding himself, and his pride put on the line, all for the greater glory of the Culinary Art.

Finally, the Dining Table has become the linchpin of political, literary, financial, and commercial matters. Promotions, academic successes, business dealings, negotiations all take place at the dining table, or at least get started there; and Lord knows that the Host who wants to meet with his guests' approval has every reason to serve them splendidly refined fare.

Thus, whether one considers fine dining from the perspective of art or from that of human nature, it seems to us a fact that Culinary Art has made undeniable Progress in the past twenty years, which is what we wanted to demonstrate in as many words.

From *The Host's Manual* (1808)

A Treatise on the Dissection of Meats: General Principles

A Host who does not know how to carve, nor to serve, is like someone who has a fine library and cannot read. The one is almost as shameful as the other.

Our fathers thought the art of carving well to be essential, indispensable in fact for rounding out a well-born, wealthy man's proper education. A young man's last preceptor was therefore a carving master, who would oversee daily practice on all sorts of flesh, combining concrete examples with principles, and who would only leave when his pupil had finished a complete course in this difficult art, and become conversant with all cuts of meat, and all joints of game and fowl.

Armed with this knowledge, and possessing the skill, strength, and agility needed to practice it well, Hosts in days past would almost always prove worthy of their carving masters; and, those who could not have analyzed a single line of Virgil or Cicero, not even with open book, would know every last sinew of a duck, goose, or even wild goose.

Above all, proficiency in this challenging art was the hallmark of someone born to wealth. Never at a loss to do the honors at home and even elsewhere, he took pride in carving up and serving the largest and most difficult specimens himself, discharging these duties with such ease and dexterity that there could be no doubt he was born in the upper class, and thus familiar since childhood with choice cuts.

The art of the Carving Squire was prized even more in the past than during the last years of the reign of Louis XV. At Court, and in the chief Noble households, this would be practiced *ad hoc* by a man who held top rank among the household's servants, and would only carry out these duties with his sword by his side. In Royal and Princely households, these duties were always carried out by a gentleman.

This position fell out of favor during the splendid reign of Louis XIV, and since then Hosts have taken matters into their own hands, and are proud to carve their finest meats by themselves. Only the Germans have had the good sense to retain a Carving Squire, and in their households Hosts only serve meats that have already been carved.

It is no doubt most unfortunate that in our country, such arduous duties have ceased to be fulfilled by a man devoted solely to them, who through long practice had acquired such mastery that he might carve up a turkey at the end of his fork, without ever putting it down. Moreover, carving upon a separate table, completely in control, out of sight of the guests, working on a wooden board and never on the serving platter, focused entirely on the task at hand, he would doubtless have carried this out far better than a Host who must perform before a thousand watchful, curious eyes; whose head is filled with so many other concerns; and, who is subject to so many irksome distractions. The roast and the guests benefitted tremendously from this old method: carved better and faster, meats were more appetizing and hotter; and, freed from this burden, the Host could concentrate instead on stimulating and satisfying his guests' appetite.

But since this is no longer our custom—indeed Carving Squires now exist only in history books—and since the Revolution has shifted wealth, few Hosts today had their educations completed with a course in the dissection of meats; it is thus essential to recall the principles of this art, to reveal its secrets, and to cultivate its practice in the younger generation, which is beginning to realize that nothing is more shameful for a master of the house than not to know how to carve. One might as well not know how to write.

First of all, a Host eager to carve well needs to have knives and forks of different sizes, and proportionate to the cuts upon which he shall operate. The knives must have keen edges, and be honed daily on a wet stone. The steel forks must have sharp points, and be strong yet slender. As it is very hard to carve well on a serving platter, it is a good idea for the Host to have within his reach a scrupulously clean, mahogany credenza, and for him to perform his duties on this sort of workbench. He should place the roast squarely in front of him, and not be afraid to stand up if needed. His hands should be deft and sure, his arms should be held comfortably open and remain flexible; his napkin should cover his entire chest, so that fear of splattering shall not keep him from performing freely. Mindful of the task at hand, he should attend only to this, and imagine that he is alone, and that no one is watching him. For their part, guests should avoid focusing their attention on this operation, which shall be accomplished better and faster as a result.

As soon as a limb, a filet, or any other portion is detached, it should be put on the serving platter, and arranged symmetrically. When all has been thus divided, the credenza is taken away; the Host puts away his napkin and tools, only to take them up again, impeccably cleaned, to undertake a new dissection.

Then, either he serves each of the guests one of the pieces carved, or he fills several plates and passes them round, or else he passes the serving platter itself, so that each guest can serve himself as he wishes, if he is not too timid—and one must never be at the dining table, at the risk of starving to death, even at a four-course dinner.

Such are the general Principles that we thought best to set forth first, before entering into specifics; by following them exactly, one can be assured of being on the right path toward establishing the reputation of one's dining table and household, indeed to being considered a Host well-versed in the art of *Savoir-Vivre*, whose education is lacking in no respect. We shall now survey the different sorts of meat and even of fish likely to need carving; indicate the most elegant and surest way to divide them up properly; and, spare nothing so that each person—with the help of our descriptions, our principles, and the Plates that illustrate our commentary, and with a little aptitude, determination, and skill—might, in short order become, if not a first-rate Carving Squire, at least a deft enough carver to garner the praise and affection of the most demanding guests.

Before concluding this chapter, we shall add that the great art of carving is not only necessary for Hosts: on more than one occasion it has proven quite beneficial for guests, indeed it can often suffice for them to be considered clever and amiable. As long as he is otherwise presentable, a man who knows how to carve and serve well is not only welcome everywhere, but in many households is given preference. If, like most of his counterparts today, a Host is uninitiated in this art, he shall be all the more eager to have

Pt. I. P. 33.

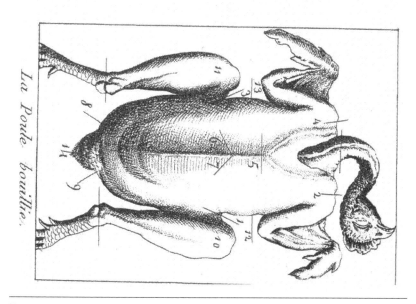

Figure 9   *Boiled Piece of Meat; Boiled Hen (La pièce de bouillie; La poule bouillie)* from Grimod de la Reynière, *The Host's Manual* (1808). Courtesy of Department of Special Collections, Stanford University Libraries.

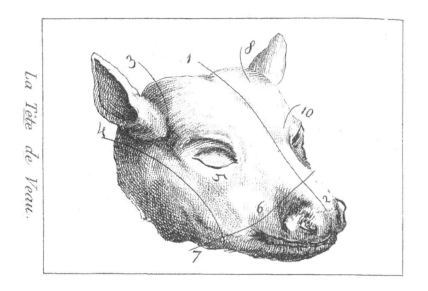

Pl. III. P. 3 9.

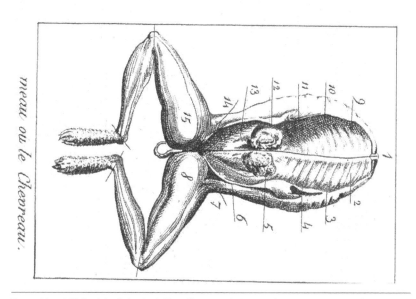

Figure 10 *Calf's Head; Lamb (La tête de Veau; L'Agneau ou le chevreau)* from Grimod de la Reynière, *The Host's Manual* (1808). Courtesy of Department of Special Collections, Stanford University Libraries.

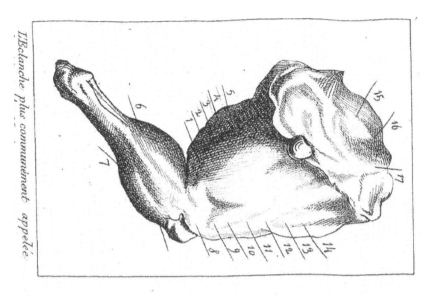

PL. IV. P. 41.

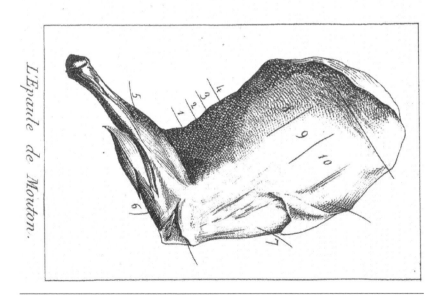

Figure 11 *Leg of Mutton; Shoulder of Mutton (L'éclanche plus communément appelée le gigot de mouton et l'epaule de mouton)* from Grimod de la Reynière, *The Host's Manual* (1808). Courtesy of Department of Special Collections, Stanford University Libraries.

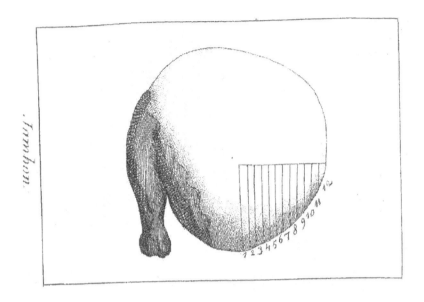

Pl. V. P. 45.

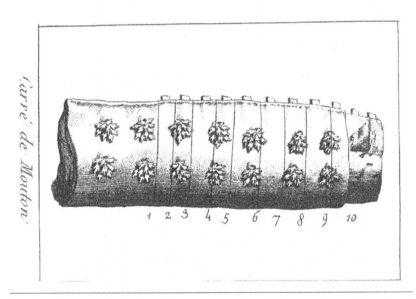

Figure 12 *Ham; Mutton Loin (Jambon; Carré de mouton)* from Grimod de la Reynière, *The Host's Manual* (1808). Courtesy of Department of Special Collections, Stanford University Libraries.

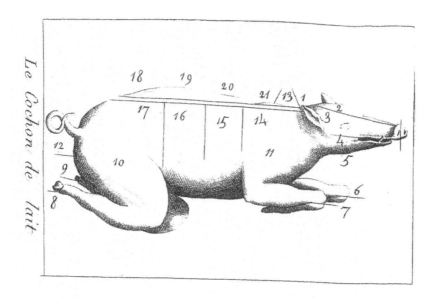

Pl. VI. P. 45.

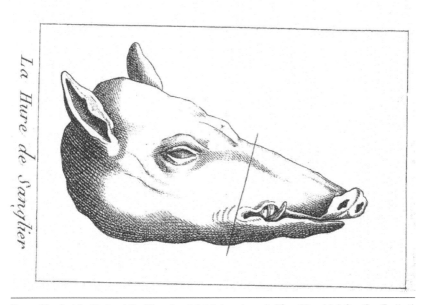

Figure 13   *Suckling Pig; Boar's Head (Le cochon de lait; La hure de sanglier)* from Grimod de la Reynière, *The Host's Manual* (1808). Courtesy of Department of Special Collections, Stanford University Libraries.

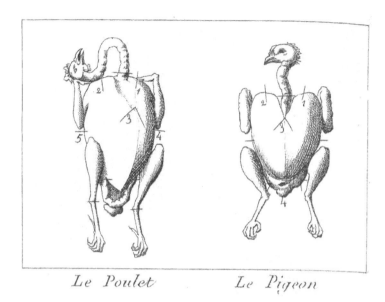

Le Poulet   *Le Pigeon*

Pl.XII. P.89.

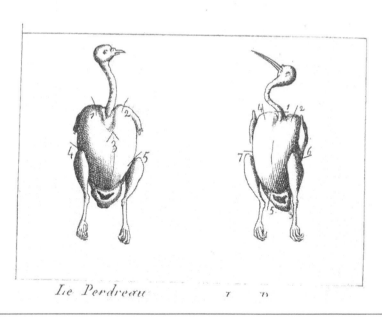

Le Perdreau   *L   D*

Figure 14 *Chicken; Pigeon; Young Partridge; Woodcock (Le poulet, le pigeon; Le perdreau ou la perdrix, la bécasse)* from Grimod de la Reynière, *The Host's Manual* (1808). Courtesy of Department of Special Collections, Stanford University Libraries.

Figure 15 *Turbot; Barbel; Carp (Turbot; barbeau; carpe)* from Grimod de la Reynière, *The Host's Manual* (1808). Courtesy of Department of Special Collections, Stanford University Libraries.

someone who masters it at his table, and shall invite him often, to put his talents to good use.

Definitions and General Principles Concerning Menus

The word *Menu*, when used as a noun, is one of those terms peculiar to the French language, which may well have no equivalent elsewhere. It has various meanings, but we shall only deal with it here in relation to dining; and, considered from this point of view, it would be difficult to find a synonym for it, and thus to define it without resorting to circumlocution.

The *Menu* of a meal is generally understood to mean the summary of its components. Such is the definition given for this word in the Dictionary of the Academy, but it is a bit vague—indeed, strictly speaking, it lacks precision for, starting with the wine list, there are many things which are part of a meal, yet do not figure on the Menu, such as the dessert, the soup course, etc.

The Menu is thus limited to whatever comes out of the kitchen, and goes onto the table.

In well-ordered households, where the Host oversees personally the composition of each meal, the Maître-d'hôtel or, if there is none, the cook, must bring him each morning the day's dinner Menu, and append at least an overview of that for the following day. This is the time for the Host, whom we assume to possess all the knowledge that this title requires, to discuss item by item the dishes that make up the menu, and often his ideas may provide inspiration, even for the most skillful of artists. These consultations shall not be without benefit for the culinary art if, on the one hand, the Host chooses no dish without careful deliberation and if, on the other, the cook proposes none without knowing for sure that he can do it justice.

In short, composing and discussing a Menu is no small matter. The first endeavor requires a superior mind, deep and varied knowledge, and quite extensive reflection; the second, considerable experience, a sure and refined sense of taste, and expert judgment. As these assertions suggest, cooks capable of drawing up sophisticated Menus, and Hosts able to discuss them fully, are rare indeed—privileged souls, in a sense.

Yet, despite the great importance now accorded everything related to the art of fine dining, there is still far from enough emphasis placed on the subject at hand. Most menus are drawn up out of habit, and adopted out of inexperience, carelessness, or thoughtlessness. In many households noted today for their opulence, the cook is even allowed complete freedom to compose Menus according to his whim, and only upon sitting down at the table does the Host become acquainted with his dinner.

This is not the way to make a name for oneself as a true Host—indeed, deserving such a reputation takes more care, vigilance, and hard work than most honors in this world. We cannot emphasize enough that money alone does not suffice to serve excellent food. The most skillful of cooks will soon lapse into mediocrity if in the service of a careless master, who has neither the feeling, nor the taste, nor the judgment, nor the experience that true gourmandise requires.

Menus necessarily vary according to the seasons, since they are made up of the foodstuffs that Nature's bounty provides us at more or less set periods in each climate. A skillful cook needs to seize the moment, and use each of these provisions when it is at its best; nothing second-rate should end up on a great artist's Menu, for pretty much the same is true of a Menu as of a sonnet. Comus

> Forbade a weak *dish* ever to appear,
> Nor a *delicacy*, once served, to reappear.[36]

While it is sometimes tolerable for appetizers or entremets to repeat, this is only the case for meals served to more than sixty people, where it would otherwise be impossible to maintain a proper proportion of these dishes to the number of guests.

One ought to make a clear distinction between daily Menus for small but well-appointed gatherings, and those for official, holiday, and family events—all those, in short, which bring together a large number of guests for a festive occasion.

A cook should take great care that each dish on the first type of Menu bespeak, in all respects, the work of a great artist. It would no doubt be desirable for him to do the same for the second kind, but this would be asking the impossible. Usually, he settles for paying particular attention to the main appetizers and selected entremets; preparing the rest is left in less distinguished hands, which is almost always a catastrophe. One should therefore not expect to find subtle, delicate, superlative fare at heavily-attended gatherings, and be happy if it is simply good, copious, and wholesome.

The menus which we offer here as examples, and which several skillful practitioners helped us to compose, shall doubtless not teach culinary artists anything new, but may be useful to Hosts, compensate for their inexperience, or refresh their memory when they need to order dinners they would like to be proud to offer. We provide examples for fifteen, twenty-five, forty, and sixty place-settings; these are fairly common proportions for festive dinners. It would moreover be easy to modify these Menus for meals smaller than the first of these, or larger than the last, by taking away or adding dishes; in the latter case, one could choose among items on the first three Menus to add to the fourth, and go as high as, say, a hundred place-settings; but such cases are exceedingly rare. In extremely large gatherings, it is customary to increase the number rather than the size of the tables; this is better in all respects, for it makes serving easier, and the dinner better and hotter.

We should note that the names of certain stews, which sound odd and whose origin seems difficult to explain, actually derive from the names of their inventors, which in turn were corrupted by artists who make no claim to being grammarians. Restoring these names to their pristine state, and thus affirming the identity of such dishes' inventors, would be a tribute paid to these illustrious Fathers of the Church of Gourmandise. This is a job for scholars, and we freely relinquish the trouble of undertaking it, and the resulting glory, to those members of the former Academy of Inscriptions and Belles-Lettres who might feel called to such an illustrious enterprise. Scholarship shall repay our debt through the renewed recognition of these inventors—and who could be more truly deserving, since they are the true founders of a great part of our national glory?[37]

Elements of Gastronomic Etiquette: Preliminary Considerations

Far be it for us to try giving etiquette lessons here; this fine art can be learned much more effectively through practice than in theory, and those who live in high society are far greater experts in this respect than Men of Letters, whose studious and sedentary way of life often leaves them unaware of the very formalities that are a socialite's principal preoccupation.

But the customs specific to the manducatory art constitute a Code of etiquette which should not be confused with the larger one, even though a part of it; we should like to focus here on these customs alone. It seems to us that, since the rules of this Code are so vague and changeable, everyone ends up practicing them differently, which represents a significant drawback for true Gourmands, and can often prove seriously detrimental to their appetite. We therefore propose, in the third Part of this modest Work, to standardize these rules; to choose, among diverse customs, those that discriminating minds consider best; to establish a more direct relationship between Hosts and guests; in short, to do everything we can to facilitate the practice of the great art of *savoir-vivre*, by clarifying the ambiguities which have frozen the former's generosity, and daunted the latter's appetite. We shall not forget that in this sort of discussion, as in all others, it is best to be brief.

Finally, whatever personal reasons we may have for cursing the French Revolution, we shall not suggest that it alone is to blame for the confusion that now reigns within this *Code of Gastronomic Etiquette*, nor for the lost sense of respect and duty that once governed relations between Hosts and their guests, nor for the general decline in the ways and customs of fine dining. No doubt it played a large role in this; but a part of this transformation must also be attributed to contemporary mores, indeed Time alone would have brought this about, a bit later perhaps, but inevitably, for as we all know, change is one of the hallmarks of this God, eternal devourer of people and things.

It would therefore not be reasonable to expect contemporary Hosts and guests to return completely to the way things were done thirty years ago; but, by taking from each period whatever it has to offer that seems best, most sensible, in short most favorable toward progress in the art of gourmandise, we shall draw up a series of principles, which we shall be all the more delighted to see put into practice, since love of this art alone has motivated us to publish them.[38]

Notes

1. For a stimulating discussion of eighteenth-century mechanisms and the company that made Grimod's false hands, see Jessica Riskin, "Eighteenth-Century Wetware," *Representations* 83 (2003): 97–124 (110–12).
2. *L'École des gourmands, vaudeville en un Acte, par* [*André René Polydore Alissan de*] *Chazet, Lafortelle et Francis; Représenté pour les premières fois, sur le théâtre Montansier, les 30 Thermidor, 1, 2, 3, 4, 5 et 6 fructidor an 12* [*1803*]. (Paris: Mad. Cavanagh, 1804).
3. The *Fermier général* was a tax farmer under the Ancien Régime (Old French Monarchy), who was responsible for "farming" the taxes of a particular district. This much detested position was abolished in 1790, immediately following the French Revolution.
4. A butler, or headwaiter of a restaurant.
5. A clever or witty saying; a repartee.
6. Above all brief: this is quite essential at the dining table where, according to the judicious advice Madame Geoffrin offered a young provincial, one must be equipped with knives that are long, and stories that are short. [Grimod]
7. A "galantine" is a type of *charcuterie* made from poultry or other white meat (like veal or even suckling pig) which has been deboned (but usually with the skin left on), stuffed with forcemeat, cooked, covered with aspic and served cold; a "saveloy" is a dish made from veal, chicken, or other white, boneless meat that is tied, boiled, and served cold; a mortadella is a large, spiced pork sausage, originally from Bologna.
8. Bleeding was a medical practice, popular through the eighteenth and into the nineteenth century, as was "evacuation" through the use of emetics, mentioned below.
9. Literally, a white food to be eaten; from the Middle Ages this was composed of fowl and other meat, minced with cream, rice, almonds, sugar, and eggs; Grimod probably intended the more modern version of the sweetmeat, boiled with milk, in the shape of an opaque, white jelly.
10. A small amount of cheese, with bread crumbs, eggs, and other ingredients, baked and served in a mold.
11. A reference to the *Dictionnaire de l'académie française*, first published in 1694 (and in subsequent editions of 1718, 1740, 1762, 1798, 1835, etc.). The French Academy, created in 1635 by Cardinal Richelieu (Prime Minster of France from 1585–1642) and sanctioned by Louis XIII, was a learned society of leading Men of Letters charged with the task of codifying the vocabulary and grammar of the French language to make it "pure" and "comprehensible."
12. Pierre Joseph André Roubaud (1730–91), *Nouveaux synonymes français* (Paris: Moutard, 1785).
13. A reference to the first encyclopedia (*L'encyclopédie, ou, dictionnaire raisonné des sciences, des arts et des métiers*) by Denis Diderot (1713–84) and Jean le Rond d'Alembert (1717–83), published in thirty-two volumes from 1751 to 1777.
14. This precaution is all the more necessary since there are people who believe themselves quite well known, and who are in fact, but whose address is unfamiliar to the guest they have invited for the first time, who finds himself obliged to inquire bluntly. This is precisely what happened to the Author of this Work, with someone quite well known today. [Grimod]
15. Cf. note 2, above.

16. To put our conscience at ease, we should point out that we have taken this high praise of Cahors solely on faith; but it is up to its inhabitants to provide us the means to judge its various specialties more authoritatively. [Grimod]

17. Salep, made from the powdered root of various wild orchids, is a tasty and nourishing warm winter drink that was known for boosting immunity against colds and coughs.

18. The very skillful son of a most skillful father who, about forty years ago, returned silver and gold smithing to its former glory, for this art seemed to have been lost in France since the time of the Germanic tribes. His workshops are located opposite the Carrousel. [Grimod]

19. We shall not even mention those who, when they stay at a Host's country residence, make off with items provided for their convenience, like slippers, combs, hair curlers, etc. [Grimod]

20. Distraction is either feigned, or comes naturally. In the first instance, it is a mark of foolishness; in the second, a veritable handicap. Distracted people are thus never good for anything, especially at the dining table. [Grimod]

21. There are many instances when one would vex a Host greatly by trying to reciprocate in kind. Any man who has a good Cook and serves excellent meals is glad to excuse others for not inviting him, because he eats better at home on a regular basis than elsewhere on special occasions. Indeed, it is a nasty trick to play on someone, to invite him and feed him less well than he would have eaten at home: better to remain in his debt than to try foolishly to repay him with inadequate means. The Author of this Work is so thoroughly committed to these principles, that he would refrain from inviting this or that person in whose home he had enjoyed excellent dinners, for this would be cruel punishment for their generosity. They know this, and are glad to forgive him his apparent ingratitude. General rule: those inferior in wealth or worth should almost never take the liberty of inviting their superiors. [Grimod]

22. Since there can only be true agreement, in any sort of discussion, when parties agree on a precise definition of terms, it will be useful here to articulate what we mean by the three of these, the last of which has not even been recognized by the Academy, and cannot be found in any Dictionary. An *Invitation* is the act whereby a Host asks someone to dine at his home; in the interest of both caution and consistency, it should always be done in writing and in advance. A *Commitment* is an obligation that the guest agrees to honor when he accepts the invitation. It should be sacred to a true Gourmand, who never gives his word in vain. *Dis-Invitation* is the act whereby a Host informs you that the meal to which you had been summoned shall not take place or that, for whatever reasons, he is relieving you of your obligation, and requesting that you not come. This is the height of impoliteness, and nothing justifies a Host *Dis-Inviting* one or more guests. Finally, *Relinquishment* takes the form of a note (for this must always be done in writing) in which a guest lets you know that he cannot come, and asks you to release him from his obligation. This is also extremely improper and, while never justified, may in rare instances be excusable. [Grimod]

23. Pierre Augustin Caron de Beaumarchais (1732–99). The distinction between *savoir-faire* (tact or the instinctive knowledge of behaving appropriately to any situation) is here contrasted with *savoir-vivre* (knowledge of the world, living well, and the customs of good society).

24. We have never met any lady of the house who knew better than Madame Caron de Beaumarchais (née Villers) how to officiate at a well-populated and well-served table. She had so refined this art that, during a four-hour long dinner with twenty guests, each could believe that she had tended only to him, for she knew how to apportion her warmth and attention with such grace and discernment. We shall never cease to hold her up as a model for Hostesses today. [Grimod]

25. The name of a white wine exported from the south of Spain.

26. Grimod draws on the stereotype of the Gascon as a braggart or boaster.

27. Literally, on the "ambiguous": a form of entertainment from the seventeenth and eighteenth centuries where the food and dessert are all served up together.

28. A female slave in an Eastern harem, esp. as in the seraglio of the Sultan of Turkey.

29. The "Béchamel," a white creamy sauce, is named after its inventor, the Marquis de Béchamel, steward of Louis XIV; the "quenelle" is a seasoned ball made of meat or fish reduced to a paste; a "fricassee" is fried or stewed sliced meat, served with a sauce; an "émincé" is a dish made from left-over roast or braised meat, thinly sliced, put in an ovenware dish, and served with sauce; "à la reine" is another term for "à la française."

30. *Quod Erat Demonstratum*, meaning what was to be demonstrated has been, was traditionally written at the end of a mathematical proof.

31. The central dish of a meal; the "relevé" referred to below is a "remove" of top and bottom dishes, generally one in which large joints of meat or game replace soup and fish.

32. Never have Changes been more frequent in the profession of notary than since the Revolution. Its members have changed almost entirely over the past twenty-five years, indeed at the moment we are writing this, out of one-hundred thirteen notaries [in Paris], there remain only twelve who were in practice before 1789. This did not used to be so; it was an honorable profession in which one grew old, and in which young people were not in the majority. It is true that, in the past, Notaries shared with the Parish Priests of Paris and Sergeants in the Royal Guard the honor of being considered the most respectable professional body in Paris . . . . . . Far from the case today!!! [Grimod]

33. The expression is no doubt a strong one, when speaking of such an establishment, but we would appeal here to all who frequented it after the elder M. Robert's departure. [Grimod]

34. An Eastern sect of people who look back to the past as a better time; the phrase is used by Horace in *Ars Poetica*, line 173, though Horace uses the singular (*laudator*), as printed in the edition by C. O. Brink (Cambridge: Cambridge University Press, 1971), 61.

35. These were all leading chemists of the time: Antoine François, Comte de Fourcroy (1755–1809), Jean-Antoine Chaptal, Comte de Chanteloup (1756–1832), and Louis Nicolas Vauquelin (1763–1829).

36. A parody of Nicolas Boileau, *L'art poétique* (1674), Chant II, 91–92: "Défendit qu'un vers faible y pût jamai entrer / Ni qu'un mot déjà mis osât s'y remontrer."

37. In polite society, it is often debated whether the dinner Menu should be given to the guests, or left a mystery. In the first instance, guests adapt their appetites according to the nature of the dishes offered, which interferes with and slows down service. In the second, they let loose on the first courses, so that the roast and entremets often end up neglected. These are both significant drawbacks, but since the latter is the lesser, as a true Gourmand always has room for choice items, we feel that the Menu should remain a secret between the cook and Host. [Grimod]

38. There exists a Manuscript in four folio volumes, entitled M. AZE'S RULES, which includes a Summary of all the Rules of Politeness, and indicates the best way to act and the right path to follow in all social circumstances. This is an extremely valuable Work, yet known to very few. We plan to publish it some day, and would wager that the public shall be all the more grateful for a volume so keenly awaited. For now it shall have to suffice to note that the great M. Aze, born in 1725, and the father of twenty children, whose addresses alone (printed in M. Caillot-du-Val's *Philosophical Correspondence*) fill more than a half page in small roman typeface, is a practicing Philosopher who, at the dining table as elsewhere, has always preached by example, and thus whose authority concerning Precepts and *Rules* is far mightier than that of most contemporary Preachers. [Grimod]

2
William Kitchiner (1775[?]–1827)

Apicius Redevivus, or The Cooks Oracle; Actual Experiments Instituted in the Kitchen of a Physician (London, 1817)

Peptic Precepts, Pointing Out Agreeable and Effectual Methods to Prevent and Relieve Indigestion, and to Regulate and Strengthen the Action of the Stomach and Bowels (London, 1821)

Introduction

The British physician, Dr. William Kitchiner, adopted the French fashion for treating food as a fine art and cooking as a medium for self-expression and self-invention. His cookbook, *Apicius Redevivus; or the Cook's Oracle* (1817) was prefaced by an essay in the style of the gastronomical treatise. Its prefaces multiplied along with the number of editions, introducing his book as a compendium of empiricist experiments in taste. For him, the art of cookery was "an Occupation neither unbecoming nor unworthy [of] Philosophers of the highest class." Each recipe he claimed to have been submitted to a professional "Committee of Taste," modeled on Grimod de la Reynière's Tasting Jury. Kitchiner's was not the first gastronomical essay to appear in English, but it was the most influential, transporting French gastronomy into English and introducing British readers to the concept of the "rational epicure."

Throughout the 1820s and 1830s, Kitchiner was considered a leading authority on cookery, and his preface acknowledged that "increasing demand for *The Cook's Oracle*, amounting in 1822 to the extraordinary number of upwards of 15,000, has been stimulus enough to excite any man to submit

57

to the most unremitting study." One society lady compared the book favorably to contemporary best-selling literary works, remarking that "Neither Walter Scott nor Lord Byron have had so quick and profitable a sale."[1] Walter Scott himself, author of *Waverly* (1814), *Rob Roy* (1817), *Ivanhoe* (1819), and other historical novels, observed how much Kitchiner's work outstripped the generic collection of recipes.[2] The essayist Charles Lamb boasted of his ability, "Doctor Kitchener-like to examine the good things at table," and his fictional persona in "A Dissertation Upon Roast Pig," sounds much like Kitchiner in his taste for suckling pig. "To gain the praise of Epicurean Pig-Eaters," writes Kitchiner in words Lamb would echo, "the CRACKLING must be *nicely crisped* and delicately *lightly browned*, without being either blistered or burnt."[3]

Far from the typical cookbook, Kitchiner's *Cook's Oracle* was considered by one reviewer in 1842 a "mass of eccentricity"; two years later, another referred to it as "an odd confused *olla podrida* of receipts, observations, maxims, and remarks, drawn from all sources, ancient and modern, foreign as well as domestic."[4] Gastronomers today continue to describe it as "the raciest, most opinionated, least practical cookery book ever written."[5] The text is peppered with literary allusions to poets such Milton, Pope, Southey, and Byron, and it denounces all previous cookery books as no more helpful to the practicing cook "than reading *Robinson Crusoe* would enable a Sailor to steer safely from England to India." In response to this perceived neglect, *The Cook's Oracle* initiates the English gastronomical tradition as a philosophico-literary genre of writing about food.

Kitchiner, who as the son of a well-to-do coal merchant was financially independent, devoted himself to the study of science at home, hosting elaborate dinners for a circle of literary and intellectual friends. His kitchen was his laboratory, and his experiments with the "science" or "art" of cookery (alternately so called) took place there. He was assisted in his labors by Henry Osborne, the distinguished chef of Sir Joseph Banks, President of the Royal Society of London. Reviewing Kitchiner's book for *The Edinburgh Review* in 1821, Richard Chenevix supposed that his recipes "were actually written down by the fire-side, with a spit in the one hand, and a pen in the other; in defiance to the combined odoriferous calefaciant repellants of roasting and boiling, frying and broiling."[6] Applying his scientific knowledge to cookery, Kitchiner claims that he would never have "*presumed to recommend one Receipt that has not been previously and repeatedly proved in His own Kitchen*." All of his recipes were "approved by the most accomplished Cooks" and "eaten with unanimous applause by a COMMITTEE OF TASTE, composed of some of the most illustrious Gastrophilists of this luxurious Metropolis." Like taste philosophers of the eighteenth century, Kitchiner was an empiricist, committed to the pursuit of correct judgment through disinterested experimentation.

The very title of his book alludes to Baltasar Graciáns *The Oracle: A Manual of the Art of Discretion*, which aesthetic philosophers starting with Joseph Addison in 1711 took as a point of origin for the concept of taste.

Unlike French cookery, modeled on the courtly model, Kitchiner's brand of gastronomy stressed economy in language as well as in culinary art. He chose to discard "a farrago of unappropriate and unmeaning terms, many corrupted from the French," in common use among culinary writers. His aim was to "render Food acceptable to the Palate, without being expensive to the Purse...constantly endeavouring to hold the balance even, between the agreeable and the wholesome, the Epicure and the Economist." Kitchiner also showed the gastronomical penchant for antiquarian research, and he claimed to have "patiently pioneered through more than TWO HUNDRED COOKERY BOOKS before he set about recording these results of his own Experiments!!!!" Of the numerous books to which he alludes, however (one diligent contemporary counts over two hundred and fifty), he does not mention any by the leading French chefs practicing in England at the time, Eustache Ude and Charles Elmé Francatelli. Both of these men were in turn critical of him for his "hackneyed terms" and "economical makeshifts."[7] As subsequent writers have noted, Kitchiner was not a professional chef. His contribution to food history is mainly epicurean.

Kitchiner himself was moderate in his habits, convinced that health depends upon the proper preparation of food. He explains that "The Editor is now in his forty-third year, and has been from his youth occasionally afflicted with [stomach] disorders; sometimes without being able to imagine what has produced them," such he describes as "'NIGHTMARE,' 'Globus Hystericus,' 'Spasms,' 'Cramp,' or 'Gout,' in the Stomach, with which few who have passed the Meridian of Life,[8] are so fortunate as not to be too well acquainted." His desire to relieve others from similar complaints—and from the fatigue attending the performance of the role of host or Amphitryon—motivates his *Peptic Precepts*.

The following extracts are from the 1831 London edition of *The Cook's Oracle* and the third (1822) edition of *Peptic Precepts*.

From *The Cook's Oracle* (1817)

Introduction

The following Receipts are not a mere marrowless collection of shreds and patches, of cuttings and pastings,—but a *bonâ fide* register of Practical Facts;—accumulated by a perseverance not to be subdued or evaporated by the igniferous terrors of a Roasting Fire in the Dog-days,—in defiance of the odoriferous and calefacient repellents, of *Roasting,—Boiling,—Frying,—*and *Broiling;*—moreover, the Author has submitted to a labour no preceding Cookery-Book-maker, perhaps, ever attempted to encounter,—having *eaten* each Receipt before he set it down in his book.

They have all been heartily welcome by a sufficiently well-educated Palate, and a rather fastidious Stomach;—perhaps this certificate of the reception of the respective preparations—will partly apologise for the Book containing a smaller number of them than preceding writers on this gratifying subject have transcribed—for the amusement of "every man's Master," the STOMACH.[9]

Numerous as are the Receipts in former Books, they vary little from each other, except in the name given to them; the processes of Cookery are very few,—I have endeavoured to describe each, in so plain and circumstantial a manner, as I hope will be easily understood even by the Amateur, who is unacquainted with the practical part of Culinary concerns.

OLD HOUSEKEEPERS may think I have been tediously minute on many points which may appear trifling:—my Predecessors seem to have considered the RUDIMENTS OF COOKERY quite unworthy of attention. These little delicate distinctions constitute all the difference between a common and an elegant Table, and are not trifles to the YOUNG HOUSEKEEPERS, who must learn them either from the communication of others,—or blunder on till their own slowly accumulating and dear-bought experience teaches them.

A wish to save Time, Trouble and Money, to inexperienced Housekeepers and Cooks,—and to bring enjoyments and indulgences of the Opulent within reach of the middle Ranks of Society,—were my motives for publishing this book;—I could accomplish it only by supposing the Reader (when he first opens it,) to be as ignorant of Cookery,—as I was when I first thought of writing on the subject.[10]

I have done my best to contribute to the comfort of my fellow-creatures;—by a careful attention to the directions herein given, the most ignorant may easily learn to prepare Food, not only in an agreeable and wholesome,—but in an elegant and economical manner.

This task seems to have been left for me, and I have endeavoured to collect and communicate in the clearest and most intelligible manner, the whole of the heretofore abstruse Mysteries of the Culinary Art, which are herein, I hope, plainly developed, that *the most inexperienced* student in the occult Art of Cookery, *may work from my Receipts with the utmost facility.*

I was perfectly aware of the extreme difficulty of teaching those who are entirely unacquainted with the subject, and of explaining my ideas effectually by mere Receipts, to those who never shook hands with a Stewpan.

In my anxiety to be readily understood,—I have been under the necessity of occasionally repeating the same directions in different parts of the book, but I would rather be censured for repetition than for obscurity,—and hope not to be accused of Affectation, while my intention is Perspicuity.

Our neighbours in France are so justly famous for their skill in the affairs of the Kitchen, that the adage says, "*As many Frenchmen as many Cooks.*" Surrounded as they are by a profusion of the most delicious Wines, and seducing Liqueurs offering every temptation to render drunkenness delightful, yet a tippling Frenchman is a "*rara avis*" [rare bird].

They know how, so easily, to keep Life in sufficient repair by good eating, that they require little or no screwing up with liquid Stimuli.—This accounts for that "*toujours gai*," and happy equilibrium of the animal spirits which they enjoy with more regularity than any people:—their elastic Stomachs, unimpaired by Spirituous Liquors, digest vigorously the food they sagaciously prepare and render easily assimilable, by cooking it sufficiently,—wisely contriving to get half the work of the Stomach done by Fire and Water, till

> The tender morsels on the palate melt,
> And all the force of Cookery is felt.

The cardinal virtues of Cookery, "CLEANLINESS, FRUGALITY, NOURISHMENT, AND PALATEABLENESS," preside over each preparation; for I have not presumed to insert a single composition, without previously obtaining the "*imprimatur*" of an enlightened and indefatigable "*COMMITTEE OF TASTE*" (composed of thoroughbred GRANDS GOURMANDS of the first magnitude,) whose cordial co-operation I cannot too highly praise; and here do I most gratefully record the unremitting zeal they manifested during their arduous progress of proving the respective Recipes,—they were so truly philosophically and disinterestedly regardless of the wear and tear of teeth and stomach, that their Labour—appeared a Pleasure to them.—Their laudable perseverance has enabled me to give the inexperienced Amateur an unerring guide how to excite as much pleasure as possible on the Palate, and occasion as little trouble as possible to the Principal Viscera, and has hardly been exceeded by those determined spirits who lately in the Polar expedition braved the other extreme of temperature, &c. in spite of Whales, Bears, Icebergs, and Starvation.

Every attention has been paid in directing the proportions of the following Compositions, not merely to make them inviting to the Appetite, but agreeable and useful to the Stomach—nourishing without being inflammatory, and savoury without being surfeiting.

I have written for those who make Nourishment the chief end of Eating,[11] and do not desire to provoke Appetite beyond the powers and necessities of Nature;—proceeding, however on the purest Epicurean principles of indulging the Palate as far as it can be done without injury or offense to the Stomach, and forbidding[12] nothing but what is absolutely unfriendly to Health.

> That which is not good, is not delicious
> To a well-govern'd and wise appetite.—MILTON.[13]

This is by no means so difficult a task as some gloomy philosophers (un-initiated in Culinary Science) have tried to make the world believe—who seem to have delighted in persuading you, that every thing that is Nice must be noxious;—and that everything that is Nasty is wholesome.

How charming is Divine Philosophy!
Not harsh, and crabbed, as dull fools suppose,
But musical as is Apollo's lute,
And a perpetual feast of nectar'd sweets,
Where no crude surfeit reigns.—MILTON.[14]

Worthy William Shakespeare declared he never found a philosopher who could endure the Toothache patiently,—the Editor protests that he has not yet overtaken one who did not love a Feast.[15]

Those *Cynical* Slaves, who are so silly as to suppose it unbecoming a wise man to indulge in the common comforts of Life, should be answered in the words of the French philosopher. "Hey—What, do you Philosophers eat dainties?" said a gay Marquess, "*Do you think*," replied DESCARTES, "*that God made good things only for Fools?*"

Every individual, who is not perfectly imbecile and void of understanding, is an *Epicure* in his own, way—the Epicures in boiling of Potatoes are innumerable,—the perfection of all enjoyment depends on the perfection of the faculties of the Mind and Body, therefore—*the Temperate Man is the greatest Epicure*—and the only *true Voluptuary*.

THE PLEASURES OF THE TABLE have been highly appreciated and carefully cultivated in all Countries and in all Ages,[16]—and in spite of all the Stoics,—every one will allow they are the first and the last we enjoy,—and those we taste the oftenest,—*above a Thousand times in a Year, every Year of our Lives!*

THE STOMACH is the mainspring of our System,—if it be not sufficiently wound up to warm the Heart and support the Circulation,—the whole business of Life will, in proportion, be ineffectively performed,—we can neither *Think* with precision,—*Walk with vigour*,—*Sit down* with comfort,—nor *Sleep* with tranquillity.

There would be no difficulty in proving that it influences (much more than people in general imagine) all our actions:—the destiny of Nations has often depended upon the more or less laborious digestion of a Prime Minister.[17]

The philosopher *Pythagoras* seems to have been extremely nice in eating; among his absolute injunctions to his disciples, he commands them "to abstain from Beans."

This ancient Sage has been imitated by the learned who have discoursed on this subject since,—who are liberal of their negative,—and niggardly of their positive precepts—in the ratio, that it is easier to tell you not to do this, than to teach you how to do that.

Our great English moralist Dr. S. JOHNSON, his biographer Boswell tells us, "was a man of very nice discernment in the science of Cookery," and talked of good eating with uncommon satisfaction. "Some people," said he, "have a foolish way of not minding, or pretending not to mind what they eat; for my part, I mind my belly very studiously and very carefully, and I look upon it that he who does not mind his Belly, will hardly mind any thing else."

The Dr. might have said, *cannot* mind any thing else—the *energy of our* BRAINS *is sadly dependent on the behaviour of our* BOWELS[18] —those who say, "Tis no matter what we eat or what we drink,"—may as well say, "Tis no matter whether we eat, or whether we drink."

The following Anecdotes I copy from BOSWELL'S *Life of* JOHNSON.

Johnson.—"I could write a better Book of Cookery than has ever yet been written;—it should be a book on philosophical principles.—I would tell what is the best Butcher's meat,—the proper seasons of different Vegetables,—and then, how to roast and boil, and to compound."[19]

Dilly.—"Mrs. Glasse's Cookery, which is the best, was written by DR. HILL."[20]

Johnson.—"Well, Sir—this shews how much better the subject of Cookery[21] may be treated by a Philosopher;[22]—but you shall see what a book of Cookery I shall make, and shall agree with Mr. Dilly for the Copyright."

Miss Seward.—"That would be Hercules with the distaff indeed!!"

Johnson.—"No, Madam; Women can spin very well,—but they cannot make a good book of Cookery."[23]

Mr. B. adds, "I never knew a man who relished good eating more than he did: when at Table, he was totally absorbed in the business of the moment: nor would he, unless in very high company, say one word, or even pay the least attention to what was said by others, until he had satisfied his Appetite."

The peculiarities of his Constitution were as great as those of his Character:—Luxury and Intemperance are relative terms, depending on other circumstances than mere quantity and quality. Nature gave him an excellent Palate, and a craving Appetite, and his intense Application rendered large supplies of nourishment absolutely necessary to recruit his exhausted spirits.

The fact is, this great Man had found out that *Animal and Intellectual Vigor,*[24] *are much more entirely dependent upon each other than is commonly understood*; especially in those constitutions, whose digestive and chylopoetic organs are capricious and easily put out of tune, or absorb the "*pabulum vitæ*" indolently and imperfectly,—with such, it is only now and then that the "*sensorium commune*" vibrates with the full tone of accurately considerative or creative energy. "His favourite dainties were, a leg of pork boiled till it dropped from the bone, a veal-pie with plums and sugar, or the outside cut of a salt buttock of beef." "With regard to Drink, his liking was for the strongest, as it was not the *Flavour*, but the *Effect* that he desired."[25]

Thus does the HEALTH always, and very often the LIFE of invalids, and those who have weak and infirm STOMACHS, depend upon the care and skill of the Cook. Our Forefathers were so sensible of this, that in days of Yore no man of consequence thought of making a day's Journey without taking his "MAGISTER COQUORUM" [master cook] with him.

...

MY RECEIPTS are the results of experiments carefully made, and accurately and circumstantially related;

The TIME requisite for dressing being stated;

The QUANTITIES of the various articles contained in each composition being carefully set down in NUMBER, WEIGHT, and MEASURE.

The WEIGHTS are *Avoirdupois;* the MEASURE, *Lyne's* graduated Glass, i.e. a Wine pint divided into sixteen ounces, and the Ounce into eight Drachms:—by a *Wine-glass* is to be understood two ounces liquid measure;—by a large or *Table-Spoonful*, half an ounce;—by a small *or Tea-Spoonful*, a drachm, or half a quarter of an ounce, i.e. nearly equal to two drachms avoirdupois.[26]

At PRICE'S glass warehouse, near Exeter 'Change, in the Strand you may get measures divided into Tea and Table-Spoons.—No Cook should be without one, who wishes to be regular in her business.

This precision has never before been attempted in Cookery books, but I found it indispensable from the impossibility of *guessing* the quantities intended by such obscure expressions as have been usually employed for this purpose in former works:—

For instance: a bit of this—a handful of that—a pinch of t'other,—do 'em over with an Egg,—and a sprinkle of salt,—a dust of flour,—a shake of pepper,—a squeeze of lemon,—or a dash of vinegar, &c. are the constant phrases; season it to your Palate, (meaning the Cook's,) is another form of speech: now, if she has any,—it is very unlikely that it is in unison with that of her employers,—by continually sipping *piquante* relishes, it becomes blunted and insensible, and loses the faculty of appreciating delicate flavours,—so that every thing is done at random.

These Culinary technicals[27] are so very differently understood by the learned who write them, and the unlearned who read them, and their "rule of Thumb" is so extremely indefinite, that if the same dish be dressed by different persons, it generally be so different, that nobody would imagine they had worked from the same directions, which will assist a person who has not served a regular apprenticeship in the Kitchen, no more than reading "Robinson Crusoe" would enable a Sailor to steer safely from England to India.

It is astonishing how cheap *Cookery Books* are held by practical Cooks: when I applied to an experienced artist, to recommend me some books that would give me a notion of the rudiments of Cookery, he replied with a smile—"You may read *Don Quixote,* or *Peregrine Pickle,* they are both very good books."

Careless expressions in Cookery are the more surprising, as the Confectioner is regularly attentive, in the description of his preparations, to give the exact quantities, though his business, compared to Cookery, is unimportant, as the Ornamental is inferior to the Useful.

The maker of Blanc-mange, Custards, &c. and the endless and useless collection of puerile playthings for the palate (of First and Second childhood, for the *Vigour of Manhood seeketh not to be sucking Sugar, or sipping Turtle,*) is scrupulously exact, even to a grain, in his ingredients; whilst Cooks are unintelligibly indefinite, although they are intrusted with the administration of our FOOD, *upon the proper quality and preparation of which, all our Powers of Body and Mind depend;—their Energy, being invariably in the ratio of the performance of the restorative process,* i.e. the quantity, quality, and perfect digestion of what we Eat and Drink.

Unless *the Stomach* be in good humour, every part of the machinery of *Life* must vibrate with languor:—can we then be too attentive to its adjustment?!!

Invitations to Dinner

In *"the affairs of the Mouth"* the strictest punctuality is indispensable;—the GASTRONOMER ought to be as accurate an observer of Time, as the ASTRONOMER. *The least delay produces fatal and irreparable Misfortunes.*

Almost all other Ceremonies and Civil Duties may be put off for several hours without much inconvenience, and all may be postponed without absolute Danger. A little Delay may try the patience of those Who are waiting; but the act itself will be equally perfect and equally valid. Procrastination sometimes is rather advantageous than prejudicial. It gives time for Reflection—and may prevent our taking a step which would have made us miserable for Life; the delay of a Courier has prevented the conclusion of a Convention, the signing of which might have occasioned the ruin of a Nation.

If, from Affairs the most important, we descend to our Pleasures and Amusements, we shall find new arguments in support of our assertions. The putting off of a Rendezvous, or a Ball, &c. will make them the more delightful. To *hope* is to *enjoy.*

Man never is, but always to be blest.[28]

The anticipation of Pleasure warms our imagination, and keeps those feelings alive, which possession too often extinguishes.

'Tis *Expectation* only makes us blest;
Enjoyment disappoints us at the best.

Dr. Johnson has most sagaciously said, "Such is the State of Life, that *none are happy, but by the anticipation of Change*: the change itself is nothing; when we have made it, the next wish is, immediately to change again."[29]

However singular our assertions may have at first appeared to those who have not considered the subject, we hope by this time we have made converts of our readers, and convinced the *"Amateurs de Bonne Chère"* of the truth and importance of our remarks; and that they will remember, that DINNER is the only act of the day which *cannot be put off with Impunity, for even* FIVE MINUTES.

In a well-regulated family, all the Clocks and Watches should agree; on this depends the fate of the Dinner; *what would be agreeable to the Stomach, and restorative to the System, if served at* FIVE *o'clock,—will be uneatable and innutritive and indigestible at* A QUARTER PAST.

The Dining-room should be furnished with a good going clock;—the space over the Kitchen fire-place with another, vibrating in unison with the former, so placed, that the Cook may keep one Eye on the Clock, and the other on the Spit, &c. She will calculate to a minute the time required to roast a large Capon or a little Lark, and is equally attentive to the degree of heat of her Stove, and the time her sauce remains on it, when to withdraw the Bakings from the oven, the Roast from the spit, and the Stew from the pan.

With all our love of punctuality, the first consideration must still be, that the dinner *"be well done, when 'tis done."*[30]

It is a common fault *with Cooks who are anxious about Time, to overdress every thing*—the Guests had better wait than the Dinner—a little delay will improve their appetite;[31] but if the Dinner waits for the Guests, it will be deteriorated every minute:—The Host who wishes to entertain his friends with food perfectly well dressed, while he most earnestly endeavours to impress on their minds the importance of being punctual to the appointed hour,—will still allow his Cook a quarter of an hour's grace.

The old Adage that "the Eye is often bigger than the Belly," is often verified by the ridiculous vanity of those, who wish to make an appearance above their fortune—nothing can be more ruinous to real comfort than the too common custom of setting out a table, with a parade and a profusion, unsuited not only to the circumstances of the Hosts, but to the number of the Guests;—or more fatal to true Hospitality, than the multiplicity of dishes which luxury has made fashionable at the tables of the Great, the Wealthy—and the Ostentatious,—who are often neither great nor wealthy.

Such pompous preparation, instead of being a compliment to our Guests, is nothing better than an indirect offence; it is a tacit insinuation, that it is absolutely necessary to provide such delicacies to bribe the depravity of their palates, when we desire the pleasure of their company; and that Society in England, now, must be purchased, at the same price SWIFT told POPE, he was obliged to pay for it in Ireland—"I should hardly prevail to find one Visitor, if I were not able to hire him with a bottle of Wine."[32]

When twice as much Cooking is undertaken as there are Servants, or conveniences in the Kitchen to do it properly, Dishes must be dressed long before the Dinner hour, and stand by spoiling —the poor Cook loses her credit, and the poor guests get Indigestions. Why prepare for eight or ten *Friends,* more than sufficient for twenty or thirty *VISITORS?* "*Enough is as good as a Feast,*" and a prudent provider, who sensibly takes measure of the Stomachic, instead of the Silly ocular, appetite of his Guests, may entertain his Friends,—three times as often, and ten as well.

It is Your SENSELESS SECOND COURSES—ridiculous variety of WINES, LIQUEURS, ICES,[33] DESSERTS, &C.—which are served up merely to feed the Eye, or pamper palled appetite that *overcome the Stomach, and paralyse Digestion*, and seduce "children of a larger Growth" [34] to sacrifice the health and comfort of several days,—for the Baby-pleasure of tickling their tongue for a few minutes, with Trifles and Custards!!! &c.&c.

INDIGESTION will sometimes overtake the most experienced Epicure; when the gustatory nerves are in good humour, Hunger and Savoury Viands will sometimes seduce the Tongue of a "*Grand Gourmand*" to betray the interests of his Stomach in spite of his Brains.

On such an unfortunate occasion, when the Stomach sends forth eructant[35] signals of distress, the *Peristaltic Persuaders* are as agreeable and effectual assistance as can be offered; and for delicate Constitutions, and those that are impaired by Age or Intemperance, are a valuable Panacea.

· · ·

The Cloth[36] *should be laid in the Parlour*, and all the paraphernalia of the dinner-table completely arranged, at least *half an hour before dinner-time*.

The Cook's labour will be lost, if the Parlour-table be not ready for action, and the Eaters ready for the Eatables, which the least delay will irreparably injure:—therefore, the GOURMAND will be punctual for the sake of gratifying his ruling passion; the INVALID, to avoid the danger of encountering an *Indigestion* from eating ill-dressed food; and the RATIONAL EPICURE, who happily attends the Banquet with "*mens sana in corpore sano*," will keep the time not only for these strong reasons, but that he may not lose the advantage of being introduced to the other Guests. He considers not only what is on the Table, but Who are around it: his principal inducement to leave his own Fireside, is the charm of agreeable and instructive Society, and the opportunity of making connexions, which may augment the interest and enjoyment of existence.

It is the most pleasing part of the Duty of the Master of the Feast (especially when the Guests are not very numerous[37]), to take advantage of these moments to introduce them to one another, naming them individually in an audible voice, and adroitly laying hold of those ties of acquaintanceship or profession which may exist between them.

This will much augment the pleasures of the Festive Board,—to which it is indeed as indispensable a Prelude as an Overture is to an Opera: and the Host will thus acquire an additional claim to the gratitude of his Guests. We urge this point more strongly, because from want of attention to it, we have seen more than once, persons whom many kindred ties would have drawn closely together, pass an entire day without opening their lips to each other, because they were mutually ignorant of each other's names, professions, and pursuits.

To put an end at once to all ceremony as to *The Order in which the Guests are to Sit*, it will save much time and trouble, if the Mistress of the Mansion adopts the simple and elegant method of placing the name of each Guest in the plate which is intended for him.—This proceeding will be of course the result of consideration, and the Host will place those together whom he thinks will harmonise best.

Le Journal des Dames informs us, that in several fashionable houses in Paris, a new arrangement has been introduced in placing the company at a Dinner-table.[38]

"The Ladies first take their places, leaving intervals for the Gentlemen; after being seated, each is desired to call a gentleman to sit beside her; and thus the, Lady of the house is relieved from all embarrassment of étiquette as to rank and pretensions," &c.

But without doubt, says the Journalist, this method has its inconveniences.

"It may happen that a bashful Beauty dare not name the object of her secret wishes; and an acute observer may determine, from a single glance, that the *elected* is not always the *chosen*."

If the Party is large, the Founders of the Feast may sit in the middle of the Table, instead of at each end thus they will enjoy the pleasure of attending equally to all their Friends; and being in some degree relieved from the occupation of Carving, will have an opportunity of administering all those little attentions which contribute so much to the comfort of their Guests.

If the Guests have any respect for their HOST, or prefer a well-dressed-dinner to one that is spoiled, instead of coming *half an hour after*, they will take care to make their appearance *a quarter of an hour before* the time appointed.

The operations of the Cook are governed by the Clock; *the moment the Roasts, &c. are ready*, they must go to the table, if they are to be eaten in perfection.

An invitation to come at FIVE o' clock seems to be generally understood to mean *Six*; FIVE PRECISELY, half-past Five;—and NOT LATER THAN FIVE (so that Dinner may be on the table within five minutes after, allowing this for the variation of watches) FIVE O'CLOCK EXACTLY.

Be it known to all Loyal Subjects of the Empire of Good-living, that the COMMITTEE OF TASTE have unanimously resolved, that "*an invitation to* ETA. BETA. PI *must be in Writing*, and sent at least ten days before the Banquet—*and must be answered in Writing (as soon as possible after it is received)—within Twenty-four hours at least*"—especially if it be not accepted—then, in addition to the usual complimentary expressions of thanks, &c. the best possible reasons must be assigned for the non-acceptance, as a particular pre-engagement, or severe indisposition, &c. Before the bearer of it delivers it, he should ascertain if the person it is directed to is at home—if he is not, when he will be—and if he is not in town to bring the summons back.

Nothing can be more disobliging than a refusal which is not grounded on some very strong and unavoidable cause,—except not coming at the appointed hour;—"according to the Laws of Conviviality, a certificate from a Sheriff's Officer, a Doctor, or an Undertaker are the only Pleas which are admissible. The duties which Invitation imposes do not fall only on the Persons invited, but, like all other Social duties, are reciprocal.

As he who has accepted an Invitation cannot disengage himself from it; the Master of the Feast cannot put off the entertainment on any pretence whatever. Urgent Business—Sickness,—not even Death, can dispense with the obligation which he is under of giving the Entertainment, for which he has sent out invitations, which have been accepted; for in the extreme cases of compulsory Absence, or Death, his place may be filled by his Friend or Executor."[39]

It is the least Punishment that a blundering ill-bred Booby can receive, who comes half an hour after the time he was bidden, to find the Soup removed, and the Fish cold: moreover, for such an offence, let him also be *mulcted* in a pecuniary Penalty, to be applied to the FUND FOR THE BENEFIT OF DECAYED COOKS. This is the least punishment that can be inflicted on one whose silence, or violation of an engagement, tends to paralyse an entertainment, and to draw his friend into useless expense.

BOILEAU, the French satirist, has a shrewd observation on this subject. "I have always been punctual at the hour of dinner," says the Bard; "for I knew, that all those whom I kept waiting at that provoking interval, would employ those unpleasant moments, to sum up all my faults.—Boileau is indeed a man of Genius—a very honest man; but that dilatory and procrastinating way he has got into, would mar the virtues of an Angel."[40]

There are some who seldom keep an appointment—we can assure them they as seldom "'scape without whipping," and exciting those murmurs which inevitably proceed from the best-regulated Stomachs, when they are empty, and impatient to be filled.

The most amiable Animals when hungry become ill-tempered—our best Friends employ the time they are kept waiting, in recollecting and repeating any real faults we have, and attributing to us a thousand imaginary ones.

Ill-bred Beings, who indulge at their own caprice, regardless how they wound the feelings of others, if they possess brilliant and useful talents, may occasionally be endured as convenient Tools; but deceive themselves sadly, even though they possess all the Wisdom, and all the Wit in the World, if they fancy they can ever be esteemed as Friends.

From *Peptic Precepts* (1821)

THE STOMACH is the centre of Sympathy;—if the most minute fibre of the human frame be hurt, intelligence of the injury instantaneously arrives;—and the Stomach is disturbed, in proportion to the importance of the Member, and the degree in which it is offended.

If either the Body or the Mind be fatigued,—the Stomach invariably sympathizes;—if the most robust do any thing too much, the Stomach is soon affronted,—and does too little:—unless this main-spring of Health be in perfect adjustment, the machinery of life will vibrate with languor;—especially those parts which are naturally weak, or have been injured by Accidents, &c. Constipation is increased in costive habits—and Diarrhœa in such as are subject thereto—and all Chronic complaints are exasperated, especially in persons past the age of 35 years.

Of the various helps to Science, none perhaps more rapidly facilitate the acquirement of knowledge, than analogical reasoning; or illustrating an Art we are ignorant of, by one we are acquainted with.

THE HUMAN FRAME may be compared to a Watch, of which the Heart is the Mainspring—the Stomach the regulator,—and what we put into it the Key by which the machine is wound up;—*according to the quantity,—quality,—and proper digestion of what we Eat*[41] *and Drink, will be the pace of the Pulse, and the action of the System in general:*—when we observe a due proportion between the quantum of Exercise and that of Excitement, all goes well.—If the machine be disordered, the same expedients are employed for its re-adjustment, as are used by the Watch-maker; it must be carefully cleaned, and judiciously oiled.

Eating *Salads* after Dinner,—and chilling the Stomach, and checking the process of digestion by swilling cold Soda Water—we hold to be other Vulgar Errors.

It is your superfluous SECOND COURSES,—and ridiculous variety of Wines,—Liqueurs,—Ices, Desserts, &c.—which (are served up more to gratify the pride of the Host, than the appetite of the Guests, that) *overcome the Stomach, and paralyze Digestion*, and seduce "Children of larger Growth" to sacrifice the health and comfort of several days—for the Baby-pleasure of tickling their tongue for a few minutes, with Trifles and Custards!!

Most of those who have written on what—by a strange perversion of language—are most non-naturally termed the non-naturals,—have merely laid before the Public a nonsensical register of the peculiarities of their own Palate, and the idiosyncracies of their own Constitution.[42]

Some omnivorous Cormorants have such an ever-craving Appetite, that they are raging with hunger as soon as they open their Eyes,—and bolt half a dozen hard Eggs before they are well awake:—Others are so perfectly restored by that "chief nourisher in Life's feast," Balmy Sleep, that they do not think about Eating,—till they have been up and actively employed for several hours.[43]

Some Minute Philosopher has published an 8vo. pamphlet of 56 pages! on the omnipotent *"virtues Of a Crust of Bread eaten early in the morning fasting*!![44] We have no doubt it is an admirable Specific—for that grievous disorder of the Stomach called Hunger.

The strong Food, which the strong action of strong bodies requires, would soon destroy weak ones,—if the latter attempt to follow the example of the former,—instead of feeling invigorated, their Stomachs will be as oppressed, as a Porter is with a load that is too heavy for him,—and, under the idea of swallowing what are called strengthening nourishing things,—will very soon make themselves ready for the Undertaker.

Some people seem to think, that the more plentifully they stuff themselves, the better they must thrive, and the stronger they must grow.

It is not the quantity that we swallow,—but that which is properly digested, which nourishes us.

A Moderate Meal well digested, renders the body vigorous,—glutting it with superfluity, (which is only turned into excrement instead of aliment, and if not speedily evacuated,) not only oppresses the System, but produces all sorts of Disorders.

Some are continually inviting *Indigestion*,—by eating *Water-cresses*, or other *undressed* Vegetables,[45] "to Sweeten their Blood,"—or Oysters "to enrich it."—Others fancy their Dinner cannot digest till they have closed the orifice of their Stomachs with a certain portion of Cheese,—if the preceding Dinner has been a light one, a little bit of Cheese after it may not do much harm, but its character for encouraging concoction is undeserved,—there is not a more absurd Vulgar Error, than the often quoted proverb, that

> Cheese is a surly Elf,
> Digesting all things, but itself.

A Third never eats Goose, &c. without remembering that *Brandy* or *Cayenne* is the Latin for it.

A much less portion of Stimulus is necessary after a hearty meal of califactive materials, such as good Beef or Mutton—than after a maigre Dinner of Fish,.&c.

Another *Vulgar Error* in the school of Good Living, is, that "*Good eating requires Good drinking.*"—Good eating generally implies *high* seasoned Viands,—the savoury Herbs, and stimulating Spices with which these Haut-Goûts are sprinkled and stuffed, &c. are sufficient to encourage the digestive faculties to work "*con amore*" without any "*douceur*" of Vinous irrigation,—but many persons make it a rule, after eating Pig, &c. to take a glass of *Liqueur,* or *Eau de Vie*, &c.—or, as when used in this manner, it would be as properly called, "*eau de mort.*"

INDIGESTION, or, to use the term of the day, A BILIOUS ATTACK,—*as often arises from over-exertion*, or ANXIETY OF MIND,—as from refractory Food; it frequently produces FLATULENCE[46], and flatulence produces *Palpitation of the Heart*; which is most difficult to stop, when it comes on about an hour or two after a Meal;—the Stomach seems incapable of proceeding in its business, from being over-distended with wind, which pressing on the Heart and larger vessels, obstructs the Circulation:—as soon as this flatulence is dispelled, all goes well again:—inflating the Lungs to the utmost, *i.e.* taking in as much breath as you can, and holding it as long as you can, will sometimes act as a counterbalance, and produce relief....

To Chew long, and leisurely, is the only way to extract the essence of our food—to enjoy the taste of it, and to render it easily convertible into laudable Chyle, by the facility it gives to the gastric juices to dissolve it without trouble.

The pleasure of the *Palate*, and the health of the *Stomach*, are equally promoted by this salutary habit, which all should be taught to acquire in their infancy.

The more tender meat is, the more we may eat of it.—That which is most difficult to Chew, is of course most difficult to Digest.

From 30 to 40 (according to the tenderness of the meat) has been calculated as the mean number of Munches, that solid meat requires, to prepare it for its journey down *the Red Lane*; less will be sufficient for tender, delicate, and easily digestible white meats.

The sagacious *Gourmand*, will calculate this precisely,—and not waste his precious moments in useless Jaw-work, or invite an Indigestion by neglecting *Mastication*.

I cannot give any positive rules for this, it depends on the state of the Teeth[47]; every one, especially *the Dyspeptic*, ought to ascertain the condition of these useful working tools; and to use them with proportionate diligence, is an indispensable exercise which every rational Epicure will most cheerfully perform, who has any regard for the welfare of his Stomach.[48]

It has been recommended, that those whose Teeth are defective, should mince their meat—this will certainly save trouble to both Teeth and Stomach—nevertheless, it is advisable, let the meat be minced ever so fine, to endeavour to mumble it into a pulp before it be introduced to the Stomach—on account of the advantage derived from its admixture with the SALIVA.

"By experiment, I determined the quantity of *Saliva* secreted in half an hour, to be *whilst the parts were at rest*, four drachms,—*whilst eating*, five ounces four drachms."[49]

MASTICATION is the source of all good Digestion;—*with its assistance*, almost any thing may be put into any stomach with impunity:—*without it*, Digestion is always difficult, and often impossible: and be it always remembered, it is not merely what we eat, but what we digest well, that nourishes us.

The sagacious *Gourmand* is ever mindful of his motto—
Masticate, Denticate, Chump, Grind, and Swallow.

The four first acts, he knows he must perform properly,—before he dare attempt the fifth.

Notes

1. *The Remains of the Late Mrs. Richard Trench, Being Selections from her Journals, Letters, and Other Papers*, edited by her son, 2nd ed. (London: Parker, Son, & Bourn, 1862), 471.
2. Walter Scott to Archibald Constable, Edinburgh, February 25, 1822; *The Letters of Sir Walter Scott*, 6 vols., ed. H. J. C. Grierson (London: Constable, 1934), 6: 80–81.
3. Charles Lamb, *The Letters of Charles Lamb to which are added those of his sister Mary Lamb*. ed. E. V. Lucas. 3 vols. (London: Methuen, 1935), 3: 97; Charles Lamb, *The Works of Charles and Mary Lamb*, 8 vols., ed. E. V. Lucas (London: Methuen, 1903), 1: 124; Kitchener, *Cook's Oracle*, 168.
4. Benson E. Hill, *The Epicure's Almanac for 1842; Containing a Calendar of the Months, Adorned with Cuts; Tables of the Various Dishes in Season: with a Collection of Original and Choice Recipes* (London: How & Parsons, 1842), 56; "Cookery Review," *The Foreign Quarterly Review* 33 (1844): 181–212 (203).
5. Jane Grigson, *Jane Grigson's Vegetable Book* (London: Michael Joseph, 1978), 133.
6. Richard Chenevix, "Review of *Almanach des Gourmands, Chimie du Gout, Manuel des Amphytrions, L'Almanach Comestible, Cours Gastronomique, La Gastronomie, Poëme didactique, Dictionnaire de la Cuisine, Apicius Redivivus, Peptic Precepts*, and *Tabella Cibaria*," *The Edinburgh Review* 35:69 (1821): 43–62 (60–61).
7. Charles Elmé Francatelli, *The Modern Cook; a Practical Guide to the Culinary Art in all its Branches, Adapted as well for the Largest Establishments, as for the Use of Private Families* (London: Richard Bentley, 1846), 2nd p. of preface.

8. "It is at *the commencement of Decline*, i.e. about our 40th year, that the stomach begins to require peculiar care and precaution. People who have been subject to Indigestions before, have them then more frequent and more violent; and those who have never been so afflicted, begin to suffer them from slight causes: a want of attention to which too frequently leads to the destruction of the best constitutions, especially of the studious, who neglect to take due exercise. The remedy proposed is Ipecacuanha, in a dose that will not occasion any nausea; but enough to excite such an increased action of the vermicular movement of the stomach, that the phlegm may be separated and expelled from the organ.

   "The effects of it surpassed his most sanguine hopes: by the use of it, notwithstanding he had naturally a delicate constitution, he weathered the storms of the Revolution, &c., and lived to be 84." The above is an extract from DR. [William] BUCHAN'S translation of MR. [Louis-Jean-Marie] DAUBENTON'S *Observations on Indigestion* [: *in Which it is Satisfactorily Shewn the Efficacy of Ipecacuan, in Relieving this, as well as its Connected Train of Complaints Peculiar to the Decline of Life* (London, 1809)] This treatise brought Ipecacuanha Lozenges into fashion, as the most easy and agreeable manner of taking it: they contain about one-sixth of a grain, and are prepared and sold by SAVORY and MOORE, Chemists, in Bond Street. [Kitchiner]

9. "The STOMACH is the Grand Organ of the human system, upon the state of which, all the powers and feelings of the individual depend."—See [Alexander] HUNTER'S *Culina [Famulatrix Medicinæ: or, Receipts in Modern Cookery* (1804)], p. 13.

   "The faculty the Stomach has of communicating the impressions made by the various substances that are put into it, is such, that it seems more like a nervous expansion from the Brain, than a mere receptacle for Food."—Dr. [Benjamin] WATERHOUSE'S *Lecture on Health [Cautions to Young Persons Concerning Health* (Cambridge, MA: W. Hillard, 1805)], p. 4. [Kitchiner; actually p. 8 of Waterhouse.]

10. "De toutes les Connoissances nécessaires à l'humanité souffrante, la plus agréable, la plus importante à la conservation des hommes, et à la perpétuité de toutes les jouissances de la nature, c'est la parfaite connoissance des alimens destinés à former notre constitution, à fortifier tous nos membres, à ranimer ces organes destinés à la perfection des sens, et à être les médiateurs des talens, de l'esprit, du génie, &c. &c.

   C'est du sue exprimé de nos fluides alimentaires, qu'est formé le tissu del notre frêle machine; c'est au chyle qui en provient, que notre sang, nos chairs, nos nerfs, nos organes, et tous nos sens, doivent leur existence et leur sensibilité." [Kitchiner]

11. I wish most heartily that the restorative process was performed by us poor mortals, in as easy and simple a manner as it is in *"The Cooking Animals in the Moon,"* who "lose no time at their meals; but open their left side, and place the whole quantity at once in their stomachs, then shut it, till the same day in the next month, for they never indulge themselves with food more than twelve times in a year."—See BARON MUNCHAUSEN'S *Travels*, p. 188. [Kitchiner; re. Karl Friedrich Hieronymus von Münchausen and Gottfried August Bürger, *Wunderbare reisen zu wasser und lande* (1786), pub. in English in 1870–79, indicating that Kitchiner is not quoting directly.]

   Pleasing the Palate is the main end in most books of Cookery, but *it is my aim to blend the toothsome with the wholesome*; for, after all, however the hale Gourmand may at first differ from me in opinion, the latter is the chief concern; since if he be even so entirely devoted to the pleasure of eating as to think of no other, still the care of his Health becomes part of that; if he is sick he cannot relish his Food.

   "The term *Gourmand* or EPICURE has been strangely perverted; it has been conceived synonymous with a Glutton, *'né pour la digestion,'* who will eat as long as he can sit, and drink longer than he can stand, nor leave his cup while he can lift it; or like the great eater of Kent whom FULLER places among his Worthies, and tells us that he did eat with ease *thirty dozens of Pigeons* at one meal; at another, *fourscore Rabbits* and *eighteen Yards of Black Pudding*, London Measure!—or a fastidious Appetite, only to be excited by fantastic Dainties, as the brains of *Peacocks* or *Parrots*, the tongues of *Thrushes* or *Nightingales*, or the teats of a lactiferous *Sow*.

   In the acceptation which I give to the term EPICURE, it means only the person who has good sense and good taste enough to wish to have his food cooked according to scientific principles; that is to say, so prepared that the palate be not offended—that it be rendered easy of solution in the Stomach, and ultimately contribute to Health; exciting him as an animal to the vigorous enjoyment of those recreations and duties, physical and intellectual, which constitute the happiness and dignity of his nature." For this illustration I am indebted to my scientific friend

Apicius Cælius, Jun. with whose erudite observations several pages of this work are enriched, to which I have affixed the signature *A.C. Jun.* [Kitchiner]

12. "Although AIR is more immediately necessary to life than FOOD, the knowledge of the latter seems of more importance; it admits certainly of great variety, and a choice is more frequently in our power. A very spare and simple has commonly been recommended as most conducive to Health; but it would be more beneficial to mankind if we could shew them that a pleasant and varied diet was equally consistent with health, as the very strict regimen of Arnard, or the Miller of Essex. These and other abstemious people who, having experienced the greatest extremities of bad health, were driven to temperance as their last resource, may run out in praises of a simple diet; but the probability is, that nothing but the dread of former sufferings could have given them the resolution to persevere in so strict a course of abstinence, which persons who are in health and have no such apprehension could not be induced to undertake, or, if they did, would, not long continue.

In all cases, great allowance must be made for the weakness of human nature; the desires and appetites of mankind must, to a certain degree, be gratified, and the man who wishes to be most useful will imitate the indulgent Parent, who, whilst he endeavours to promote the true interests of his children, allows them the full enjoyment of all those innocent pleasures which they take delight in. If it could be pointed out to mankind that some articles used as food were hurtful, while others were in their nature innocent, and that the latter were numerous, various, and pleasant, they might, perhaps, be induced to forego those which were hurtful, and confine themselves to those which were innocent."—*See* Dr. [William] STARK'S *Experiments on Diet,* [*The Works of the Late William Stark… with Experiments, Dietetical and Statical* (London: J. Johnson, 1788)], pp. 89 and 90 [Kitchiner]

13. John Milton, *A Masque at Ludlow Castle* (1637), lines 704–05.

14. Ibid., l. 475

15. "For there was never yet philosopher / That could endure the toothache patiently"; William Shakespeare, *Much Ado About Nothing*, 5.1.35–36, *The Riverside Shakespeare*, ed. G. Blakemore Evans (Boston: Houghton Mifflin, 1974), 356.

16. See a curious account in [Charles-Louis, Cadet de Gassicourt], COURS GASTRONOMIQUE [*ou, Les diners de Manant-ville, ouvrage anecdotique, philosophique et littéraire* (1809)], p. 145, and in [Jean-Jacques Barrthelemy] *Anacharsis' Travels*, Robinson, 1796. Vol. ii. p. 58, and *Obs.* and note under No. 493. [Kitchiner]

17. See the 2d, 3d and 4th pages of Sir WM. TEMPLE'S *Essay on the Curse of the Gout by Moxa.* See a *very curious anecdote* in the Memoirs of COUNT ZINZENDORFF in Dodsley's Annual Register for 1762. 3d edition, p. 32 [Kitchiner]; Count Zinzendorff, a minister of Emperor Charles VI, kept one of the most elegant tables in Vienna; Jeaffreson, *Book About the Table*, 288.

18. "He that would have a *clear Head*, must have a *clean Stomach.*"—Dr. [George] CHEYNE *on Health,* [*An Essay of Health and Long Life.*] 8vo. 1724, p. 34. "It is sufficiently manifest how much uncomfortable feelings of the Bowels affect the Nervous System, and how immediately and completely the general disorder is relieved by an alvine evacuation."—p. 53. [Kitchiner]

"We cannot reasonably expect tranquillity of the Nervous System, whilst there is disorder of the digestive organs. As we can perceive no permanent source of strength but from the digestion of our food, it becomes important on this account that we should attend to its quantity, quality, and the periods of taking it, with a view to ensure its proper digestion."—[John] ABERNETHY'S *Sur. Obs.* [*Surgical Observations on Injuries of the Head and on Miscellaneous Subjects*] 8vo. 1817, p. 65. [Kitchiner]

19. James Boswell, Wed. April 15, 1778, *Life of Johnson*, ed. R. W. Chapman (Oxford: Oxford University Press, 1998), 942.

20. On the supposition that the popular eighteenth-century cookery author, Mrs. Hannah Glasse, was a physician named John Hill, see Frank Schloesser, *The Greedy Book: A Gastronomical Anthology* (London: Gay & Bird, 1906), 82–85.

21. "If Science can really contribute to the happiness of mankind, it must be in this department; the real comfort of the majority of men in this country is sought for at their own fire-side; how desirable does it then become to give every inducement to be at home, by directing all the means of Philosophy to increase Domestic Happiness!"—[Charles] SYLVESTER'S *Philosophy of Domestic Economy*, 4to. 1819, p. 17. [Kitchiner]

22. The best Books of Cookery have been written by Physicians.—Sir KENELME DIGBY [*The Closet of the Eminently Learned Sir Kenelme Digbie Kt Opened: Whereby is Discovered Several*

ways for making of Metheglin, Sider, Cherry-Wine, &c. together with Excellent Directions for Cookery: As also for Preserving, Conserving, Candying, &c. (London, 1669)]—Sir THEODORE [Turquet de] MAYERNE.—See the last quarter of page 304 of vol. x. of the *Phil. Trans.* for 1675.—Professor [Richard] BRADLEY [*The Country Housewife and Lady's Director, in the Management of a House, and the Delights and Profits of a Farm* (London, 1732)]—Dr. [John] HILL [a physician whom some believe to have been the real "Hannah Glasse"]—Dr. [Guilliaume Vincent] LE COINTE—Dr. [Alexander] HUNTER, &c. [Kitchiner further quotes from the "Supplement to *Encyclop. Brit. Edin.* vol. iv. p. 344, the Article 'FOOD,'... "as the most scientific paper on the subject we have seen."]

23.   See [Boswell, *Life of Johnson*], vol. III, p. 311. [Kitchiner; see the Oxford version, p. 943.]

24.   "Health, Beauty, Strength, and Spirits, and I might add all the faculties of the Mind, depend upon the Organs of the Body; when these are in good order, the thinking part is most alert and active, the contrary when they are disturbed or diseased."—Dr. [William] CADOGAN *on Nursing Children,* [*An Essay upon Nursing, and the Management of Children: from Their Birth to Three Years of Age*] 8vo. 1757, p. 5. [Kitchiner]

25.   Mr. Smale's account of Dr. [Samuel] Johnson's Journey into Wales [*Diary of a Journey into North Wales, in the Year 1774*], 1816, p. 174. [Kitchiner]

26.   The standard system of weights in Kitchiner's time used in Great Britain for all goods except precious metals, precious stones, and medicines; the avoirdupois pound contains 700 grains.

27.   "In the present language of Cookery, there has been a woeful departure from the simplicity of our ancestors,—such a farrago of unappropriate and unmeaning terms, many corrupted from the French, others disguised from the Italian, some misapplied from the German, while many are a disgrace to the English. What can any person suppose to be the meaning of *a Shoulder of Lamb in epigram,* unless it were a poor dish, for a Penny-less Poet? *Aspect of fish* would appear calculated for an Astrologer; and *shoulder of mutton surprised,* designed for a Sheep-stealer."—A.C. *Jun.* [Kitchiner]

28.   Alexander Pope, *Essay on Man,* Epistle i.96, as printed with capitalization variants in *Poetry and Prose of Alexander Pope,* ed. Aubrey Williams (New York: Houghton Mifflin, 1969), 125.

29.   Spoken by Princess Nekayeh in chapter 47 of Samuel Johnson, *The History of Rasselas, Prince of Abissinia* (1759), as printed with punctuation variants and no italics in the edition by D. J. Enright (London: Penguin, 1985), 143.

30.   Probably a reference to Macbeth's comment that "If it were done, when 'tis done, then 'twere well / It were done quickly"; *Macbeth* 1.7.1–2, as printed in *The Riverside Shakespeare,* 1317.

31.   "Il y a trois sortes d'appétits; celui que l'on éprouve à jeûne; sensation impérieuse qui ne chicane point sur le mets, et qui vous fait venir l'eau à la bouche à l'aspect d'un bon ragoût. Je le compare au désir impétueux d'un jeune homme qui voit sourire la beauté qu'il aime. *Le second* appétit est celui qui l'on ressent lorsque, s'étant mis à table sans faim, on a déjà goûté d'un plat succulent, et qui a consacré le proverbe, *l'appétit vient en mangeant*: je l'assimile a l'état d'un mari dont le cœur tiède s'échauffe aux premières caresses de sa femme. *Le troisième* appétit est celui qu'excite un mets délicieux qui paraît à la fin d'un repas, lorsque, l'estomac satisfait, l'homme sobre allait quitter la table sans regret. Celui-là trouve son emblème dans les feux du libertinage, qui, quoique illusoires, font naître cependant quelques plaisís réels. La connoissance de cette métaphysique de l'appétit doit guider le Cuisinier habile dans la composition du premier, du second, et du troisième service."—*Cours Gastronomique,* p. 64. [Kitchiner; minor errata corrected.]

32.   Vide Swift's Letters to Pope, July 10th, 1732. [Kitchiner re. Swift's Letter to John Gay and the Duchess of Queensberry: "I have a large house, yet I should hardly prevail to find one visitor, if I were not able to hire him with a bottle of wine: so that, when I am not abroad on horseback, I generally dine alone, and am thankful if a friend will pass the evening with me"; *Correspondence of Jonathan Swift,* ed. F. Elrington Ball, vol. 4. (London: G. Bell & Sons, 1913), 314.]

33.   Swilling cold Soda Water immediately after eating a hearty dinner, is another very unwholesome custom—take good Ginger Beer if you are thirsty, and don't like Sir John Barleycorn's cordial. [Kitchiner]; Barleycorn's cordial is a name for any distilled drink.

34.   "Men are but Children of a larger Growth"; John Dryden, *All for Love,* IV.i.44; see edition by N. J. Andrew (London: Ernest Benn, 1975), 75.

35.   The *Strong Peppermint or Ginger Lozenges,* made by Smith, Fell Street, Wood Street, Cheapside, are an excellent help for that flatulence with which some aged and Dyspeptic people are afflicted three or four hours after Dinner. [Kitchiner]

36. *Le Grand Sommelier*, or CHIEF BUTLER, in former times was expected to be especially accomplished in the Art of folding Table Linen—so as to lay his napkins in different forms every day—these transformations are particularly described in [Giles] Rose's Instructions for the Officers of the Mouth [*A Perfect School of Instructions for the Officers of the Mouth: Shewing the Whole Art of A Master of the Household, A Master Carver, A Master Butcher, A Master Confectioner, A Master Cook, A Master Pastryman*], 1682, p. 111 &c. "To pleat a napkin in the form of a Cockle-shell Double"—"In the form of a Hen and Chickens"—"shape of two capons in a Pye"—or "like a Dog with a Collar about his Neck"—and many others equally whimsical. [Kitchiner]

37. "Depuis long-temps, le nombre des Graces ou celui des Muses a réglé les dîners aimables; passé ce dernier nombre, il n'y a plus ni intimité, ni conversation générale."—*Cours Gastronomique*, p. 311. [Kitchiner]

38. Founded in 1759 the *Journal des dames* was suppressed in 1778 for its radical tendencies.

39. *Vide le Manuel des Amphitryons*, 8vo. *Paris*, 1808; and *Cours Gastronomique*, 1809; to which the reader is referred for further Instructions. [Kitchiner re. Grimod de la Reynière's and de Gassicourt's works, respectively]

40. Nicolas Boileau (Despreaux) (1636–1711); unidentified.

41. "It is but INCREASING or *diminishing* the velocity of certain fluids in the animal machine,—to elate the Soul with the gayest hopes,—or to sink her into the deepest despair; to depress the HERO into a *Coward*—or advance the *Coward* into a HERO."—[William Melmoth,] FITZOSBORNE'S *Letters, On Several Subjects* [London, 1750)], I. viii. [Kitchiner; actually from Letter 13 (not 1), entitled "To Philotes.—Written in a fit of the spleen."]

42. "SALT, PEPPER, and MUSTARD, ay, VINEGAR too, / Are quite as unwholesome as CURRY I vow, / All lovers of Goose, Duck, or Pigs, he'll engage, / That eat it with Onion, Salt, Pepper or Sage, / Will find ill effects from 't," and therefore no doubt/ Their prudence should tell them,— best eat it without! / But, alas! these are subjects on which there's no reas'ning, / For you'll still eat your Goose, Duck, or Pig, with its seas'ning; / And what is far worse—notwithstanding his huffing, / You'll make for your Hare and your Veal a good stuffing: / And I fear, if a Leg of good Mutton you boil, / With Sauce of vile Capers, that Mutton you'll spoil; / And tho', as you think, to procure good Digestion, / A mouthful of Cheese is best thing in question: / "In *Gath* do not tell, nor in *Askalon* blab it, / You're strictly forbidden to eat a *Welsh Rabbit*." / And *Bread,* " the main staff of our life," some will call / No more nor less,—than " the worst thing of all."—See THE LADY'S Address to Willy Cadogan in his Kitchen, [*The Doctor Dissected; or Willy Cadogan in the Kitchen*] 4to. 1771. [Kitchiner]

43. William Shakespeare, *Macbeth*, II.ii.37, as printed with capitalization variants in *The Riverside Shakespeare*, 1320.

44. Nicholas Robinson, *Treatise on the Virtues and Efficacy of a Crust of Bread Eaten Early in a Morning Fasting* (London: 1756)

45. Are very crude indigestible materials for a weak Stomach, unless warmed (No. 372);—with the assistance of which, and plenty of pepper, you may eat even *Cucumber* with impunity. [Kitchiner]

46. DR. [Charles Bland] RADCLIFFE [1822–89], who succeeded better by speaking plainly to his Patients, than some of his successors have by the most subtle Politeness,—when asked what was *the best Remedy for Wind in the Stomach*, replied, "That which will expel it quickest"—inquiring of the Ventose subject whether the Wind passed *per Ascensum, vel per Descensum,* observing,—that the former is the most aggravated of *Ventriloquism*, the latter a sign that the Bowels are recovering their Healthful Tone. [Kitchiner]

47. In no branch of the practice of physic, is there more *Dangerous Quackery*, than in this department—the only means we can furnish our friends with to avoid this—is to recommend them to apply to a scientific Dentist of acknowledged integrity and experience.—Our own Mouth is under considerable obligations to Mr. EDMONDS, of Conduit Street, Hanover Square. [Kitchiner]

48. "Slave-dealers are well acquainted with the characteristic signs of perfect Health—any defect of which much diminishes the value of a Slave. The want of *a Tooth* makes a Slave worth two Dollars less."—[Leonhard Ludwig] FINKE'S *Medical Geography* [*Versuch einer allgemeinen medicinisch-praktischen Geographie* (1792)] vol. i. p. 449. [Kitchiner]

49. STARK on Diet, p. 99. [Kitchiner]; cf. note 12 above.

3
Launcelot Sturgeon (Pseudonym)

Essays, Moral, Philosophical, and Stomachical, on the Important Science of Good-Living (London, 1822)

Introduction

The pseudonymous Launcelot Sturgeon's "gastronomic tour on the Continent" and his acquaintance with "that very erudite work, the *Almanach des Gourmands*" yields what may be the most original attempt in English to "stimulate the powers of discriminating appetites" in a moral and philosophical, not to mention comical, manner. Whereas Dr. Kitchiner's gastronomical writings were bound into the more traditional form of the cookbook, Sturgeon's concern is appetite rather than cookery. He breaks free from the genre of the British cookbook into the first full-length English work on the gastronomical model. Sturgeon identifies himself on the title page to his book as a "Fellow of the Beef-Steak Club, and an Honorary member of several Foreign Pic Nics, &c. &c. &c." In this, he resembles other gastronomers, including Brillat-Savarin, who identifies himself a "Professor" and "Member of Numerous Scholarly Societies" on the 1826 title page to his *Physiologie du goût*, and Fredrick Accum, who defends his *Culinary Chemistry* in 1821 as a serious endeavor by listing his professional qualifications: Operative Chemist, Lecturer on Practical Chemistry, Mineralogy, and on Chemistry applied to the Arts and Manufactures; Member of the Royal Irish Academy; Fellow of the Linnaean Society; Member of the Royal Academy of Sciences, and of the Royal Society of Arts of Berlin, &c. &c.[1] As a practicing English epicure, Sturgeon also boasts "professional" qualifications that suggest a lifetime's labor devoted to attainment in the gastronomical arts.

MEDITATIONS OF AN EPICURE.

Figure 16 *The Meditations of an Epicure* (cf. Figure 5) from Launcelot Sturgeon, *Essays, Moral Philosophical and Stomachical* (1823). Courtesy of the author.

Whether his pseudonym derives from the imperial fish of the Caspian Sea so highly esteemed by the ancient Romans, or the royal fish of Great Britain (traditionally offered to the monarch when caught in British waters), Sturgeon was to be sure no ordinary fish: he too staked a claim to elite exceptionality. He had a familiarity with Grimod's *Almanach des gourmands*, a flair for adaptation, and literary ambitions for his own gastronomical work beyond the ordinary. His talents are on a par with (if they do not exceed) those of Brillat-Savarin who would gain lasting literary fame four years later. Nineteenth-century gastronomical authors in English concealed their identities under generic masks such as "The Epicure" or "The Alderman" (based on the latter's reputation for public festivity). Indeed, some wondered whether "Kitchiner," meaning cook, was a pseudonym too. British gastronomical tradition leaves much to the imagination, and while speculations have been made as to Sturgeon's true identity, perhaps its most interesting aspect is its pseudonymity itself.

Charles Lamb owned a copy of the second (1823) edition of Sturgeon's *Essays*, and at the sale of Lamb's library in 1858 following his death, it passed into the hands of one Captain Francis Jackson of Red House, Mare Street, Hackney. Lamb published an essay called "Captain Jackson" in the *London Magazine* in 1824, and though its namesake remains uncertain, the eccentric bachelor Richard Charles Jackson claims to have been his grandson. The younger Jackson lived alone among 8,000 books and catalogued Lamb's copy of Sturgeon as No. 133 in his "Lamb Collection of Books." A note in his hand (now at Pennsylvania State University) "surmised that this book is from the pen of Charles Lamb—my father told me that my grandfather would say that our immortal Charles was author of two or three other works, for which he had paid the cost of publication." Lamb published all of his fictional essays under pseudonymns—of which his most famous (Elia) may be an acronym for "a lie." A letter from a friend describes the joy Lamb took in his pseudonymous identity:

> No one had the slightest conception who "Elia" was. He was talked of everywhere, and everybody was trying to find him out, but without success. At last, from the style and manner of conveying his ideas and opinions on different subjects, my brother began to suspect that Lamb was the individual so widely sought for, and wrote some lines to him, anonymously, sending them by post to his residence, with the hope of sifting him on the subject. Although Lamb could not *know* who sent him the lines, yet he looked very hard at the writer of them the next time they met, when he walked up, as usual, to Lamb's desk in the most unconcerned manner, to transact the necessary business. Shortly after, when they were again in conversation, something dropped from Lamb's

lips which convinced his hearer, beyond a doubt, that his suspicions were correct. He therefore wrote some more lines (anonymously, as before), beginning: "I've found thee out, O Elia!" ... at their next meeting Lamb produced the lines, and after much laughing, confessed himself to be *Elia*.[2]

His friends may have discovered Elia, but no one seems to have found out Sturgeon. Stylistic elements of the text, however, including the author's use of the word *gusto*, his view of the hog as a member of society, and his confusions between the human and the pig, suggest that Sturgeon could well have been Lamb.

Another copy of Sturgeon's 1822 *Essays* was owned by William Beckford, and the Yale University Library has catalogued the book under his authorship as No. 100 of the Beckford Collection. The authority for the attribution to Beckford is the bibliographer Guy Chapman, who catalogued William Beckford's library at Fonthill in conjunction with John Hodgkin and who claims that "Mr. Hodgkin also suspects the hand of Beckford" in Sturgeon's *Essays*.[3] Beckford's library contained a number of gastronomical texts from the Romantic period, including *The School for Good Living* (1814), *Tabella Cibaria; the Bill of Fare* (1820), and Dick Humelbergius Secundus's *Apician Morsels; or Tales of the Table, Kitchen, and Larder* (1829).

Whoever Sturgeon was, we know that he was familiar with the work of Grimod de la Reynière. His essay on "The Fatal Consequences of Pride Considered on its Effects Upon Dinners" is copied from Grimod's *Almanach des gourmands*, and his essay "On Mustard, Philosophically Considered; and on the Use of Garlick as a Perfume" also derives from that work (though Grimod concentrates on syrop, or cordials, instead of garlic as a complement to mustard). In addition, Sturgeon's essay "On the Nature and Properties of the Braise; with a Concise Account of its Origin," is based on a story told by Grimod, though adapted in interesting ways. The frontispiece to his work, moreover, engraved by William Hughes, is a direct copy of *Les méditations d'un gourmand*, designed by Grimod de la Reynière for the fourth year of his *Almanach* (fig. 16). The image features a gourmand seated at his desk in his dressing robe, in a room decorated *à la moderne*. The Gourmand, or Epicure, is in the process of writing, but as Grimod points out, he seems distracted, reflecting on the objects that occupy his thoughts, above all the calf's head on the table "whose stony face profoundly occupies the scene." Several treatises on the alimentary arts, including the *Patisserie of Health*, *The Talents of Comus*, and *The Modern Confectioner*, lay scattered around him, as the bookshelves have been converted into a culinary amphitheater, storing *Légitimations* that must wait their turn to pass in scrutiny before the epicure.

Sturgeon, following Grimod, sought to transform the traditional taste object (the literary text or objet d'art) into an item to be literally tasted.

The *Essays* below are from the 1823 London edition.

From *Essays, Moral, Philosophical, and Stomachical* (1822)

Introduction

The pleasures of the table have ever held a distinguished rank amongst all those which man experiences in a state of society. It has been justly observed, that they are the first of which we are susceptible, the last that we quit and those that we can most frequently enjoy: in spite of all the Stoics can say, every one must admit, that a stomach which is proof against all trials is the greatest of all blessings; and it would be easy to demonstrate, that it exercises an extended influence over the moral destinies of life.

But, without involving ourselves in the intricacy of metaphysical discussions—which belong rather to philosophy than to cookery, and are, besides, injurious to digestion—we shall confine ourselves to the more important object of illuminating the paths of epicurism, and guiding the votaries of good-cheer through the labyrinth of enjoyment to which they lead.

But ere we commence this pleasing task, we must beg leave to enter our most solemn protest against the indiscriminate application of the terms *Epicurism* and *Gluttony*; which are but too commonly applied synonymously, with a degree of ignorance, or of malignity, worthy only of the grossness of mere beef-eaters, or of the envy of weak appetites.

Hume being told by a lady, that she had heard he was a great epicure—"No, madam," replied the historian, "I am only a glutton!" Gluttony is, in fact, a mere effort of the appetite, of which the coarsest bolter of bacon in all Hampshire may equally boast with the most distinguished consumer of turtle in a corporation; while Epicurism is the result of that "choicest gift of Heaven," a refined and discriminating taste: this the peculiar attribute of the palate, that of the stomach. It is the happy combination of both these enviable qualities that constitutes that truly estimable character, the real epicure. He is not only endowed by nature with a capacious stomach and an insatiate appetite, but with a delicate susceptibility in the organs of degustation, which enables him to appreciate the true relish of each ingredient in the most compound ragoût, and to detect the slightest aberration of the cook; added to which advantages, he possesses a profound acquaintance with the rules of art in all the most approved schools of cookery, and an enlightened judgment on their several merits, matured by long and sedulous experience. In him, all the senses should be in unison with that of taste: his eye should be penetrating, to direct him in the first choice or rejection of what is before him; his ear quick, to catch, from the farthest end of the table, the softest whisper in praise of any particular dish; his extended nostrils, uncontaminated with snuff, should faithfully convey the savoury intelligence of what surrounds him; and his ample tongue should dilate each copious mouthful, both to protract the enjoyment of mastication and to aid the powers of deglutition. But the concentration of such various perfections is rare: few men are able to do equal justice to a dinner—

Ab ovo usque ad mala—

from the soup to the coffee;[4] that demands a universality of taste, and a profundity of judgment, which fall to the lot of only some favoured individuals. Such gifted beings do, however, exist: they are entitled to our highest respect; and, whenever it is our good fortune to meet them, we should endeavour to collect their opinions, and to follow, at however humble a distance, their splendid example. We have, ourself, made this our constant study; and although the axiom that "no man is wise but through his own experience," can never be more properly applied than to the science of good-living, yet are we not without hopes, that the labours of a long life, incessantly directed to that sole object, will not be without profit to those who mean to devote themselves to the same commendable pursuit. We trust, too, that we shall not be accused of unbecoming vanity, or of unfounded pretensions, if we add, that our claims to the confidence of the epicurean world are hereditary.

Descended from an opulent family, settled for ages in the very heart of the city of London, and which has given more than one alderman to the corporation, our father was, himself, a distinguished member of the Fishmongers' Company, and many years deputy for the ward of Port-soken. He died gloriously on the field of honour:—that is to say, of an indigestion after a Lord Mayor's feast. Had be been merely an honorable or a good man, his name would not deserve to occupy a place in this work: but he was no common person: he possessed a delicacy of palate, and a superiority of tact in all that concerned the table, which have been but seldom approached, and never surpassed. His discernment was equally various and unerring: it extended over every particle of aliment without exception: fish, flesh, fowl, game—whether furred or feathered,—fricassées, ragoûts, entremets and dessert, all passed in succession through the ordeal of his jaws; and his opinion on each was just as decisive. Nor was he less eminent in the important department of the bottle: from imperial Tokay, or royal Burgundy, to humble Port, he was not to be deceived even in a vintage; and the cellar which he left at his death was the most glorious monument that could be erected to his memory.

Educated at such a table as his, daily imbibing the precepts of such a professor along with the more solid elements of his art, and inheriting from him, not alone his ample fortune, but his disposition, also, to enjoy it—we surely may be allowed some title to the "*ed io anche*" of Michael Angelo. We do not, indeed, affect to rival, so much as to emulate, our illustrious parent; nor have we altogether trusted to our own *savoir-vivre*. An occasional residence in Paris, while on a gastronomic tour on the Continent, has enabled us to appreciate the real merits of French cookery, and French wines; and to select from that very erudite work, the "*Almanach des Gourmands*," those precious receipts which may more particularly stimulate the powers of discriminating appetites. Not that we pretend to present the public with a system of cookery, or a dissertation on the juice of the grape: far be from us any such ambitious aim: that belongs to the pages of science, and the research of successive ages: it presents too vast a field for the experience of one short life; and while we sincerely wish that its rich harvests may be reaped by our readers, we must ourself be content with the more humble department of a mere gleaner. Our present object, indeed, is rather to inform the fresh-man than to add to the experience of the rubicund professor; more to direct the taste, than to satisfy the palate. But we have culled with care, not alone the receipts, but the maxims also, of most essential use, to which we have added the results of our own experience; reserving some minor details, as a *bonne-bouche* for a future occasion. Before, however, we enter on the marrow of our subject, we request particular attention to a few fundamental principles, without which all our instructions will be in vain; and which, indeed, should form the bases of the conduct of every man who places a just value on the interests of his stomach.

Moral Maxims and Reflections

As eating is the main object of life, so, dining being the most important action of the day, it is impossible to pay too great attention to every thing which has any affinity to it.

It is convenient to dine late; because, the more trivial concerns of the morning being by that time despatched, all our thoughts may then be concentrated upon our plate, and our undivided attention may be bestowed on what we are eating.

A true epicure would as soon fast as be obliged to hurry over a good dinner.

Five hours are a reasonable time to remain at table, when the dinner is tolerable: but, as a well-bred man never looks at his watch in company, so, no man of sense ever regulates the period of his sitting by aught but the quality of the entertainment; and time is never so well employed as in doing justice to good-fare.

Punctuality is, in no transaction of life, of such importance as in cookery: three turns too many may spoil a haunch: the *critical minute* is less difficult to be hit in the boudoir than in the kitchen; and every thing may be put into a stew—except the cook.

He, therefore, who keeps dinner waiting, commits an irreparable injury. Even should he not have been waited for, yet, if he arrive after the company have sat down, he disturbs the arrangement of the table; occasions a useless waste of time in empty compliments and excuses; retards the first course; puts the removes in jeopardy; and occasions many troublesome distractions from the great object at stake. Such men should be looked upon as the common enemies of society.

As a fricassée of chickens cannot be perfect if it consists of more than three, so, a dinner of thorough amateurs should never exceed ten covers.

Some people are alarmed if a saltcellar be overturned at table; and if the company are *thirteen* in number. The number is only to be dreaded when the dinner is provided but for *twelve;* and as for the salt, the main point is, that it does not fall into a good dish.

As every one's attention should be entirely given up to what is on the table, and not to what *surrounds it*—ladies should not expect particular notice until the dessert is served; the sex then recovers all its rights, and its empire is never less disputed.

Every thing has its value in this world, and more especially a good dinner. If then a guest cannot return the obligation in kind, he should in some other manner; the most common is to amuse the company when he cannot regale them more substantially. This, indeed, is paying in *monkey's coin;* but it is current in London.

It is contrary to every acknowledged principle of moral rectitude, to speak ill of the man at whose house you have dined—*during a space of time proportioned to the excellence of the fare.* For an ordinary dinner, a week is generally sufficient; and it can, in no case, exceed a month; at the expiration of which time, the tongue is once more at liberty. But it is always in the power of the host to chain it again, by an invitation given in due time: and of all the modes to prevent slander, this has been found the most efficacious; for, the gratitude of an epicure having its source in his stomach, there can be no doubt of its sincerity.

It is commonly said, that new wine, a family dinner, and a concert of amateurs, are three things to be equally avoided. As to the concert, however, one may go to sleep at it; and even new wine is better than none; but a bad dinner admits of no palliative: a man may as well be starved as poisoned. He, therefore, who invites you take *pot-luck,* is your enemy. However specious his apparent motive, be assured that he bears you some latent grudge, or he would not attempt to do you so wanton an injury; beware of such perfidious friends:—

Hic niger est, hunc tu, Romane! caveto.
This man is vile; here, Roman! fix your mark, "his sole is black."
—*Francis's Horace*[5]

Fish, it has been remarked, should swim three times—in water—in sauce—and in wine. It may be added, that once it appears upon the table, it should be sacred from steel: the man who could touch turbot with a knife, would feel no compunction at cutting your throat.

It is the surest proof of a weak understanding, to waste the period of action in frivolous conversation; and a man who is capable of such a misapplication of time, will never rise in the world: – wherefore, never enter into any discussion until the second course be removed.

As the greatest outrage that can be committed, is, to interrupt a man in the exercise of his jaws—never address an observation, that requires an answer, to any one whilst he is eating; and if any one put a question to you—unless it be to ask you to take wine—reply to him merely with a significant nod. If he repeat it, he means to spoil your dinner; and, as that is an injury which no one can be expected to forgive, you may either resent it accordingly, or cut his acquaintance.

Digestion, is the affair of the stomach: indigestion, that of a doctor; and the cure, that of chance.

It is better to pick full pockets than empty teeth.

On the Advantages of Giving Dinners, and the Qualifications and Duties of Amphytrions; With some Interesting Particulars of the Illustrious Count Zinzendorff

[Loosely adapted from Grimod de la Reynière's "On Hosts"][6]
The principles and the habits in which we have been educated, lead us to revere the institutions of society as they exist among us, and to pay to every class that degree of respect to which it is generally considered as entitled: thus, we venerate the clergy, honour the magistracy, look with deference to the nobility, and with regard to our equals; but far above all do we esteem those truly respectable persons who give dinners. But we claim no peculiar merit to ourselves in this; for we must do the public at large the justice to admit, that no people appear to be held in such general estimation as those who keep what is termed "a good table." And, what proves that it is to that alone that all their consideration is owing—whenever one of them ruins himself with giving entertainments, it is instantly discovered by those who never spoke of him before but as "a devilish pleasant, sensible, good, fellow"—that "poor man! he is really a great bore;"—and out of twenty who

were proud to call him friend, scarcely one in a dozen will deign to give him a nod of recognition. If any giver of dinners doubts this, let him only—instead of giving invitations—give out that he is completely done up; put down his carriage, and advertise his house and cellars to be disposed of; then, about a fortnight afterwards, let him stroll down Bond Street in a thread-bare coat, with an embarrassed air and an unassured step, and he will find—that when his friends can no longer cut his mutton, they will cut him. It is, therefore, manifestly the interest of those who wish to acquire, and to maintain, an influence in society, to give frequent and good dinners. The politician who is striving to get into power, or he already in office who wishes to keep his place; the doctor who wants patients, and the lawyer who wants clients; the poet who is anxious for praise, and the Crœsus who is desirous of being known, have no means so infallible to secure their object; and it has been demonstrated, that no play would ever be damned, if the author could but afford to give a dinner to the pit.

Thus the most glorious part that a man can play in this world is that of an Amphytrion. But, like other distinguished stations, it is difficult to be maintained with eclat: money alone is not sufficient to keep a good table, and one may spend a fortune and yet give execrable parties, while another with only a moderate income, shall give famous dinners. It is, in fact, far easier to acquire a fortune rapidly, than to learn how to spend it scientifically. To become a thorough Amphytrion, a man should pass through all his degrees, from that of B.A. or *amateur of banquets*, up to D.D. or *donor of dinners*. He should, besides, have a natural talent for eating: not that undiscriminating kind of beef and mutton appetite that belongs to the vulgar, but that delicacy of palate which is the attribute of real genius: then he should have been educated in the sound principles of good cheer at a first-rate table; and he should have all the faculties, both natural and acquired, which we have already enumerated as distinguishing an accomplished epicure. And here we cannot refrain from doing justice to the memory of one of the greatest men of the last age; who has, indeed, been already often mentioned in history, as a statesman, but whose more brilliant qualities, as a host, have been passed over with that ingratitude which ever attends the memory of past dinners.

Lewis, Count Zinzendorff, one of the ministers of the Emperor Charles VI, kept the most elegant, as well as the most profuse, table in all Vienna. Although formed to shine with distinguished lustre in the cabinet, yet he was less jealous of his reputation there, than of that more solid renown which he might acquire by giving the most splendid entertainments of any minister in Europe. He was equally acquainted with Asiatic and European luxury: his curries rivalled those of the great Mogul; his olios exceeded those of Spain; his pastry was more delicate than that of Naples; his macaroni was made by the Grand Duke's cook; his liver-pies were prepared at Strasburgh and Toulouse, and his Périguex patés were really brought from thence, nor was there in any country a grape of the least repute, but a sample of it in wine was, for the honour of its vineyards, to be found on his sideboard. His kitchen was an epitome of the universe; for there were cooks in it from all nations, and rarities from every quarter of the globe. To collect these, he had agents appointed in each place of any note for its production: the carriages on which they were laden, came quicker and more regularly than the posts; and the expenses of the transport of his dinners ran higher than those for secret correspondence. In his general conversation, the Count was cautious: in his conferences with other ministers, he was reserved: but at his table all his state machinery was thrust aside: there he discoursed at large, and delivered the most copious and instructive lectures on all his exotic and domestic delicacies; and here no professor was ever less a plagiary. He had his pillau from Prince Eugene, who had it from the Basha of Buda; the egg-soup was made after a receipt of the Duke de Richelieu; the roan-ducks were stewed in the style of the Cardinal du Bois; and the pickled-lampreys came from a great minister in England. His dishes furnished him with a kind of chronology: his water-souchy[7] was borrowed from the Marshal d' Auverquerque's table, when he was first in Holland; the partridge stuffed with mushrooms and stewed in wine, was a discovery made by that prince of good livers, the Duke de Vendôme, during the war of the succession; and the Spanish Puchero was the only solid result of the negotiation with Riperda.[8] In short, with true Apicean eloquence, he generously instructed the novices in the arts of good living; and, as Solomon discoursed of every herb, from the cedar of Lebanon to the hyssop on the wall, so, he began with a champignon no bigger than a Dutchman's waistcoat button, and ended with a wild boar, the glory of the German forest.

There was always an hour in his public days when he was totally inaccesible. The politicians were astonished at a retirement for which they could assign no reason, until an inquisitive foreigner, by giving a large gratuity to one of his servants, was let into the secret. Being placed in a chamber between the chamber of audience and the room where the Count was, he saw him seated in an elbow chair: when, preceded by a page with a cloth on his arm and a drinking glass, one of his domestics appeared, who presented a salver of many little pieces of bread, elegantly disposed; and was followed by the first cook, who, on another salver with as many different kinds of gravy. His Excellency then, tucking his napkin his cravat, first washed and gargled his mouth, then dipped a piece of bread successively into each of the sauces, and having tasted it with much deliberation, carefully rincing his palate after every one, to avoid confusion, he at length, with inexpressible sagacity, decided on the destination of them all.

"He was indeed a host! take him for all in all, we ne'er shall look upon his like again."[9]

But were a man endowed with all the talent, the science, and the experience of the Count, together with that equally indispensable qualification—his fortune, he should still possess that penetration and tact in the selection of the company whom he means to invite together, and the nice discernment in the arrangement of their places at dinner, without which it is impossible to form a pleasant party. Out of the five hours which pass at the table, we seldom employ more than two in eating; and when we can in length turn our attention from our plate to our neighbour, nothing is more annoying than to find ourself seated next to some one who has no ideas in common with us, or who will not communicate those—if any—of which he is in exclusive possession. One might as well be in the situation of a friend of ours,—an amateur landscape painter,—who advertised for an agreeable companion in a postchaise to Edinburgh, and was joined by a mountain of a man, whose enormous bulk wedged the unfortunate dilettante into a corner of the carriage, and who proved to be a Newcastle collier, without a single thought that did not centre in a coal mine.

Our readers will perceive, from this slight sketch, that it is not so easy a matter to ruin oneself with credit, as they might have imagined. But if any one among them feels that irresistible impulse, which is the sure indication of true nobility of soul, to run the glorious career of an Amphytrion, and wishes, not only to go through it with reputation, but to protract it beyond the ordinary limits—let him apply the hints he will find in our fifth and sixth essay; let him, instead of confiding in ignorant butlers and knavish cooks, trust to no nose or palate but his own; and keep as strict an account of the wines in his cellar, as he does of the cash at his Bankers—when he has any—and he will go far to solve the problem that Harpagon's steward proposed to Maître Jaques,[10] which no cook, either past or present, has ever clearly understood, and which will probably always remain an enigma to them—that of *providing good dinners with little money.*

On Modern Manners;
Containing Hints to Grown Gentlemen

The poor Irish are said to be more in want of breeches than bibles; and some people may think, that dinners are more wanting than directions how to eat them. But this, though a prevalent, is a very erroneous idea; and as the bible society, very properly, provide for the latter end of neighbours with gospel rather than corderoy, so, we deem it our duty to whet the appetite of our readers, but by no means to fill their stomachs. We trust, however, that we shall not be considered guilty of the presumption of my Lord Chesterfield,[11] (who seems to have written his principles of politeness for the instruction of footmen rather than of their masters,) if we address a few friendly hints to those gentlemen, whose occasional distractions at table render them sometimes suspected of not having always breathed the atmosphere of fashion.

In the first place, we shall suppose you, though perhaps not quite at home in Portman or Grosvenor Squares, yet sufficiently *au fait* to the usages of good society, to be neither much dazzled at the splendor of fashionable apartments, nor greatly alarmed at finding yourself in the immediate vicinity of "titled folk;" and then, with attention to the few following rules, you may at least pass muster in a large party without being remarked for awkwardness or ill-breeding.

To commence with your entrance into the drawing room—don't stand bowing at the door, as if you had a petition to present; but stride confidently up to the lady of the house, and so close before you make your obeisance, that you nearly thrust your head into her face.

When dinner is announced—if you should follow a lady to the dining room, don't tread upon her train, nor step back, to avoid it, upon the toes of her behind you; and if it should be your lot to hand one to her seat—endeavour to avoid tumbling over the chairs in your hurry to place her.

When seated—don't stare up at the lamps, as if you were an oilman calculating their contents; but look inquisitively round the table, and if you have got an eye glass—which, by the bye is a great help to gentility—apply it steadily to the object that is nearest to you: those at a distance require no such help.

Whatever may be your inclination, cautiously abstain from being helped a second time from the same dish: a man's character has been damned in society in consequence of being stigmatized as "*one of those fellows who call twice for soup!*"

If you should happen to be seated next to some country acquaintance—don't let former recollections betray you into asking him to *hobnob*: it is tantamount to a public declaration that you are a Goth.

If the wine should be on the table, and your neighbour should offer to help you—don't cant up your glass to prevent his filling it: and don't let your own eagerness to help the lady next you, induce you to enter into competition with the gentleman on her other side, and thus bring the decanters into collision, and smash them.

Drink your wine instead of spilling it on the table cloth; and if either yourself, or any other booby, should overturn his own or his neighbour's half-filled-glass—don't display your chemical knowledge by covering the stain with salt.

When constrained to speak, abridge all superfluous words as waste of valuable time: thus, if you wish to take wine with any one, instead of making a formal request to that effect, just bend the body quietly, and merely say,—"honour of some wine?" and if the same broken sentence be addressed to you, make no reply; but gently bob your head and fill your glass. But, if either want of appetite, or want of sense, should lead you into a warm discussion during dinner—don't gesticulate with your knife in your hand, as if you were preparing to cut your antagonist's throat.

If you should, unhappily, be forced to carve,—neither labour at the joint, until you put yourself into a heat, and hack it so that one might with justice exclaim, "mangling done here!" nor make such a desperate effort to dissect it, as may put your neighbours in fear of their lives. However, if an accident should happen, make no excuses, for they are only an acknowledgment of awkwardness. We remember to have seen a man of high fashion deposit a turkey in this way in the lap of a lady; but, with admirable composure, and without offering the slightest apology, he finished a story which he was telling at the same time, and then, quietly turning to her, merely said—"Madam, I'll thank you for that turkey."

If any one ask for some of the dish before you—don't help him as you would like to be helped yourself; but take that opportunity to show your breeding at his expense, and send him about as much as your sister gives to her favourite kitten.

Drink no malt liquor: if you have the least pretension to epicurism, you will find better employment for your stomach; and if not, it betrays vulgar habits.

It formerly was considered well-bred to affect a certain indifference for the fare before you; but fashion has acquired more candour; and there is now no road to the reputation of a man of ton, so sure as that of descanting learnedly on the composition of every dish. If you have ever been in France—were it only to travel by the Diligence from Dieppe to Rouen and back—it affords you a famous opportunity to praise French cookery; and if you wish to appear particularly well informed, endeavor to recollect the names and ingredients of a few rare dishes, such as, *Côtellettes à la purée de bécasses, Rognons au vin de Champagne, Dindes aux truffes,* &c.; but beware of your nomenclature; and take care not to torture his most Christian Majesty's French, with your own Cockney pronunciation.

Nothing partakes more of the very essence of high-breeding, than a nonchalant disregard of every thing but your own comfort: therefore, when finger glasses are brought, not only rince your mouth, but gargle your throat, just as if you were in your dressing-room; and if you have got good teeth, you may take that opportunity to admire them in the mirror of your tooth-pick-case.

So also, when the ladies have retired, and you are at length relieved from all etiquette, clap both your hands into your breeches pockets, and stretch yourself out in your chair, as if you had just awoke from a long nap: there is no other limit to the extent to which you may advance your legs, but that of not breaking the shins of your opposite neighbour.

In fine, if you wish to acquire the character of a thorough-bred man of ton, you must affect—even if it should not be natural to you—the most decided egotism, and total want of feeling: laugh at the distresses of your friends, and pretend not to understand those of the public; term all those whom you consider, or whom you wish to be thought, beneath you, the canaille, the plebs, and the mob; and talk as if you considered it a matter of course, that all men, of a certain class, drink claret, keep horses, have an intrigue, and have fought, or are ready to fight, a duel: but be very cautious how you allow the latter point to be brought to the test in your own person.

On the Theory and Practice of Dinatory Tactics

Of all the actions of life, dining is that which we perform with the greatest alacrity. The table is a centre which attracts around it men of the most opposite characters and dispositions; and although some affect to hold it in contempt, they all equally submit to its influence. The portly vicar, who rails in the pulpit against sensual indulgence, walks straight home to a comfortable dinner, and scolds the cook if it be not done to a turn. The doctor, who exclaims against luxury as the root of all disorders, sits four hours at table, eats of every dish, and never flinches a bumper. The M.P.'s, who so pathetically deplore the miseries of starvation, that you would think they had not broken their own fast for the last eight-and-forty hours, have just arranged their speech while swallowing beef-steaks and claret at Bellamy's; and ministers decide upon schemes of retrenchment at cabinet dinners of three courses. The judge, who condemns a starving culprit for stealing a loaf, and lectures him to boot on the enormity of his offence, hurries from the bench lest the haunch that awaits him should be spoiled; and—

Wretches hang that Jurymen may dine.[12]

In short, a coquette would rather renounce the pleasure of being admired; a poet that of being praised; a tailor that of cheating; or a dandy that of getting into his debt—parsons would sooner abandon their tythes, and lawyers and physicians their fees—nay, a bailiff would sooner let you out of his clutches without a bribe, than seven-eighths of the inhabitants of London would forego a good dinner.

A tender assignation, a marriage, or a funeral, may generally be put off without much inconvenience, and often with advantage. The assignation may end in swinging damages; the marriage would sometimes be "more honoured in the breach than in the observance;" and as for the funeral, no one ever yet complained of not being buried. Even a battle, on which the fate of a nation may depend, had better sometimes be deferred—as every man to be engaged in it will tell you. But if, by some unlooked-for accident, dinner be only retarded a single hour beyond that appointed, how every visage lengthens; how the most animated conversation flags of a sudden; how every one's aspect becomes clouded, and every eye is instinctively turned towards the door. And when, at length, that is opened by the butler with the joyful intelligence that "dinner is on the table!" what a talismanic effect does not that single sentence instantly produce: it restores serenity, gaiety, and wit; every heart beats with expectation; and no bridegroom ever betrayed greater impatience to fly to the arms of his bride, than the guests do to take possession of their plates.

But this moment of general exultation is one that demands the greatest circumspection; for on that depends all your future happiness; that is to say, your comfort during the whole period of dinner. Endeavour therefore to command your feelings, and retain possession of all your sang-froid, that you may be enabled to decide with judgment upon that most important point of good generalship—the selection of the ground on which the battle is to be fought—in other words, the choice of your seat. The instant you enter the dining parlour, throw a scrutinizing eye over the whole scene of operations, and determine the point of attack with the promptitude and decision of a veteran. Avoid the vicinity of large dishes: but, above all, sedulously shun the perilous distinction of being seated next the mistress of the house, unless you choose to incur the risk of being forced to waste your most precious moments in carving for others instead of for yourself. Never could it be more truly said than on such an occasion, that "the post of honour is place of danger."

Yet, as it is the peculiar attribute of superior minds to change events apparently the most unpropitious into real advantages, should your untoward fate force you into that unenviable station, or ensconce you behind a joint, a turkey, or a goose, let not a mistaken notion of politeness induce you to part with all the choice bits before you help yourself. Endeavor to rise above such prejudices, of which weak minds are alone the dupes; and turn a deaf ear to every request for any particular part on which you may have set your own inclination. We remember to have dined, some years ago, with a country corporation;[13] a very prominent member of which was placed opposite to a noble haunch of venison, which, as may easily be supposed, was in universal request. He carved it with an alacrity, and disposed of it with a degree of good humour that was truly magnanimous; until a sleek, red-faced gentleman in a bob-wig, at the other end of the table, sent his plate, a second time, for another slice of fat: to which our friend, eyeing him with some disdain, replied, "*Another* slice of fat, Sir! Hum!—pray, Sir, do you suppose that a man is to take the trouble of carving such a joint as this here, and not to retain a morsel for himself?—*another* slice of fat, indeed!—no, Sir!—there is but one slice left that is worth eating, and you cannot be so unconscionable as to expect it." Whereupon he very composedly helped himself to what remained. His conduct was very generally applauded; and, for our own part, we conceived the highest opinion of his judgment, and have ever since held him in the greatest respect.

We are all liable to error, and although a real epicure is rarely guilty of keeping dinner waiting, it may yet happen that he, unconsciously, arrive late; in which case, he is probably reminded of his transgression, by hearing the lady of the mansion exclaim, ere he be well announced—"John, you may desire the cook to send up dinner *now!*" with a peculiar emphasis on the last word. Should that unfortunately happen to you, your most prudent course will be, not to affect to notice it; make no excuses, for they will not be credited, and may rather aggravate than allay the irritation you have excited; in short, let the storm blow over. But we advise you not to approach the fair enragée; for your reception will certainly be as cold as the dinner you have delayed. Make your *bow à la distance*[14] and wait until the middle of the second course before you attempt to address her; you may then ask her to take wine; and, should there be champagne on the sideboard, you may confidently expect your pardon.

We have mentioned the second course, on the presumption that you never accept of invitations to any other than such dinners—when you can get them. As to those houses where one finds nothing but the family joint, the bare idea of which makes us shudder—a man had better swallow one of his own legs than put his foot into them.

On the Nature, the Intent, and the Value of Invitations

[Adapted from Grimod de la Reynière, "On the Importance of Invitations"][15] It has been profoundly observed by a philosopher of deep penetration, "that the difficulty is not so great in eating a good dinner, as in getting it," and the justness of the remark has been generally felt. The subject of invitations is, therefore, of too great importance to be passed over in silence. It offers indeed, nearly equal difficulties to both the givers and the receivers. The former, led away by the warmth of their feelings during the circulation of the bottle, are too apt to offer impromptu invitations, of which they repent on reflection; or, they are exposed to find the engagement overlooked by some of those thus lightly invited, their dinner spoiled in waiting for them, and their table only half filled. While the latter, accepting them with equal want of consideration, are not unfrequently caught in the snare of a family dinner, for which they perhaps undergo the further mortification of having declined a regular party; or, on arriving full-dressed at the appointed hour, find the house as dark as Erebus, and, after thundering for half an hour at the door, are at length informed by some wondering booby, who has first duly reconnoitred them from the area, that "Master dines out."

To obviate these mutual disappointments, it should be a fixed rule with all Amphytrions, never to ask any one to dinner but through the medium of a card, penned in the morning, fasting, after as mature reflection, and as much hesitation, as if it were an invitation to Chalk Farm;[16] and they should require as categorical a reply. It sometimes, however, will happen, that country friends, quite unaware of the importance attached to the regularity of a London dinner-party, will only return for answer, "I'll come if I can"—that is, (well understood) if nothing more agreeable occurs: but if to this be made the retort courteous, "then I shall not expect you," it will be generally found to produce an immediate and unequivocal acceptance.

As to the receiver, he should be quite as cautious in accepting an invitation, as if it were a bill of exchange. It should be in due form, and at a proper date and hour. If it be a first engagement, he should warily enquire into the credit of the party's dinners; and if that does not stand high, he should refuse acceptance as peremptorily as his banker would to his own draft without funds. As to a general invitation, where the day is not fixed, nothing more is meant by it than mere empty politeness; just as a man tells you to command his services, or to make his house your own. But if you have a pique against him, it affords you a glorious occasion to indulge it, by taking him at his word, and naming the day yourself. You must in that case, however, take care not to let him off; for you may be assured that he will afterwards be upon his guard, and never afford you another opportunity. Indeed, they who the seldomest give real dinners, are always the most forward to press this kind of invitation with an apparent cordiality that is often mistaken for genuine: it at once satisfies their vanity, and lays you under a kind of undefined obligation, without putting themselves to the slightest inconvenience....

It is not alone of the insincerity of invitations that we have to complain. Even when your host has got over his selfish reluctance to entertain you, and you are fairly seated at his table; if towards the close of dinner, there should happen to be a joint yet uncut, an undissected turkey, or a virgin pye, with what tremulous apprehension does his lady ask if you will be helped to some! And when, about an hour after "the women" have retired, and you are just beginning to cotton comfortably to your wine, the butler announces the hated intelligence, that "coffee is ready," how faintly are you pressed to partake of another bottle! In law, no tender is valid unless it be made in actual cash; and so at table, no offer should be considered sincere, unless the article be produced *in naturâ*—the meat dissected, and the wine decanted. There can be no good reason why a man's stomach should be defrauded by an illusory offer any more than his purse; and we are quite sure that there is not a sound lawyer in Westminster Hall, who would be of a contrary opinion. We have, indeed, heard some eminent counsel declare, that it is an indictable offence;

and that persons who are guilty of such frauds, should be placed by the legislature on the same footing with the utters of base coin.

But if we feel indignant at the hollowness of general invitations, we are equally shocked at the little regard paid to the substantial tender of a precise engagement. The extreme levity of the young people of the present age, makes them attach too little consequence to nutritive invitations; they even affect to consider the obligation on either side as equal; and pretend that the ephemeral honor of their company is an equivalent for the solid advantages of a good dinner. This is the effect of the modern philosophy, which is corrupting the hearts and turning the heads of the rising generation; and is even undermining the corporation dinners and parish feasts. Unlike our ancestors, amongst whom a grand entertainment was talked of for a month before-hand; its digestion was not completed within a week; and the visits to the host, dictated by the gratitude of his guests, occupied the following fortnight. Either a man's principles or his stomach must be very unsettled, who is insensible to the real value of the pleasures of the table; and we may be assured, that no constitution stands so much in need of radical reform, as that of him who can view a good dinner with indifference, or repay it with ingratitude.

On Modern Architecture, and the Comparative Miseries and Comforts of Dining-Rooms

The man who resides in London, leads the life of a lamp-lighter.[17] The houses are so confined and lofty, that the rooms are necessarily perched above each other like the nests in a dovecot; and he is eternally up and down on the same ladder—for our staircases deserve no other name. He ascends to a bed-chamber in the clouds, where he sleeps "aloft in air," exposed to be blown out of his bed by the first high wind, or to be crushed in it by the fall of some tall stack of chimneys: if he escape these dangers, and live till morning, he must descend forty steps of cold stone enclosed in a narrow funnel—which serves as a channel to convey the steams from the kitchen and blasts from the hall-door—ere he can be seated in the breakfast room: does he want a book to glance through as he sips his tea—his library is still further down the same dreary chasm; and should he wish to consult his cook, on the theatre of his operations, he must seek him "five fathom deep" below the habitable world.

But all this is nothing in comparison with the inconveniencies of our dining parlours. Instead of being placed in the most secluded part of our mansions—far removed from noise and interruption—they are generally situated in the very front of the house, exposed to all the racket of the street, and open directly on the hall, unprotected by an anti-room: so that, your head is stunned with the rattle of carriages, the knocks at and clapping of doors, the screams of ballad-singers, and the horns of news-boys; and, as if this were not sufficient annoyance, your legs are blown from under you every time the door of the room opens, unless, indeed, you should have had the precaution to secure a seat at a distance from it.

But here, again, the parade of symmetry pursues you. If you have had the good fortune, as you suppose, to place yourself with your back to the fire—the table is probably so near to it, that your spine is melted, and your appetite destroyed, before you have got through the first course; and if experience of this mistake should have directed you to the opposite side—you run the risk of being frozen, the powers of your stomach become torpid, and it will not be in the power of cayenne itself to restore them.

"How, then, is all this to be avoided?" How?—why, place your dining-room at the back of your house, and let it be approached through an anti-room; make it the very *penetralia* of your household gods, where you may meditate without distraction on the worship peculiar to the place; shield your table from all draughts but those of wine; leave a vacuum—the only one that ever should be left at dinner—on that side of it next the fire, so that every one may have a view of it; and in the corner next your sideboard place a German stove, that may at once serve as a hot-closet for your butler, and an air-warmer for your guests: – thus shall you be in possession of a temple and an altar, both worthy of the sacrifice to be consummated.

Let us only picture to ourselves a dining-room thus arranged, well warmed, and carpeted—scarlet furniture—lamplight—table enclosed within an ample screen—deep, well stuffed, elbow chairs—party not exceeding ten, nor the dishes sixteen (exclusive of the soups, vegetables, entremets, and dessert), and these served up separately—dinner hot—wines cool—appetite keen—stomach clear:—the imagination can hardly conceive an idea of human felicity to exceed such a scene, and he who can realize it need never envy the joys of Paradise.

> Let scarlet hangings clothe the parlour walls,
> And dinners snug be served in well-warmed halls:
> Let Turkey carpets o'er the floors be laid,
> And whitest damask on the tables spread.
> With loads of massy plate let sideboards shine,
> And crystal vases fill with gen'rous wine—
> Thus feast the Gods who in Olympus dine.
> VIRGIL, *Aeneid* VII

On the Physical and Political Consequence of Sauces

If we say of a doctor, while smirking from within the comfortable enclosure of his varnished pill-box, that "his science is in the gold head of his cane;"—of a parson, that "it is the surplice makes the divine;"—and of a judge, that "the wisdom's in the wig;"—how much more aptly may we apply the old proverb— "it is the sauce that passes the fish!"—a profound observation, containing a great moral truth, from which we may deduce the vast importance of this delicate branch of culinary science. Sauces form not only an essential addition to, and even an integral part of, most meats; they do not alone vary the taste and form in which they are presented to us, and impart that relish which enables a man to eat three times as much as he could without them, but they decorate them with an attractive embellishment which may justly be compared to the finishing touch of the painter, or the toilette of a pretty woman.

The duty of a good sauce is, to titillate the capillaceous extremities of the maxillary glands, and thus to flatter and excite the appetite. If it be too mild, it causes no sensation, and its object is not attained; and if it be too pungent, it excoriates instead of arousing that gentle stimulation of the palate, the source of those undescribable feelings in which the enjoyment of a real epicure consists, and which an experienced and accomplished cook can alone produce.

Physicians indeed tell us, that sauces should be avoided—"because they induce us to eat to repletion!"— not perceiving that the objection constitutes the finest eulogium that could be passed on them. Were we guided by such reasoning as this, it would undermine the constitution and destroy the whole system of modern cookery; it would absolutely reduce us to a diet of plain roast and boiled, and condemn us for the remainder of our lives to the regimen of a family-joint. But, putting aside the impotent logic of these sons of Æsculapius, we may safely refer to their own practice; and, if we are not forced to refrain from the use of sauces until we see them refuse lobster with their turbot, swallow venison without jelly, take beef-steaks without oysters, or reject turtle and ragoûts, we need be in no dread of being speedily compelled to abstinence; and we may say to them, as Brutus to his brother Cassius—

There is no terror, Doctor! in your threats....[18]

On the Importance of Forming Good Connexions; and on the Moral Qualities of the Stomach

[Adapted from Grimod de la Reynière's "On Connexions"][19]
Society offers various degrees of connexion, all founded upon interests or passions by which they are continually liable to be interrupted. Thus, we have—

Family Connexions, which are commonly frigid;
Matrimonial Connexions, generally interested;
Illicit Connexions, always frail;
Political Connexions, ever hollow;
Commercial Connexions, often ruinous;
and, finally, *Friendly Connexions*, which are seldom sincere, and the
   semblance of which lead to so many *Equivocal* and even *Dangerous*
   Connexions.

The world, indeed, affords but one kind of connexion that is not exposed to
some of these disadvantages, and, consequently, that is worth forming—that
is, *the Connexion of Sauces*. The art of forming these is one of the greatest
mysteries in the whole arcana of the sciences, and its acquirement is the very
acme of the culinary art. Its elements indeed are simple, consisting chiefly of
gravy or of cream, as those of ordinary connexions do of interest or affection;
their object, too, is to cement the union of various, and often discordant,
qualities: it is their employment which is difficult. As, in a happy marriage,
the interests, the temper, and the wishes, of each, must mutually yield to the
other, in order to produce that harmony which forms the basis of connubial
happiness and of social order; so, in a good ragoût, the substance, the seasoning, and the sauce, should all be blended in that exquisite concord which
constitutes the foundation of good cookery and of all rational enjoyment.
The importance of an art which thus binds the whole fabric of society must
be at once apparent, and we are more earnest in soliciting attention to it, as
it is one in which the generality of cooks are most lamentably deficient: like
many of their masters, they cheat us with false appearances, and give their
sauces the semblance of richness, by the aid of mere colouring matter, while
they, in fact, possess neither flavour nor substance.[20]

The consideration of this subject leads us to that of *Social Connexions*,
which spring from it as naturally as horns from a connexion of another
kind. The table is a magnet which not only attracts around it all those who
come within its influence, but connects them together by ties which no one
ever wishes to dissolve. These are much stronger among epicures than other
persons; not only from the principle of attraction in a conformity of taste,[21]
but because epicures are more sociably disposed, more frank and cordial,
and are, in fact, better than any other of the human species. However this last
assertion may occasion a sneer of disbelief on the wan visage of some water-
drinking cynic, it is susceptible of the most incontrovertible demonstration.
Thus—no man abstains from the pleasures of the table, unless forced to do
so by some constitutional defect:—the greatest defect in the constitution
is a bad stomach:—if the stomach be unsound, the heart which is lodged
in it must be corrupted: it therefore follows, that all abstemious people are

persons of bad heart; and the converse of this proposition evidently is, that all bon-vivants are persons of a good heart, as well as a sound constitution. The truth of this axiom is confirmed by the daily experience of society: your sober people, not having the power to digest sufficient food and wine to support the system and stir the generous current of the blood, are cold in manners as in constitution, and from being pursued with the eternal consciousness of their deficiencies, they are ever envious and malignant; while the jolly votary of the table, reveling in the full tide of enjoyment, feels no corroding anxiety check the warm impulse which expands his mind to hilarity and his heart to friendship; and, as good cheer is the nurse of good humour and wit—a good stomach is the parent of every social virtue.

Let us be assured, therefore, that the connexion between a good sauce, whereby the powers of the food are cemented, and a good stomach, wherewith the constitution is supported and the social system maintained, possesses the only legitimate title to respect, and is, in fact, the real secret of the HOLY ALLIANCE.

On Roasting Beef, Including Considerations on its Domestic and National Importance, with an Entire Plan for Its Improvement

There is but one rib to which every man is uniformly constant: that is, a rib of beef. Its attractions, unlike the fading beauties of the person, or the variable qualities of the mind, ever retain the freshness of their first impression on our senses, and neither time nor circumstance can estrange our affections from this earliest object of our ardent love, and latest of our matured attachment. It is this which may truly be denominated "bone of our bone, and flesh of our flesh," and from which no man of sound principles or good appetite would ever wish to be separated. If any lean and atrabilarious [sic] contemner of the solid joys of life should be so insensible to its charms as to wish to divorce it a *mensâ*—no ecclesiastical court would entertain the suit; if appeal were made to the Lords—the Bench of Bishops would declare it to be contrary to every orthodox principle; the Judges would decide that all precedent was opposed to it; the house would unanimously reject the petition as dangerous to the constitution; and even the Chancellor himself would feel no hesitation in pronouncing judgment. It is interwoven with all our most cherished recollections and our sweetest sympathies: let an Englishman be taken from his native country to any quarter of the globe, surround him with all the seductions of France or Italy—he still sighs for it—no reveille ever animated the soldier with half the ardour that does the drum when, a quarter of an hour before dinner, it beats the inspiring air of "Oh! the roast beef of old England!"—it was to its honored remains that the sentimental muse of Moore addressed the pathetic song which ends with these expressive lines—

Around the dear ruin each wish of my heart
Shall entwine itself verdantly still;[22]

and it is of such a rib that every man may truly say, he wishes—"to cut, and come again." But it is not alone as an object of our fondest care that it should be regarded: the national character is involved in that of our beef; and not only our love, but our pride also, is interested in preserving its reputation untainted, and in presenting it in the most fascinating garb. It is with this double object in view, that we venture to suggest an important improvement in the art of dressing it, to which we request that serious attention which the subject so well deserves; and while we submit it to be weighed in the even scale of public opinion, we trust that our readers will "sink the offal" of prejudice, and judge it with all the impartiality of a Smithfield umpire.

According to the present vitious mode of roasting—before a tolerably sized piece of beef can be sufficiently done, the greater part of its succulent and invaluable juices are wasted in the dripping-pan, and confiscated to the profit of the cook. This has long been matter of poignant regret to those who are best enabled to appreciate the value of the loss, and various have been the plans proposed to remedy the evil; but the honor of complete success was reserved to the nineteenth century, already so fruitful in great events. Like most other inventions of general utility, it is equally simple and comprehensive. The object being, to close the pores of the meat, and thus, by preventing the escape of its juices, to retain all its most nutritive qualities, and to heighten its flavor—all these desirable objects are at once attained by merely *immersing the joint in rendered tallow*.

On a little reflection, our readers cannot fail to be struck with all the advantages which must necessarily result from this process; and we doubt not that it will be immediately, and universally, adopted. There is but one objection that we have anticipated, and that is, the inconvenience of the operation; but for this we have provided in a manner that we are equally sure must meet with general approbation.

There can be no doubt of the intimacy of your kitchen-maid with the tallow-chandler:—let her seek him in his melting moments; and, submitting her ribs to the warm embraces of his vat, leave them plunged in the soft effusion for about half an hour, in which time the operation will generally be completed. When sufficiently impregnated with the unctuous mass, let them be placed in a cool situation, in order that it may form an impenetrable coating, equally impervious to the external air and retentive of the internal moisture: thus, they will be preserved in all their primitive freshness until the period of their maturity; when put to the fire, the gradual decomposition of the tallow will preserve them from being scorched without, or drained within; and when placed upon the table, the first incision of the carving-knive will be followed by an inundation of gravy that will richly compensate the cares of its conservation.

In presenting this receipt to our country as an object of truly national importance, we have yet to regret, that the merit of the discovery belongs to France. We confess, that we do not make this acknowledgment without some degree of confusion:—we feel as if invaded, as it were, in our own territory:—while the strong hold of roast-beef was exclusively our own, we felt securely entrenched—knuckle deep—in a substantial fort, from which we might look with a certain degree of indifference on the lesser outposts occupied by our rivals, and could at any time make a sally upon them without fear of reprisal; but the new mode of attack which we have just detailed, fills us with alarm for the undivided dominion of this most antient and most valuable British possession. Never can that approved military maxim—*"fas est ab hoste doceri"*[23]—be more aptly applied; and devoutly do we hope, that the experience of the enemy will, in this instance at least, redound to our own advantage. There is but one slight inconvenience attending its employment, and that arising solely from its superior excellence:—such is the relish which it imparts, that a Baron of Beef prepared in this manner will scarcely suffice for half a dozen men of moderate appetite.

On the Virtues, the Qualifications, and the Consequence of the Ancient Family of Hogs

It is not to the bipeds who bear this title that we allude:—the amiable quadruped known by it is a far more estimable personage: and, though decried and despised, is, in fact, one of the most estimable members of society. His various good qualities are, indeed, felt by all, but acknowledged by few; and in no instance is the ingratitude of the world more glaring than in the contempt with which his modest merits are rewarded. For our own part, we never meet him without taking off our hat with all the respect which is due to real worth in whatever garb we find it.

He is the prince of all the animals that "chew *not* the cud," and although the majority of the Christians of the present age are as great Jews as ever lived, yet none of them adhere to the Levitical law in regard to him.[24] Nature has been so bountiful to this her favored child, that every part of him is equally valuable:—arms and the arts contend with the kitchen for his spoils; and if the fame and fortune of many a pork-butcher is due to his flesh, his bristles have been the instruments of the glory of many a celebrated painter, as his hide is ever the seat of honor of the warrior. Were he banished from our tables—neither ham, nor brawn, nor bacon, nor smoked chops, nor

Brunswick or Bologna sausages, nor forced-meat, nor black-puddings, nor pickled petitoes, nor standing pies, would ever greet our sense; the Christmas chine, the harslet and the crackling, griskins and spare-ribs would be seen no more;[25] pease-pudding, apple-sauce, and savoury sage, would partake in his disgrace; and sucking-pigs would cease to smile upon our boards. We have recapitulated these few traits of his innumerable excellencies from the same feeling that would lead us to rescue the character of a valued friend from obloquy; and we trust, that the slanderers of this truly respectable animal, will in future admit—"that they have ta'en the wrong sow by the ear."

The metamorphoses which the flesh of the hog undergoes, are as various as those described by Ovid; and if he had but employed his pen to record them, his works, instead of being only found in the hands of school-boys, would be read with more enthusiasm than those of Sir Walter Scott or Lord Byron. We shall not attempt to detail them: they would, alone, occupy the pages of a folio, and they more properly form the subject of a profound treatise than of a mere elementary essay. But we cannot refrain from touching upon that long contested and still unsettled point—*the best mode of dressing ham.*

A noble peer, whose experience on this interesting subject has been displayed with great erudition in his truly instructive travels, and whose critical acumen in culinary science can no more be questioned than his knowledge of military tactics, has furnished one invaluable receipt which must be within the recollection of every reader of taste; and we remember to have been ourself present, at the table of another noble and truly amiable bon-vivant, when an animated discussion took place on the comparative merits of stewing a ham in champagne, or of baking it in the center of a dunghill when in a state of fermentation. Our own opinion inclined to the latter: the champagne has the inconvenience of penetrating the brain of your cook rather than the flesh of the ham; while there can be no doubt of the pungent effluvia of the compost communicating to it a very high flavor. A preferable mode to either is, in our humble estimation, to thoroughly roast it in a paste, after having soaked it for four-and-twenty hours in syrup strongly impregnated with garlick-vinegar; due allowance being made, in the latter respect, for the different treatment required by a ponderous Westphalian, and the more delicate native of Guimaraens or the mountains of Galicia. But ham should never be eaten hot; nor cold, unless smothered in a savoury jelly.

We shall not advert to that highly valued delicacy of the ancients—stewed sow's teats—because the avarice of modern times opposes itself to the slaughter of the animal at the period when they are in perfection, and a prejudice exists against those which die in parturition. But we think we shall render a great public service by recording the modern Portuguese method of dressing a loin of pork:—

Steep it, during an entire week, in red wine, (*claret in preference,*) with a strong infusion of garlick and a little spice; then sprinkle it with fine herbs, envelope it in bay-leaves, and bake it along with Seville oranges *piquées de girofle*.

We strongly recommend this dish to the Society for the Conversion of the Jews, as a more effectual means of making proselytes than any they have yet adopted; and we must here remark, to the honor of the pig, that there is no example upon record of a real epicure having been converted to Judaism.[26]

Naturalists may say what they please of the lion—the wild boar is the real monarch of the forest; and no one who has seen him, towering at the head of the table in proud pre-eminence above all lesser game, could doubt for a moment of his rank, or of the respect to which he is entitled. Indeed few potentates can vie with him in the love and admiration which he commands; and there is none whose head is so well spoken of. To mention the various gracious forms in which he condescends to appear in those countries where he yet reigns, would only be to excite vain regrets, and to make our mouths water fruitlessly; we shall therefore spare our readers and ourself the tantalizing recital; but it is consolatory to reflect that, by only just going to Poland or Hungary, or even to Hanover, we may yet see him in all his glory—and few travelers have in view an object so truly worthy of pursuit. We presume that no one will be either so simple, or so unjust, as to confound this noble animal with the common *bores* to be every day met at the very best tables in this country.

Having made this feeble attempt to do justice to the merits of the hog, and the splendor of his great ancestor, it now only remains for us to mention his nephew, and the heir to all his virtues—for progeny of his own he has none—the gentle sucking-pig. And with regard to him, we have merely to recommend, that he be treated as a tender mother does her darling infant—that is to say—that he be well stuffed; and while dressing, let him be watched with as much solicitude as a daughter in her teens; but, above all, let him be well done; for, as to under-roasted pig—a man might just as well eat a raw child.[27]

A modern professor of some reputation in the practical arts of the kitchen, recommends that, when dressed, it should be divided longitudinally, and dished up conjugally—that is, *back to back*.

With regard to the antiquity of this family—they who have been weak enough to waste their time upon literature need not be told, that the foundation of the Roman Empire was due to the fortunate omen offered to Aeneas by a sow:—

> Wond'rous to tell!—she lay along the ground:
> Her well-fed offspring at her udders hung;
> She white herself, and white her thirty young!
> —Dryden's Virg. Aen. b. viii.

And we have the authority of Varro for the fact, that the remains of this venerable prophetess were preserved in brine, and shewn, by the priests of Juno, at Lavinium, in his time; that is to say—about seventeen hundred years after her decease.[28] It is, therefore, clearer than many a pedigree in the Heralds' College, that the origin of pickled-pork remounts at least as high as the Trojan war. Nay, her descendants are to this day distinguished in our universities by collegiate honors—better merited, by the bye, than some bestowed there—as many a fellow of Queen's Coll. Oxon. can testify:—

Caput apri defero, &c.&c.[29]

On Coffee, and Liqueurs

Our readers must have already perceived, that we are unfriendly to excesses of any kind. Our instructions are pointed to the use, not the abuse, of good-cheer. We would close our own dining-room, as mysteriously as if it were a second temple of Eleusis,[30] against all but the elect; and if any gross revelers think to find "warrant for their orgies" in the rites of which we treat, we say to them, in the language of its priests—

Hence, ye profane! Far, far away remove.[31]

But you, gentle reader! we take to be, "like him we love"—that is to say, ourself—a moderate man; and we therefore suppose you—resisting with fortitude all temptations to prolong the sitting, whether in the commands of your host, the jeers of six-bottle men, or, above all, the smiling entreaty of another rosy batch—to have retired to the drawing-room as soon as possible after you have dispatched your fourth bottle. But here other snares await you: the mistress of the house—"delighted to find one man gallant enough to desert his wine for the ladies"—immediately proposes to you—"to cut into a rubber." You might with truth, perhaps, excuse yourself on the plea—"that you are cut already;" but at all events, cut out if you wish to avoid being cut up: or, at least, excuse yourself until you have taken coffee, which of all beverages is the best calculated to clear the head, and to fit a man for the learned society of the Greeks. This will, besides, afford you an opportunity for displaying one of the most valued qualities, and one the rarest to be found, in all societies—that of a patient listener: for, unless you abstain from all conversation, on your own part, until you can count every light in the center chandelier without either blinking or doubling one of them—a task not easily performed after the fourth bottle—you had better not think of whist for that night. Search, therefore, for some garrulous giver of good dinners; throw yourself on the sofa beside him, and whilst he, "good easy man," flatters himself that you are relishing his vapid stories, and snuffs up the incense of your silence, do you sip the cordial of your coffee-cup in complete abstraction; and, while fumigating your brain with its aromatic steam, secure to yourself the certainty of an invitation to his choicest parties:—this is what wary people call "killing two birds with one stone."

Coffee, besides stimulating the reasoning faculties, is one of the best digestives with which we are acquainted; and we owe to it the inappreciable advantage of being enabled to eat much more than we could venture to do, with safety, were it not for the benign influence of its salutary aid. But then it must be swallowed hot, strong, and without any infusion of that viscous compound which is, in London, misnamed cream. It is a melancholy fact, however, that in not one house in ten, throughout England, do you ever meet with it of even tolerable quality: it is usually foul, flat, weak, and cold: nay, we doubt not that some of our readers must have seen a simpering miss, whilst presiding at the tea-table, pour from the half-cold urn a quart of water over about an ounce of burnt powder placed in the fusty woolen bag of a machine ycleped a biggin; then, when she had drenched the surrounding tabbies with the precious decoction, replenish the machine with another libation, and so on, so long as they consented to be thus physicked; and this the young lady would call—"making coffee!"—but, "*mutato nomine*," &c. &c.[32] It once fell to our own lot to witness this profanation, in company with a French count, who, in his own country, had been accustomed to the very essence of mocha. He seemed to watch the progress of the operation with some degree of curiosity; but when a cup-full of the potion was presented to himself, he started back with surprise and horror, and would, of course, have declined it, had not the lady of the house had the cruelty to tax his politeness by declaring that, "it was prepared expressly for him." There was no longer any possibility of escape: he shuddered involuntarily, "grinned horribly a ghastly smile,"[33] and accepted it with that kind of desperate resolution which a man may be supposed to exert who is forced to swallow a dose of poison. We observed him with a mixture of pity and anxiety: he took two or three gulps with much the same contortions that a child does rhubarb, when a violent fit of coughing, either real or affected, gave him a pretext to set down the cup with such violence as to break it, and at the same time to spill the remaining contents over the robe of his fair persecutress: – the revenge was deep, but suited to the injury, and no man can say that it was unjustifiable.

. . .

Liqueurs follow coffee as naturally as night follows day: their influence too is in some measure to be compared to that of the sable goddess; for they come like "balmy sleep," after the fatigues of a long dinner, as the "tired stomach's sweet restorers."[34] They embalm it with the spicy fragrance of their odour, and strengthen it with the tonic influence of their salutary spirit; while they titillate the palate with their delicious flavor, and produce those voluptuous extasies which are the ne plus ultra of all human enjoyment. It is a reproach to our country, that we yet possess none which deserve the title; unless indeed, we elevate to that rank our humble cherry-bounce and raspberry brandy.[35] Of those which we receive from abroad, it would puzzle Sir Isaac Heard himself to regulate the precedence:— each has its peculiar pretensions and partisans:—Kirchwasser, Dantzick, and Turin, Cinnamon and gold-waters, and Geneva-cordial are vaunted by those who give the preference to strong tonics; Curaçoa, the elixir of Garus, and the Anisette of Bordeaux, are in request as more gentle stimulants; while the various *Crêmes,—de Moka, d'Arabie, de Mexique, de Rose, de Jasmin, de Mille-fleurs,* and *d'Orange,* the *Huile de Venus,* and *Parfait Amour,* find constant advocates among the ladies. For our own part, we consider none of these as comparable to the Noyeau of Martinique—when it can be procured genuine; but that, alas! is scarcely to be hoped for, and we have never tasted an imitation that even approaches the seducing original of the far-famed Madame Chassevent. In the regretted absence of this queen of cordials—which may be truly termed *bottled velvet*—we would ourself assign the palm to the Maraschino of Zara; but here, again, we must protest against counterfeits; and more especially against that Neapolitan drug Rosoglio, or, as our honest tars in the Mediterranean not unaptly term it, "*Roll-your-soul-out!*" But, "*palmam qui meruit ferat,*" it is not for us to decide a contest of such moment; we shall therefore leave our readers to wander through this wilderness of sweets,[36] and cull a flower from each according as taste or fancy may direct; only entreating them to bear in mind that, as moderation is the essence of real enjoyment—*they should never exceed six cups of coffee and eight glasses of liqueur.*

On the Nature and Properties of the Braise; with a Concise Account of its Origin, and Application

[Adapted from Grimod de la Reynière's "Braised Turkeys"][37]
We are so much the creatures of habit, that we daily perform many of the most important functions of life without being able to account for the impulse by which we are guided; and are just as little acquainted with the hidden motives which govern us, as the lank-haired, long-eared, parish clerk is with the reason for his crying "Amen" with the same nasal twang at the end of a funeral prayer, a marriage blessing, or a sentence of excommunication. Thus, we every day eat our meat à la braise, without knowing any more of the manner of preparing it, than we do of the prescriptions which apothecaries poison us; and, although the braise is one of the most momentous operations of the kitchen, its principles are, generally, as little understood as those of the most abstruse mathematical science, or of the operation of the sinking fund. We shall endeavour to explain it, according to the rules laid down by

the President of the Royal Society, in the interesting chemical lecture which he delivered at his initiatory dinner.

In the common mode of dressing our carneous aliments, either those particles which constitute the chief portion of their savour evaporate on the spit as fruitlessly as the sighs of an absent lover, or their nutritive juices are drained into the pot with as little advantage to our stomachs as if they had been drawn into the vortex of the exchequer. To remedy these inconveniences, recourse is had to the braise, which is thus performed:—The bottom of a stewpan is strewed with slices of bacon and of beef, chopped carrots, onions, celery, fine-herbs, salt, pepper, mace, and allspice: upon this bed—more fragrant than if it were of roses—is laid, in soft repose, the joint which is the special object of your care; which is then wrapped in a downy covering of the same materials, and the curtain of the lid is cautiously closed upon it. It is then placed in the warm chamber of the portable furnace, and left to slumber in a state of gentle transpiration, under the guardian protection of a sylph of the kitchen, during as many hours as the priestess of the temple may deem salutary. When at length taken up, it rivals the charms of Diana newly risen from the bath; and when dressed in all its splendor—that is, dished with its sauce—we question whether the homage paid to the most admired beauty on her first presentation in the drawing-room was ever half so ardent or sincere as that which it receives when it makes its entrée at the table. The most homely leg of mutton acquires, in this way, a degree of refinement which fits it for the highest society: it may indeed be conjectured, that it cannot remain long in such intimate union with the piquant associates we have mentioned, without acquiring a certain portion of taste; and it strongly exemplifies the truth of that ancient adage—"tell me your company and I'll tell you your manners." Nor are these its only advantages: it imparts a certain yielding tenderness, peculiarly agreeable to those who begin to feel the effects of time upon their masticatory powers, and who, although as fervent as ever in their admiration, do not altogether possess the vigor which distinguished the devotions of their youth.

The origin of this truly great improvement in the culinary art, was, as we have been assured by a learned friend of deep research in such matters as follows—

There existed, at Paris, a "CONSTITUTIONAL ASSOCIATION" whose object was, not the persecution of printers, but the encouragement of cooks. The members, more attentive to the preservation of their own constitution than that of the state, attempted no interference with any government but that of the kitchen; they supported not party but that of dinner; professed no principles but those of good fellowship and attachment to the table; and were actuated by no exclusive feelings of preference for any administration but that of the best maître d'hôtel. They had long reflected with concern on the apathy which seemed to reign among the cooks, and had deliberated on the means of giving some stimulus to their invention, but without coming to any determination, until the alternate appearance of boiled and roast turkey on four successive club-days shewed the absolute necessity for taking decisive measures. The president, therefore, after an elaborate speech, in which he detailed, with equal perspicuity and force, the lamentable deficiency of the ancient system, and pathetically deplored the disappointment it had occasioned, proposed—that the silver gridiron of the society should be offered for the best essay on a new mode of dressing turkey. The resolution passed unanimously, and was attended with the desired effect. A young artist—called Le Gacque—whose name deserves to be handed down to posterity—warmed by the offer, his imagination heated with the prospect of distinction, and himself burning with emulation in his profession, conceived the fortunate idea of the braise. But his plan was not adopted without opposition: the maître d'hôtel, a man of great experience and distinguished reputation, and withal sharp-set against reformers, represented to the club, that it would be a dangerous innovation on the established principles which the society was particularly bound to support; that no turkey was ever so treated before; and as it was a measure which probably would fail in the execution, his character was interested in not countenancing it. To these observations the president replied—that the club had not come to so serious a determination without that mature deliberation which the importance of the subject required; that however the innovation might appear to be a solecism in cookery, yet the association felt itself above public opinion, and, notwithstanding the failure of some other trials, had resolved to incur the risk of the experiment; and that, whatever might be the result, it took the honor of the maître d'hôtel under its special protection: in fine, that its mandate was conclusive—a turkey must be braised; but in order to afford the fairest opportunity of judging the more comparative merits of the different modes, two other turkeys should be dressed at the same time—one boiled, the other roasted.

Monsieur Le Gacque got not a wink of sleep that night: he turned as often in his bed as if he had been himself upon the spit; and he contemplated the approaching trial of his skill with all the anxiety that may be supposed to agitate an author on the first representation of his play. The maître d'hôtel—with a rare disinterestedness in the head of a department—threw no official impediments in the way; and on the appointed day, the several candidates smoked upon the board. The interval which elapsed before their pretensions were finally discussed, was the most anxious of Monsieur Le Gacque's existence; nor was he entirely relieved from suspense on being summoned to hear the decision, as he could not but perceive, that the three turkeys had wholly disappeared among the thirteen members of the committee to whom the judgment was referred. But this was soon explained by the chairman as the consequence of that rigid impartiality which required that every particle of the evidence produced should be examined with scrupulous attention, without which they could not do justice to the merits of each, and, consequently, that no accurate conclusion could be arrived at until they had picked every bone. He proceeded to say—that having gone through that arduous duty with entire satisfaction to themselves, it only remained of him to declare, that the sense of the committee was so decidedly in favour of the discovery of Monsieur Le Gacque, that it felt not the least hesitation in recommending it to the adoption of the association, and unanimously awarded him the grid-iron.

This resolution was confirmed at a subsequent general meeting of the club, and a minute was inserted on their registers, concluding with the followiong remarkable lines, which we have translated literally from the original:-

That "turkey boil'd
Is turkey spoil'd,
And turkey roast
Is turkey lost; —
But, for turkey braised,
The Lord be praised!"

We must however observe, that a note appears upon the protocol of this record—but in a different hand from the original—that there was an exception made in favour of roasted turkey, "*when stuffed with truffles.*"

This last decision will no doubt be admitted as the most convincing proof of the equity, the moderation, and the discernment of this truly valuable association.

On the Philosophy of the Stomach; With Rules for the Better Regulation of Appetite and Digestion

There is an old proverb which has always appeared to us to concentrate more good sense and profound reflection than all other maxims of morality put together—"*eat to live, AND live to eat.*"[38] We are aware that some designing persons substitute the word "*not*" for "*and,*" by which they destroy the meaning and the whole value of the axiom; but no reflecting man will be at a loss to discover, that it is an interpolation of those envious reformers who, having nothing to eat themselves, would persuade us to stint our own precious stomachs, in order to ruin the revenue, and to deprive ministers of cabinet dinners; whereas the object of every good citizen ought to be, to multiply dinners by every means in his power. These men have no bowels, and are quite as ferocious as those political economists who tell us that we should cut each other's throats to avoid starvation. For our own part, we hear more frequent complaint of the want of appetite than of food—indeed we have it from the highest authority, that whatever distress there may be in the country is entirely owing to too great plenty!—and so far from abetting the unnatural system of starving the finances through ourselves, we always look upon those persons whose stomachs appear to be bomb-proof, and who commit as great havoc at a dinner as a Cossack while laying waste an enemy's country, as not only the most loyal subjects of the state, but the most valuable members of society, and the most favored mortals of the creation. Such men may eat as often as they please, and thus multiply their joys in endless succession: but persons of weaker constitution, or those whose stomachs at length begin to submit to the toils of a long protracted warfare, should husband their forces with more caution. A valetudinarian is, indeed, placed between the alternative of abstinence and medicine; and is, in fact, in a situation directly the reverse of that of an ass between two bundles of hay.

These veterans should only take the field during the general engagement of dinner, and should abandon the outpost skirmishes of second breakfast, luncheon, tea, and supper, to younger and less experienced combatants; always bearing in mind that "prudence is the better part of valour," and that an epicure whose stomach is out of order, is of no more use than a grenadier at the hospital. Let them eat but once a day:—alas! So fragile is our nature, that this is not the only instance in which our enjoyments are thus limited:—but let them dine well; solidly, leisurely, and with all the calm of the most perfect self-possession; let them display vigour in their attack, deliberation in their aim, ardour in the pursuit; and when obliged to quit the field, let their retreat be cool and steady.

So far the appetite: but that gained and satisfied, the day is not yet won until the digestion be complete; and this grand point will never be attained without due attention to the mode of conducting the previous operations, so as to secure the full benefit of their final advantages. Not only is it wholly destructive of all rational enjoyment to swallow down one's meat without taking proper time to comment upon its merits, and expatiate upon the happiness it procures us—or, in other words, to chew it with measure and reflection, and turn it as often as a minister does a new measure of finance before he can render it palatable—but, on this trituration depends not alone the ineffable pleasure to be derived from expressing and compounding the juices of viands and the flavor of the sauces, but the important object, also, of their undisturbed repose during the process of digestion.

It has been calculated by a learned physician, who devoted the greatest part of a long life to experiments upon his own stomach, that a mouthful of solid meat requires thirty-two bites, of a perfect set of teeth, to prepare it for deglutition. Now it unfortunately happens, that but few of those who have arrived at that period of life when the substantial joys of the table supersede more evanescent pleasures, possess their masticators unworn by the edge of time and service; it is, therefore, impossible to lay down any fixed rule on the subject. But, as a man who plays at hazard should be perfect master of the odds on every main and chance, in order to enable him to bet and hedge with advantage, so, every one who sets at the great game of dinner should accurately calculate the respective number and strength of his grinders and incisors, in order to determine, in the first place, the steak on which he will venture, and in the next the quantum of labour to be bestowed on it. It is inconceivable how much valuable time may thus be saved, which would otherwise be wasted in unprofitable speculation; and while you are actively employed on one dish with your teeth, you may devour the remainder with your eyes.

The next point to be attended to is, that repose which will afford the digestive faculties the undisturbed exercise of their powers. By repose we do not mean sleep; that could be obtained by listening to some of the prosing stories which we have already supposed you to have affected to lend a patient ear to while taking your coffee; or by reading a political pamphlet, or the last new poem; or, in short, in a hundred other ways, all equally effective as laudanum: no; what we allude to, is that perfect composure of the mind which is unbroken by any effort of imagination, and unobtruded upon by any thing that can be called an idea. To obtain this enviable degree of tranquility, you may either visit the opera, or a conversazione; or, if you happen to be an M.P., and there should be a debate on the supplies, you may stroll to the house; for having already secured your own share, it cannot afford you any anxiety. But, as you value your comfort that night, and your appetite the next day, we charge you to avoid the perusal of the correspondence you may find upon your table on your return home: for, whether it consist of attorneys' letters, tradesmen's bills, or billets-doux, you may be assured that they are all filled with either threats, solicitations, or reproaches; and will be equally fatal to the serenity of your temper and the renovation of your stomach. If, however, notwithstanding these our injunctions, the dæmon of curiosity should tempt you to their inspection, and that your nerves should consequently be agitated by either dread, regret, or ire—those enemies to repose—we recommend to you the following draught, as an opiate, to be taken on retiring to rest—take equal parts of brandy and rum, (*each a large wine glass-full*) half a glass of arrack, and the same quantity of curaçoa: to these, add the juice of two small limes, and the rind (*peeled thin*) of one, with quantity sufficient of refined sugar to render the whole palatable; then pour in double the quantity of strong decoction of gunpowder-tea (*boiling hot*) with two glasses of warm calf's feet jelly; stir well together, and swallow instanter. This mixture will be found by no means unpleasant; and if it fail of the desired effect, it can only be, because either your conscience, or your stomach, is overloaded.

On the Financial Importance of Teeth, Containing Some Valuable Hints to Statesmen

The consideration of the subject of which we have treated in the preceding essay, has led us to that of the general use and value of teeth; and the more we have reflected on it, the more surprise have we felt that it should hitherto have escaped the vigilance of the Chancellor of the Exchequer. If it be a maxim in taxation "that luxuries are its fittest objects," where shall we find any greater?—and if universal use, and ease in the collection, be further inducements, we know of none that come more immediately within that description, or that may be made more largely productive to the revenue—than teeth. As we throw this out merely as a hint, it is no part of our object to discuss the amount of the assessment, or the various modifications to which it must necessarily be subject; but we would submit, that the charge ought to be *per tooth*, with a proportionate reduction for stumps, and that some allowance should be made to those who give satisfactory proof that they are unremittingly afflicted with the tooth-ache.

On the other hand, we would increase the rates on some particular species—as, for instance, *liquorish-teeth*, and colt's-teeth; and we would press heavily on *false-teeth* as articles of the highest luxury. Indeed, the latter we think, ought to be rated, like the assessed taxes, by a progressively encreasing scale; with a clause in the act, allowing a full set to be compounded for. There should also be a clause, subjecting persons to heavy fines who should be proved guilty of having willfully had their teeth drawn, with a view to defraud the revenue; and it should be highly penal, in future, for any person to knock another's teeth down his throat.

Where there are no other means of compelling payment, collectors of the taxes might be empowered to put a distress into the mouth of the defaulter, and to take the amount in kind: they have all been too long accustomed to every mode of screwing, to feel in the least a loss in wrenching a man's teeth out of his head.

It has been observed to us, that some ill-natured fellows might seize this opportunity to deprive their wives for ever of the means of snapping at them, and, with that view, might leave them to pay the tax in kind; but the Chancellor of the Exchequer—who, whatever some people may think, certainly has got his eye-teeth about him—is not to be bitten in that way, and would of course make them answerable in their own persons.

There was also another objection started, which, we confess, somewhat puzzled us: that was, the injustice of making aliens liable to it who came into the country for a short time only, and the difficulty of preventing frauds if they were to be exempted. But, upon mentioning this to a particular friend, who is a Commissioner of the Customs, he at once relieved our embarrassment, by proposing—with all that liberality and discernment for which the board to which he belongs is so conspicuous—to extend to such persons the benefit of the bonding system; that is, that on their arrival in this country, they may enter their teeth for exportation, by which means—on merely submitting to have them drawn—they may be warehoused until their departure, when they would be returned without duty. To an arrangement so equitable as this, of course no objection could be found; and the whole plan has already received the decided approbation of every one to whom we have communicated it, with the exception of one country gentleman, who, indeed, muttered something about grinding, and seemed to think that teeth would soon become useless. There are no doubt persons who, entertaining a deep-rooted antipathy to all taxation, will make observations upon it equally hollow and unsound; will draw false conclusions from our strongest premises, and extract a wrong sense from the plainest meaning; and will, in short, oppose every operation of the ministry both tooth and nail. Such men keep their wits on edge to torture the meaning of the fast friends of order and regular government, and to put words into their mouths from which they may be considered as the instruments of oppression; and so loose are their principles, that they would not hesitate to root out all revenue, and thus destroy the nerves, and plug up the resources of the state. But we flatter ourself that the suspicion of wishing to place any impediment in the way of the free exercise of the jaws can never be thrown in our teeth: indeed, our disinterestedness in submitting the plan thus publicly to Ministers is self-evident; while we shall also be peculiarly exposed to its operation, for, whatever allowance we might expect in our own person or that of our family, on the score of stumps, will be more than counterbalanced by the extra charge on false-teeth, which we have, notwithstanding, had the magnanimity to suggest. We may also observe, that whatever the enemies of the measure may assert, they cannot call that which will oblige every man in the kingdom to open his mouth—*a gagging act*: and as it will, we have no doubt, be brought forward in the next session, and passed in spite of their teeth, we strenuously advise the opposition to chew the cud upon it during the recess, and neither by picking out technical flaws, or snapping at trifling objections, "to shew their teeth before they can bite;" nor yet, should they chop upon a stray majority on the first reading—"to hollow before they are out of the wood."

On Education, and the Application of the Science of Mnemonics; Together with Some Hints to Travellers, and Public Societies

It has often afforded matter of surprise to us, that, while all our schools seem fully sensible of the inconvenience of filling the stomachs of the pupils with wholesome beef and mutton, they yet see no impropriety in cramming their heads with hard and indigestible Greek and Latin; and force them to waste their time in poring over musty authors, which they never afterwards remember, or which, if remembered, are not worth the pains, while our shelves are loaded with valuable treatises on cookery, which, when once read, can never be forgotten. We cannot help thinking, that it would be productive of the most important results to society, if children, instead of reading Ovid's Metamorphoses, were instructed in those of Mrs. Glasse, and then proceeded through a regular course of culinary classics, including the whole range of English literature from "Murrel's Kickshawes" and "May's Accomplishede Cooke," down to "NUTT'S COMPLETE CONFECTIONER," "APICIUS REDIVIVUS," and "SIMPSON'S BILLS OF FARE," until they reached the French "*Cours Gastronomique*," and were able to enjoy the "*Almanach des Gourmands*," as a book of amusement as well as study.[39] We have ourself pursued this plan with a boy whom we have been led to suppose our own; and who, indeed already displays all the distinctive qualities of his illustrious grandsire. So well has he profited by the lessons he has received, that before he had well attained his thirteenth year, he had acquired the envied appellation of alderman—a presage, we trust, of his future greatness:—after perfecting him in all that was worth learning in England, we have sent him to France, where, such are his powers, he complains that the table of the college where he is placed, does not afford scope enough for the exercise of his talents; and we make no doubt, that if removed to the University of Paris, he would cut a distinguished figure amongst the disciples of Professors Very and Beauvilliers.[40]

But it has more particularly occurred to us, that the science of Mnemonics, which has lately attracted such attention in this country, could be adapted to some of the purposes of education with much greater effect than has been yet attempted. Our present application of the science is generally obscure, often absurd, and sometimes even unintelligible. Thus, who can discover any analogy between ladies and loose-fish, or between the gentlemen of Essex and their calves? Why is it that a leech should be supposed to remind us of an attorney, or a rat of an M.P.? Whence arises it, that, if you see a fellow reeling through the streets, you say—"he is as drunk as a lord"—although it is very well known that lords never get drunk at all! Or that, when you perceive a precise-looking, formal gentleman, with a measured step and a set countenance, talking common-place morality in a solemn tone of dictatorial consequence, you call him "a saint," although you are persuaded that he is only a hypocrite? These, to be sure, are all rather extravagant instances; but our readers will easily recollect others not less inapplicable, and as such assimilations are generally arbitrary, they are often calculated to lead us astray. The study of geography alone appears to us not liable to this objection, and we flatter ourself with being able to show, that Mnemonics are susceptible of being applied to it in a manner that has not hitherto occurred to the learned professor who has distinguished himself by that method of instruction.

The object of Mnemonics being, to imprint one recollection on the mind by its association with another, the more agreeable the symbol is made to the imagination, the more likely will it be to take root in the memory:—such is the theory on which it is founded. We propose to go a step farther, and to ensure its indelible impression, by implanting it in the stomach.[41] Thus, on commencing with an infant, we would imprint Shrewbury and Banbury on his mind through the medium of their cakes; the Isle of Wight by its cracknels, Kent by its cherries; Norfolk by its biffins;[42] and Sussex through its dumplings. As he advanced in taste and erudition, and after the several remarkable places in his own land had thus been rendered familiar to him, we would have him proceed with those of foreign countries, and there are few but would afford him the most agreeable recollection of their names through their distinctive products in either liquors or eatables; of which especial care should be taken to make him taste regularly as he went on. Such a mode of study would, besides, be attended with these peculiar advantages:—it would, doubtless, be pursued with more eagerness than the meager plan at present adopted; the instruction to be received by it would be solid; and even persons of mature age, whose education had been neglected in their youth, would find it neither dry nor unprofitable.

In this manner, geography, which has hitherto been little more than a mere science of empty names, would be engrafted on one of real utility: travelers would no longer find it so necessary to carry astronomical, as culinary instruments; instead of planetary they would make alimentary observations; they would visit markets in preference to libraries; and in lieu of discussions with academicians, they would have consultations with cooks. While those of the old school would be torturing their brains to decipher the unintelligible fragments of some worthless inscription, these would be comforting their stomachs with the substantial contents of a good dinner; instead of returning at last with musty old manuscripts which no one understands, and with the mutilated legs and arms of statues which, though nobody can eat, every body seems to grudge us—they would come home with receipts for new dishes and specimens of foreign dainties, far more agreeable to a man of real taste, and which they could acquire without robbing either churches or temples;

and thus we should become at once good geographers and excellent cooks. We know of only two travelers who have as yet distinguished themselves in this way; but the information displayed in the "forced journey" of the one, and the "sporting tour" of the other, is far more valuable than that afforded by all the rest of the classical tourists of the age put together. Their deserved celebrity will, we trust, serve to excite the emulation of those who are bitten by the touromania of the day, and tend eventually to enrich their country with all the delicacies of every quarter of the globe.

We leave our readers to meditate on this text: the intelligent and enlightened, but above all, the gastronomical, among them, will be at no loss to extend the commentary: indeed we think the hint well worthy the attention of government; and we would venture to suggest, that no voyage of discovery should in future be undertaken without a special instruction on this subject. We do not know whether this may not have been already done in the case of the expedition to the north pole. These adventurous navigators do not, indeed, seem to have, as yet, met with much success in that respect; but we understand there is a race of people bordering on the arctic regions, who are eminently skilled in the dressing of the fins and tails of whales, and the preservation of bears' paws; and, if a communication could be once opened with them, we have no doubt of some important results being yet obtained from the voyage.

We also beg leave most respectfully to submit to that philanthropic body, the Missionary Society, the expediency of promoting this great object through the medium of their agents and correspondents in the East. Enlightened as the age is, we are yet utterly in the dark respecting that far-famed delicacy, the birds' nests of the Chinese; our catalogue of curries is lamentably deficient; and our cooks are as ignorant of the true method of boiling rice as of the tenets of the Braminical faith. Now, if instructions were given to those reverend gentlemen, who seem to be wasting their logic and their time among the Hindoos, just to bestow a little attention on these important subjects, they would convert more Christian unbelievers in the utility of their mission than they now do heathens, and there can be no doubt of the subscriptions being greatly augmented the moment it is known that there is an attainable object in view.

We likewise strenuously exhort those pious persons, the Branch-Bible-Society's Committee-Ladies—who have so charitably relinquished the mending of their own stockings for the sake of patching their neighbours' souls—to contribute their now useless stock of household receipts to be printed for the general benefit. Such a publication would better establish the fame of the society than all the windy speeches in which the members echo each others praises throughout the Egyptian Hall, and would render a much more essential service than most of the crude and undigested homilies that daily issue from the press for our admonition; while our fair instructresses might say—what few of the most orthodox can boast—that their precepts would merit attention, for that, in truth, *they practise as they preach.*

Such subscriptions would besides, possess the inappreciable advantage of not taking any money out of their husband's pockets; and would relieve themselves from the imputation of belonging to a sect—

> More peevish, cross, and splenetick,
> Than dog distract, or monkey sick;
> Who quarrel with minc'd pies, and disparage
> Their best and dearest friend, plum-porridge;
> Fat pig and goose itself oppose,
> And blaspheme custard through the nose![43]

On the Qualifications of Cooks

The assemblage of qualifications requisite in a perfect cook, renders the profession one of the most arduous, as it unquestionably is the most important, in the whole range of the sciences.

A cook, to be thoroughly accomplished, should not only be deeply versed in all the arcana of the kitchen, but should possess an intimate knowledge of ichthyology, zoology, anatomy, botany, and chemistry; should be endowed with profound observation, solid, judgement, unremitting vigilance, and incorruptible sobriety; but, above all, should be impressed with a strong sense of the value of the art, and stimulated by the ardor of professional emulation.

We have heard a great deal of the power of the esprit de corps in the army: but, for our part, we look upon it to be something like wind in the stomach—more vapour than substance—nor do we know of any value it possesses but that of getting men spitted like larks, and sent out of the world before their time; whereas, the same spirit infused into a legion of cooks, tends to the preservation of life, instead of its destruction, and is productive of the most salutary results to political, as well as domestic, economy. The statesman, who looks only to its general effect, should therefore encourage it in preference, as promoting that greatest of all national objects the support of the constitution, the strength of which can in no way be so well maintained; and it is, doubtless, this which all very loyal men have in view when they talk of devoting their lives and fortunes; for, in fact, who would hesitate between the choice of a bullet or a beef-steak in the thorax, or between having his guts run through with cold steel or filled with a hot dinner? But, as the spirit of the army would lie dormant unless roused by the voice of public approbation, so, the emulation of our cooks is repressed by the want of that powerful stimulant to great actions. Whatever may be the praises bestowed on a dinner, the host never thinks of declaring the name of the artist who produced it; and while half the great men in London owe their estimation in society solely to the excellence of their tables, the cooks on whose talents they have risen languish "unknown to fame" in those subterraneous dungeons of the metropolis termed kitchens. In France, on the contrary, a man's cook is his pride; he glories in his feats beyond all the exploits of his ancestors; and, indeed, the most zealous devotee of musty genealogies must admit—that a live cook is at any time worth a dead general. To this it is that the French are indebted for those professors of the art who have raised the national glory to that pitch which is now their greatest boast; and until we imitate them in this respect, we must either be content to be dependent on them for all our tolerable artists, or to put up with the plain roast and boiled, and the meager catalogue of made-dishes of our own fat kitchen-wenches. We would rather fan the blaze of competition, than blow the embers of discord, between the cooks of the respective countries; and it is merely with a view to kindle the former, and to show of what self-devotion a cook is capable—as well as a soldier—when his zeal for the honor of his profession is properly encouraged, that we relate the following instance of *culinary esprit de corps*.

The history of the reign of Lewis the Fourteenth—so fertile in great men of every class—has preserved the record of one eminent professor of the science of cookery, whose name will descend to posterity with the honors of martyrdom, and to whose fame we feel a just pride in adding the tribute of our admiration and regret.

CHARLES AUGUSTUS ARMAND WATEL [VATEL] was descended from an ancient family, of cooks, long settled in the University of Toulouse, so celebrated for its learning and its pâtés of ducks' livers. History is silent on the subject of his early education; and we only learn, that from his most tender years he evinced a decided preference for the science of eating. But we may conjecture that he was brought up in the most orthodox culinary principles; for the memoirs of the times represent him as having taken an important degree in the kitchen of an archbishop at a time of life when few of his young associates had advanced beyond the rank of under graduate. From that period he advanced rapidly to the highest honors of his profession, until, at length, we find him chief cook to the great Prince of Condé—a master hardly less distinguished in the annals of history than himself. Here it was that he immortalized himself by the invention of the *Côtellettes à la Maintenon*, and the discovery of Catsup, to which we owe so much of our real enjoyments; and here, alas! it was that he ended his brilliant career, at a moment when science had still to expect from him the noblest efforts of his genius. There are various accounts of the circumstances which led to the catastrophe; but the statement most to be relied upon, is as follows:—

The Prince had invited a large party of the first nobility to dine with him, and the repast was ordered in all the profusion which reigned in those days, and all the magnificence which became the entertainer and his guests. At that period sea-fish (never plentiful at Paris) was a rarity of most difficult attainment, and, consequently, in the highest request. Watel, determined, on this occasion, to out-do all his competitors, and to raise his master to the very pinnacle of fame, had arranged an entire course of fish—to consist of forty-eight dishes—and, to make sure of having each in perfection, he had dispatched a special messenger to the nearest sea-port, whose return was so calculated as that he should arrive in Paris with his convoy on the morning of the fête. But the most important events of life are often subordinate to the most trivial occurrences:—the messenger got drunk on the road, and overstaid his time; the appointed morning arrived, but along with it no fish made its appearance. The hours rolled on, and hope sustained the sinking spirits of Watel until hope itself could cheat him no longer: he then took a step which at an earlier hour might have been attended with some success—he went to market—but it was too late—all the fish was gone. Thus foiled in all his plans, deprived of his last resource, fevered by the state of agitation in which he had been held, and goaded, it is said, by the taunts of a fellow-cook, who envied his reputation, and who reproached him with the "pretty kettle of fish he had made of it," he, in a moment of despair, resolved not to survive his disgrace; and, retiring to the pantry—stabbed himself to the heart with a silver skewer.

Thus fell Watel! Contemporary authors speak of him, as they do of other great characters, in terms rather dictated by party spirit than the dignified impartiality of history; and one—who evidently never partook of a dinner prepared by him—has even ventured to affirm, that he was poisoned by one of his own ragoûts. Whatever our own admiration of the course he meditated, we shall not attempt to palliate that which he adopted; and although our respect inclines us to draw a veil over his infirmities, we must yet admit, that his memory would have been freer from reproach, if he had dished up dinner before he dished himself.[44]

Peace to his illustrious shade! He has proved that the spirit of honor reigns in the kitchen as well as the camp, and fires the breasts of cooks as well as soldiers; and although, in this philosophic age, his successors seem to prefer the pleasure of living at their masters' expense to the glory of dying for their reputation, yet may we hope that his generous self-devotion will rouse their emulation, or, at least, remind them—never to forget the fish.

On the Health and the Morals of Cooks

[Adapted from Griimod de la Reynière's "On the Health of Cooks"][45]
Every master of a house who has the least regard for his own reputation will
doubtless be equally attentive to that of his cook: we deem it, therefore, quite
unnecessary to enforce those minute enquiries respecting natural abilities,
education, acquirements, and experience, which every one of common sense
will, of course, make regarding the person to whom they are about to commit
their dearest interests. The point to which we request attention, is—not the
acquisition of cooks, but the conservation of their degustative faculties in that
healthful state without which no dinner can be dressed with precision; and
this, we shall endeavour to shew, depends mainly on their being frequently,
attentively, and copiously physicked. Some unreflecting persons may perhaps
be at a loss to conjecture how the delicacy of a table can depend upon the
plethora of the cook: nothing, however, is more simple. The fore-finger of an
experienced cook travels incessantly from the stewpan to the mouth; for it is
only by tasting the ingredients in it every moment, that the critical point of
their perfection is to be ascertained. The organs of sense should, therefore, be
preserved in a state of the extremest delicacy, as on that depends the flavour
of your sauces, the seasoning of your ragoûts, the coction of your meat, and,
in short, all your terrestrial happiness. But the heat and smoke of the fires,
the confined air of kitchens, and perhaps, also, a little occasional intemperance, which these inconveniencies render excusable, gradually induce a slight
attack of slow fever, which usually manifests itself in that most alarming
symptom, an insensibility in the organs of the palate. The ordinary stimulants
no longer produce the same effect, and the consequence is, that your dishes
are unnaturally seasoned. The moment, therefore, that you detect a shake
too much of the pepperbox, be assured that the temperament of your cook
is deranged, and that no time is to be lost if you wish to restore the palate to
the proper degree of susceptibility. The cook may probably be unconscious
of disease, and reluctant to submit to the necessary regimen: but listen to no
remonstrance—overpower all opposition—trust to no apothecary, lest there
should be collusion—and proceed as follows; taking especial care to witness
the whole operation yourself.

Remove the patient from the precincts of the kitchen, and out of the way
of all temptation to indulge in animal food: administer a gentle emetic, and
chamomile tea *ad lib.*: confine to a strict diet and cooling drinks for the two
following days, then throw in a brisk cathartic, and allow nothing but weak
chicken broth for the next twenty-four hours. The following day, you may
try the effect of these remedies on a couple of white fricassees, a brown soup,
some vegetable and fish curries, and a few other made dishes; but you must
not allow the powers of your cook to be exhausted on a regular dinner. The

mode in which these are dressed will ascertain the state of convalescence: if the same faults prevail, you must repeat the operation, and draw about twenty ounces of blood from the left arm, which will be generally found sufficient to reduce the system to a proper equilibrium.

No cook who aspires to any thing beyond mediocrity will ever object to this mode of treatment; but, as some may, no doubt, be found so insensible to fame and so unreasonable as to start objections, it ought ever be made a positive condition of their engagement, that they should implicitly submit to be physicked and bled at the option of their masters: and to those who value themselves on the superiority of their tables, we cannot too often repeat—*physick your cooks.*

Notes

1. The quotation is from the preface to Fredrick Accum's *Culinary Chemistry*; his titles are listed on the title page to *A Treatise on Adulterations of Food, and Culinary Poisons, Exhibiting the Fradulent Sophistications of Bread, Beer, Wine, Spiritous Liquors, Tea, Coffee, Cream, Confectionery, Vinegar, Mustard, Pepper, Cheese, Olive Oil, Pickles, and Other Articles Employed in Domestic Economy and Methods of Detecting Them* (London: Longman, Hurst, Rees, Orme, & Brown, 1820).
2. Charles and Mary Lamb, *The Letters of Charles and Mary Anne Lamb*, ed. Edwin W. Marrs, Jr. 3 vols. (Ithaca, NY: Cornell University Press, 1975), 3: 84.
3. Guy Chapman, *A Bibliography of William Beckford at Fonthill by Guy Chapman in Conjunction with John Hodgkin* (London: Constable, 1930), 89.
4. Actually, the Latin reads "from the egg to the apple," which was the Roman tradition for dinner, starting with eggs and ending with fruit, as expounded in Horace, *Satires*, i.3.6. and Cicero, *Ad Familiares*, ix. 20; cf. Kitchiner, *Cook's Oracle*, 28. Sturgeon hints at two traditions, for Grimod writes "from soup to coffee"; see this volume, 14.
5. Book I, Satire 4, line 85. *The Satires of Horace in Latin and English*, ed. Philip Francis, vol. 3 of the 4 in *A Poetical Translation of the Works of Horace: with the original text, and critical notes collected from his best Latin and French commentators.* 4th ed. (London: A Millar, 1750).
6. Grimod, "Des Amphitryons," in *Almanach des gourmands*, 2: 34–41. Sturgeon's direct translation of Grimod begins in the final sentence of the first paragraph and continues through the middle of the second; after this random echoes or paraphrases are the only similarity.
7. Fish (properly perch) boiled and served in its own liquor. (*OED*).
8. Juan Guillermo, Duque de Riperda (1680–1737); Duc de Vendôme was the military officer Louis Joseph (1654–1712); the Spanish Puchero is a composite stew of meat and vegetables.
9. Adapted from Shakespeare, *Hamlet*, I.ii.188–89, as printed in *The Riverside Shakespeare*, 1145.
10. See the Avare of Molière. [Sturgeon; referring to Molière's five-act 1668 comedy, *l'Avare*]
11. Philip Dormer Stanhope, Fourth Earl of Chesterfield (1694–1773) was an English politician best remembered for his *Letters to His Son* (1774), which gave advice on manners and morals to his illegitimate son, Philip Stanhope.
12. Alexander Pope, "The Rape of the Lock," Canto iii, line 21.
13. A reference to a provincial municipal corporation, which includes the collected body of civic authorities of a borough or incorporated town or city, including the mayor, aldermen and councillors. Aldermen were legendary in gastronomical literature and other writing of the nineteenth century for their love of feasting. The Lord Mayor was the Head of the corporation, and the Lord Mayor's feast, discussed by Sturgeon in his introduction, was known as the most sumptuous annual civic feast in London from early times.
14. "*A-la-distance*"— modern French, lately imported, and quite as good as that usually spoken in London. [Sturgeon]
15. Grimod, "L'Importance des Invitations," in *Almanach des Gourmands*, 3: 7–12.

16. At the time, an outlying area of London, located to the northwest near Camden Town.
17. When this was written, street lights in London used gas and required a lamp lighter to climb the lampost to light them.
18. An adaptation of "There is no terror, Cassius, in your threats"; William Shakespeare, *Julius Caesar*, 4.3.66, as printed in *The Riverside Shakespeare*, 1125.
19. Grimod, "Des liaisons," in *Almanach des gourmands*, 6:26–33; to the categories of connections listed at the start of the essay, Grimod adds connections of pleasure, which he finds little durable (*de plaisir, peu durables*); connections of interest which are suspect (*d'intérèt, si suspectes*); and connections of friendship, which are very rare (*d'amitié, si rares*). The category of "Matrimonial Connexions, generally interested" is added by Sturgeon.
20. Grimod adds a paragraph here detailing the culinary-chemical composition of sauces.
21. From this point, where Grimod concludes, Sturgeon's text is original.
22. Slightly misquoted from Thomas Moore's poem, "Believe Me, If All Those Endearing Young Charms," from his *Irish Melodies* (1808–34).
23. A maxim generally attributed to the Romans, meaning "Never adverse to learn from a foe."
24. This comment bears a certain resemblance to the remarks made by Charles Lamb, in his essay "Imperfect Sympathies" (1821), about Jews, Christians, and their dining practices.
25. Harslet, or haslet, refers to a piece of meat to be roasted, particularly the entrails of a hog; griskin, or grisking, refers to the lean part of the loin of a bacon pig.
26. See footnote 23, above.
27. A reference to Swift's "A Modest Proposal for Preventing the Children of poor People in Ireland, from being a Burden to their Parents or Country; and for making them beneficial to the Publick" (1729); see *The Prose Works of Jonathan Swift*, ed. Herbert Davis, 14 vols. (Oxford: Blackwell, 1957–68), 12:116.
28. Varro, *Rerum rusticarum de agri cultura*, 2.4.18: huius suis ac porcorum etiam nunc vestigia apparent, quod et simulacra eorum ahenea etiam nunc in publico posita, et corpus matris ab sacerdotibus, quod in salsura fuerit, demonstratur (Even today there are still traces of this sow and her piglets, because even now bronze statues of them have been set up in public, and the body of the mother, which has been preserved in brine, is exhibited by the priests).
29. A line from the "Boar's Head Carol," an English traditional song, first published in 1521.
30. The first temple of Eleusis was the site of the secretive cult of Demeter in ancient Greece, where priestesses performed mysteries that the uninitiated could not watch.
31. St. Chrystostom says, "When we celebrate the Mysteries, we send away those who are not initiated, and shut the doors, a deacon exclaiming, 'Far from hence, ye profane! Close the doors! Thy Mysteries are about to begin. Things Holy for the saints, hence all dogs" (Hom 33, Matt.).
32. Part of an aphorism, *mutato nomine de te fabula narratur*, which means "with the name changed the story applies to you."
33. This is Death's expression in Milton, *Paradise Lost*, 2.846.
34. Adapted from the opening line of Thomas Young, *Night Thoughts* (1741).
35. Cherry-bounce is a colloquial expression for cherry-brandy.
36. The Latin phrase *Palmam qui meruit ferat* translates "Let him bear the palm who has deserved it." A "wilderness of sweets" is a reference to Milton, *Paradise Lost*, 5.294.
37. Cf. Grimod, *Almanach des gourmands*, 2: 266–72. Sturgeon transforms Grimod's Wednesday Society (Société des Mercredis) into a "Constitutional Association," with ironic political overtones that his British readers would not miss. Sturgeon keeps the episode set in France, commenting derisively on its members who care little for their nation in relation to their gustatory pleasure. Sturgeon attributes the Turkey adventure to the apathy of cooks, unlike Grimod who treats it as a dignified culinary experiment in overcoming the challenges of tough turkey.

    In Grimod's text, it is not entirely clear whether the members of the society themselves do the cooking, and Le Gacque (the innovator and chef at the famous Parisian restaurant *Rocher de Cancale*, where Grimod's Société des Mercredis met) may in fact be a member of the society, rather than simply a provider. Grimod's Le Gacque is too concerned for his honor to try something as potentially disastrous as braising a turkey. But the President of the Society convinces him to give it a try, for the sake of his art. There is no hint of competition for Grimod, and in the end everyone finds Le Gacque's turkey delicious. Sturgeon's version of the story, on the other hand, mocks the club and the emasculating obsession its members have with the quality of their food, implying that such an interest is foreign to (British) male virtue. I am grateful to Eliza Ridgeway for this analysis, and for that in note 45 below.

38. The dictum that one ought to eat to live, not live to eat (*esse oportet ut vivas, non vivere ut edas*) commonly attributed to Socrates, occurs in Nestor's speech in Homer's *Iliad* (4.39).

39. Sturgeon refers successively to Hannah Glasse, *The Art of Cookery Made Plain and Easy; Which far exceeds any Thing of the Kind yet published.* [by Mrs. Glasse] 3rd ed. By a Lady; Printed for the Author, 1748; Robert May's *The Accomplisht Cook, or the Art and Mystery of Cookery* (London: Nathaniel Brooke, 1660) and Hannah Woolley's *The Cook's Guide; or, Rare Receipts for Cookery … Whereby Noble Persons and Others in their Hospitalities may be Gratified in their Gusto's* (London: Peter Dring, 1664); Frederick Nutt, *The Complete Confectioner; or, The whole art of confectionery: forming a ready assistant to all genteel families; giving them a perfect knowledge of confectionery; with instructions, neatly engraved on ten copper-plates, how to decorate a table with taste and elegance, without the expence or assistance of a confectioner* (London, Printed for the author, and sold by J. Matthews, 1790); John Simpson, *A Complete System of Cookery, on a plan entirely new, consisting of every thing that is requisite for cooks to know in the kitchen business; containing bills of fare for every day in the year, and directions to dress each dish; being one year's work at the Marquis of Buckingham's from the 1st of January to the 31st of December, 1805* (London, Printed for W. Stewart, 1806).

40. The Véry brothers, Jean Baptiste and Jean François, and Antoine Beauvilliers were among the most famous early nineteenth-century restaurateurs of Paris.

41. Cracknels are a type of light, crisp biscuit, of a curved or hollowed shape, and biffins a variety of cooking apple, cultivated especially in Norfolk.

42. Cf. Grimod de la Reynière, "Essay on Gourmand Geography" (1806) in this volume, 16–18.

43. *Hudibras*, Canto 1 [Sturgeon's note]; loosely adapted from Samuel Butler, *Hudibras*, 1.209–10, 225–28, as printed in the edition by John Wilders (Oxford: Clarendon Press, 1967).

44. Madame De Sévigné records the event of Vatel's famous death in her letters: "Only listen to what I learned upon arriving here, that Vatel, the great Vatel, maître d'hôtel of Monsieur Fouquet, this man, with a capacity distinguished above all others, whose splendid head was capable of managing the affairs of a state, this man, on account of the non-arrival of a fish at the proper hour, rushed to his room and stabbed himself with his sword. You can picture to yourself the horrible disorder into which this accident has thrown our fête. And only imagine that while be was drawing his last breath, the fish arrived. This is all I know at present, and I think you will find it enough. The confusion here is very great. It is a grievous thing to happen in the middle of a fête costing fifty thousand crowns." Letter of April 24, 1671, in *Letters from the Marchioness de Sévigné to her Daughter the Countess de Grignan*, 7 vols. (London: J. Sewell, 1801), 1: 125–25. Her next letter, from Paris on Sunday, April 26, 1671, provides further detail; *Letters*, 1: 126–29. Grimod dedicated the eighth year of his *Almanach des gourmands* (1812) to the shade or ghost (*l'ombre*) of Vatel, *Almanach*, 2: v–xiv.

45. Grimod, "De la santé des cuisiniers," in *Almanach*, 2: 216–22: these texts are very similar with one notable divergence. When they treat specifically of how to treat cooks, Sturgeon focuses on the foods with which the cook should be doctored, "remedies" such as brown soup and fish curry. But the joke, one realizes, is that these are not being fed to the cook; rather, he is gradually allowed to prepare them. Grimod is less autocratic toward the cook, allowing that timing and manner of purging depends on individual circumstances, and more pragmatically prescriptive, providing a short list of medicines to effect purging, and the name of an apothecary (M. Folloppe) who is available to dose one's cook.

4
Charles Lamb (1775–1834)

"A Dissertation Upon Roast Pig" and "Grace Before Meat," from *Elia, Essays which have appeared under that title in the London Magazine* (London, 1823). Originally published in September 1822 and November 1821, respectively.

Introduction

Strange to say, the Romantic writer Charles Lamb has never been read within the gastronomical genre that sprung up in Britain in the 1820s, though he was certainly influenced by it and influenced later writers in that vein. He owned (if he did not himself write) Sturgeon's *Essays, Moral, Philosophical, and Stomachical* (see chap. 3, editor's introduction). And it was less than one month after his trip to Paris with his sister Mary that he published the essay for which he is best known, "A Dissertation Upon Roast Pig" (1822). Lamb recognized the degree to which the trip to France was registered upon his palate in a letter of September 22 of that same year to his friend Barron Field: "I & sister are just returned from Paris!! We have eaten frogs. It has been such a treat! You know our monotonous general Tenor. Frogs are the nicest little delicate things—rabbity-flavoured. Imagine a Lilliputian rabbit! They fricassee them; but in my mind, drest seethed, plain, with parsley and butter, would have been the decision of Apicius." Lamb admired the work of the Roman cook Apicius, as he did Heliogabulus whom he praises for having "started nightingales brains and peacock's tongues as a garnish."[1] The scholar Fred V. Randel, who remarks that virtually every one of Lamb's essays makes some reference to eating or drinking, has put together an impressive list of foodstuffs specifically mentioned by his fictional character, Elia.[2] If we extend this list to include the other miscellaneous essays and essays, it would go on much longer.

Lamb describes to his friend Samuel Taylor Coleridge the joys of eating pig in a letter of March 1822: "You all had some of the crackling—and brain sauce," he asks, "did you remember to rub it with butter, and gently dredge it a little, just before the crisis? Did the eyes come away kindly with no Oedipean avulsion? Was the crackling the colour of the ripe pomegranate?" If Lamb's praise of pig is familiar to lovers of literature, his delightful discernment of fish, though more obscure, is equally insightful. He compares the golden haddock, for example, a fish nicknamed the John Dory, to the turbot: "it hath not that moist mellow oleaginous gliding smooth descent from the tongue to the palate, thence to the stomach &c. as your Brighton Turbot hath, which I take to be the most friendly and familiar flavor of any that swims." To Lamb's delicate palate, the John Dory is as distinct from turbot as it is from cod: "nor has it on the other hand that fine falling off flakiness, that obsequious peeling off (as it were like a sea onion) which endears your cods head & shoulders to some appetites, that manly firmness combined with a sort of womanish coming-in-pieces which the same cods head & shoulders hath."[3] Lamb was even capable of choosing his friends for their gastronomical acumen: "I like you for liking hare. I esteem you for disrelishing minced veal. Liking is too cold a word, I love you for your noble attachment to the fat unctuous juices of deers flesh & the green unspeakable of turtle."[4] Lamb himself was a "true son of Epicurus," and in his literary pose as Elia he approached the world as a "judicious epicure."

Although Lamb is usually associated with his love of roast pig, it is worth noting that in a brief series of essays called "The Lepus Papers," he drops the signature "Elia" in favor of "Lepus," which is Latin for hare. "Time was," he admits in "Thoughts on the Presents of Game," speaking of himself in the third person, "when he was not arrived at his taste, that he preferred to all luxuries a roasted Pig. But he disclaims all such green-sickness appetites in future." Later in life, instead of the "grossness" of pig, he prefers the swiftness of hare: "how light of digestion we feel after a hare! How tender its processes after swallowing! What chyle it promotes! How etherial! as if its living celerity were a type of its nimble coursing through the animal juices." The hare's nimble coursing through the alimentary tract, its "living celerity," resembles what Lamb calls the "fine madnesses of the poet … Thence is he hare-brained."[5] Lamb's essays are "hare-brained" insofar as they are a fine poetical madness, the dietary decoction of a low-urban poet in prose.[6]

The following text is from Lamb's 1823 edition of *Elia*.

A Dissertation Upon Roast Pig

Mankind, says a Chinese manuscript, which my friend M. was obliging enough to read and explain to me, for the first seventy thousand ages ate their meat raw, clawing or biting it from the living animal, just as they do in Abyssinia to this day. This period is not obscurely hinted at by their great Confucius in the second chapter of his Mundane Mutations, where he designates a kind of golden age by the term Cho-fang, literally the Cooks' holiday.[7] The manuscript goes on to say, that the art of roasting, or rather broiling (which I take to be the elder brother) was accidentally discovered in the manner following. The swine-herd, Ho-ti, having gone out into the woods one morning, as his manner was, to collect mast for his hogs, left his cottage in the care of his eldest son Bo-bo, a great lubberly boy, who being fond of playing with fire, as younkers of his age commonly are, let some sparks escape into a bundle of straw, which kindling quickly, spread the conflagration over every part of their poor mansion, till it was reduced to ashes. Together with the cottage (a sorry antediluvian make-shift of a building, you may think it), what was of much more importance, a fine litter of new-farrowed pigs, no less than nine in number, perished. China pigs have been esteemed a luxury all over the East from the remotest periods that we read of. Bo-bo was in the utmost consternation, as you may think, not so much for the sake of the tenement, which his father and he could easily build up again with a few dry branches, and the labour of an hour or two, at any time, as for the loss of the pigs. While he was thinking what he should say to his father, and wringing his hands over the smoking remnants of one of those untimely sufferers, an odour assailed his nostrils, unlike any scent which he had before experienced. What could it proceed from?—not from the burnt cottage—he had smelt that smell before—indeed this was by no means the first accident of the kind which had occurred through the negligence of this unlucky young fire-brand. Much less did it resemble that of any known herb, weed, or flower. A premonitory moistening at the same time overflowed his nether lip. He knew not what to think. He next stooped down to feel the pig if there were any signs of life in it. He burnt his fingers, and to cool them he applied them in his booby fashion to his mouth. Some of the crums of the scorched skin had come away with his fingers, and for the first time in his life (in the world's life indeed, for before him no man had known it) he tasted—*crackling*! Again he felt and fumbled at the pig. It did not burn him so much now, still he licked his fingers from a sort of habit. The truth at length broke into his slow understanding, that it was the pig that smelt so, and the pig that tasted so delicious; and, surrendering himself up to the new-born pleasure, he fell to tearing up whole handfuls of the scorched skin with the flesh next it, and was cramming it down his throat in his beastly fashion, when his sire entered amid the smoking rafters, armed with retributory cudgel, and finding how affairs stood, began to rain blows upon the young rogue's shoulders, as thick as hail-stones, which Bo-bo heeded not any more than if they had been flies. The tickling pleasure, which be experienced in his lower regions, had rendered him quite callous to any inconveniences he might feel in those remote quarters. His father might lay on, but he could not beat him from his pig, till he had fairly made an end of it, when, becoming a little more sensible of his situation, something like the following dialogue ensued.

"You graceless whelp, what have you got there devouring? Is it not enough that you have burnt me down three houses with your dog's tricks, and be hanged to you, but you must be eating fire, and I know not what—what have you got there, I say?"

"O father, the pig, the pig, do come and taste how nice the burnt pig eats."

The ears of Ho-ti tingled with horror. He cursed his son, and he cursed himself that ever he should beget a son that should eat burnt pig.

Bo-bo, whose scent was wonderfully sharpened since morning, soon raked out another pig, and fairly rending it asunder, thrust the lesser half by main force into the fists of Ho-ti, still shouting out "Eat, eat, eat the burnt pig, father, only taste—O Lord,"—with such-like barbarous ejaculations, cramming all the while as if he would choke.

Ho-ti trembled every joint while he grasped the abominable thing, wavering whether he should not put his son to death for an unnatural young monster, when the crackling scorching his fingers, as it had done his son's, and applying the same remedy to them, he in his turn tasted some of its flavour, which, make what sour mouths he would for a pretence, proved not altogether displeasing to him. In conclusion (for the manuscript here is a little tedious) both father and son fairly sat down to the mess, and never left off till they had despatched all that remained of the litter.

Bo-bo was strictly enjoined not to let the secret escape, for the neighbours would certainly have stoned them for a couple of abominable wretches, who could think of improving upon the good meat which God had sent them. Nevertheless, strange stories got about. It was observed that Ho-ti's cottage was burnt down now more frequently than ever. Nothing but fires from this time forward. Some would break out in broad day, others in the nighttime. As often as the sow farrowed, so sure was the house of Ho-ti to be in a blaze; and Ho-ti himself, which was the more remarkable, instead of chastising his son, seemed to grow more indulgent to him than ever. At length they were watched, the terrible mystery discovered, and father and son summoned to take their trial at Pekin, then an inconsiderable assize town. Evidence was given, the obnoxious food itself produced in court, and verdict about to be pronounced, when the foreman of the jury begged that some of the burnt pig, of which the culprits stood accused, might be handed into the box. He handled it, and they all handled it, and burning their fingers, as Bo-bo and his father had done before them, and nature prompting to each of them the same remedy, against the face of all the facts, and the clearest charge which judge had ever given,—to the surprise of the whole court, townsfolk, strangers, reporters, and all present—without leaving the box, or any manner of consultation whatever, they brought in a simultaneous verdict of Not Guilty.

The judge, who was a shrewd fellow, winked at the manifest iniquity of the decision; and, when the court was dismissed, went privily, and bought up all the pigs that could be had for love or money. In a few days his Lordship's town house was observed to be on fire. The thing took wing, and now there was nothing to be seen but fires in every direction. Fuel and pigs grew enormously dear all over the district. The insurance offices one and all shut up shop. People built slighter and slighter every day, until it was feared that the very science of architecture would in no long time be lost to the world. Thus this custom of firing houses continued, till in process of time, says my manuscript, a sage arose, like our Locke,[8] who made a discovery, that the flesh of swine, or indeed of any other animal, might be cooked (*burnt*, as they called it) without the necessity of consuming a whole house to dress it. Then first began the rude form of a gridiron. Roasting by the string, or spit, came in a century or two later, I forget in whose dynasty. By such slow degrees, concludes the manuscript, do the most useful, and seemingly the most obvious arts, make their way among mankind.—

Without placing too implicit faith in the account above given, it must be agreed, that if a worthy pretext for so dangerous an experiment as setting houses on fire (especially in these days) could be assigned in favour of any culinary object, that pretext and excuse might be found in roast pig.

Of all the delicacies in the whole *mundus edibilis*, I will maintain it to be the most delicate—*princeps obsoniorum*.

I speak not of your grown porkers—things between pig and pork—those hobbydehoys—but a young and tender suckling—under a moon old—guiltless as yet of the sty—with no original speck of the amor immunditiæ,[9] the hereditary failing of the first parent, yet manifest—his voice as yet not broken, but something between a childish treble, and a grumble—the mild forerunner, or *præludium*, of a grunt.

He must be roasted. I am not ignorant that our ancestors ate them seethed, or boiled—but what a sacrifice of the exterior tegument!

There is no flavour comparable, I will contend, to that of the crisp, tawny, well-watched, not over-roasted, *crackling*, as it is well called—the very teeth are invited to their share of the pleasure at this banquet in overcoming the coy, brittle resistance—with the adhesive oleaginous—O call it not fat—but an indefinable sweetness growing up to it—the tender blossoming of fat—fat cropped in the bud—taken in the shoot—in the first innocence—the cream and quintessence of the child-pig's yet pure food—the lean, no lean, but a kind of animal manna—or, rather, fat and lean (if it must be so) so blended and running into each other, that both together make but one ambrosian result, or common substance.

Behold him, while he is doing—it seemeth rather a refreshing warmth, than a scorching heat, that he is so passive to. How equably he twirleth round the string!—Now he is just done. To see the extreme sensibility of that tender age, he hath wept out his pretty eyes—radiant jellies—shooting stars—

See him in the dish, his second cradle, how meek he lieth!—wouldst thou have had this innocent grow up to the grossness and indocility which too often accompany maturer swinehood? Ten to one he would have proved a glutton, a sloven, an obstinate, disagreeable animal—wallowing in all manner of filthy conversation—from these sins he is happily snatched away—

Ere sin could blight, or sorrow fade,
Death came with timely care —[10]

his memory is odoriferous—no clown curseth, while his stomach half rejecteth, the rank bacon—no coalheaver bolteth him in reeking sausages—he hath a fair sepulchre in the grateful stomach of the judicious epicure—and for such a tomb might be content to die.

He is the best of Sapors. Pine-apple is great. She is indeed almost too transcendent—a delight, if not sinful, yet so like to sinning, that really a tender-conscienced person would do well to pause—too ravishing for mortal taste, she woundeth and excoriateth the lips that approach her—like lovers' kisses, she biteth—she is a pleasure bordering on pain from the fierceness and insanity of her relish—but she stoppeth at the palate—she meddleth not with the appetite—and the coarsest hunger might barter her consistently for a mutton chop.

Pig—let me speak his praise—is no less provocative of the appetite, than he is satisfactory to the criticalness of the censorious palate. The strong man may batten on him, and the weakling refuseth not his mild juices.

Unlike to mankind's mixed characters, a bundle of virtues and vices, inexplicably intertwisted, and not to be unravelled without hazard, he is—good throughout. No part of him is better or worse than another. He helpeth, as far as his little means extend, all around. He is the least envious of banquets. He is all neighbours' fare.

I am one of those, who freely and ungrudgingly impart a share of the good things of this life which fall to their lot (few as mine are in this kind) to a friend. I protest I take as great an interest in my friend's pleasures, his relishes, and proper satisfactions, as in mine own. "Presents," I often say, "endear Absents." Hares, pheasants, partridges, snipes, barn-door chicken (those "tame villatic fowl"),[11] capons, plovers, brawn, barrels of oysters, I dispense as freely as I receive them. I love to taste them, as it were, upon the tongue of my friend. But a stop must be put somewhere. One would not, like Lear, "give every thing." I make my stand upon pig. Methinks it is an ingratitude to the Giver of all good flavours, to extra-domiciliate, or send out of the house, slightingly, (under pretext of friendship, or I know not what) a blessing so particularly adapted, predestined, I may say, to my individual palate—It argues an insensibility.

I remember a touch of conscience in this kind at school. My good old aunt, who never parted from me at the end of a holiday without stuffing a sweet-meat, or some nice thing, into my pocket, had dismissed me one evening with a smoking plum-cake, fresh from the oven. In my way to school (it was over London bridge) a grey-headed old beggar saluted me (I have no doubt at this time of day that he was a counterfeit). I had no pence to console him with, and in the vanity of self-denial, and the very coxcombry of charity, school-boy-like, I made him a present of—the whole cake! I walked on a little, buoyed up, as one is on such occasions, with a sweet soothing of self-satisfaction; but before I had got to the end of the bridge, my better feelings returned, and I burst into tears, thinking how ungrateful I had been to my good aunt, to go and give her good gift away to a stranger, that I had never seen before, and who might be a bad man for aught I knew; and then I thought of the pleasure my aunt would be taking in thinking that I—I myself, and not another—would eat her nice cake—and what should I say to her the next time I saw her—how naughty I was to part with her pretty present—and the odour of that spicy cake came back upon my recollection, and the pleasure and the curiosity I had taken in seeing her make it, and her joy when she sent it to the oven, and how disappointed she would feel that I had never had a bit of it in my mouth at last—and I blamed my impertinent spirit of alms-giving, and out-of-place hypocrisy of goodness, and above all I wished never to see the face again of that insidious, good-for-nothing, old grey impostor.

Our ancestors were nice in their method of sacrificing these tender victims. We read of pigs whipt to death with something of a shock, as we hear of any other obsolete custom. The age of discipline is gone by, or it would be curious to inquire (in a philosophical light merely) what effect this process might have towards intenerating and dulcifying a substance, naturally so mild and dulcet as the flesh of young pigs. It looks like refining a violet. Yet we should be cautious, while we condemn the inhumanity, how we censure the wisdom of the practice. It might impart a gusto—

I remember an hypothesis, argued upon by the young students, when I was at St. Omer's,[12] and maintained with much learning and pleasantry on both sides, "Whether, supposing that the flavour of a pig who obtained his death by whipping (*per flagellationem extremam*) superadded a pleasure upon the palate of a man more intense than any possible suffering we can conceive in the animal, is man justified in using that method of putting the animal to death?" I forget the decision.

His sauce should be considered. Decidedly, a few bread crums done up with his liver and brains, and a dash of mild sage. But, banish, dear Mrs. Cook, I beseech you, the whole onion tribe. Barbecue your whole hogs to your palate, steep them in shalots, stuff them out with plantations of the rank and guilty garlic; you cannot poison them, or make them stronger than they are— but consider, he is a weakling—a flower.

Grace Before Meat

The custom of saying grace at meals had, probably, its original in the early times of the world, and the hunter-state of man, when dinners were precarious things, and a full meal was something more than a common blessing; when a belly-full was a windfall, and looked like a special providence. In the shouts and triumphal songs with which, after a season of sharp abstinence, a lucky booty of deer's or goat's flesh would naturally be ushered home, existed; perhaps, the germ of the modern grace. It is not otherwise easy to be understood, why the blessing of food—the act of eating—should have had a particular expression of thanksgiving annexed to it, distinct from that implied and silent gratitude with which we are expected to enter upon the enjoyment of the many other various gifts and good things of existence.

I own that I am disposed to say grace upon twenty other occasions in the course of the day besides my dinner. I want a form for setting out upon a pleasant walk, for a moonlight ramble, for a friendly meeting, or a solved problem. Why have we none for books, those spiritual repasts—a grace before Milton—a grace before Shakespeare—a devotional exercise proper to be said before reading the Fairy Queen?—but the received ritual having prescribed these forms to the solitary ceremony of manducation, I shall confine my observations to the experience which I have had of the grace, properly so called; commending my new scheme for extension to a niche in the grand philosophical, poetical, and perchance in part heretical, liturgy, now compiling by my friend Homo Humanus, for the use of a certain snug congregation of Utopian Rabelæsian Christians, no matter where assembled.[13]

The form, then, of the benediction before eating has its beauty at a poor man's table, or at the simple and unprovocative repasts of children. It is here that the grace becomes exceedingly graceful. The indigent man, who hardly knows whether he shall have a meal the next day or not, sits down to his fare with a present sense of the blessing, which can be but feebly acted by the rich, into whose minds the conception of wanting a dinner could never, but by some extreme theory, have entered. The proper end of food—the animal sustenance—is barely contemplated by them. The poor man's bread is his daily bread, literally his bread for the day. Their courses are perennial.

Again, the plainest diet seems the fittest to be preceded by the grace. That which is least stimulative to appetite, leaves the mind most free for foreign considerations. A man may feel thankful, heartily thankful, over a dish of plain mutton with turnips, and have leisure to reflect upon the ordinance and institution of eating; when he shall confess a perturbation of mind, inconsistent with the purposes of the grace, at the presence of venison or turtle. When I have sate (a *rarus hospes*) at rich men's tables, with the savoury soup and messes steaming up the nostrils, and moistening the lips of the guests with desire and a distracted choice, I have felt the introduction of that ceremony to be unseasonable. With the ravenous orgasm upon you, it seems impertinent to interpose a religious sentiment. It is a confusion of purpose to mutter out praises from a mouth that waters. The heats of epicurism put out the gentle flame of devotion. The incense which rises round is pagan, and the belly-god intercepts it for his own. The very excess of the provision beyond the needs, takes away all sense of proportion between the end and means. The giver is veiled by his gifts. You are startled at the injustice of returning thanks—for what?—for having too much while so many starve. It is to praise the Gods amiss.[14]

I have observed this awkwardness felt, scarce consciously perhaps, by the good man who says the grace. I have seen it in clergymen and others—a sort of shame—a sense of the co-presence of circumstances which unhallow the blessing. After a devotional tone put on for a few seconds, how rapidly the speaker will fall into his common voice; helping himself or his neighbour, as if to get rid of some uneasy sensation of hypocrisy. Not that the good man was a hypocrite, or was not most conscientious in the discharge of the duty; but he felt in his inmost mind the incompatibility of the scene and the viands before him with the exercise of a calm and rational gratitude.

I hear somebody exclaim,—Would you have Christians sit down at table, like hogs to their troughs, without remembering the Giver?—no—I would have them sit down as Christians, remembering the Giver, and less like hogs. Or if their appetites must run riot, and they must pamper themselves with delicacies for which east and west are ransacked, I would have them postpone their benediction to a fitter season, when appetite is laid; when the still small voice can be heard, and the reason of the grace returns—with temperate diet and restricted dishes. Gluttony and surfeiting are no proper occasions for thanksgiving. When Jeshurun waxed fat,[15] we read that he kicked. Virgil knew the harpy-nature better, when he put into the mouth of Celæno any thing but a blessing. We may be gratefully sensible of the deliciousness of some kinds of food beyond others, though that is a meaner and inferior gratitude: but the proper object of the grace is sustenance, not relishes; daily bread, not delicacies; the means of life, and not the means of pampering the carcass. With what frame or composure, I wonder, can a city chaplain pronounce his benediction at some great Hall feast, when he knows that his last concluding pious word—and that in all probability, the sacred name which he preaches—is but the signal for so many impatient harpies to commence their foul orgies, with as little sense of true thankfulness (which is temperance) as those Virgilian fowl! It is well if the good man himself does not feel his devotions a little clouded, those foggy sensuous steams mingling with and polluting the pure altar sacrifice.

The severest satire upon full tables and surfeits is the banquet which Satan, in the Paradise Regained, provides for a temptation in the wilderness:

A table richly spread in regal mode,
With dishes piled, and meats of noblest sort
And savour; beasts of chase, or fowl of game,
In pastry built, or from the spit, or boiled,
Gris-amber-steamed; all fish from sea or shore,
Freshet or purling brook, for which was drained
Pontus, and Lucrine bay, and Afric coast.[16]

The Tempter, I warrant you, thought these cates would go down without the recommendatory preface of a benediction. They are like to be short graces where the devil plays the host.—I am afraid the poet wants his usual decorum in this place. Was he thinking of the old Roman luxury, or of a gaudy day at Cambridge? This was a temptation fitter for a Heliogabalus.[17] The whole banquet is too civic and culinary, and the accompaniments altogether a profanation of that deep, abstracted, holy scene. The mighty artillery of sauces, which the cook-fiend conjures up, is out of proportion to the simple wants and plain hunger of the guest. He that disturbed him in his dreams, from his dreams might have been taught better. To the temperate fantasies of the famished Son of God, what sort of feasts presented themselves?—He dreamed indeed,

—As appetite is wont to dream,
Of meats and drinks, nature's refreshment sweet.
But what meats?—

Him thought, he by the brook of Cherith stood,
And saw the ravens with their horny beaks
Food to Elijah bringing, even and morn;
Though ravenous, taught to abstain from what they brought.
He saw the prophet also how he fled
Into the desert, and how there he slept
Under a juniper; then how awaked
He found his supper on the coals prepared,
And by the angel was bid rise and eat,
And ate the second time after repose,
The strength whereof sufficed him forty days:
Sometimes, that with Elijah he partook,
Or as a guest with Daniel at his pulse.[18]

Nothing in Milton is finelier fancied than these temperate dreams of the divine Hungerer. To which of these two visionary banquets, think you, would the introduction of what is called the grace have been most fitting and pertinent?

Theoretically I am no enemy to graces; but practically I own that (before meat especially) they seem to involve something awkward and unseasonable. Our appetites, of one or another kind, are excellent spurs to our reason, which might otherwise but feebly set about the great ends of preserving and continuing the species. They are fit blessings to be contemplated at a distance with a becoming gratitude; but the moment of appetite (the judicious reader will apprehend me) is, perhaps, the least fit season for that exercise. The Quakers who go about their business, of every description, with more calmness than we, have more title to the use of these benedictory prefaces. I have always admired their silent grace, and the more because I have observed their applications to the meat and drink following to be less passionate and sensual than ours. They are neither gluttons nor wine-bibbers as a people. They eat, as a horse bolts his choppt hay, with indifference, calmness, and cleanly circumstances. They neither grease nor slop themselves. When I see a citizen in his bib and tucker, I cannot imagine it a surplice.

I am no Quaker at my food. I confess I am not indifferent to the kinds of it. Those unctuous morsels of deer's flesh were not made to be received with dispassionate services. I hate a man who swallows it, affecting not to know what he is eating. I suspect his taste in higher matters. I shrink instinctively from one who professes to like minced veal. There is a physiognomical character in the tastes for food. C—holds that a man cannot have a pure mind who refuses apple-dumplings. I am not certain but he is right. With the decay of my first innocence, I confess a less and less relish daily for those innocuous cates. The whole vegetable tribe have lost their gust with me. Only I stick to asparagus, which still seems to inspire gentle thoughts. I am impatient and querulous under culinary disappointments, as to come home at the dinner hour, for instance, expecting some savoury mess, and to find one quite tasteless and sapidless. Butter ill melted—that commonest of kitchen failures—puts me beside my tenour.—The author of the Rambler used to make inarticulate animal noises over a favourite food.[19] Was this the music quite proper to be preceded by the grace? or would the pious man have done better to postpone his devotions to a season when the blessing might be contemplated with less perturbation? I quarrel with no man's tastes, nor would set my thin face against those excellent things, in their way, jollity and feasting. But as these exercises, however laudable, have little in them of grace or gracefulness, a man should be sure, before he ventures so to grace them, that while he is pretending his devotions otherwhere, he is not secretly kissing his hand to some great fish—his Dagon—with a special consecration of no ark but the fat tureen before him.[20] Graces are the sweet preluding strains to the banquets of angels and children; to the roots and severer repasts of the Chartreuse;[21] to the slender, but not slenderly acknowledged, refection of the poor and humble man: but at the heaped-up boards of the pampered and the luxurious they become of dissonant mood, less timed and tuned to the occasion, methinks, than the noise of those better befitting organs would be which children hear tales of, at Hog's Norton.[22] We sit too long at our meals, or are too curious in the study of them, or too disordered in our application to them, or engross too great a portion of those good things (which should be common) to our share, to be able with any grace to say grace. To be thankful for what we grasp exceeding our proportion, is to add hypocrisy to injustice. A lurking sense of this truth is what makes the performance of this duty so cold and spiritless a service at most tables. In houses where the grace is as indispensable as the napkin, who has not seen that never settled question arise, as to *who shall say it;* while the good man of the house and the visitor clergyman, or some other guest belike of next authority from years or gravity, shall be bandying about the office between them as a matter of compliment, each of them not unwilling to shift the awkward burthen of an equivocal duty from his own shoulders?

I once drank tea in company with two Methodist divines of different persuasions, whom it was my fortune to introduce to each other for the first time that evening. Before the first cup was handed round, one of these reverend gentlemen put it to the other, with all due solemnity, whether he chose to *say any thing.* It seems it is the custom with some sectaries to put up a short prayer before this meal also. His reverend brother did not at first quite apprehend him, but upon an explanation, with little less importance he made answer that it was not a custom known in his church: in which courteous evasion the other acquiescing for good manner's sake, or in compliance with a weak brother, the supplementary or tea-grace was waived altogether. With what spirit might not Lucian have painted two priests, of *his* religion, playing into each other's hands the compliment of performing or omitting a sacrifice,—the hungry God meantime, doubtful of his incense, with expectant nostrils hovering over the two flamens, and (as between two stools) going away in the end without his supper.[23]

A short form upon these occasions is felt to want reverence; a long one, I am afraid, cannot escape the charge of impertinence. I do not quite approve of the epigrammatic conciseness with which that equivocal wag (but my pleasant school-fellow) C. V. L., when importuned for a grace, used to inquire, first slyly leering down the table, "Is there no clergyman here?"—significantly adding, "Thank G——."[24] Nor do I think our old form at school quite pertinent, where we were used to preface our bald bread and cheese suppers with a preamble, connecting with that humble blessing a recognition of benefits the most awful and overwhelming to the imagination which religion has to offer. *Non tunc illis erat locus.*[25] I remember we were put to it to reconcile the phrase "good creatures," upon which the blessing rested, with the fare set before us, wilfully understanding that expression in a low and animal sense,—till some one recalled a legend, which told how in the golden days of Christ's, the young Hospitallers were wont to have smoking joints of roast meat upon their nightly boards, till some pious benefactor, commiserating the decencies, rather than the palates, of the children, commuted our flesh for garments, and gave us—*horresco referens*—trowsers instead of mutton.[26]

Notes

1. Lamb, Letter to Charles Chambers; September 1, 1817, in *Letters*, ed. Marrs, 3: 253.
2. Fred V. Randel, *The World of Elia: Charles Lamb's Essayistic Romanticism* (Port Washington, NY: Kennikat Press, 1975), 114.
3. Lamb, *Letters*, ed. Marrs, 3: 253.
4. Ibid., 3: 254.
5. Lamb, *Works*, 1: 343–34.
6. For a more detailed discussion of Lamb's use of contemporary discourses of diet to suit his own purposes, see my chapter on Lamb in *Taste: A Literary History* (New Haven, CT: Yale University Press, 2005), 89–116.
7. Lamb's creative imagination is at work here.
8. British philosopher, John Locke (1632–1704).
9. *Amor immunditiæ* is "love of dirt," a reference to original sin.
10. See Coleridge's "Epitaph on an Infant": "Ere Sin could blight or Sorrow fade, / Death came with friendly care; / The opening bud to Heaven conveyed, / And bade it blossom there."
11. A reference to John Milton, *Samson Agonistes*, line 1695.
12. A Jesuit College, originally founded as a medieval monastery in France.
13. See Rabelais, *Gargantua and Pentagruel*, Book 1, chapters 52–57.
14. "When for their teeming flocks, and granges full, / In wanton dance they praise the bounteous Pan, / And thank the gods amiss"; Milton, *A Masque*, 175–77.
15. Deuteronomy 32.15.
16. John Milton, *Paradise Regained*, II.340–47; the last two lines above are elided from: "And exquisitest name, for which was drained / Pontus, and Lucrine bay, and Afric coast."

17. A gaudy day was a feast day; Heliogabalus was a notorious Roman Emperor-Gourmand of the third century A.D.
18. John Milton, *Paradise Regained*, II.264–78.
19. "C—" is a reference to Coleridge; Samuel Johnson was the author of *The Rambler*.
20. Dagon was the fish god of the Philistines (see Judges 16.23 and 1 Samuel 5).
21. The Chartreuse was the monastery of the Carthusians, an order of silent monks in France.
22. In traditional English folklore Hog's Norton was a place "Where Folks say Pigs play on the Organs"; Edward Ward *The fidler's fling at roguery* (London: W. Smith, 1734), line 284.
23. Lucian's *Dialogues*; a flamen was a priest in the service of a particular god.
24. A reference to Charles Valentine le Grice (1773–1858), a clergyman and friend of William Wordsworth and Charles Lamb.
25. From Horace, *Ars poetica*, 19: "Sed nunc non erat his locus," (but that was not the occasion for such things) in *Opera omnia* (Oxford: Clarendon Press, 1891), page 391, line 19.
26. "I tremble at the recollection"; Virgil, *The Aeneid*, II.204; *Opera*, ed. R. A. B. Mynors (Oxford: Clarendon Press, 1969), 133. Christ's Hospital is the school that Lamb and his friend Coleridge both attended. His recollections of its scanty food supply are recorded in "Christ's Hospital Five and Thirty Years Ago," in *The Last Essays of Elia* (1833).

5
Jean-Anthelme Brillat-Savarin
(1755–1826)

Physiologie du goût, ou Méditations de gastronomie transcendante; ouvrage théorique, historique et à l'ordre du jour, dédié aux gastronomes parisiens, par un professeur (1826). *[Physiology of Taste, or Meditations on Transcendental Gastronomy, An Historical, Theoretical, and Timely Work, Dedicated to Parisian Gastronomers, by a Professor]* trans. *Brillat-Savarin's Physiologie du Gout: A Handbook of Gastronomy* (New York, 1884)

Introduction

Jean-Anthelme Brillat-Savarin's *Physiologie du goût* "has gained and gains many men every day to gastronomy by the perfect wisdom of his precepts," claimed the French gastronomer Charles Monselet in 1879—and his statement still holds true today. Brillat-Savarin's gastronomical masterpiece has remained in print since its first posthumous publication in 1826. Like Grimod de la Reynière's *Almanach des gourmands*, it is a pot pourri, consisting of gastronomical aphorisms, dialogues between the author and fellow gourmands, some thirty "meditations," and an assortment of miscellaneous adventures, inventions, recipes, and anecdotes. Brillat-Savarin acknowledged his debt (if indirectly) to the works of Grimod de la Reynière, though there was one major difference between these two founding fathers of French gastronomy. While Grimod was an aristocrat of ancien-régime France, with an illustrious gourmet and avid Amphitryon for a father, Brillat-Savarin was a self-made member of the bourgeoisie. As such, he became a spokesperson for the postrevolutionary, gastronomical future of France.

Figure 17 *Les Boissons* [Beverages] by Bertall [Albert Arnoux], from Jean-Anthelme Brillat-Savarin, *Physiologie du Goût* (1868).

Born and raised in the provincial town of Belley, Brillat-Savarin led a fairly peaceful life as a country lawyer until his mid-thirties. His successor Monselet depicts him "in the fertile country of Bugey, sometimes sitting down in well-provisioned inns, where strings of poultry were roasting, sometimes opposite to some jovial curé, sometimes coping with noisy huntsmen." His friends describe him as an amiable, robust figure, inclined to study but with little apparent ambition. But the elite of Paris looked down on him because of his provincial origins. The chef Carême complained that he was too preoccupied with his digestion after eating, and the Marquis de Cussy (1766–1837) wrote in *l'Art culinare* that he "ate copiously and ill." Brillat-Savarin's own preface to *The Physiology of Taste* reveals that his textual persona as a gourmand was a conscious performance: "When I write 'I' or '*Me*' in the singular, I am merely gossiping with the reader, who may examine, discuss, doubt, and even laugh; but when I am equipped with the redoubtable '*we*' I am a professor, and every one must give in." When the professor's writings appeared after his death, contemporaries were astounded with their sophistication and learning, Honoré de Balzac doing him homage in *The Physiology of Marriage* by "borrowing the Professorial Accent." Excelling at the anecdote, his alimentary "meditations" went down easy.

The disconnected style of his book, carved up into bite-sized portions for the reader, can serve as "a metaphor of the turbulent times he witnessed during a life that covered eight different regimes: the Monarchy, the Revolution, the First Republic, the Directory, the Consulate, the First Empire, as well as the two Restorations with Charles X and Louis XVIII."[1] When the French Revolution broke out, he became a representative to the Constituent Assembly and, upon his return to Belley, was named president of the civil tribunal and then mayor. Political complications at this time caused his flight to Switzerland and ultimately America, where he lived for two years teaching French. His hunting experience in Hartford, Connecticut, is a memorable snapshot of postrevolutionary America, which has been blown up and mythologized in gastronomical tradition into a conversation with Thomas Jefferson.[2] Having avoided the worst of the Terror, Brillat-Savarin returned to France in 1796 to find that his private property and vineyard had been confiscated. He quickly joined the French Army in Germany, where he learned the language and sampled local delicacies. After several years, he returned as Commissioner to the Tribunal of the Seine-et-Oise and then became a judge in the Paris Court of Appeal. After the 18th Brumaire, he entered the Senate where he remained for the rest of his life, weathering the storms of political change.

Unlike Grimod, Brillat-Savarin did not publish at the time when Paris was rising to prominence as the gastronomical capital of the world. Instead, he scribbled his observations privately, carrying his manuscript on his person for thirty years and adding anecdotes and revisions along the way. These he only assembled into order at the end of his life: "an amusing occupation, which I reserved for my old age." Most often, he took mental notes for his work which required him (in his own words) "to be a physician, a chemist, a physiologist, and even more or less of a classical scholar." As one critic observes, Brillat-Savarin "is not a novelist, he is not a memorialist, he is not a scientist, he is not a philosopher, and yet when one considers his *Physiology of Taste*... it could be said that he could claim each of these titles."[3] He was always conscious of the literary nature of his work, borrowing foreign words freely when an appropriate French one could not be found. "What is to be done," he asks (in what can also stand as a general commentary upon gastronomy), "To borrow or steal? I do both, inasmuch as these borrowings are not subject to restitution, and as the robbery of words is not punishable by the penal code." Yet, in making *gourmandise* palatable to the many, he begs that "care should be taken not to assign me a place among compilers; if I had been reduced to this, my pen might have been quiet." Luckily for us, it was not. His book made a splash in Paris in the 1820s when the word gastronomy was on everybody's tongue, and it remains perhaps the most satisfying work on the topic.

The text below is from the first unabridged English translation of *Physiologie du Goût, A Handbook of Gastronomy* (1884). It wavers in tone between the more stilted 1854 translation by the American Fayette Robinson and the more colloquial contemporary edition, with copious notes and commentary, by M. F. K. Fisher. For more on Brillat-Savarin's colorful life and times, see Thierry Boissel, *Brillat-Savarin (1755–1826): Un chevalier candide* (Paris, 1989) and Giles MacDonough, *Brillat-Savarin: The Judge and His Stomach* (Chicago, 1992).

From *Physiologie du Goût* (1826)

Aphorisms of the Professor to Serve as Prolegomena to his Work, and as an Eternal Basis to Science.

I.   The world would have been merely nothing except for life. All that lives, feeds.

II.   Animals feed, man eats; wise men alone know how to eat.

III. The destiny of nations depends on the manner wherein they take their food.

IV.   Tell me what thou eatest, and I will tell thee what thou art.

V.   The Creator, though condemning man to eat to live, invites him to do so by appetite, and rewards him by enjoyment.

VI.   Good living is an act of our judgment by which we grant a preference to those things which are agreeable to the taste above those that have not that quality.

VII.   The joys of the table belong equally to all ages, conditions, countries, and times; they mix with all other pleasures, and remain the last to console us for their loss.

VIII.   The table is the sole locality where no one during the first hour feels himself tired.

IX.   The discovery of a new dish is more beneficial to humanity than the discovery of a new star.

X.   The dyspeptic man and the drunkard are incapable of either eating or drinking.

XI.   The order of food is from the most solid to the most light.

XII.   The order of drink is from the mildest to the most heady and the most scented.

XIII.   To say that we should not mix our liquors is a heresy. The tongue becomes saturated, and after the third glass, the finest wine only gives an obtuse sensation.

XIV.   Dessert without cheese, is like a pretty girl with only one eye.

XV.   A cook may be educated, but a "roast cook" must be born such.

XVI.   The most indispensable quality in the cook is punctuality, and such ought to be the duty of the guests.

XVII.   To wait too long for a late guest denotes a lack of consideration to all those who are present.

XVIII. He who receives guests, and pays no personal care to the repast offered them, is not worthy to have friends.

XIX.   The hostess should always assure herself that the coffee is good, and the host that the *liqueurs* are of the finest quality.

XX.   To invite any one, implies that we charge ourselves with his happiness all the time that he is under our roof.

From *Meditation II*. Of Taste

Mechanism of Taste

It is not easy to determine exactly wherein the faculty of taste consists. It is more complicated than it appears. Certainly the tongue plays a great part in the mechanism of taste, for, considering it as gifted with rather strong muscular power, it enfolds, turns, presses, and swallows the food.

Further, by means of the more or less numerous papillae, with which it is covered, it is impregnated with sapid and soluble particles from those bodies with which it comes in contact; but all this is not sufficient, and many other

Figure 18   Untitled, by Bertall, from Jean-Anthelme Brillat-Savarin, *Physiologie du Goût* (1868).

adjacent parts concur to complete the sensation, namely, the cheeks, the palate, and, above all, the nasal fossæ, whereon physiologists have perhaps not sufficiently insisted.

The cheeks, as well as the maxillary and sublingual glands, form the saliva, equally necessary for mastication and the formation of the nourishing mass. They, as well as the palate, are gifted with a portion of the appreciative faculties; I do not know if even in certain cases the gums do not participate a little in it; and without the odoration which is preserved in the back part of the mouth, the sensation of taste would be obtuse and wholly imperfect.

The persons who have no tongue, or whose tongue has been cut out, possess the sensation of taste very fairly. Many books speak of the first case; the second has been sufficiently explained to me by a wretched man whose tongue the Algerians had cut out for having, with some of his comrades in captivity, formed a project of escaping and running away.

This man, whom I met at Amsterdam, where he gained his living by running errands, had some education, and it was easy to communicate with him in writing.

After having observed that all the fore part of the tongue down to the frænulum had been cut away, I asked him if he still recognised any taste in what he ate, and if the sensation of taste had survived the cruel operation which he had undergone.

He answered, that what was most troublesome to him was the act of swallowing, which was only done with great difficulty; that he had preserved taste pretty fairly; that he appreciated, like others, what was little sapid or agreeable, but that anything which was very sour or bitter caused him intolerable pain.

He also told me that cutting away the tongue was common in some African kingdoms; that it was applied especially to those who were thought to have been chiefs of a plot, and that special instruments were used for this operation. I wanted him to describe them, but he exhibited on this topic such a sorrowful disinclination that I did not insist.

I reflected on what he had said, and, carrying my thoughts back to those centuries of ignorance, when the tongues of blasphemers were pierced and cut, I came to the conclusion that these punishments were of African origin, and imported at the return of the Crusaders.

We have seen already that the sensation of taste resides principally in the papillæ of the tongue. But anatomy tells us that every tongue has not the same number of them, and that in some tongues there are three times as many papillae as in others. This circumstance will explain why of two guests sitting at the same table one should be deliciously affected, whereas the other seems to eat from constraint; it is because the latter has a tongue imperfectly provided with papillæ, and that the empire of taste has also its blind and its deaf people.

Influence of Smell on Taste

The order I have indicated for myself has gradually brought me to the moment when I shall render to smell the rights that belong to it, and the recognition of the important services it renders to us in the appreciation of savours; for, amongst the authors whom I have perused, I have not found one who appears to have done entire and complete justice to it.

For myself, I am not only persuaded that without the participation of smell there is no perfect taste, but I am even tempted to believe that smell and taste only form one sense, of which the mouth is the laboratory and the nose the chimney; or to speak more exactly, that the tongue tastes tactile substances, and the nose gases.

This theory may be rigorously defended. Nevertheless, as I do not pretend to found a sect of my own, I only venture to expose it, to indicate to my readers a subject of thought, that they may see that I have carefully studied the subject I am treating. Now, I shall continue my demonstration on the subject of the importance of smell, if not as a constituent part of taste, at least as a necessary adjunct.

All sapid bodies must be necessarily odorous, which places them as well in the empire of smell as in the empire of taste.

We eat nothing without smelling it with more or less consciousness; and for unknown foods, the nose acts always as a sentinel, and cries, "Who goes there?"

When smell is interrupted, taste is paralysed. This is proved by three experiments, which any one may make successfully.

First Experiment. When the nasal mucous membrane is irritated by a violent cold in the head, taste is entirely obliterated. In anything we swallow, there is no taste. The tongue nevertheless remains in its normal state.

Second Experiment. If we eat whilst holding tight our nose, we are much astonished only to experience the sensation of taste in an obscure and imperfect manner. By this means, the most disgusting medicines are swallowed almost without tasting them.

Third Experiment. We see the same effect if, at the moment we have swallowed, instead of bringing back the tongue to its usual place, we keep it close to the palate. In this case, the circulation of the air is intercepted, the organs of smell are not affected, and taste does not occur.

These different effects depend upon the same cause, the lack of co-operation of the smell, which makes the sapid body to be appreciated only on account of its juice, and not for the odoriferous gas that emanates from it.

Analysis of the Sensation of Taste

These principles being thus laid down, I regard it as certain that taste gives rise to sensations of three different orders, namely: *direct* sensation, *complete* sensation, and *reflex* sensation.

Direct sensation is that first perception which arises from the immediate operation of the organs of the mouth, whilst the appreciable body is yet found on the point of the tongue.

Complete sensation is that which is composed of this first perception, and of the impression which originates when the food abandons this first position, passes into the back part of the mouth, and impresses the whole organ with both taste and perfume.

Finally, *reflex* sensation is the judgment of the mind upon the impressions transmitted to it by the organ.

Let us apply this theory, and see what takes place in a man who eats and drinks.

He who eats a peach, for example, is at first agreeably struck by the odour which emanates from it; he puts it in his mouth, and feels a sensation of freshness and of sourness which induces him to continue; but it is only at the moment when he swallows it, and when the mouthful passes under the nasal fossa, that the perfume is revealed to him. This completes the sensation which a peach ought to produce. Finally, it is only when it has been swallowed that, considering what he has just experienced, the taster says to himself, "How delicious!"

So also, when we drink, while the wine is in the mouth, we are agreeably but not perfectly impressed; it is only at the moment when we have ceased to swallow that we may truly taste, appreciate, and discover the particular bouquet of each sort; and a little interval of time is necessary before the connoisseur can say, "It is good, middling, or bad. By Jove! this is Chambertin! Good Heavens! this is Suresnes!"

We see by this that it is according to principles, and on account of a well understood practice, that real lovers of wine sip it, because at each mouthful, when they stop, they have the sum total of the pleasure which they would have experienced if they had drunk the whole glass up at one draught.

The same thing also occurs, but with much more energy, whenever the taste is disagreeably affected.

Look at this sick man, whom the faculty constrains to swallow an enormous glass of a black draught, such as was drunk in the reign of Louis XIV.

The smell, a faithful adviser, warns him against the repulsive flavour of the deceitful liquid. His eyes expand, as if at the approach of danger: disgust is on his lips, and already his stomach begins to rise. Nevertheless he is expostulated with; he takes courage, gargles his throat with brandy, holds his nose, and drinks....

So long as the detestable beverage fills the mouth and lines the organ, the sensation is confused and the condition bearable, but at the last mouthful aftertastes begin to be developed, nauseous odours arise, and the features of the patient express a horror and a disgust which is only braved through fear of death.

If the liquid be, on the contrary, merely insipid, as, for example, a glass of water, there is no taste or after-taste. Nothing is felt, nothing is thought of: we merely drink, and that is all.

Succession of the Divers Impressions of Taste

Taste is not so richly endowed as hearing: the latter can appreciate and compare many sounds at the same time; but taste, on the other hand, is actually simple—that is to say, that two flavours at once are equally inappreciable.

But it may be doubled and multiplied in succession—that is to say, that in one act of deglutition we may experience successively a second and even a third sensation, each of which gradually becomes more weak, and which are described by the words after-taste, bouquet, or fragrance. So, when a chord is struck, a skilful ear may distinguish one or many series of consonances, of which the number is as yet imperfectly known.

Those who eat rapidly and without attention do not discern secondary impressions. These are only the exclusive appanage of a small number of the elect, and it is by their means that the various substances submitted to their examination may be classified.

These transient diversities vibrate yet for a long time in the organ of taste. Without having the least idea of it, gastronomes will assume an appropriate position, and their judgments are always pronounced with outstretched neck, and with the nose upon the larboard tack.

Supremacy of Man

We have been brought up in the pleasant belief that amongst all the animals which walk, swim, creep, or fly, man is the one whose taste is most perfect.

This belief is liable to be upset.

Dr. Gall, relying on some examinations, says that there are many animals who have the organs of taste more developed and, therefore, more perfect than those of man. This is a very unpleasant doctrine, and smacks of heresy.[4]

Man, by Divine right king of all creation, and for whose benefit the earth has been covered and peopled, must necessarily be provided with organs which can adequately appreciate all that is sapid amongst his subjects.

The tongue of animals does not exceed the reach of their intelligence. In fishes, it is only a movable bone; in birds, it is generally a membranous cartilage; in quadrupeds, it is often covered with scales or asperities, and, moreover, has no circumflex motions.

The tongue of man, on the other hand, by the delicacy of its texture and the various membranes with which it is environed and surrounded, sufficiently indicates the sublimity of the operations for which it is destined.

I have, besides, discovered at least three movements unknown to animals, and which I name *spicattan, rotation,* and *verrition.* The first is when the tongue, in a conical shape, comes from between the lips that compress it; the second, when the tongue moves circularly in the space comprised between the interior of the cheeks and the palate; the third, when the tongue, curving upwards or downwards, gathers anything which remains in the semicircular canal formed by the lips and the gums.

Animals are limited in their tastes: some only live on vegetables; others only eat flesh; some nourish themselves exclusively on grain; none of them knows composite flavours.

Man, on the contrary, is omnivorous. Everything which is eatable is subject to his enormous appetite; hence, as a consequence, his gustatory powers must be proportionate to the general use he has to make of them. In fact, the power of taste is of a rare perfection in man, and we have only to convince ourselves of this by seeing it in operation.

The moment an esculent body is introduced into the mouth, it is for ever confiscated, with all its gases and juices.

The lips prevent its going back; the teeth take hold of it and crush it; the saliva imbibes it; the tongue mixes it and turns it over and over; an aspiratory motion pushes it towards the gullet; the tongue raises it up to let it slide down; the sense of smell perceives it as it goes along, and it is thrown into the stomach, to undergo ulterior transformations. But throughout this operation there is not a single particle, a drop, or an atom, which has not been submitted to the appreciative power.

It is on account of this perfection that *gourmandise* belongs exclusively to man.

This *gourmandise* is even contagious, and we impart it readily to the animals which we have appropriated to our use, and which, to a certain extent, have become our companions, such as elephants, dogs, cats, and even parrots.

If some animals have the tongue larger, the palate more developed, the gullet wider, it is because this tongue, acting as a muscle, is destined to move great weights; the palate to press, the gullet to swallow larger portions; but any sound analogy is opposed to the inference that their sense of taste is more perfect.

Besides, since taste can only be judged by the nature of the sensation which it carries to a common centre, the impression received by the animal cannot be compared with that experienced by man; this latter is clearer and more precise, and necessarily supposes a superior quality in the organ which transmits it.

Finally, can we hope for any improvement in a faculty susceptible of such a point of perfection that the *gourmands* of Rome distinguished, by taste alone, the fish caught between the bridges from that which had been caught lower down. Do we not see some in our own days that can distinguish by its superior flavour the thigh on which the partridge leans while sleeping? And have we not plenty of *gourmands* who are able to indicate the latitude under which a wine has ripened, as certainly as a pupil of Biot or Arago can foretell an eclipse?[5]

What follows from all this? That we should render to Caesar that which is Caesar's, proclaim man the great *gourmand* of nature, and not be surprised if the good doctor nods sometimes like Homer —

... *aliquando bonus dormitat Hanarus.*[6]

Method Adopted by the Author

Up to the present time we have only examined taste from a physical point of view, and, unless in some anatomical details which few will regret, we have kept to the level of science. But here does not finish the task which is imposed on us, because it is especially from its moral point of view that this reparative sense draws its importance and glory.

We have therefore arranged, in analytical order, the theories and the facts which compose the totality of this history, in such a manner that instruction without fatigue will be the result.

Thus, in the chapters which are about to follow, we shall show how sensations of taste, by being repeated and reflected, have perfected the organ and extended the sphere of its powers: how the desire for food, which was at first but an instinct, has become an important passion, which has a marked influence on all which relates to society.

We shall also show how all the sciences that have to deal with the composition of bodies classify and place in a separate category all those appreciable to taste, and how various travellers have followed in the same direction by placing before us substances that nature never had destined to come together.

We shall follow chemistry to the very moment when she has penetrated into our subterranean laboratories to enlighten our food-preparers, to lay down principles, to create methods, and to unveil causes which up till then had remained hidden.

Finally, we shall see how, by the combined power of time and experience, a new science has suddenly appeared amongst us, which feeds, restores, preserves, persuades, consoles, and, not content with throwing, with an open hand, flowers over the career of each individual, contributes also powerfully to the strength and the prosperity of kingdoms.

If, in the midst of such grave lucubrations, a piquant anecdote, a pleasant remembrance, or some souvenir of a life of many ups and downs, should come on the tip of my pen, it may slip freely to relieve a little the attention of my readers. Their number will not affright us, and we shall be glad to talk with them; for, if they are men, we are certain that they are as indulgent as well informed; and, if they are ladies, they, of course, are charming.

Here the professor, full of his subject, lets his hand drop, and rises into the higher regions. He ascends the torrent of ages, and takes from their cradle the

Figure 19   Untitled, by Bertall, from Jean-Anthelme Brillat-Savarin, *Physiologie du Goût* (1868).

sciences which have for their object the gratification of taste; he follows their progress across the night of time, and, seeing that in the pleasures they procure us early centuries were less profitable than those which followed them, he seizes his lyre, and sings, in the Dorian mode, the historical melopoea which will be found among the "Varieties" at the end of this volume.

From *Meditation III*. On Gastronomy

Origin of Gastronomy

Gastronomy has appeared, in her turn, and all the sister sciences have made way for it.

What, indeed, can be refused to a science which sustains us from the cradle to the grave, which enhances the pleasures of love and the intimacy of friendship, which disarms hatred, renders business more easy, and offers us, in the short journey of life, the only recreation which, not being followed by fatigue, makes us yet find relief from all others?

Without doubt, as long as the food-preparations were entrusted to salaried servants, and the secrets of the craft remained underground, as long as cooks alone kept the matter to themselves, and books of directions alone were written, the results of such labours were merely the products of an art.

But finally, perhaps too late, learned men approached the subject.

They examined, analysed, and classified alimentary substances, and reduced them to their most simple constituents.

They fathomed the mysteries of assimilation, and, tracing inert matter through its metamorphoses, they saw how it became endowed with life.

They studied food in its transitory or permanent effects for some days, some months, or even for a whole lifetime.

They have estimated its influence even upon the faculty of thought, whether the soul is impressed by the senses, or whether it feels without the aid of these organs, and from all these labours they have deduced a lofty theory which embraces the whole man and the whole part of the creation which can become animalised.

Whilst all these things were taking place in the studies of men of science, it was said aloud in the drawing-rooms that a science which nourishes men is probably worth at least as much as one which teaches them to kill each other; poets sang the praises of the table, and the books on good cheer displayed deeper views and maxims of a more general interest.

Such are the circumstances which have preceded the advent of gastronomy.

Definition of Gastronomy

Gastronomy is the rational knowledge of all that relates to man as an eater.

Its object is to watch over the preservation of men, by means of the best nourishment possible.

It arrives thereat by laying down certain principles to direct those who look for, furnish, or prepare the things which may be converted into food.

Thus it is gastronomy that sets in motion farmers, vinegrowers, fishers, hunters, and the numerous family of cooks, whatever may be their title, or under whatever qualification they may disguise their occupation of preparing food.

Gastronomy is connected—

With natural history, by its classification of alimentary substances;

With physics, by the investigation of their composition and of their qualities;

With chemistry, by the different analyses and decompositions which it makes them undergo;

With cookery, by the art of preparing food and rendering it more agreeable to taste;

With commerce, by the search for means to buy at the cheapest rate possible what is consumed by it, and selling to the greatest advantage that which is presented for sale.

Finally, with political economy, by the resources which it furnishes to the authorities for taxation, and by the means of exchange which it establishes among nations.

Gastronomy rules the entire life; for the tears of the new-born babe call for the breast of the nurse, and the dying man receives still with some pleasure the last cooling drink, which, alas! he can no longer digest.

It has to do, also, with all the states of society; for it presides at the banquets of assembled kings, and also calculates the number of minutes of ebullition which a fresh egg requires to be properly boiled.

The material subject belonging to gastronomy is everything which may be eaten; its direct object, the preservation of individuals, and its means of execution; cultivation which produces, commerce which exchanges, industry which prepares, and experience which invents the means of turning everything to the best account.

Various Objects Treated On by Gastronomy

Gastronomy considers taste in its pleasures as well as in its pains. It has discovered the gradual degrees of excitation of which it is susceptible; it has rendered their action more regular, and laid down limits that a man who respects himself should never overstep. It also considers the action of food on the morals of man, on his imagination, his mind, judgment, courage, and perceptions, either waking, sleeping, working, or resting.

It is gastronomy that determines the degree of esculence of every alimentary object, for all are not presentable at table under the same circumstances.

Some should be eaten before they have arrived at their entire development, as capers, asparagus, sucking-pigs, pigeons, and other animals which are eaten when they are young; others, the moment they have attained all the perfection destined for them, as melons, most fruits, mutton, beef, and all animals eaten when full grown; others, when they commence to be decomposed, as medlars, woodcocks, and especially pheasants; others, finally, after the operations of art have taken from them their deleterious qualities, as the potato, the cassava root, and others.

It is also gastronomy that classifies all these substances according to their diverse qualities, which indicates those that should go together, and which, taking into account the quantity of nourishment they contain, distinguishes those which ought to form the basis of our repasts from those that are mere accessories, and also from those which, though being no longer necessary, are nevertheless an agreeable distraction, and become the necessary accompaniment of convivial gossip.

Gastronomy takes no less interest in the drinks which are destined for us, according to time, place, and climate. It teaches us to prepare them, preserve them, and, above all, to present them in such an order, that the pleasure continually increases, until gratification ends and abuse begins.

It is gastronomy which examines men and things for the purpose of transporting from one country to another everything which merits to be known, and which orders that a feast skilfully arranged should be like the world in miniature, where each quarter of the world is typified by its representatives.

Use of Gastronomic Knowledge

Some knowledge of gastronomy is necessary to all men, inasmuch as it tends to augment the sum of happiness which is allotted to them. This utility augments in proportion as it is applied to the most comfortable classes of society; finally, it is indispensable to those who, enjoying a large income, receive much company, either because in this respect they think they must keep up an appearance, follow their own fancy, or yield to fashion.

There is this special advantage that they take even a personal interest in the manner wherein their table is kept, that they are able to superintend, up to a certain point, the compulsory guardians of their confidence, and even on many occasions to direct them.

The Prince de Soubise one day intended to give a feast which was to finish with a supper, and he asked that the bill of fare should be shown to him.

At his *levée* came the steward with a beautifully ornamented document, and the first article which caught the eye of the prince was "fifty hams."

"Hullo, Bertrand!" said he, "you must be out of your senses. Fifty hams! Do you want to feed all my regiment?"

"No, your highness, there will only appear one on the table; but the others are not the less necessary for my concentrated gravy, my *blonds*, my trimmings, my...."

"Bertrand, you are cheating me, and I cannot let this item pass."

"Ah, my lord," said the artist, scarcely able to retain his rage, "you do not know our resources. Give the order, and I will put these fifty hams that annoy you into a glass phial not much larger than my thumb."

What reply could be made to so positive an assertion? The prince smiled, nodded assent, and so the bill was passed.

Influence of Gastronomy on Business

We know that among the men who are still almost primitive, no matter of importance is treated except at table; it is in the midst of banquets that savages decide on war or peace, and we need not go far to see that villagers do all their business at the public-house.

This observation has not escaped those who frequently deal with the most weighty affairs. They saw that a man with a full stomach was very different from a man fasting; that a certain bond was formed at table between hosts and guests; that it made guests more apt to receive certain impressions and to submit to certain influences. Thus was born political gastronomy. Dinners have become a means of government, and the fate of peoples are decided at a banquet. This is neither a paradox nor even a novelty, but a simple observation of facts. If we look at any historian, from the time of Herodotus up to our own days, it will be seen that, without even excepting conspiracies, no great event ever took place that was not previously concocted, planned, and determined upon at a banquet.

Figure 20 Untitled, by Bertall, from Jean-Anthelme Brillat-Savarin, *Physiologie du Goût* (1868).

A Gastronomic Academy

Such is, at the first glance, the domain of gastronomy—a domain fertile in results of every sort, and which cannot be extended except by the discoveries and inventions of those who cultivate it. Nay, in a few years gastronomy will have its academicians, its courses of lectures, its professors, and prizes.

At first, some zealous and wealthy gastronomer will establish at his own home periodical assemblies, where the most learned theorists will unite with artists to discuss and investigate the various branches of alimentary science.

Thereupon, for such is the history of all academies, the government will interfere, codify, protect, and establish some institution; it will take an opportunity to compensate the public for all orphans made in war, for all the Ariadnes who have been made to shed tears by the summons to combat.

From *Meditation VI*. Special Kinds Of Food

Of Bouilli

Bouilli is a wholesome food, which satisfies hunger readily, is easily enough digested, but which alone does not give much strength, inasmuch as the meat has lost in the boiling a part of the animalisable juices.[7]

We may take it as a general rule in housekeeping, that beef loses half of its weight when boiled.

We may group under four categories all persons who eat *bouilli*.

Men of routine, who eat it because their ancestors ate it, and who, following this practice implicitly, expect their children to imitate them.

Impatient men, who, detesting to be inactive even at table, have acquired the habit of throwing themselves at once upon whatever is first put before them (*materiam subjectam*).

Inattentive men, who, not having received from heaven the sacred fire, look upon dining as a period of forced labour, put on the same level anything which can nourish them, and are at table like an oyster on its bed.

Gluttons, who, gifted with an appetite of which they seek to conceal the capacity, hasten to throw into their stomach the first victim they can find to appease the gastric fire which devours them, and to serve as a basis for all the different things they wish to send the same way.

Real gastronomes never eat *bouilli* on principle, and because they have heard it authoritatively stated as an incontestable truth that *bouilli* is meat without gravy.[8]

Poultry

I am a strong partisan of second causes, and I believe firmly that the entire gallinaceous order has been merely created to furnish our larders and to enrich our banquets.

In fact, from the quail to the turkey, wherever we meet an individual of this numerous family, we are certain of finding a light and savoury food, which is as suitable to a convalescent as to a man who enjoys the most robust health.

For who is there amongst us, condemned by the medical faculty to the fare of the hermits in the desert, who has not smiled at seeing a neatly-carved wing of a chicken, announcing his return to social life?

We are not satisfied with the qualities that Nature has given to the gallinaceous race. Art has taken possession of them, and, on the pretext of improving them, has made them into martyrs. They are not merely deprived of the means of reproduction, but they are kept in solitude, thrown into darkness, and forced to eat. They are thus brought to a size which Nature never intended for them.

It is true that this preternatural fat is very nice, and that this infernal skill gives them that delicacy and juiciness which make them to be the chief dishes of our best tables.

Thus improved, poultry is for the cook what canvas is for a painter, and the cap of Fortunatus for conjurors. It is served up boiled, roasted, fried, hot or cold, whole or in parts, with or without sauce, boned, grilled, stuffed, and always with the same success.

Three districts of ancient France rival for the honour of furnishing the finest poultry: Caux, le Mans, and la Bresse.

As to capons, there is always some doubt; the one a man has his fork in always appearing the best. But as regards chickens, we prefer those of Bresse, which are called *poulardes fines*, and are as round as an apple. It is a great pity that they are so rare in Paris, where they only arrive as occasional presents.

The Turkey

The turkey is certainly one of the most beautiful presents which the New World has made to the Old.

Those who always desire to be better informed than others, say that the turkey was known to the Romans, that it was served up at the wedding-feast of Charlemagne, and that therefore it is an error to attribute this savoury importation to the Jesuits.

To meet these paradoxes two objections may be made:

1. That in French the name of the bird, *Coq à Inde* or *Dindon*, proves its origin, because at one time America was called the "West Indies."
2. The shape of the bird is evidently quite foreign. No man able to judge could make a mistake in this.

But although I am already perfectly satisfied, I have made on this matter rather considerable researches, which I shall not inflict on my readers, but of which I shall only give the results:

1. The turkey first appeared in Europe towards the end of the seventeenth century.
2. It was imported by the Jesuits, who reared a large number especially on a farm which they possessed near Bourges.
3. They spread thence gradually over the whole of France, which is the reason that in many places, and in familiar speech, a turkey was formerly, and is to this day, called "a Jesuit."
4. Only in America has the turkey been found in a wild state, and in a state of nature; -- it does not exist in Africa.
5. In the farms of North America, where the turkey is very common, it is got either from eggs which have been found and hatched, or from young birds caught in the woods and tamed. The consequence is, that they are more like a wild turkey, and preserve their original plumage.

Convinced by these arguments, I owe to the good fathers a double debt of gratitude, for they also imported the chinchona, which is called in English "Jesuits bark."

The same researches taught me that the turkey is gradually becoming acclimatised in France. Well-informed observers have told me that towards the middle of the last century, out of twenty turkeys that were hatched, scarcely ten lived to maturity, while now, all things being equal, out of twenty fifteen are reared. Storms of rain are especially fatal to them; large drops of rain driven onward by the wind and striking their tender and undefended heads destroy them.

Turkey-Lovers

The turkey is the largest, and, if not the finest, at least the most savoury of our domestic birds.

It enjoys, moreover, the unique advantage of uniting around it all classes of society.

When our vine-dressers and our farmers wish to regale themselves in the long winter evenings, what do we see roasting at the brilliant fire of the kitchen where the table is spread? A turkey.

When a useful mechanic, when a laborious artist, assembles a few friends to enjoy some relaxation, which is the more prized because it is so rare, what is the dish which, as a matter of course, he sets before them? A turkey stuffed with sausages or Lyons chestnuts.

And in our most gastronomical circles, in those select companies where politics is forced to give way to dissertations on taste, what is expected, what is desired, what is always seen at the second course? A truffled turkey. A truffled turkey!... And my "Secret Memoirs" tell me that its restorative juices have more than once lighted up most diplomatic faces.

From *Meditation XI.* On Gourmandise

I have consulted the dictionaries under the word *gourmandise*, and I am not at all satisfied with what I find. There is a perpetual confusion between *gourmandise*, properly so called, and "gluttony" and "voracity," whence I infer that lexicographers, however otherwise very estimable, do not belong to those amiable scientific men who can eat gracefully a wing of a partridge *au suprême*, and then, by raising the little finger, wash it down with a glass of Lafitte or Clos-Vougeot.

They have forgotten, they were entirely oblivious of the social *gourmandise*, which includes Athenian elegance, Roman luxury, and French refinement; which arranges wisely, orders dishes to be prepared skilfully, appreciates energetically, and judges profoundly. This precious quality might almost rank as a virtue, and is very certainly the source of our purest enjoyments.

Definitions

Let us define in order that we shall understand each other.

Gourmandise is an impassioned, rational, and habitual preference for all objects which flatter the sense of taste.

Gourmandise is opposed to excess; any person who eats more than he can digest or who gets intoxicated, runs the risk of being struck out from the list of its votaries.

Gourmandise also comprises a love for tit-bits which is merely an analogous preference for light, delicate, small dishes, pastry, sweets, and so forth. This is a modification introduced in favour of ladies and men of feminine tastes.

From whatever point of view *gourmandise* is examined, it deserves nothing but praise and encouragement.

Physically, it is the result and the proof of the wholesome and perfect state of the organs destined to nutrition.

Morally, it shows implicit resignation to the commands of the Creator, who, in ordering man to eat that he may live, invites him to do so by appetite, encourages him by flavour, and rewards him by pleasure.

Advantages of Gourmandise

Considered from the point of view of political economy, *gourmandise* is the common tie which unites nations by the reciprocal exchange of various articles which are daily consumed.

It is the cause why wines, brandies, sugars, groceries, pickled and salted viands, and provisions of every kind, even eggs and melons, are sent from pole to pole.

It gives a proportionate price to things which are middling, good, or excellent, whether these qualities are artificial, or have been given to them by Nature.

It sustains the hope and emulation of a crowd of fishermen, sportsmen, gardeners, and others who every day stock the most wealthy larders with the result of their labour and their skill.

Finally, it supports an industrious multitude of cooks, pastry-cooks, confectioners, and other food-preparers, who, under different titles, all in their turn employ for their wants other and various workmen, which gives rise, at all times and at all hours, to a circulation of capital the most practised mind cannot reckon up, or calculate its quotient.

Let us also remark that this branch of industry which has *gourmandise* for its object, presents so much the more advantages, as on the one hand it derives its support from the largest incomes, and on the other from wants that spring up afresh every day.

In the state of society which we have now reached, it is difficult to imagine a race living solely on bread and vegetables. If such a nation existed, it would undoubtedly have been conquered by carnivorous armies,—like the Hindoos, who have been successively the prey of all those who cared to attack them,—or else it would be converted by the cooking of their neighbours, as the Bœotians have been who became gourmands after the battle of Leuctra.

Sequel

Gourmandise offers great resources for levying taxes, for it brings contributions to town dues, to custom-houses, to indirect taxation. Everything we eat pays a tax, and there is no exchequer of which the lovers of good living are not the firmest supports.

Shall we speak of that swarm of cooks who for many centuries past annually leave France to instruct foreign nations in *gourmandise*. The majority succeed, and then, in obedience to an instinct which never dies in a Frenchman's heart, bring back to their country the fruits of their economy. This contribution is far greater than might be supposed, and therefore these people will be honoured by posterity as others have been.

But if nations are grateful, then Frenchmen, above all other nations, ought to erect a temple and altars to *gourmandise*.

Influence of Gourmandise

By the treaty of the month of November 1815, France was compelled to pay to the allies seven hundred and fifty million francs, or about thirty millions sterling, in three years.

To this sum should be added the amount required to satisfy the demands for compensation of the inhabitants of various countries, of which the allied sovereigns had stipulated the interests to be paid, amounting to more than three hundred million francs, or about twelve millions sterling.

Finally, to this should be added the various requisitions in kind of the enemies' generals, who filled whole waggons, which they sent towards the frontiers, and for which the public treasury had eventually to pay—in all, more than fifteen hundred million francs, or about sixty millions sterling.

We ought to have felt some apprehension that such large payments daily made in hard cash would have produced a deficiency in the treasury, would have depreciated all fictitious values, and finally have brought on us all those evils which menace a country without cash and without means of procuring it.

"Alas!" said all who had anything to lose, when they saw the fatal tumbril coming for its load in the Rue Vivienne; "alas! there is all our money emigrating in a lump! Next year, we shall go down on our knees before a crown-piece; we shall fall into the deplorable condition of a ruined man; speculations of every kind will be unsuccessful; it will be impossible to borrow; there will be nothing but consumption, exhaustion, and civil death."

The result contradicted all these fears; all payments were made with ease, to the great astonishment of every financier; our credit rose, loans were eagerly caught at, and during all the time this "superpurgation" lasted, the rate of exchange, this infallible gauge of monetary circulation, was in our favour—that is to say, it was arithmetically proved that more money came into France than ever went out of it.

What power came to our aid? What divinity worked this miracle?... *Gourmandise*.

When the Britons, Germans, Teutons, Cimmerians, and Scythians made their irruption into France, they brought with them a rare voracity and stomachs of no common capacity.

They did not long remain satisfied with the official cheer which a forced hospitality had to supply them with; but they aspired to more refined enjoyments, and soon the Queen City became nothing but an enormous refectory.

Those invaders ate in restaurants, eating-houses, inns, taverns, at open-air stalls, and even in the streets.

They gorged themselves with meat, fish, game, truffles, pastry, and especially with our fruit.

They drank with an avidity equal to their appetite, and always ordered the dearest wines, in the hope of finding in them some enjoyments they had not before known, and which they were afterwards quite astonished they did not meet with.

Superficial observers did not know what to think of all this eating without end or limit, but your genuine Frenchman laughed and rubbed his hands, saying, "We have them now under the spell, and they will pay us back this evening more crowns than was counted out to them this morning from the public treasury."

It was a favourable time for all those who contribute to the enjoyments of the sense taste. Véry made his fortune; Achard laid the foundation of his; Beauvilliers made a third; and Madame Sullot, whose shop in the Palais Royal was a mere pigeon-hole, sold every day as many as twelve thousand tarts.[9]

The effect still lasts. Foreigners flow in from every part of Europe to renew during peace those delightful habits they have contracted during war. They must come to Paris; and when they are there, they must be regaled at any price; and if French funds are in favour, it is perhaps less due to the higher interest they pay than to the instinctive confidence that foreigners can scarcely prevent placing in a people amongst whom the *gourmands* find so much happiness.[10]

Women are Gourmandes

The desire of the fair sex for *gourmandise* is in some sort instinctive, because it is favourable to beauty.

A series of strictly exact observations has demonstrated that a succulent, delicate, and choice diet delays for a long time and keeps aloof the external appearances of old age.

It gives more brilliancy to the eye, more freshness to the skin, more support to the muscles; and as it is certain in physiology that it is the depression of muscles that causes wrinkles, these formidable enemies of beauty, it is equally true that, all things being equal, those who know how to eat are comparatively ten years younger than those ignorant of that science.

Painters and sculptors are deeply penetrated with this truth, for they never represent those who practise abstinence by choice or by duty, such as misers and anchorites, without giving to them the pathos of sickness, the leanness of misery, and the wrinkles of decrepitude.

Effects of Gourmandise on Sociability

Gourmandise is one of the principal links of society; it extends gradually that spirit of conviviality which unites every day different classes, welds them into one whole, animates conversation, and softens the angles of conventional inequality.

It also justifies all the trouble the host takes to receive his guests properly, as well as their gratitude when they see he has so ably occupied himself with them. Now is the time to stigmatise for ever those senseless feeders who swallow with culpable indifference the nicest tit-bits, or who with sacrilegious carelessness inhale the "bouquet" of an odoriferous and clear wine. As a general maxim, every lofty and intelligent guest requires to be specially praised, and delicate compliments should always be paid wherever a desire to please has been shown.

Note of a Patriotic Gastronomer

I observe with pride that "coquetry" and *gourmandise*, by which good society has greatly modified our most imperious wants, are both of French origin.

From *Meditation XII.* Of Gourmands

Every one who wishes it is not a Gourmand

There are individuals to whom Nature has refused that delicacy of organs, or that degree of attention, without which the most succulent dishes pass unobserved.

Physiology has already recognised the first of these varieties by showing us the tongue of these unfortunate beings badly provided with the nervous papillae destined to inhale and to appreciate flavours, they only incite in them obtuse sensations; such persons are, with regard to taste, what the blind are with regard to light.

The second of these varieties is composed of absent-minded men, chatter-boxes, persons engrossed in business or ambition, and others who want to occupy themselves with two things at the same time, and eat only to be filled.

Figure 21   *Les Aliments* [Food], by Bertall, from Jean-Anthelme Brillat-Savarin, *Physiologie du Goût* (1868).

Napoleon

Such, for example, was Napoleon; he was irregular in his meals, and ate fast and badly; but there also was to be discerned that absolute will which he carried into everything. The moment he felt hungry, it was necessary that he should be fed, and his establishment was so arranged that in any place and at any hour a chicken, cutlets, and coffee had to be served him as soon as wanted.

Gourmands by Predestination

But there is a privileged class whom a material and organic predisposition summons to the enjoyments of taste.

I have always been a disciple of Lavater and Gall, and I believe in innate tendencies.[11]

Since there are some persons who have evidently come into the world to see badly, walk badly, and hear badly, because they are born near-sighted, cripples or deaf, why should there not be others who have been predisposed to feel more especially a certain series of sensations?

Moreover, the most ordinary observer may recognise every moment in society faces that bear the unmistakeable imprint of a ruling passion, such as supercilious impertinence, self-satisfaction, misanthropy, sensuality, and many others. Truly, a very expressionless face may indicate all this; but when the physiognomy is characteristic of resolution, it is very rarely delusive.

The passions act on the muscles, and very often, although a man is perfectly silent, the various sentiments that agitate him can be read in his face. This tension, if in the slightest degree habitual, leaves at last perceptible traces, and stamps thus the countenance with permanent and recognisable characteristics.

Sensual Predisposition

Those persons predisposed to *gourmandise* are generally of middling height. They have a round or broad face, bright eyes, a small forehead, a short nose, thick lips, and a rounded chin. The women are plump, pretty rather than beautiful, with a slight tendency to corpulence.

Chiefly those who are fond of tit-bits and dainties have refined features and a very delicate appearance; they are more graceful, and above all, are distinguished by a peculiar motion of the tongue.

It is especially amongst such persons that we must look for the most agreeable guests. They accept everything that is offered them, eat slowly and taste with discrimination. They never make any haste to leave those houses where they have been treated hospitably, but they stay the whole evening, because they know all the games and pastimes which are the ordinary accessories of a gastronomical gathering.

Those, on the contrary, to whom Nature has refused an aptitude for the gratifications of taste, are long-faced, long-eyed, and long-nosed; whatever may be their height, they appear somewhat lanky. They have dark and straight hair, and look always out of condition; they also have invented pantaloons.[12]

The women whom nature has afflicted with the same misfortune, are angular, feel themselves wearied at a dinner-table, and only live on cards and scandal.

This physiognomical theory will only, I trust, find few of my readers to contradict it, inasmuch as each can verify it from his own observations. I shall nevertheless give an instance to prove the truth of it.

One day I was present at a grand banquet, and opposite to me sat a pretty young lady who had a very sensuous countenance. I turned towards my neighbour, and whispered to him that with such features it was impossible for this lady to be anything else but a *gourmande*. "How absurd!" he replied, "she is scarcely fifteen years old, and has not yet reached the age of *gourmandise*.... However, let us watch."

The beginning, was not in my favour, I was afraid of having compromised myself, for during the two first courses the young lady ate with a discretion that astonished me; and I thought we had fallen upon an exception, as there are some for every rule. But, finally, the dessert came, a dessert both magnificent and copious, and this revived my spirits. Nor did I hope in vain; not only did she eat of everything offered her, but she even had dishes brought to her that were at the other end of the table. In a word, she tasted everything, and my neighbour was surprised that so little a stomach should hold so many things. Thus my diagnosis was verified, and science triumphed once again.

A couple of years later I met the very same lady, a week after her marriage. She had become far more beautiful: showed a little coquetry, and displayed those charms permitted by fashion; she was delightful. Her husband was a sight to see, and resembled one of those ventriloquists who can laugh on one side of the face and cry on the other; that is to say, that he appeared very content to see his wife admired by every one, but was seized with a tremor of jealousy that was very apparent as soon as any one engaged in a serious flirtation with her. This last sentiment prevailed; he took his wife with him into a far-off department, and here, for me, ends her biography.

I made a similar observation on the Duke Decrès, who for so long a time was minister of marine.

He was stout, short, of a dark complexion, had curly hair, and was broad-shouldered; he had a visage at least round, a protruding chin, thick lips, and the mouth of a giant. Thus I proclaimed him at once predestined to be a lover of good cheer and of the fair sex.

I whispered this physiognomical observation to a lady I thought very pretty, and whom I believed could keep a secret. Alas! I was wrong; she was a daughter of Eve, and my secret soon leaked out. That very evening, the scientific induction I had drawn from his features was told to the duke.

The next day I received a very nice letter from the minister, in which he modestly declined the two very excellent qualities I had discovered in him.

I did not consider myself beaten. I replied that Nature had made nothing in vain; that she had evidently created him to perform certain duties, and that if he did not do so, he would be acting contrary to his destiny; that anyhow, I had no right to expect such confidence, and so on.

Our correspondence was not continued; but a short time afterwards the newspapers told the whole of Paris that a furious battle had taken place between the minister and his cook, a battle which lasted for a long time, and was doubtful in its results, as the statesman had not always the best of it. Now, if after such an adventure the cook was not sent away—which he was not—I may, I think, draw the conclusion that the duke was absolutely overcome by the talents of such an artist, and that he despaired of finding another who knew so well how to flatter his taste; otherwise he would never have been able to conquer the very natural repugnance he must have felt at being attended on by so bellicose a servant.

Whilst I was writing the above, on a fine winter's evening, M. Cartier, formerly first violin at the Opera, and an able teacher, paid me a visit, and sate down at my fireside. I was full of my subject, and looked at him with attention. Then I said, "My dear professor, how does it happen that you are not a *gourmand*, when you have all the features of one?" "I was once one of the best," he answered, "but now I abstain." "On principle?" I asked. He did not reply, but heaved a sigh after the manner of some of the heroes of Walter Scott—that is to say, almost a groan.

Gourmands by Virtue of Their Profession

If there are gourmands by predestination, there are also others who become so by virtue of their calling. These latter can be divided into four grand categories: the moneyed classes, the doctors, the men of letters, and the pious people.

From *Meditation XIV.* The Pleasures of the Table

Man is, without doubt, amongst the sentient beings that people our globe, the one who undergoes the most suffering.

Figure 22　Untitled, by Van Muyden, from Brillat-Savarin, *Physiologie du Goût*, in *Four Private Libraries of New York* by Henri Pène du Bois (1892). Courtesy of Department of Special Collections, Stanford University Libraries.

Nature has originally condemned him to sorrow by the bareness of his skin, the form of his feet, and the instinct of war and destruction that accompanies the human race wherever it has been met.

Animals have not been stricken with this curse; and excepting some combats caused by the instinct of reproduction, pain would be absolutely unknown to the majority of animals in a state of Nature; whilst man, who can only experience pleasure transiently and by a small number of organs, can at all times, and in every part of his body, suffer intense agony.

This decree of destiny has been aggravated in its fulfilment by a host of maladies, which are produced by the habits of social life; so that the most keen and the best regulated pleasure than can be imagined cannot either in intensity or duration make up for the atrocious pains that accompany certain disorders, such as gout, toothache, acute rheumatism, strangury, or that caused by the severe punishments amongst certain peoples.

This practical dread of pain has forced man, without being aware of it, to throw himself impulsively in an opposite direction, and to attach himself ingenuously to the small number of pleasures allotted to him by Nature.

For this same reason he has increased, extended, fashioned, and finally worshipped them; for, in the idolatrous ages, for many centuries, all the pleasures were secondary deities, presided over by superior gods.

The severity of modern religions has destroyed all those patrons: Bacchus, Love, Comus, Diana, no longer exist except in poetical tradition; but the thing still exists, and, under the most serious of all forms of belief, men feast occasionally at a marriage, a baptism, and even a funeral.

Origin of the Pleasures of the Table

Meals, in the sense that we give to this word, commenced in the second era of the human race, that is to say, when it ceased to live on fruits. The preparation and the distribution of foods rendered necessary a meeting of the family, when the heads distributed to their children the product of the chase, and adult children rendered in their turn the same service to their aged parents. These meetings, limited at first to the nearest relations, little by little have been extended to neighbours and friends.

Later, and when the human race had spread, the weary traveller came and sate himself down at these primitive repasts, and related what had happened in distant countries. Thus hospitality was born, with its rights held sacred among all peoples; for there is no one, however savage, who does not consider it a duty to respect the life of him with whom he has consented to share bread and salt.

It was during such meals that languages were born or improved, either because it was an occasion for meeting one another which took place often, or because the leisure during and after repasts disposes naturally to confidence and to loquacity.

Difference between the Pleasure of Eating, and the Pleasures of the Table

Such must have been, from the nature of things, the main-springs of the pleasures of the table, which we must distinguish from the pleasures of eating, its necessary antecedent.

The pleasure of eating is the actual and direct sensation of a want which is satisfied.

The pleasure of the table is a reflex sensation that arises from the various circumstances of facts, places, things, and persons present during the repast.

The pleasure of eating we have in common with animals; it only supposes hunger, and what is necessary to satisfy it.

The pleasure of the table is peculiar to the human species; it supposes care bestowed beforehand on the preparations of the repast, on the choice of the place and the assemblage of guests.

The pleasure of eating requires, if not hunger, at least appetite; the pleasure of the table is most often independent of both.

These two different kinds of pleasure can always be observed in our banquets.

At the first course, at the commencement of the meal, every one eats eagerly without speaking, without paying attention to what is said; and whatever the rank may be the guest occupies in society, everything is forgotten, and he becomes merely a workman in the grand manufactory. But when the natural wants are satisfied, reflection arises, conversation begins, another order of things is inaugurated, and he who has hitherto been merely a consumer becomes a more or less agreeable guest, according to the means which the Master of all things has bestowed upon him.

A Sketch

"But," the impatient reader will probably exclaim, "how then, in this year of grace 1825, is any feast to be spread so as to unite all the conditions necessary to the highest pleasures of the table?"

I will answer this question. Readers, please be attentive: Gasterea, the fairest of the muses, inspire me; I shall be as clear as an oracle, and my precepts will live for centuries.

Let the number of guests not exceed twelve, so that the conversation may be constantly general.

Let them be so chosen that their occupations are various, their tastes analogous, and with such points of contact that one need not have recourse to that odious formality of introductions.

Let the dining-room be brilliantly lighted, the cloth as white as snow, and the temperature of the room from sixty to sixty-eight degrees of Fahrenheit.

Let the men be witty and not pedantic, and the women amiable without being too coquettish.[13]

Let the dishes be exquisitely choice, but small in number, and the wines of the first quality, each in its degree.

Let the dishes be served from the more substantial to the lighter; and from the simpler wines to those of finer bouquet.

Let the eating proceed slowly, the dinner being the last business of the day, and let the guests look upon themselves as travellers who journey together towards a common object.

Let the coffee be hot, and the liqueurs be specially chosen.

Let the drawing-room to which the guests retire, be large enough to permit those who cannot do without it, to have a game of cards, while leaving, however, ample scope for post-prandial conversation.

Let the guests be detained by social attraction, and animated with expectation that before the evening is over, there will be some further enjoyment.

Let the tea not be too strong, the toast artistically buttered, and the punch made with care.

Let the signal for departure not be given before eleven o'clock.

Let every one be in bed at midnight.

If any man has ever been a guest at a repast uniting all these conditions, he can boast of having been present at his own apotheosis; and he will have enjoyed it the less in proportion as these conditions have been forgotten or neglected.

Notes

1. Fabrice Teulon, "Gastronomy, *Gourmandise* and Political Economy in Brillat-Savarin's *Physiology of Taste*," *The European Studies Journal* 15:1 (1998): 41–53 (42).
2. Abraham Hayward, *The Art of Dining* (New York: G. P. Putnam's Sons, 1899), 59.
3. Teulon, "Gastronomy," 41.
4. Franz Josephe Gall (1758–1828), together with Johann Caspar Lavater (1741–1801), founded the science of phrenology, which analyzed human identity based on skull shape.
5. Jean-Baptiste Biot (1774–1862) and Dominique François Arago (1786–1853) were both leading astronomers of their day.
6. "Good Hanarus feels sleepy at some time."
7. Brillat-Savarin defines pot-au-feu as beef put into boiling water, with a little salt, to extract its soluble parts; bouillon as the fluid that remains after the operation; and *bouilli* the flesh deprived of its soluble parts.
8. This is a truth that is beginning to be understood, and *bouilli* has disappeared in first-class dinners. It is replaced by a piece of roast meat, a turbot, or a *matelotte*. [Brillat-Savarin]

9. When the army of invasion traversed Champagne, it took six hundred thousand bottles of wine from the cellars of M. Moet, of Epernay, well known for his excellent cellars. He consoled himself for this tremendous loss when he found that the thieves had retained a taste for his wines, and because he receives now from the North twice as many orders as before their visit. [Brillat-Savarin]

10. The calculations whereon this article is based have been communicated to me by M. Jean-Marie Boscary, an aspiring gastronome, and who is not in want of sufficient titles for this denomination, for he is a financier and a musical amateur. [Brillat-Savarin]

11. See note 4 above.

12. A reference to the Venetian character Pantalone from contemporary Italian comedy, represented as a lean and foolish old man, wearing spectacles, pantaloons and slippers. Hence applied in contempt to mean dotard, old fool.

13. I write this in Paris, between the Palais-Royal and the Chaussée d'Antin. [Brillat-Savarin]. This was an extremely fashionable section of Paris, near the restaurant district.

6
Dick Humelbergius Secundus
(Pseudonym)

Apician Morsels; or, Tales of the Table, Kitchen, and Larder: Containing, a New and Improved Code of Eatics; Select Epicurean Precepts; Nutritive Maxims, Reflections, Anecdotes, &c. Illustrating the Veritable Science of the Mouth; Which includes the Art of Never Breakfasting at Home, and Always Dining Abroad (1829)

Introduction

Like good portions of this text, the identity of its author has its origin elsewhere. The name Humelbergius is an allusion to Apicius's annotator, Gabriel Hummelberger, who edited the Roman cook's tenth book on spice and condiments from *Arte Coquinaria* in 1542. Dick Humelbergius Secundus compares himself to the cook who derives his ingredients from elsewhere and who is, therefore, "a mere gatherer of other people's stuff," which he uses to "dress up his finest flavoured dishes." Just as there were no original ingredients for the nineteenth-century chef, common wisdom held there to be no such thing as an original combination of ingredients: skill in executing a recipe distinguished the chef up through the time when the Romantic Carême began to cultivate originality in the culinary arts. In his concluding "Trio: The Cook, the Author, and the Bookseller," Humelbergius joins a time-honored tradition of comparing books to edibles. As he writes, they are both "of various complexions and dimensions, suited to as various tastes and caprices." He scrambles together his literary hodgepodge of *Apician Morsels* without any great pretense of authorial authenticity, but with little doubt that

175

MR. EATINGTOWN IN THE ACT OF RECEIVING AN
INVITATION FOR 5 O'CLOCK *very* PRECISELY.——

Figure 23 *Mr. Eatington in the Act of Receiving an Invitation for 5 O'Clock Very Precisely*, by Robert Cruikshank, from Dick Humelbergius Secundus, *Apician Morsels* (1834). Courtesy of the author.

they will "go down." And down they went in several editions in England and America, making this book the best-known gastronomical text in English of the nineteenth century.

Like Kitchiner's *Apicius redevivus*, the title of *Apician Morsels* alludes to the Roman chef Apicius Coelius (some believe there to have been three brothers of this name) who wrote down his recipes, preserving the glories of Roman gastronomy for later ages. The morsels gathered by Humelbergius include tidbits from Grimod de la Reynière and Brillat-Savarin, organized in gastronomical categories, such as a "Code of Eatics," "Epicurean Precepts," and "Nutritive Maxims, Reflections, Anecdotes." The title page of the 1836 New York edition signals familiarity with French gastronomical culture by including the slogan of the first French restaurateur, "O vos qui stomacho laboratis, accurrite, et ego vos restaurabo!"[1] It also includes a maxim from Grimod's Code Gourmand: "Always breakfast as if you did not intend to dine; and dine as if you had not broken your fast." The first half of the volume traces the gastronomical habits of the Romans and the subsequent history of cuisine up through the present, when the text veers off into the more distinctively Romantic literary genre of gastronomy.[2]

In addition to original essays on various aspects of cookery and good living, Humelbergius includes healthy portions of letters printed in *The Art of Cookery: In Imitation of Horace's Art of Poetry*, written by William King to Martin Lister, the early eighteenth-century editor of Apicius. Several of his "Nutritive Varieties" are imported from Grimod's *Almanach des gourmands*, as are his treatments of meals in "The Knotty Point," his explanation of "Table Ceremonies between Host and Guest," and his thoughts on invitations to both town and country meals. Robert Cruikshank engraved two illustrations for the book, one of which, "The Roman Senate Debating in the Turbot," is copied from the frontispiece to Joseph Berchoux's 1803 poem, *La gastronomie; ou l'homme des champs à table* (fig. 24). It depicts the emperor Domitian petitioning the Roman Senate for advice on what sauce to serve with a giant turbot (in other versions of the story, a sturgeon). Also borrowed from Berchoux's work is his *Prière du soir d'un poëte* prefixed to his poem, which Humelbergius translates as "Prayer of a Half-Starved Hungry Poet."[3]

Here, as in the case of Sturgeon, the Gothic novelist William Beckford has been suggested as the man behind the pseudonym. Beckford's library at Fonthill Abbey included a first edition of *Apicius in re quoquinaria* (1498), Lister's edition of *Apicius coelius de arte coququinaria cum annotationibus Martini Lister et notis variorium* (1709), and relevant texts from which Humelbergius draws, including Berchoux's *La gastronomie*.[4] Beckford's librarian, Ange Denis Macquin (1758–1823), was himself a food connoisseur who published anonymously a clever poem in Latin with extensive notes, entitled *Tabella cibaria* (1820), or Bill of Fare. It was written in response to a challenge to express "in *decent* Latin verses, the curious and pleasingly *tangible* variety of dishes which French eating-houses and hotels lavishly display upon their long and hardly intelligible *Bills of Fare*." A copy of the poem owned by Beckford has also been (wrongly) attributed to him.[5] Beckford owned several editions of *Apician Morsels*, which the Yale University

THE ROMAN SENATE DEBATING ON THE TURBOT.

Figure 24   *The Roman Sentate Debating on the Turbot*, by Robert Cruikshank, from Dick Humelbergius Secundus, *Apician Morsels* (1834). Courtesy of the author.

Library catalogues under his authorship. One of these, the 1829 London edition, is in pristine condition—uncut in its original boards as if its author had no need to read it.

Another possible identity for Humelbergius may be proposed: the Irish-born writer of French extraction, Richard Chenevix (1774–1830). Beckford's extensive library did not contain any volumes of Grimod's *Almanach des gourmands* (1803–12), which were creatively plagiarized by Humelbergius. But Chenevix knew the book well since he had reviewed it in 1821 for *The Edinburgh Review*. In this review, he discussed nine other cookery books, some even more obscure works of French gastronomy, such as the 1809 *L'Almanach comestible cours gastronomique* and the 1814 *Dictionnaire de la cuisine*. A Fellow of the Royal Society of Edinburgh, the Irish Academy, and several other learned societies on the continent, Chenevix spent a year in Paris in 1808 at the height of Grimod's publishing fame, and he authored more than one anonymous review with a comparativist focus on Britain and France.[6] Although he is known today primarily for his scientific writings, Chenevix was also a prolific poet (reviewed in *The Edinburgh Review* in

1812), playwright (*Mantuan Revels, Henry VII*), and essayist (e.g., *An Essay Upon National Character*, 1830). He certainly had enough gastronomical materials at hand to compose *Apician Morsels*, and it may be telling that his 1821 cookery review not only refers to the obscure Humelbergius but cites one precept ("'Digestion,' the French say, 'is the stomach's affair;' indigestion, 'that of the Doctor'") that also occurs in Dick Humelbergius Secundus.[7] Were Richard Chenevix the author, it would account for Humelbergius's incongruous first name, Dick.

The text below is from the 1834 London edition of *Apician Morsels*.

From *Apician Morsels* (1829)

Stomach and Appetite

The stomach has frequently a great deal more laid to its charge than it is guilty of; for it is just as tractable as any other part of the system when well used, and is often considerably more indulgent. It certainly possesses the most exquisite sympathy, and is feelingly alive to all the injuries inflicted on any of its dependencies; but that it is either a pudding-bag[8] intended to be filled, or like a pair of saddle-bags, built for stowage, and to be crammed as full as it can hold, is a mistaken, and often a fatal notion.

The stomach then, anatomically and physiologically considered, for the want of a better simile, may not inappropriately be likened to a pair of Scotch bagpipes, which, having an entrance and an exit for the necessary quantity of air they ought to receive and contain, without being distended beyond their natural elasticity, it submits to the functions it has to perform with ease and harmony. In like manner, the stomach has its conducting tube (oesophagus) for the aliment it is destined to hold and digest; so also has it its common sewer or drain (the intestinal canal) through which all superfluous matter is carried away. By this succession of changes the health and strength of the animal economy is maintained.

Appetites are often capricious when left to the imagination; and the stomach, when accustomed to artificial stimuli, plays such fantastic tricks, "before high Heaven," as not unfrequently make even gourmands themselves weep.

According to gastronomers, there are three sorts of appetite; two of which come more immediately under the consideration of the gourmand:—

1. That which we feel upon an empty stomach: a sensation so imperious, that it does not quibble much with the quality of the food offered to it, but which at the sight of a ragout, makes the mouth water.

2. That, which is felt when, sitting down to a dinner without being hungry, we taste some succulent dish, which realizes the proverb, "appetite comes by eating;" and which may be compared to a husband whose lukewarm heart grows more kindly on the first caresses of his wife.

3. That appetite excited by some delusive viand, which makes its appearance towards the end of a meal, when, the stomach already satisfied, the temperate man is about to retire without reluctance. This may be typified by the gross desires of libertinage, which, although illusory, or feeding only in the mind, give rise nevertheless to some real pleasures.

A knowledge of stomachical metaphysics, ought to direct a skilful cook how to prepare the first, second, and third courses; the last of which usually consists of a ridiculous variety of wines, liquors, fruits, confectionary, &c., to feed the eye, to overcome the stomach, paralyze digestion, and seduce children of a larger growth, to sacrifice the health and comfort of several days, for the infantine though no less gourmand pleasure of tickling their palates with these newfangled lollypops.

The stomach, nevertheless, though the mainspring of our system, ought not unnecessarily to engage more of our attention than is requisite to the due performance of its necessary functions, and the maintenance of health, any more than it ought not, by any means to become a mere matter of secondary importance; because, if it be not sufficiently wound up to warm the heart and support the circulation, the whole business of life will be ineffectually performed; we can neither think with precision, sleep with tranquillity, walk with vigour, or sit down with comfort, if there be any thing wrong in the victualling office. But let no man make so far "a god of his guts," as to give them precedence of other equally paramount duties which he owes alike to himself and society.

Every convive will best know how to regulate his appetite, by the quality and quantity of the food his stomach is calculated to bear. The best rule is to leave off with an appetite; and the bon vivant will always prefer hilarity from wine, than heaviness from repletion.

If variety of food be at all necessary, it is from the mutual advantages which vegetable and animal food have in correcting each other. Whatever this variety may consist of, it does not appear, that any inconvenience arises from their mixture, or difficulty of assimilation, provided a moderate quantity be taken at a time; and the quantity of nutriment in each, is either absolute or relative—absolute, as regards the quantity it really contains, sufficient powers being given to extract it;—relative, with respect to the assimilating powers of those who use it.

A Short Dissertation on the Origin of Dentiscalps, or Toothpicks

It is generally supposed by those most conversant in the philosophy of the mouth, that the use of dentiscalps are of great antiquity, and that their origin was first dictated by instinctive Nature, which, in cases of emergency, is the best preceptress.

The Egyptians, it is well known, were a people excellent for their philosophical and mathematical observations—they searched into all the springs of action; and though their superstition must be condemned, posterity cannot do otherwise than applaud their inventions. This people had a vast district that worshipped the crocodile, which is an animal, whose jaws being very oblong, give him the opportunity of having a great many teeth; and his habitation and business lying most in the water, he like our modern Dutch whitsters in Southwark,[9] had a very good stomach, and was extremely voracious. It is certain that he had the water of Nile always ready, and consequently the opportunity of washing his mouth after meals; yet he had farther occasion for other instruments to cleanse his teeth, which are *serrate*, or like a saw,—to this end, nature has provided an animal called the Ichneumon, which performs this office, and is thus maintained by the product of his own labour.

Seeing such an useful sagacity in the crocodile, which they so much reverenced, they soon began to imitate it—great examples easily drawing the multitude—so that it became their constant custom to pick their teeth and wash their mouth after eating and drinking....

Although the Egyptians often extended their conquests into Africa and Ethiopia, and though the Caffree blacks have very fine teeth, yet it does not appear that they made use of any such an instrument, as a toothpick; nor does Ludolphus, though very exact as to the Abyssinian Empire, give any account of a matter so important; for which he is to blame.

Dr. Heylin says, in the third book of his cosmography, that the Chinese eat their meat with two sticks of ivory, ebony, or the like; and do not touch it at all with their hands: consequently, they are not very great soilers of linen. This, however, is contradicted by Dr. King, in his treatise of forks[10] and napkins. "The use of, silver forks, among us, came from China into Italy, and thence into England; although gastronomers have not agreed on this subject. For the first use of these sticks is not so much to save linen, as, from pure necessity, arising from the length of their nails, which persons of great quality, and, at the present day, with almost idlers of every quality, wear at a prodigious length, to prevent all possibility of working, or being serviceable to themselves or others: and, therefore, if they would, they could not easily feed themselves with these talons; and there is good authority to suppose that in the East, and especially in Japan, the princes have the meat put into their mouths by their attendants. Besides, these sticks are of no sort of use but of their own sort of meat, which, being *pilau,* is all boiled to rags. But of what use would these sticks be in carving a turkey, or a round beef? Our forks, therefore, are of quite a different shape—the steel ones being bidental, and the silver ones generally tridental, which leaves reason to suppose that they are as ancient to Pluto, and the latter to Neptune.

It is certain that Pedro della Valle, a famous Italian traveller, carried his knife and fork with him to the East Indies; and he gives an account that at the court of an Indian prince, he was admired for his neatness in that respect, and his care in wiping both, before he returned them to their respective repositories.[11]

The Origin of Forks at Table

The use of forks at table did not prevail in England till the reign of James I, as we learn from a remarkable passage in Tom Coryat. The reader will laugh at the solemn manner in which this important discovery or innovation is related.

"Here I will mention a thing that might have been spoken of before in discourse of the first Italian towne. I observed a custom in all those Italian townes and cities, through which I passed that is not used in any other country that I saw in my travels, neither do I think that any other nation of Christendome doth use it, but only Italy. The Italian and also most strangers that are common and in Italy, doe always at their meals use a little forke when they eate their meate; for while with their knife, which they hold in one hand, upon the same dish, so that whatsoever he be that sitting in the company of any others at meate should unadvisedly touch the dish of meat with his fingers, from which all the table doe cut, he will give occasion of offence unto the company, as having transgressed the lawes of good manners, in so much that for his error he shall be at least brow-beaten, if not reprehended in wordes. This form of feeding, I understand, is generally used in all parts of Italy, their forks for the most part being made of yronn, steele, and some of silver, but those are used only by gentlemen. The reason of this their curiosity is, because the Italian cannot by any means endure to have his dish touched with fingers, seeing all men's fingers are not alike cleane. Hereupon I myself thought good the Italian fashion by this forked cutting of meate, not only while I was in Italy, but also in Germany, and often times in England since I came home: being once quipped for that frequently using my forke, by a certain learned gentleman, a familiar friend of mine, Mr. Lawrence Whitaker; who in his merry humour doubted not to call me at table Furcifer, only for using a fork at feeding, but for no other cause."[12]

The Knotty Point

A Question, hitherto undecided in this all-consuming world, and particularly with gourmands, connected with the philosophy of the stomach, is, do we eat to live, or live to eat? The temperate man adopts the first; the man of appetite the other. Now, as there are few people, of whatsoever country, calling, or sect, who would not prefer a good dinner to an indifferent one, and one of an indifferent quality to none at all; we maintain that it is nearly as rational for a man to live to eat, as it is for him to eat to live; nay, did we only eat to live, how little would satisfy nature,—"man's life," as the poet says, "would then be as cheap as beasts." But eating and drinking have such irresistible appeals to the palate and stomach, that insensible indeed must be the nerves of either the one or the other that could withstand the *argumentum* of a smoking Sir Loin, or round of good English beef, even upon a Good Friday, were the appetite jaded to eat.

A good dinner being one of the greatest enjoyments of human life, is it to be wondered that so many *ruses de guerre* are adopted to procure one abroad, when it is not convenient to find one at home? Besides, ought we not to be grateful to those benefactors, who are open to such satisfactory accommodation, and who take so much trouble to make us eat and drink their substance? Far, indeed, from jesting, or treating such hospitality with levity, we should endeavour to pay our host with appropriate encomia on every thing set before us; and to settle our reckoning, with sallies of wit and humour, short and amusing stories, anecdotes, a thousand times told, glees, catches, compliments, and conundrums; in short, to secure another invitation, feel the pulse of the Amphitrion, get hold of his weak side, his hobby; you then invest the main post, and if ever you lose it, it will be your own fault; flatter him to the skies—say *yes* and *no*— But stop—we are proceeding rather too fast; let us first say

Something About Breakfast

[Adapted from Grimod de la Reynière's "On Breakfast."][13]
An early breakfast belongs chiefly to the lower orders, and middling classes of people; it is nevertheless the invariable symptom of a good appetite, and of temperance the preceding evening. Happy are those who thus enjoy an early stomach; they require no whets to rouse a sleeping palate, no invention to debauch the treat. Such appetites are natural; not depending upon either caprice or fashion, they promote the growth, happiness, and independence of man. But late breakfasts, our *déjeunés à la fourchette* belong to the haut-ton, men of fashion, and (we were going to say men of sense) such as, having no breakfast of their own, are glad to chime in any where, at any hour, to get one.

To those who are in the habit of dining late, a dish of tea or coffee, with the usual accompaniments at an English breakfast table, would not be sufficient to stay the stomach, which stands in need of more substantial materials, both as regards meat and drink, to prevent this important bowel from grumbling. Hence probably the origin of breakfasts *à la fourchette*, at one time as much deprecated as they are now lauded and enjoyed by the epicures and bons-vivants of the day. If any hot viands are permitted at this repast, they generally—particularly at Paris, where they are in great reputation consist of the legs and wings of poultry, (*en papillotes de Madame Hardy,*) and fowls (*à la Tartare*), or at least, small pies (*au jus de M. Rouget,*) kidneys and sausages, "*Les pièces de résistance, les salades de volaille, et les pâtés de gibier,*"—"these," says the Almanach des Gourmands, "act the principal parts at this preparatory meal, of which the oysters of the celebrated Rocher de Cancale are, during nearly the whole winter, the necessary preface." But this opulent regimen is not convenient to the man of limited income, nor to the modest nursling of the Muses; the income of the first, at this rate, would not last him ten days; and the imagination of the other would soon become paralysed by the habitual use of such solid nutriment. When Boileau said that

Horace a bu son saoul quand il voit les Ménades,[14]

he did not allude to these kinds of breakfasts. If it is proved that abstinence slackens the circulation of the blood, confuses the ideas, and extinguishes the poetic vein, they are no less paralyzed by rich and solid food taken to excess. The hour of dining being with them nearly the same, it became necessary for them to seek some means of waiting, without suffering, till this time arrived, and to seize a medium between a cup of tea and a rump steak—to find a substance, light and substantial—friendly to the stomach and the imagination—agreeable to the taste, and not expensive, easy to be got ready, and which, within a small compass, should include particles sufficiently nutritive to let them wait without impatience a late dinner, and, at the same time, not substantial enough to prevent them from doing honour to it when the hour arrived. Such is the problem it was necessary to explain; "and," says the Almanach already cited, "chocolate has resolved it."

Chocolate, which, about forty or fifty years ago, was only used as a breakfast for old people, constitutes, at the present day, that of every one who wishes to preserve the brilliancy of the imagination, or whose faculties cannot be raised above the standard of a common dunce. But such, indeed, are the adulterations to which chocolate is submitted, that it can rarely be obtained genuine; hence the reason it does not agree with every one; and often occasions a weight, or, in other words, lies heavy at the stomach, difficulty of digestion, and sometimes obstructions. These, in short, are the too ordinary consequences of such unwholesome, and often deleterious, preparations.

Dinner Time

[Adapted from Grimod de la Reynière's "On Dinner."][15]
Dinner is the most interesting daily action of our lives; as being that which is performed with most eagerness, pleasure, and appetite. Sooner would a coquet renounce to please, a poet to be praised, a blackleg to be believed upon his oath,[16] a comedian to be applauded, a rich citizen to be flattered, than seven-eighths of the Londoners to make a good meal. We have always been much surprised that in this diversified, book-making age, no author has ever taken upon himself the task of treating this subject with the gravity it deserves, or to have written on dinners in a philosophical manner. How many things might there be to relate upon this memorable act, which is renewed 365 times in the year!

If, by any unforeseen accident, any fortuitous circumstance, the moment of dining be put off for only one hour, just look at your guests, and twig what long faces they make; see how the most animated conversation languishes, how blue every one looks, how all the zygomatic muscles are paralysed, in short, how every eye appears mechanically turned toward the dining-room! Is the obstacle removed? the master of the hotel, a napkin under his arm, comes to announce that all is ready and served up; the words act like a charm—they have a magical effect which restores to each his serenity, his gaiety, and wit. An appetite is read in every eye, hilarity in every heart; and the tumultuous impatience with which each runs to take possession of his plate, is a manifest and certain sign of the unanimity of wishes and the correspondence of sensations. Nature then resumes all her rights: and at that moment of the day, the flatterer himself suffers his thoughts to be read in every feature of his countenance. The longing looks, the smacking of lips, the anxious expectation, which are every where visible, paint the conflict of the *belly*-gerent powers, eager for the attack. Boiling hot broth or soup (just as it ought to be,) has no effect upon the general action; every palate, in fine, might be said to be, paved *en mosaïque* or that they possess the privileges of the incombustible or fire-proof man. The host, nevertheless, who ought to be less engaged in reasoning upon the variety of dishes, than in supplying the plates of his guests, divides, *secundum artem*, the smoking sirloin, surrounded with a vegetable cordon. The highest seasoned sauces serve as a stimulus to the first course, the foundation of every solid dinner, and the only one which never tires although reproduced every day in the year.

In the mean time, the side dishes disappear, and those which succeed give the necessary time to carve those which follow. In Germany, Switzerland, and throughout almost all the north of Europe, this dissection is confided to an officer *ad hoc*, who acquits himself with uncommon dexterity—a most valuable custom, which saves a great deal of time, not only to the father of the feast, but to the guests, which may be much better employed.

On Table Ceremonies Between Host and Guest

[Adapted from Grimod de la Reynière's "On Obligations Respecting Convives"][17]

During every manducatory act, among gourmands, all ceremony ought to be banished. This is a precept we will never cease to repeat; and the reasons for it are easily guessed. In the first place, good living establishes between persons who meet for the first time a sudden acquaintaince, because, towards each other, gourmands are never strangers. This similarity of taste is the best foundation of a lasting friendship; hence we seldom see real gourmands quarrel with their friends. They leave coolness, quarrelling, and disputing, to sweethearts, and they live together as the worthy children of Epicurus.

Consequently, it is proved that all ceremonies observed at table go to the deterioration of the service, for the entrees and entremets languish during these superfluous compliments. Nevertheless, as English politeness will never suffer them to be entirely banished from the commerce of life, even at dinner time, we deem it useful to lay down a few rules on this subject; which, probably, may conciliate that which is due to civility, with that exacted by good living; which will be found wonderfully adapted to every appetite.

He was certainly neither a man of wit, nor a man of business, who first said that punctuality was the beau-ideal of fools. We think, on the contrary, that it is the virtue of all those who know the value of time; and we will not do fools the honour of classing them in this rank. The gourmand either is, or ought to be, par excellence, a punctual man, as it would be easy for us to prove that, of all acts of civility, a dinner is that to which delay is most prejudicial. Any other business maybe put off for a few hours without much inconvenience; but when there is a piece of roast meat, a goose, turkey, sucking-pig, or what not, upon the spit, a pie in the oven, a saucepan on the range, there is only a set time for them to remain there; once this precious moment elapsed, the substance, whatever it may be, must lose of its flavour, and become rigid and dry—there is no other remedy.

A gourmand, and all who aspire to deserve this sacred title, ought then to be punctual in their engagements, and (come to the scratch) precisely at the appointed hour; and it is also the duty of every Amphitrion to fix that hour in a punctual manner, and to arrange matters so that the soup, or first dish, may be upon the table thirty minutes after the time appointed.

It is of importance here to make an observation as regards the time. At Paris they have three ways of determining this affair, which it is good to know, in order to arrive neither too soon nor too late. For instance, five o'clock for six; five o'clock precisely, for half-past five; and five o'clock very precisely, for five o'clock exactly. With this invariable rule, one will neither be deceived nor waited for.

Suppose, then, the dinner be named for five o'clock precisely, you must be at the spot by half-past five, where, either the host (Amphitrion), himself, or some of his family, will do the honours of the waiting room, which should be a well warmed saloon or chamber, according to circumstances, in which the morning and evening papers ought to be present.

The first compliments between gourmands ought to be very laconic; and instead of the common-place salutation of "how d'ye do?" the first question should be, "have you a good appetite to-day?" Half an hour after the appointed time, by the note of invitation, the master of the house arrives, a napkin under his arm, to announce that dinner is up. From that time, he who is nearest the door moves on in silence in order to pass into the dining-room; the others pass in succession, without stopping; the host closes the march, to accelerate those who are to follow.

As regards placing yourself at table, no ceremonies are necessary, when the name of each guest is written upon his plate. The Amphitrion ought to occupy the centre of the table, as much to be within reach of serving his guests, as that he may superintend their appetites, without suffering the plates themselves to direct his attention. After *grace* has been said, either mentally, or in the common way, he distributes the soup, or the first *entrée*; it belongs to the Amphitrion to bless the table in an audible voice, according to the *formula*, of gourmands. The soup is served in proper soup plates, which are piled up before him. The first, when filled, he gives to his right hand neighbour, the second to that on the left; he then returns to the right hand, then to the left, and so on alternately. Every one remains served in his turn, without passing the plate. It is the same in every other respect with the dishes served by the Amphitrion. With respect to the side-dishes, every one helps himself, or asks his neighbours who are in proximity with those of which he wishes to partake; but, be it observed, always in silence, and *sans cérmonie*.

The common wines, if such a liquid be used at table, are either placed on the table, or are served by dumb-waiters; on this point no compliments are necessary—every one helps himself according to his thirst: all, at most, that is permitted, is to offer to serve one's neighbour.[18] It is well understood that water is never proposed. The coup de milieu, the wine which accompanies the entremets, and those of the dessert, are always served by the master of the house in the same order as the soup, &c.

It is the same with respect to punch, wine, coffee, liqueurs, &c., if they be upon the table; in any other place, as in the *salon*, these are served, without distinction, to all who present their cup; and, as regards liqueurs, every one helps himself as he likes.[19]

Two or three hours after dinner, the guests, silently, and furtively, escape, one by one. It would be as impolite to take your leave in a formal manner, as not, in the course of eight days afterwards, at least, to pay what is called a visit of digestion.

As regards these regulations, the presence of ladies makes no difference. Every where else, their sway is acknowledged; but at table they are subjects, and, consequently, amenable to all the laws of gastronomy.

The custom of singing at table is still observed among all ranks of society; and where this harmless relaxation is confined within proper rules, and regulated by good taste, such harmonical *winds*-up of a good dinner has nothing censurable in it; and, as such, will always be more or less tolerated. Here the Amphitrion should direct the taste of his guests, by giving two or three stanzas of some popular or peculiar air, which in a manner will decide the consequences.

To Procure Town Invitations

Vanity, which acts so principal a part in societies, extends even to the denominations which they have attained. In every town, the union of some men and women of the privileged class, is called *the world*. In all great cities, the world, in this sense, is divided into what is called the *beau monde*, or fashionable world, and the *grand monde*, or great folks. Wit, fashion, and an easy intercourse, are the rules of the one; etiquette, ignorance, and falsehood, are those of the other: besides, with some few trifling exceptions, the customs are the same.

Parties and dinners at Paris occupy the greatest half of human life. For many, the recreations are composed of *days of invitation*, and days of *custom* or *habit*: in the latter, liberty and confidence are commonly the expences of a meal, where acquaintances meet periodically at the same table. These dinners have nothing in common with those meals upon fixed days, where the master of the house, whose name and quality, frequently, are all that is known, receives, as at the dinner of an inn, people who, not knowing where to pass the evening, come and begin it at his house, precisely at the dinner hour.

Dinners by invitation are, at the present day, what they have always been—a kind of lottery, where the favourable chances are not the most common; and of which those complain the most who risk nothing, and those who formerly made a fortune by them. Besides, it is not at dinners by special invitation, that we ought principally to aim at, but at those established quotidian dinners, given by an individual too happy if any one will have the goodness to come and help him to eat and drink his fortune, and to kill time for him into the bargain. The day you intend to make yourself the guest of such a person, in order to amuse you in your turn, your host might not be pleased to dine, because he appears to have placed his appetite in your stomach. In order perfectly to obtain this object, make friends with the ladies, rather than with the gentlemen; for, through the medium of the women every thing that can be wished for from the men is to be obtained. Even though the latter are, for the most part, so much preoccupied with their personal affairs as to neglect yours; nevertheless the ladies think of them incessantly, were it even from indolence itself.

Speak, the preceding evening, to a lady, who takes any interest in your affairs, about an invitation that would please you; the next day, at her piano, or upon her sofa, her favourite romance in her hand, you will find her ruminating upon the means of obtaining for you the desired invitation. But with those whom you believe able to serve you, take care how you seek to be any thing else than a friend; for, to be lovers, as soon as there are any suspicions, quarrels, and fallings-out, all is lost. Good by invitations—consequently dinners.

Be, then, towards the women, assiduous, complaisant,—yea, even gallant, if you wish it; but nothing more, mind ye.

At Paris, an Amphitrion of the cast we have just been speaking, and of whom I could wish any of our qualified readers to be the perpetual guest, reckons in his *salle à manger* upwards of a hundred seats of different kinds, independent of half a dozen small cushions and canopies, for the use of the dogs and cats belonging to the house, when they want to sleep, and on which an honest man should take good care not to sit. Only once accustom the proprietor of this establishment to see your irresistible physiognomy upon one of these hundred seats, and by your tardy loco-motion, you become one of the obliging ornaments of the saloon; you, in fact, wriggle yourself into a niche that ever afterwards secures you against the cravings of your appetite.

There are some faces so felicitously constructed that they are equal to any piece of furniture in an apartment, and who ultimately supersede an arm-chair, where the eye has contracted the habit of looking at them. Have you, for instance, ever been in an apartment where pompous curtains display their double fringes? Let all these ornaments be suddenly removed, your eyes will become sorrowful, and will experience, for some time, a kind of widowhood. Become, then, a curtain—make yourself a fringe—metamorphose yourself, if you can, into an arm-chair of this person's dining-room; for this purpose, a little perseverance is all that is necessary, in order to get yourself considered as constituting a part of his rich furniture. You will see that he will become attached to you in the same manner and degree as he would to some fancy article of his household, or to some precious stone; in short, he will no longer be able to do without you. Good by, on your side, with a pleasure or an honour of seeing you again—a simple *good night*, in fact, a simple departing salutation, would produce the effect upon him, the same as a sudden breaking up of his establishment.

There is, then, only one means left for you to parry this, which he will be more afraid of than thunder and lightning; that will be to inform you that from that moment a knife and fork will every day be laid for you at his table, and that he must understand you will always be there at the precise hour. Consequently, you will thenceforward so arrange matters, that, on his return from the Exchange, or any other place, you are the first object that meets his eyes, the first individual which this worthy inviter sees in his dining-room, at *five o'clock precisely* (fig. 23). You must always take care to occupy the same place at table, sit upon the same seat, to unfold and place your napkin in the same invariable manner, and to say grace, should you be requested to do so, as loud as a dissenting clergyman. Always break your bread on the same side, lay hold of the bottle with the same hand; do not touch the decanter, if the host himself does not drink water; and let your jaws and masticators keep pace with his, and go through the same evolutions which they do; in a word, execute, whether it be in asking, offering, or receiving, the same movements, the same gestures, the same thanks as his; the whole for the better identifying yourself with his person, so that your habits, classifying themselves symmetrically in his brain, may become, in some measure, his own.

Should any serious indisposition cause you for only once to absent yourself at the appointed hour, (for no other motive could possibly justify you, as you interfere with no other business,) you will be informed on the following day, when you return, what a vacuum you made in the looks of your Amphitrion, accustomed as he is to see your figure sitting opposite to him. Be persuaded, then, of one thing: he must have been peevish with his wife; he must have scolded his servants, and have found every thing detestable about him; the meat must have been underdone; the sauces badly made; the wine stale, the coffee cold—it must, in short, have been impossible for him to dine; he must have kicked his dog, and given a—to his cook; it is even probable, that the following morning you might yourself feel the counter shock.—Why?—because you were not there the preceding evening.

But all this is nothing, in comparison with the power which you will be able to acquire over him, if you have, at dinner time, the talent or ingenuity to take upon yourself some special functions; it will then be no longer a habit which he has of seeing you at his house; it will be a necessity or want of the first kind.

How comfortable it is to be a functionary at a splendid table! There an employment costs no sacrifice of conscience, no mean-spirited concession. A *capon* has no opinion; *hams* have never denounced any one. After having made a noble use of the knife and *truel* you will be able nobly to lay down your spoon and fork, and, without fearing to place your hand upon that part which separates the belly from the breast, you will only find it, at most, loaded with one liver of a stuffed goose. Who would dare to reproach a similar meal with the delicacy of an honest mess-mate? Every one pays in his own way: the latter, with money, because he cannot do otherwise; the former, with a "long yarn," which he causes to be told by another; but you, when any one gives you a dinner, acquit yourself more nobly, and in a more useful manner for the public good......carve.

Nutritive Varieties

From Maxims, —Reflections, —Anecdotes, —and Epicurean Whims.

[Adapted from Grimod de la Reynière's "Nutritive Maxims and Reflections"][20]

... The *visit of digestion* is a sacred duty, in which every man, who knows the world, and has not lost his appetite for another occasion, never fails. The extent of this visit is regulated in some countries, by the quality of the repast; some have lasted as long as three hours. There are many Amphitrions who would gladly dispense with so long a mark of gratitude.

There is an article in the famous regulations, already mentioned, of M. Aze,[21] strictly obligatory, which forbids us to slander the man at whose table we dine; and that for a time commensurate with the quality of the dinner: for an ordinary dinner, the term is eight days; but it never can exceed six months; after that, M. Aze allows the tongue its full play. Though it is always in the power of the Amphitrion to tie it up again, by an appropriate and timely invitation. Hence it is unanimously agreed, among gourmands, that of all the ways of preventing any one from speaking ill of another, this is by no means the least amiable.

The extreme levity of the manners of the present day, is the reason why so little importance is frequently attached to what are called nutritive invitations. Leaving behind us the time when there were more dinners than diners, it was then thought that acknowledgments of the kind ought to be reciprocal; and to justify this species of ingratitude, it is asked, what would the Amphitrion do with such a large dinner? Bad logic! the reasoning of a false and corrupt heart!—for this identical great dinner would not have existed had he invited no one; and it is only to fatten his guests that he expects them, and for which he has put himself to such expense. The gratitude of a real gourmand is of more consequence; and, as it has its origin in the belly, no one can doubt his sincerity.

In many places, a large dinner is a state affair; it is spoken of three months before hand, and it takes nearly as long to digest it after it is over.

Epicurean Parallel, &c.

[Adapted from Grimod de la Reynière's "Gourmand Madness."][22]
A celebrated gourmand, who was dining in company, where some profane
subjects, as they are called, were present,—namely, some young, sober
persons, were engaged in a discussion, the consequences of which brought
him to establish a parallel between women and good cheer. It may be readily
conceived that, in his capacity of a gourmand, he gave the preference to the
table. The following is the manner in which he undertook to establish and
prove his opinion. "Let us lay down the principles," says he; "you will agree
in the first place, gentlemen, that the pleasures which good cheer procures,
are those which are soonest known, latest relinquished, and which one may
taste the oftenest. Now, can you say as much of the others?

"Is there a woman, as handsome as you suppose her to be, even had she
the head of Mrs. A—, the majestic air of Mrs. B—, the enchanting graces of
Miss C—, the splendour, and killing embonpoint of Mrs. D—, the mouth
and smile of Miss E—, &c. who would be worth those admirable partridges,
the odour of which is superior to the perfumes of Arabia? Would you put
her upon a parallel with these pies made of the livers of geese and ducks, to
which the towns of Strasburgh, Toulouse, and Auch, owe the greater part
of their celebrity? What is she then by the side of Yorkshire hams, Epsom
sausages, Stilton, Gloucester and Cheshire cheeses, for which Old England is
so much renowned; and those morsels which have acquired so much glory
in the person of the hog?—or can you compare her with all the luxuries of
the table, brought far and near, from every quarter of the habitable globe.
Where, in fact, is the gourmand so depraved as to prefer a silly meagre beauty,
to those enormous and succulent rounds of English beef, which inundate
those who carve them, and which throw into a swoon those who eat them?
Incomparable pieces of roast beef! O the roast beef of Old England! It is
from your vast loins, the source of every vital principle and true sensation,
that the gourmand inhales his existence, the musician his talent, the lover
his tenderness, and the poet his creative genius![23]

Having drawn an endless comparison with every good thing, solid and
fluid, in this world, prepared by the cooks of England and New France, torri-
fied by the roasters of the London Tavern, carved, in fact, by British butlers,[24]
our gourmands call upon us to agree with him, that the enjoyments which
good cheer procure for a rich epicure, ought to be placed in the first rank; that,
quite differently prolonged than those which are tasted by breaking the sixth
commandment, they bring on neither languor, disgust, fear, nor remorse;
that the source or spring, whence they incessantly rise, never dries; that far
from enervating the constitution or weakening the brain, they become the
happy principle of firm health, brilliant ideas, and more vigorous sensations.

Thus, far from begetting regret, disposing to hypochondriasm, and ultimately rendering a man insupportable to himself, and to others, we are, on the contrary, indebted to them for that merry-making face, the distinctive mark of all the children of Comus—very different from the pale and squalid visage, the common mark of decrepit love, and dessicated manhood.

Such, in fine, was the discourse of our celebrated gourmand. We are not aware that he made many proselytes; but what we positively know is, that the next morning were reckoned in that society, more than *one* Ariana, and *five* or *six* indigestions.[25]

The Useless Sop; or, the Convalescent Gourmand Outwitted

[From Grimod de la Reynière's "The Useless Sop."][26]
Mons. De L. B., in his time, was the most illustrious gourmand in all Paris. He was exceedingly rich, and only had his appetite to satisfy, when he could find one. His house was abundantly stocked with every article of luxury that could be procured, far and near, for either love or money; in which he enjoyed himself with the most exquisite sensibility. But his wife, who no doubt was afraid of becoming a widow too soon, was incessantly opposing him in his various tastes, so that he was compelled, in order to luxuriate with ease and satisfaction, to shut himself up in a private room. At length he fell sick, and the first remedy which the physicians prescribe for a gourmand is abstinence. This was, for ours, the worst of all; and doubtless it would have been very differently observed by him, had he not been watched by his wife, who, having taken possession of all the keys, and established herself as a nurse, took him under her tutorship, in the same manner as any other person forced to keep his bed. The remedies operate, and our gourmand becomes convalescent; he is at length permitted to eat; and the physician who knew his weak side, scrupulously prescribed the quantum of food he was to eat; which, for the first time, consisted of a new laid egg, and one small morsel of bread for him to sop in it. Mons. de L. B. could heartily have wished that this egg had been laid by an ostrich, rather than a hen; but he made good this disparity by the sop of bread: he caused the longest loaf that could be formed in all Paris to be bought, so that his sop was about an ell in length,[27] and weighed nearly a pound. His wife was going to quarrel with him, about going against the doctor's orders; but what could she do, since he had followed the prescription to the letter. The egg was brought in, in grand style; the cloth spread upon his bed, and he got ready to dine, as one truly convalescent: but in sucking the white of the egg, he inhaled so strongly, that he swallowed the yolk at the same time!—an unfortunate accident—most deplorable precipitation! which rendered his sop entirely useless! so much so, that Madame de L. B. very gravely caused it to be taken away, with the shell of the egg; at the thought of which, our gourmand had nearly fallen sick again with despair.

The Cunning Capuchin

[From Grimod de la Reynière's "The Cunning Capucin."][28]
Some rather waggish young men wished one day to amuse themselves at the
expense of an old Capuchin friar. A nice roasted sucking pig was served up,
which they begged the friar to carve; and just as he was about to commence,
the most robust of the company spoke to the following effect, and said to
him: "My very reverend father, take care what you are going to do! for we
have made up our minds to treat you absolutely in the same manner as you
do the animal; and you may depend upon it, that if you cut one limb of the
sucking pig, that moment will you be deprived of one yourself." The friar,
without betraying the smallest symptom of fear, did to the pig, what people
usually do when they try the sweetness of poultry, and to see it is not turned,
or tainted; then addressing his young messmates, he said, "Gentlemen, I beg
you will now all do the same to me, in the terms of your threat; you see it
does not frighten me." Who was the greatest fool now? The knowing ones,
no doubt; and thus will be treated every one who attempts to make fun at
the expense of a gourmand.

Of Indigestions Occasioned by Inebriety, and Other Causes, &c.

[Partly adapted from Grimod de la Reynière's "On Digestion"; see this
volume, 11–12]
Like a young girl, who suffers herself to be seduced by some gay deceiver,
a guest who suffers from indigestion, is more to be pitied than blamed. In
short, those who are unfortunate enough, after having done homage to a
respectable meal, to find themselves, before having taken coffee, forced to
leave the table, independent of the sorrow they ought to feel, and to experience the accidents, more or less serious, which result from intemperance,
or rather from their want of method, in the manner of eating, are much to
be pitied. A skilful guest never gets intoxicated, or suffers from indigestion,
unless from some accidental cause, and independent of his will, such as a
bad habit of body.

Among the means of avoiding indigestion, there is one, quite simple;
namely, to eat very moderately of some dishes, and to know how to pay proper
respect to others. But this prescription has nothing caustic in it. In proposing
it, we assume the air of Doctor Sangrado,[29] in his government of Baratraria,
extending his long wand over each dish, which instantly disappears.

Do not imagine, my good readers, that we wish to preach you a sermon
on abstinence. On the contrary, this long lesson is intended to always secure
you an appetite, and to point out to you the means of never losing it; for we
do not write for those who, having no appetite, have it no less in their power

to satisfy it, but for those who, having always hunger at their command, do not know where to appease it. We shall limit ourselves here to trace out in a summary manner the art of eating well, and of digesting well, whenever an opportunity presents itself.

The means of avoiding indigestion are the result both of theory and practice. The first consist in examining well the nature of the food, and the strength of the stomach destined to receive it. It is in some measure the action of the one, and the reaction of the other, which constitute a good or bad digestion.

Besides, there are antipathies of the stomach, of which no account can be rendered; but you must keep an exact account in order not to expose this useful servant from receiving lodgers with which it cannot agree.

It has been said that a man at forty is either a fool or a physician; the meaning of which is, that the experience that he has acquired up to that time, ought to inform him whether or not the stomach stands in need of a heavy, a tenacious, or a light kind of nourishment—one of an aromatic, a vegetable, or animal nature. There are stomachs which must be ballasted at the same time they are fed; and those, honest deputies, sent yearly from Limoges to Paris, to build passages and palaces, will tell you that they prefer rye bread, because it *sticks* to the ribs.

A young, delicate lady, on the contrary, lives only on wings of poultry, and other dainty morsels; and the reason for this difference of regimen is founded on the different course of their lives. The one rises with the sun, fatigued by continual exercise, devours, at meal-time, which is impatiently expected, a coarse bread, watered by the sweat of his brow, and exhales a part of his digestion by means of the insensible perspiration: the other, sleeps till mid-day, and gets up weary with the very means of rest, and reposes herself from her past state of inaction by a new species of indolence; she neither knows the pleasures of fatigue, nor the delights of hunger; and even digestion itself, every thing, with her, is the result of art.

Do you wish then to prepare your digestion? Take a walk in dry weather, when exercise is indispensable with you; do not fatigue yourself; the fresh air, combined with loco-motion, will furnish you with muscular energy, and fortify the whole system, by giving it that oscillatory movement, which mixes and purifies the fluids, invigorates the solids, raises the appetite, and prepares it to be well satisfied. The celebrated Tronchin prescribed to the young noblemen of his day, to scrub their apartment, and more than one incurable indigestion yielded to this active recipe.

Such people have many means of taking exercise; tennis, billiards, riding, fencing, &c.; so have the poor, such as walking, running, dancing, skipping, and those connected with their trade or calling. Why then should not the rich and the poor make a temporary exchange, by which they would reciprocally be benefited?

Let the rich man relieve the wants of the poor, who will teach him the value of exercise. Would the former blush, indeed, to dig the earth which supports him, or to cut down and saw the wood that warms him? And if, after having, for his health and amusement, executed a part of the task of the indigent, who would repose himself by his side, pouring out big blessings upon him, if he were not to quit him without slipping a piece of money into his hand; he would soon acknowledge that he sat down to his dinner with that loyal appetite which always results from useful fatigue; at the same time he would be actuated with the pleasing recollection of having done a good action. Such, then, are the only means of avoiding indigestion. We shall now say something on the means of curing this modern bugbear.

Notwithstanding all the preceding precautions, it frequently happens, either from neglecting these rules, particular disposition, antipathy for certain meats, or, indeed, from excesses or the bad quality of the food, the stomach, too much distended, or tormented with cholic or remorse, can no longer re-act upon itself: a painful sense of oppression succeeds that hilarity which animated the coloured face of a guest who has sufficiently satisfied himself; the fumes of the viands excite nausea; wine itself, by means of which one endeavours to promote digestion, only inspires disgust; vapours arise from the over-heated stomach, and threaten a speedy eruption; the lava runs: it is now time to throw water on the flames; but take care how you use tea; this fatal and favourite potion (with the English in particular) sets the nerves on edge, and irritates the whole animal economy. Here it is the remedy you employ which aggravates the disease.

As regards intoxication, it would be a delicate subject indeed for us to handle, for the very simple reason that few people are really acquainted with its causes, effects, and results, which one is almost always disposed to confound with drunkenness.[30] If intoxication were to produce no other effect than that of depriving one momentarily of their reason, of exciting a temporary effervescence, and afterwards of provoking sleep, the inconvenience would be trifling; but serious accidents are the ordinary consequences of such a state. Not only does it absorb and attack all the intellectual faculties, but it paralyses the most solid physical qualities. The head becomes heavy, memory flies, the sight is troubled; the legs totter, the hands shake; an internal fire lacerates and devours them; they are incapacitated for any thing; they are plunged, as it were, into the most uncomfortable conditions that can be possibly imagined—they are, in short, completely paralysed both in body and mind: and God knows to what a pitiful plight such a condition may lead to after an excellent dinner, where many amiable ladies may be present. Guests never get fuddled!

We do not here mean to reprehend those little indulgences granted to the rosy god which, seldom permitted, reanimate the play of the system; but, their re-action only suits those vigorous stomachs whose energies are, at least, equal to those of the healthy labourer.

The ancients, who, in affairs of the kitchen, as in those of literature, in gluttony as in sobriety, have left us great examples and useful lessons, thought that the establishment of a *vomitorium* (or vomitory) entered into the plan of the places where they held their feasts, and it was not considered extraordinary, with this sensual people, to see a guest descend from his *triclinium* (or bed, where he lay and ate), to lighten his stomach, to gargle his mouth with perfumed water, and resume the sitting *ab ovo*. For us, cold parodists of these hot governors of nations, we are far from recommending any such culinary refinements.

If indigestion be only felt some hours after a meal, it is then more dangerous, because the work of digestion is stopped. It is in proportion to the advance this process has made, that we ought to decide whether or not an emetic ought to be given. An emetic, injudiciously prescribed here, might be attended with dangerous consequences, as well as an useless convulsion of the whole system. The essential point in this case is to accelerate the mechanical action of the stomach, and nothing adds more to its energy of dissolution than warm water—water alone; for if any other substance be added to this fluid, it loses, by acting upon it, a part of its property. After the first draught, second the dissolving action of the water by means of an aperient clyster, (we hope our readers will pardon the word, for the sake of its utility,) composed of a little common salt and linseed tea. On a little chicken broth, seasoned with cinnamon and a little orange-flower water, betake yourself to bed; and a renovating sleep, may happily close this disagreeable scene, both by the commotion it impresses upon the organism, and by the assumption of weakness and avidity which it leaves upon the unfortunate patient.

The subsequent regimen ought to be regulated by the accident; if, for instance, it has been caused by taking too much fish, or game, the patient should abstain from these articles for some time, and he ought to use that kind of food which influences the digestion of the first. It is thus that milk soup is the appropriate digestive of oysters, as a piece of good Gloucester cheese is that of fish, which, *en passant*, always stands in need, in order to be easily digested, to be associated with some more solid aliment; such, for example, as ham, in order, that we may finish the quotation as, we began it.

It is very frequently less owing to excess than to the quality of the food, which produces indigestion. One man shall eat ten times as much as another without any inconvenience; and another shall be greviously incommoded for having used a single substance which does not agree with him. It is for a gourmand to study the nature of his stomach, and to see that it be supplied with only homogeneous articles. Milk pottage, hot pastry, &c. which agree pretty generally with women, do not always succeed with robust feeders, who would digest an ox, and probably turn pale at the sight of a little blanc-manger.

But when, by repeated experience, you have a perfect knowledge of the caprices of your stomach, one may then fearlessly give way to the appetite. There is one essential difference between a gourmand and a voracious man. The former chews his food more and better; because the act of mastication is a real pleasure, and the longer the food remains on the palate the greater is the enjoyment. Again, mastication constitutes the first digestion; in this manner the saturated food reaches the gullet, and is fitter to undergo the subsequent processes which ought to assimilate a part of it with our proper substance.

It is necessary then to chew long and well; to divide the compact substances, such as tough meats, pie-crusts, &c. by mixing them frequently with good stale bread, to swallow only small mouthfuls, and quaff small draughts.[31] With these precautions one will rarely be incommoded, even after the largest and most solid dinner.

Moderate exercise (or at least a vertical position after a meal) is a good means of favouring and even of hastening digestion. Nothing can be more contrary to this disposition, than lolling in an arm-chair, and, particularly after dinner, to sit in a bent position, which, by compressing the viscera, must necessarily stop the work of digestion. For this reason, people who are obliged to write after a meal, would do well to stand instead of sit. It is also most essential to favour the heat of the stomach at that time, by securing it from external cold, which, in people of delicate health, is often enough to suspend its functions. A flannel waistcoat, which ought not to be inconsiderately relinquished when it has become habitual, is very beneficial to weak stomachs.

By adopting these precautions, one will be enabled to eat more and longer without any inconvenience—precisely what, above all other things, a gourmand ought to have most at heart; for a disease which requires several days of abstinence is, for him, more than any thing else, a truly sorrowful case; it is so much, in fact, taken from his existence; and whose existence is that which can be compared with a gourmand's? It is, upon earth, a true image of Mahomet's paradise.[32]

The pleasures of the table, when the stomach is debilitated, should not be so freely indulged in. The gourmand connoisseur will know how to lay a judicious and well-timed embargo on his appetite, by early relinquishing his seat, and not prolonging his banquet beyond the possibility of enjoyment. This, however, is not at all times an easy sacrifice—good old customs are not either soon abolished or restrained—a specimen of which may be gathered from the following lines:–

As wealth flow'd in, and plenty sprang from peace,
Good humour reign'd and pleasure found increase.
'Twas usual, then, the banquet to prolong
By music's charms and some delightful song:
When every youth in pleasing accents strove
To tell the stratagems and cares of love;
How some successful were, how others crost;
Then to the sparkling glass would give his toast:
Whose bloom did most in his opinion shine,
To relish both the music and the wine!

The Ultimatum; or, Chapter Last

A Trio: The Cook, the Author, and the Bookseller

The resemblance between cooks and authors has been started by several ingenious writers: and as there are continual variations in the culinary as well as the *literary arts*, new traits of similitude between them may be pointed out, from time to time, by means of a sagacious investigation, from the *garret* to the *kitchen*; that is, from the *author* to the *cook*.

Cooks are often *inflamed*; so are *authors*. Cooks sometimes burn *their fingers*; so do *authors*, especially when they take it in into their heads, engaged in a *hot service*, to *roast* a *prime minister*, and spit a *courtier*. Cooks *live upon the fat of the land*—here, indeed, the progress of resemblance is interrupted, as authors may think themselves very well off to get as much of *the lean of the land* as will just serve to support existence—Cooks, that is, *cooks of condition*, are perpetually employed in *disguising nature*; and by how many authors in this merry, miserable, and moping metropolis, is nature every day most absurdly, and abominably *disguised*?

Cooks generally garnish their dishes with *natural*, and authors decorate their dramas with *artificial* flowers. And yet, with all the pains which our literary cooks take to please the *public taste*, they find it extremely difficult to make certain fastidious *critics*, with very nice *palates*, heartily relish the *banquet* of the night. If all the *ingredients*, be they ever so well *mixed up*, are, upon the whole, not highly seasoned, the *composition is damned*, and the poor *garretteer*, perhaps, is doomed to sup with the *devil*, in the shape of a bailiff, watching for the fate of his farce.

Surely, of all the trades in which men are engaged to provide for themselves and their families a subsistence, undoubtedly that of a man of letters is the worst. His whole stock in trade is confined and huddled together within the narrow boundaries of his own head, and from thence he spins out his scanty materials, as spiders work their webs. The market he carries his work to, is always overstocked; and, consequently, he is frequently obliged to place his dependence in the generosity and magnanimity of his bookseller. This is not the case of the present times only. It has always been so. Homer, poor and blind, used to wander up and down the streets and squares, and repeat his verses to get bread. Plautus, the comic poet, got his livelihood by turning a mill; and it is within our recollection of a German count and a French baron being reduced to the humble necessity of turning a spit for the same purpose. Aldus Manitius was so poor, that he became insolvent, and was obliged to borrow money to transport his valuable library to Rome, where it was sent for. Arch-bishop Usher, and a multitude of literati, died poor. Agrippa breathed his last in a hospital; and Miguel Cervantes, the celebrated author of *Don Quixote*, is said to have died for want. Tasso was reduced so low as to entreat his cat, in a pretty sonnet, to lend him the light of her eyes in the night for him to compose his verses by; and the condition of our countryman, Dryden, is sufficiently well known. A scholar, therefore, who depends on his writings for his support, is the arrant slave of the public, whose understandings are enlightened, and, in the present instance, whose palates are roused, from the miserable wrecks of his brain, and the yearnings of his empty bowels. It must, nevertheless, be confessed, that the poverty of scholars frequently arises from their attaching themselves solely to one particular branch of science, which, perhaps, few but themselves understand, and which still less they are inclined to read. Hence, a literary man should, in some measure, resemble a good cook, who, knowing the palates of his different masters, seasons their dishes accordingly, cautiously avoiding either to pall the appetite or clog the stomach. Such a literary cook, perhaps, might succeed something better than many of his predecessors.

It is a common complaint amongst the learned, that booksellers love to print trifling productions in preference to works of real value. They should not, however, complain of the booksellers, but of their readers; for, if the publishing of valuable books was as lucrative as that of those insignificant scrawls, no doubt the booksellers would prefer good works to bad ones.

The greatest admirer of a great writer is hardly ever one whose admiration pleases most. He is generally some friend, of no extraordinary parts himself, whose zeal, and, sometimes, his vanity, make him enthusiastic in admiring what he does not always *taste* or understand. But, indeed, the greatest admirer of a great writer is, commonly, himself. He has a greater interest than any other person in such admiration; to which interest is a powerful seducer. He sees, perhaps, better than the alert critic or connoisseur, his own defects, and failings; but then he does not judge of them as they do; and to see and judge are, in every case, widely different, more especially when one's own faults are under consideration. In counting them right we wish them wrong; and thus it is that self-love is at once both enlightened and indulgent. Too much wit, say the people of taste, is a fault in a work; and perhaps they are in the right; but it is remarkable that many of these people of *taste* have themselves but very little wit. *De gustibus non est disputandum*, to say the least. The artificial reputation which some authors acquire, first with the *"trade"* (a cant phrase to denote the booksellers), then with the public, in spite of his ignorance in the most essential sciences; the numerous errors and inconsistencies in their writings and character; and the loathsome turgidity and quaintness both of their temper and style, is one of those paradoxes which are exhibited as it were to puzzle us in every stage of history. The *trade* is not always deceived; for it is common to hear the most sensible men (*raræ aves*) among the booksellers exclaim, "What, in the name of goodness, is there in such a one? he is a mere gatherer of other people's stuff—a collector of shreds and patches! but the book sells, certainly—that's all we want—." Thus the cook may dress up his finest flavoured dishes, and thus they may go down; but whose are the ingredients, whose are the art that deceives the palate and pleases the eye? They are not his own—they nevertheless swallow well, and better than if they had been of his pure invention. Books, then, like dishes, are of various complexions and dimensions, suited to as various tastes and caprices. The imitation of the one is compatible with the resemblance of the other: and happy is the cook, happy the author, and most happy the bookseller, when they can mutually and sympathetically put their hands in their pockets, and calmly say

Opus Coronat Finis.

Notes

1. See introduction to this volume, xxix.
2. The second London edition of the book retains the same content, but changes the title to focus on what seems to have been the more popular portion of the book: *Apician Morsels; or, Tales of the Table, Kitchen, and Larder: With Reflections on the Dietic Productions of Early Writers; on The Customs of the Romans in Eating and Drinking; on Table Ceremonies, and Rules of Conviviality and Good Breeding; with Select Epicurean Precepts, Gourmand Maxims and Medicines, &c. &c* (1834).
3. See Joseph Berchoux, *La gastronomie; ou l'homme des champs à table*, 2nd ed (Paris: Ciguet et Michaud, 1803), 17–22.
4. *Catalogue of the First Portion of the Beckford Library, removed from Hamilton Palace. Which will be sold by Auction and by Messrs. Southeby, Wilkinson, and Hodge, Auctioneers* (London: Dryden Press, 1882).
5. A. D. Macquin. *Tabella Cibaria; The Bill of Fare: A Latin Poem, Implicitly Translated and Fully Explained in Copious and Interesting Notes, Relating to the Pleasures of Gastronomy, and the Mysterious Art of Cookery* (London: Sherwood, Neely, Jones, 1820), iii; Howard B. Gotlieb, *William Beckford of Fonthill: Writer, Traveller, Collector, Caliph (1760-1844); A Brief Narrative and Catalogue of an Exhibition to Mark the Two Hundredth Anniversary of Beckford's Birth* (New Haven, CT: Yale University Library, 1960), 49.

6. See, for example, Richard Chenevix, "Review of *Voyage of H.M. Ship Alceste along the Coast of Corea, to the Island of Lewchew; with an Account of Her Subsequent Shipwreck,* by John Mc Leod, 2nd ed. (London: J. Murray, 1818) and *Naufrage de la fregate la meduse…* by Alexandre Corréard and J. B. Henri Savigny, 2nd ed. (Paris, 1818)," in *The Edinburgh Review* 30 (1818): 388–406. In Advertisement of October 26, 1831 to Richard Chenevix's *An Essay Upon National Character: Being an Inquiry into some of the Principal Causes which Contribute to Form the Characters of Nations in the State of Civilisation* (London: James Duncan, 1832), Thoms Pery Knox writes that "he had written several articles in the Edinburgh and Quarterly Reviews, on the comparative state of England and France, which attracted much attention at the time of their appearance." His *Essay Upon National Character* also focuses on a comparison of the British and French empires of his day, concluding that "while they are great in trifles, they remain, generally, little in what is great" (1: 505).

7. Richard Chenevix, "Cookery," *The Edinburgh Review* (March 1821): 43–62 (47 and 62).

8. See p. 49 of a clever little work by Dr. [John] Stevenson, on *Nervous Diseases. [Religious Revivals in Relation to Nervous and Mental Diseases]* [Humelbergius]

9. A person who whitens walls; a bleacher or whitesmith.

10. Knives and forks make a curious article in Tom Coriat, who says, his familiar friends scrupled not to call him Furcifer, for using a fork. *Fines Morrison,* in his travels, advises leaving off the fork in England, as being a piece of refinement or foppery. The following is the passage:—"Also, I admonish him, after his return home, to renew his old friendships: and, as soldiers in a good commonwealth, when the warre is ended, to return to the works of their calling, (like the followers of Mercury as well as of Mars,) so that he returning home, lay aside the spoone and fork of Italy, the affected gestures of France, and all strange apparell: yea, even those manners, which with good judgement he allows, if they be disagreeable to his countrymen." [Humelbergius]

11. Dr. King, in his "Art of Cookery," in a letter to Dr. Lister, observes, "I could wish Dr. Wotton, in the next edition of his modern learning, would shew us how much we are improved since Dr. Heylin's time, and tell us the original of modern learning, with which young heirs are suffered to mangle their own pudding; as likewise of silver and gold knives, brought in with the dessert, for carving jellies and orange butter; and the indispensable necessity of a silver knife at the sideboard, to mingle salad with, as is, with great learning, made out in a treatise, called *acetaria,* concerning dressing of salads—a noble work! but I transgress; and yet, pardon me, good Doctor, I had almost forgot a thing that I would have not done for the world, it is so remarkable. I think I may be positive from this verse of Juvenal, where he speaks of Egyptians —
    Porrum et cepe nefas violare, et frangere morsu,
    that it was a sacrilege to chop a leak, or bite an onion: nay, I believe, that it amounts to a demonstration, that Pharaoh-Necho could have had no true *lenten porridge,* nor any carrier's sauce to his mutton; the true receipt of making which sauce I have from an ancient Ms. remaining at the Bull Inn in Bishopsgate-street, which runs thus:
    "'Take seven spoonfuls of spring water, slice two onions of moderate size, into a large saucer, and put in as much salt as you can hold at thrice betwixt your fore-finger and thumb, if large, and serve it up. *Probatum est.* Hobson, Carrier to the University of Cambridge.'
    "The effigies of that worthy person remain still at the Inn; and I dare say, not only Hobson, but old Brick, and many others of that musical and delightful profession, would rather have been labourers at the Pyramids with that *regale,* than to have reigned at Memphis, and have been debarred of it." [Humelbergius]

12. Humelbergius is quoting from Thomas Coryate, *Coryat's Crudities; hastily gobled up in five moneths travells in France, Savoy, Italy, Rhetia commonly called the Grisons country, Helvetia alias Switzerland, some parts of high Germany and the Netherlands; newly digested in the hungry aire of Odcombe in the county of Somerset, and now dispersed to the nourishment of the travelling members of this kingdome,* first published in 1611.

13. Grimod de la Reynière, "Du déjeuner," *Almanach des gourmands,* 2: 41–48. Grimod doesn't attribute the rising importance of breakfast to class specifically, though he does see it as a result of changing patterns of life in postrevolutionary, bourgeois France. For him, the dinner remains the most important meal (indeed, event) of the day, for which our appetite must be maintained. Grimod also includes longer sections on chocolate and the chemists who prepare it. Basically, he claims that while apothecaries could be trusted to make fine chocolate, the contemporary popularity of chocolate has made it available to less trustworthy vendors. He asserts that there

are some chocolates in Paris that have everything except cocoa (a criticism that has been in the news recently as the European Union has forced France to accept impure chocolates made with vegetable oils, to the despair of many gourmands). A close translation is provided by August von Kotzebue (1761–1819), *Travels from Berlin, through Switzerland to Paris, in the Year 1804* (London, Printed for R. Phillips, 1804), 85–90. John Pinkerton also offers commentary (with a paragraph lifted from Grimod) in his *Recollections of Paris in the Years 1802-3-4-5*, 2 vols. (London: Longman, Hurst, Rees, & Orme, 1806), 2: 195–216 (201).

14. Horace drank his fill when he saw the Maenads; also quoted by Grimod, *Almanach*, 2: 44.

15. Grimod, "Du Diner," *Almanach,* 2: 48–56.

16. A blackleg is a swindler.

17. This is a fairly exact translation of Grimod de la Reynière, "Des devoirs respectifs des convives," in *Almanach,* 2: 273–80.

18. It should, however, be remarked, that it is not consistent with politeness to force or excite others to drink; this privilege belongs only to the master of the table; and if he does not do it, it is to be supposed that he has reason for dispensing with it. It is the same with respect to punch, wine, coffee, liqueurs, &c., if they be upon the table; in any other place, as in the salon, these are served, without distinction, to all who present their cup; and, as regards liqueurs, every one helps himself as he likes. [Humelbergius]

19. Grimod adds a section here on aperitifs, and at the end on singing at table. The final paragraph of Humelbergius as printed here is original.

20. Grimod de la Reynière, "Maximes et réflexions nutritives," in *Almanach*, 2: 121–25; Humelbergius's translation is, in general, very exact, though he eliminates Grimod's list of French locales.

21. A close friend of Grimod de la Reynière's, who claimed that he wrote four quarto volumes of rules of conduct. Grimod often cited these works, but nothing of Aze's own writing survives; see chap. 1, note 38.

22. Grimod, "Folie gourmande," in *Almanach,* 127. Another fairly faithful translation, except in places where Humelbergius cuts Grimod's list of French locales, changes local French names to more universal initials or global names, and continental place names to English ones.

23. "The things we eat by various juice controul / The narrowness or largeness of our soul. / Onions will make ev'n heirs or widows weep, / The tender lettuce brings on softer sleep; / Eat beef or pie-crust, if you'd serious be; / Your shell-fish raises Venus from the sea; / For Nature, that inclines to ill or good, / Still nourishes our passions by our food." [Humelbergius; not in Grimod]

24. This passage does not occur in Grimod.

25. Ariana is a tattle-tale character in Eliza Haywood's *The Female Spectator* (1744–46), who in Book XIII determines to expose a case of adultery; see the edition by Patricia Meyer Spacks (New York: Oxford University Press, 1999), esp. 147–54 The sixth commandment mentioned above is "Thou shalt not commit adultery."

26. A faithful rendering of Grimod, "La Mouillette inutile," *Almanach*, 2: 136–38.

27. A measure of length that varies in different countries; the English "ell" is 45 inches.

28. A faithful rendering of Grimod, "Le Capucin subtil," *Almanach*, 2: 142–43.

29. A misattribution: Doctor Pedro Resio de Agüero, not Sangrado, is the character described in this episode of *Don Quijote*; see Miguel de Cervantes Saavedra, *Don Quixote of La Mancha*, trans. Walter Starkie (London: Macmillan, 1957), 855–57.

30. We hope not to promote this vice, by the information our readers have received relative to the "Imperial Marine Tincture," which absolutely, in the course of a few minutes, disintoxicates any individual labouring under the excessive influence of spirits. [Humelbergius]

31. "King Hardicanute, midst Dane and Saxon stout, / Caroused on nut-brown ale, and din'd on *grout*; / Which dish its pristine honour still retains, / And when each prince is crown'd, in splendour reigns." *The Art of Cookery.* [Humelbergius]

32. This and the previous four paragraphs are copied from Grimod de la Reynière, "On Indigestion"; see this volume, 11–12.

7

Thomas Walker (1784–1836)

"Aristology, or the Art of Dining," from The Original (1835)

Introduction

"We know not a more amusing and racy volume than 'The Original,' by Mr. Walker," writes one reviewer in 1844.[1] Although "Aristology, or the Art of Dining" was not the only subject treated in his volume (which also contained related essays on the "Art of Attaining High Health"), it was by far the most popular. Walker himself, a barrister and lifelong bachelor, began publication of his weekly *The Original* in May 1835, which he continued for twenty-nine numbers through December of that same year. As the son of a Manchester manufacturer, he favored a simple style of dining. His editor Felix Summerly (Sir Henry Cole) observes that he likely would have learned simplicity in a city whose typical businessman prior to 1800 was also "a grocer and cheesemonger almost living in kitchen, parlour, and all."[2]

Ultimately, Walker submitted to the fate of those who would combine the literary and gastronomical arts. In the final issue of *The Original*, he explains that "London living and authorship do not go on well together. My writings have latterly drawn upon me more numerous and cordial invitations than usual, which is a gratifying sign of approbation, but of somewhat ruinous consequences. Conviviality, though without what is ordinarily called excess, during the greater part of the week, and hard fagging during the remainder,[3] with a sacrifice of exercise and sleep, must tell; ... If one could but succeed in uniting the advantages of solitude with those of society, it would be glorious." Walker intended to diet, sleep, and exercise his way back to health, but he died a few months later. His essays on dining were collected and published

Figure 25 Untitled [Title Page], by Bertall, from Eugène Briffault, *Paris à Table* (1846).

separately, and *The Original* continued to be republished through the Victorian era.

The following selections are from Henry Renshaw's 1836 edition of *The Original*, to which text heads have been added to assist the reader.

From *Aristology; or the Art of Dining* (1835)

According to the Lexicons, the Greek for dinner is Ariston, and therefore, for the convenience of the terms, and without entering into any inquiry, critical or antiquarian, I call the art of dining Aristology, and those who study it, Aristologists. The maxim that practice makes perfect, does not apply to our daily habits; for, so far as they are concerned, we are ordinarily content with the standard of mediocrity, or something rather below. Where study is not absolutely necessary, it is by most people altogether dispensed with; but it is only by an union of study and practice, that we can attain any thing like perfection. Anybody can dine, but very few know how to dine, so as to ensure the greatest quantity of health and enjoyment—indeed many people contrive to destroy their health and as to enjoyment, I shudder when I think how often I have been doomed to only a solemn mockery of it; how often I have sat in durance stately, to go through the ceremony of dinner, the essence of which is to be without ceremony, and how often in this land of liberty I have felt myself a slave!

There are three kinds of dinners—solitary dinners, everyday social dinners, and set dinners; all three involving the consideration of cheer, and the last two of society also. Solitary dinners, I think, ought to be avoided as much as possible, because solitude tends to produce thought, and thought tends to the suspension of the digestive powers. When, however, dining alone is necessary, the mind should be disposed to cheerfulness by a previous interval of relaxation from whatever has seriously occupied the attention, and by directing it to some agreeable object. As contentment ought to be an accompaniment to every meal, punctuality is essential, and the diner and the dinner should be ready at the same time. A chief maxim in dining with comfort is, to have what you want, when you want it. It is ruinous to have to wait for first one thing and then another, and to have the little additions brought, when what they belong to is half or entirely finished. To avoid this a little foresight is good, and, by way of instance, it is sound practical philosophy to have mustard upon the table before the arrival of toasted cheese. This very omission has caused as many small vexations in the world, as would by this time make a mountain of misery. Indeed I recommend an habitual consideration of what adjuncts will be required to the main matters; and I think an attention to this on the part of females, might often be preventive of sour looks and cross words, and their anti-conjugal consequences. There are not only the usual adjuncts, but to those who have any thing of a genius for dinners, little additions will sometimes suggest themselves, which give a sort of poetry to a repast, and please the palate, to the promotion of health. As our senses were made for our enjoyment, and as the vast variety of good things in the world were designed for the same end, it seems a sort of impiety not to put them to their best uses, provided it does not cause us to neglect higher considerations. The different products of the different seasons, and of the different parts of the earth, afford endless proofs of bounty, which it is as unreasonable to reject, as it is to abuse. It has happened, that those who have made the gratification of the appetite a study, have generally done so to excess, and to the exclusion of nobler pursuits; whilst, on the other hand, such study has been held to be incompatible with moral refinement and elevation. But there is a happy mean, and as upon the due regulation of the appetite assuredly depends our physical well-being, and upon that, in a great measure, our mental energies, it seems to me that the subject is worthy of attention, for reasons of more importance than is ordinarily supposed. I shall continue this article in my next number.

[*On Attendance*]

There is in the art of dining a matter of special importance,—I mean attendance—the real end of which is to do that for you, which you cannot so well do for yourself. Unfortunately this end is generally lost sight of, and the effect of attendance is to prevent you from doing that, which you could do much better for yourself. The cause of this perversion is to be found in the practice and example of the rich and ostentatious, who constantly keep up a sort of war establishment, or establishment adapted to extraordinary, instead of ordinary occasions, and the consequence is, that, like all potentates who follow the same policy, they never really taste the sweets of peace; they are in a constant state of invasion by their own troops. It is a rule at dinners not to allow you to do any thing for yourself, and I have never been able to understand how even salt, except it be from some superstition, has so long maintained its place on table. I am always in dread, that, like the rest of its fellows, it will be banished to the sideboard, to be had only on special application. I am rather a bold man at table, and set form very much at defiance, so that if a salad happens to be within my reach, I make no scruple to take it to me; but the moment I am espied, it is nipped up from the most convenient into the most inconvenient position. That such absurdity should exist amongst rational beings, and in a civilized country, is extraordinary! See a small party with a dish of fish at each end of the table, and four silver covers unmeaningly staring at the sides, whilst every thing pertaining to the fish comes, even with the best attendance, provokingly lagging, one thing after another, so that contentment is out of the question; and all this is done under pretence that it is the most convenient plan. This is an utter fallacy. The only convenient plan is to have every thing actually upon the table that is wanted at the same time, and nothing else; as for example, for a party of eight, turbot and salmon, with doubles of each of the adjuncts, lobster sauce, cucumber, young potatoes, cayenne, and Chili vinegar, and let the guests assist one another, which, with such an arrangement, they could do with perfect ease. This is undisturbed and visible comfort. I am speaking now only with reference to small parties. As to large ones, they have long been to me scenes of despair in the way of convivial enjoyment. A system of simple attendance would induce a system of simple dinners, which are the only dinners to be desired. The present system I consider strongly tainted with barbarism and vulgarity, and far removed from real and refined enjoyment. As tables are now arranged, one is never at peace from an arm continually taking off, or setting on a side dish, or reaching over to a wine-cooler in the centre. Then comes the more laborious changing of courses, with the leanings right and left, to admit a host of dishes, that are set on only to be taken off again, after being declined in succession by each of the guests, to whom they are handed round. Yet this is fashion, and not to be departed from. With respect to wine, it is often offered, when not wanted; and when wanted, is perhaps not to be had till long waited for. It is dreary to observe two guests, glass in hand, waiting the butler's leisure to be able to take wine together, and then perchance being helped in despair to what they did not ask for; and it is still more dreary to be one of the two yourself. How different, where you can put your hand upon a decanter at the moment you want it! I could enlarge upon, and particularize these miseries at great length; but they must be only too familiar to those who dine out, and those who do not, may congratulate themselves on their escape. I have been speaking hitherto of attendance in its most perfect state; but then comes the greater inconvenience, and the monstrous absurdity of the same forms with inadequate establishments. Those who are overwhelmed with an establishment, are, as it were, obliged in self defence to devise work for their attendants, whilst those, who have no such reason, ape an example, which under the most appropriate circumstances is a state of restraint and discomfort, but which, when followed merely for fashion's sake, becomes absolutely intolerable. I remember once receiving a severe frown from a lady at the head of her table, next to whom I was sitting, because I offered to take some fish from her, to which she had helped me, instead of waiting till it could be handed to me by her one servant; and she was not deficient, either in sense, or good breeding, but when people give into such follies they know no mean. It is one of the evils of the present day, that every body strives after the same dull style—so that where comfort might be expected, it is often least to be found. State, without the machinery of state, is of all states the worst. In conclusion of this part of my subject, I will observe, that I think the affluent would render themselves and their country an essential service, if they were to fall into the simple, refined style of living, discarding every thing incompatible with real enjoyment; and I believe, that if the history of overgrown luxury were traced, it has always had its origin from the vulgar-rich—the very last class worthy of imitation. Although I think a reduction of establishment would often conduce to the enjoyment of life, I am very far from wishing to see any class curtailed in their means of earning their bread; but it appears to me that the rich might easily find more profitable and agreeable modes of employing the industrious, than in ministering to pomp and parade.

[*On Ornamentation*]

In order to bring the dinner system to perfection according to my idea, it would be necessary to have a room contrived on the best possible plan for eight persons, as the greatest number. I almost think six even more desirable than eight; but beyond eight, as far as my experience goes, there is always a division into parties, or a partial languor, or sort of paralysis either of the extremities, or centre, which has more or less effect upon the whole. For complete enjoyment a company ought to be One; sympathizing and drawing together, listening and talking in due proportions—no monopolist, nor any ciphers. With the best arrangements much will depend upon the chief of the feast giving the tone, and keeping it up. Panlus Æmilius, who was the most successful general, and best entertainer of his time, seems to have understood this well; for he said that it required the same sort of spirit to manage a banquet as a battle, with this difference, that the one should be made as pleasant to friends, and the other as formidable to enemies, as possible. I often think of this excellent saying at large dinner parties, where the master and mistress preside as if they were the humblest of the guests, or as if they were overwhelmed with anxiety respecting their cumbrous and pleasure-destroying arrangements. They appear not to have the most distant idea of the duties of commanders, and instead of bringing their troops regularly into action, they leave the whole army in reserve. They should at least now and then address each of their guests by name, and, if possible, say something by which it may be guessed who and what each person is. I have witnessed some ridiculous and almost incredible instances of these defects. I remember once at a large dinner-party at a great house, the lion of the day not being called out once, and going away without the majority of the company suspecting who he was. On a similar occasion, as a very distinguished man left the drawing-room, a scarcely less distinguished lady inquired who that gentleman was, who had been so long talking to her,—though she had sat opposite to him at dinner. It appears to me that nothing can be better contrived to defeat its legitimate end than a large dinner-party in the London season—sixteen, for instance. The names of the guests are generally so announced that it is difficult to hear them, and in the earlier part of the year, the assembling takes place in such obscurity, that it is impossible to see. Then there is often a tedious and stupifying interval of waiting, caused perhaps by some affected fashionable, some important politician, or some gorgeously-decked matron, or it may be by some culinary accident. At last comes the formal business of descending into the dining-room, where the blaze of light produces by degrees sundry recognitions; but many a slight acquaintance is prevented from being renewed by the chilling mode of assembling. In the long days the light is more favourable, but the waiting is generally more tedious, and half the guests are perhaps leaving the park, when they ought to be sitting down to dinner. At table, intercourse is prevented as much as possible by a huge centrepiece of plate and flowers, which cuts off about one-half the company from the other, and some very awkward mistakes have taken place in consequence, from guests having made personal observations upon those who were actually opposite to them. It seems strange that people should be invited, to be hidden from one another. Besides the centrepiece, there are usually massive branches, to assist in interrupting communication; and perhaps you are placed between two persons with whom you are not acquainted, and have no community of interest to induce you to become so, for in the present overgrown state of society, a new acquaintance, except for some particular reason, is an encumbrance to be avoided. When the company is arranged, then comes the perpetual motion of the attendants, the perpetual declining of what you do not want, and the perpetual waiting for what you do, or a silent resignation to your fate. To desire a potato, and to see the dish handed to your next neighbour, and taking its course in a direction from you, round an immense table, with occasional retrograde movements, and digressions, is one of the unsatisfactory occurrences, which frequently take place; but perhaps the most distressing incident in a grand dinner is, to be asked to take champagne, and, after much delay, to see the butler extract the bottle from a cooler, and hold it nearly parallel to the horizon, in order to calculate how much he is to put into the first glass to leave any for the second. To relieve him and yourself from the chilling difficulty, the only alternative is to change your mind, and prefer sherry, which, under the circumstances, has rather an awkward effect. These and an infinity of minor evils are constantly experienced amidst the greatest displays, and they have from sad experience made me come to the conclusion, that a combination of state and calculation is the horror of horrors. Some good bread and cheese, and a jug of ale, comfortably set before me, and heartily given, are heaven on earth in comparison. I must not omit to mention, amongst other obstacles to sociability, the present excessive breadth of fashionable tables for the purpose of holding, first, the cumbrous ornaments and lights before spoken of; secondly, in some cases, the dessert, at the same time with the side dishes; and lastly, each person's cover with its appurtenances; so that to speak across the table, and through the intervening objects, is so inconvenient, as to be nearly impracticable. To crown all, is the ignorance of what you have to eat, and the impossibility of duly regulating your appetite. To be sure, in many particulars you may form a tolerably accurate guess, as that, at one season, there will be partridges in the third course, and at another, pigeons, in dull routine. No wonder that such a system produces many a dreary pause, in spite of every effort to the contrary, and that one is obliged, in self-defence, to crumble bread, sip wine, look at the paintings, if there are any, or if there are not, blazon the arms on the plates, or, lastly, retreat into oneself in despair, as I have often and often done. When dinner is over, there is no peace till each dish in the dessert has made its circuit, after which the wine moves languidly round two or three times, and then settles for the rest of the evening, and coffee and small talk finish the heartless affair. I do not mean to say that such dinner parties as I have been describing have not frequently many redeeming circumstances. Good breeding, wit, talent, information, and every species of agreeable quality are to be met with there; but I think these would appear to much greater advantage, and much oftener, under a more simple and unrestrained system. After curiosity has been satisfied, and experience ripened, I imagine most people retire from the majority of formal dinners rather wearied than repaid, and that a feeling of real enjoyment is the exception, and not the rule. In the long run, there is no compensation for ease; and ease is not to be found in state and superabundance, but in having what you want, when you want it, and with no temptation to excess. The legitimate objects of dinner are to refresh the body, to please the palate, and to raise the social humour to the highest point; but these objects, so far from being studied, in general are not even thought of, and display and an adherence to fashion are their meagre substitutes. Hence it is, that gentlemen ordinarily understand what pertains to dinner-giving so much better than ladies, and that bachelors' feasts are so popular. Gentlemen keep more in view the real ends, whereas ladies think principally of display and ornament, of form and ceremony—not all, for some have excellent notions of taste and comfort; and the cultivation of them would seem to be the peculiar province of the sex, as one of the chief features in household management. There is one female failing in respect to dinners, which I cannot help here noticing, and that is, a very inconvenient love of garnish, and flowers, either natural, or cut in turnips and carrots, and stuck on dishes, so as greatly to impede carving and helping. This is the true barbarian principle of ornament, and is in no way distinguishable from the "untutored Indian's" fondness for feathers and shells.[4] In both cases the ornament is an encumbrance, and has no relation to the matter on which it is placed. But there is a still worse practice, and that is pouring sauce over certain dishes to prevent them from looking too plain, as parsley and butter, or white sauce over boiled chickens. I cannot distinguish this taste from that of the Hottentot besmearing himself with grease, or the Indian with red paint, who, I suppose, have both the same reason for their practice. To my mind, good meat well cooked, the plainer it looks the better it looks, and it certainly is better with the accessories kept separate till used, unless they form a part of the dish. In my next number I shall give my ideas of what dinners ought to be.

[*The Table, the Dinner, and the Mode of Conducting It*]

Suppose a party of eight assembled in a room and at a table arranged according to what I have said in this and the preceding number, to a dinner either plain or costly, and, in the latter case, either of few dishes or of considerable variety; I would have every dish served in succession, with its proper accompaniments, and between each dish there should be a short interval, to be filled up with conversation and wine, so as to prolong the repast as much as possible, without inducing excess, and to give time to the digestive powers. By means of such intervals, time would be given to the cook, and to the attendants, so that nothing would have to wait for the guests, nor would the guests have to wait for any thing, due preparation being made for each dish before its arrival, without bustle or omissions. In dinners of few dishes they ought to be of rather a substantial kind; but, when composed of variety, the dishes should be of a lighter nature, and in the French style. It must be confessed that a French dinner, when well dressed, is extremely attractive, and, from the lightness felt after a great variety of dishes, it cannot be unwholesome; though I do not think, from my own experience and observation, that the French mode of cookery is so favourable to physical power as the English. If I might have my choice, I should adopt the simple English style for my regular diet, diversifying it occasionally with the more complicated French style. Although I like, as a rule, to abstain from much variety at the same meal, I think it both wholesome and agreeable to vary the food on different days, both as to the materials and the mode of dressing them. The palate is better pleased, and the digestion more active, and the food, I believe, assimilates in a greater degree with the system. The productions of the different seasons and of different climates point out to us unerringly that it is proper to vary our food; and one good general rule I take to be, to select those things which are most in season, and to abandon them as soon as they begin to deteriorate in quality. Most people mistake the doctrine of variety in their mode of living. They have great variety at the same meals, and a great sameness at different meals. Let me here mention, what I forgot before, that after the dinner on Christmas day we drank mulled claret—an excellent thing, and very suitable to the season. These agreeable varieties are never met with, or even thought of, in the formal routine of society, though they contribute much, when appropriately devised, to the enjoyment of a party, and they admit scope for invention. I think, in general, there is far too little attention paid to varying the mode of dining according to the temperature of the seasons. Summer dinners are for the most part as heavy and as hot as those in winter, and the consequence is, they are frequently very oppressive, both in themselves and from their effect on the room. In hot weather they ought to be light, and of a cooling nature, and accompanied with agreeable beverages well iced, rather than with pure wine, especially of the stronger kinds. I cannot think there is any danger from such diet to those who use it moderately. The danger, I apprehend, lies in excess from the pleasure felt in allaying thirst and heat. The season, in which nature produces fruit and vegetables in the greatest perfection and abundance, is surely that in which they ought to be most used. During the summer that cholera was the most prevalent, I sometimes dined upon pickled salmon, salad, and cider, and nothing else; and I always found they agreed with me perfectly, besides being very agreeable. Probably, if I had taken them in addition to more substantial food, so as to overload my appetite, it might have been otherwise, and yet that course would have been adopted by many people by way of precaution. In hot weather the chief thing to be aimed at is, to produce a light and cool feeling, both by the management of the room and the nature of the repast. In winter, warmth and substantial diet afford the most satisfaction. In damp weather, when the digestion is the weakest, the diet ought to be most moderate in quantity, but rather of a warm and stimulating nature; and in bracing weather, I think plain substantial food the most appropriate. By studying to suit the repast to the temperature, the greatest satisfaction may be given at the cheapest rate. Iced water is often more coveted than the richest wine.

One of the greatest luxuries, to my mind, in dining, is to be able to command plenty of good vegetables, well served up. But this is a luxury vainly hoped for at set parties. The vegetables are made to figure in a very secondary way, except, indeed, whilst they are considered as great delicacies, which is generally before they are at their best, and then, like other delicacies, they are introduced after the appetite has been satisfied; and the manner of handing vegetables round, is most unsatisfactory and uncertain. Excellent potatoes, smoking hot, and accompanied by melted butter of the first quality, would alone stamp merit on any dinner; but they are as rare on state occasions, so served, as if they were of the cost of pearls. Every body of genuine taste is delighted with a display of vegetables of superior order; and if great attention was bestowed upon that part of dinners instead of upon the many other dishes, dinners would be at once more wholesome and more satisfactory to the palate, and often less expensive. I have observed, that whenever the vegetables are distinguished for their excellence, the dinner is always particularly enjoyed; and if they were served, as I have already recommended, with each dish, as they are most appropriate and fresh from the dressing, it would be a great improvement on the present style. With some meats something of the kind is practised, as peas with ducks, and beans with bacon, and such combinations are generally favourites; but the system might be much extended, and with great advantage, by due attention. With respect to variety of vegetables, I think the same rule applies as to other dishes. I would not have many sorts on the same occasion, but would study appropriateness and particular excellence. There is something very refreshing in the mere look of fine vegetables, and the entrance of a well-dressed dish of meat, properly accompanied by them and all their adjuncts, would excite a disposition to enjoyment much greater than can the unmeaning and unconnected courses now placed before our eyes. This is a matter of study and combination, and a field for genius. It is a reasonable object of attention, inasmuch as it is conducive to real enjoyment, and has nothing to do with mere display. In French cookery vegetables meet with attention much more proportionate to their importance than in ours, and appropriateness in serving them is much more studied.

I think I have now said all I had to say respecting dinners. My object has been to point out what I consider to be the true philosophy, and to put people upon the right scent of what ought to be done, rather than to particularize it. Those who wish to succeed, can only do so to much extent, by first getting into the right course, and then thinking for themselves, with such aids as they can derive from observation, and the best treatises on cookery. The chief point to be aimed at, is to acquire a habit of thinking only of the real object of dining, and to discard all wish for state and display in a matter which concerns our daily enjoyment of health and pleasure. I consider my observations on the art of dining as part of what I had to say on attainment of high health, from the necessary dependence of our health upon the judicious and satisfactory manner in which we make our principal meal. I think the art of dining, properly understood, is especially worthy the attention of females of all classes, according to their respective means. It comes peculiarly within the province of domestic economy, and is indeed one of its most important features. But females ought to be especially on their guard, in this essential affair, not to divert their views from realities to show, to which they have a strong propensity. There are many things, in which they can indulge their taste for ornament, provided it is not carried too far, with advantage to themselves and to the satisfaction of others; but in the article of dinners it is misplaced, because destructive of something of much more importance; and the realities, when in full force, have quite sufficient attractions without any attempt to heighten them by "foreign aid." In conformity with my dislike to show or display in every thing connected with dinners, I prefer a service of plain white ware—the French manufacture, I believe, or an imitation of it—to plate or ornamented china. There is a simplicity in white ware, and an appearance of cleanliness and purity, which are to me particularly pleasing, besides which it is, I always think, indicative of a proper feeling, and a due attention in the right direction. As to desserts I am no great friend to them. I enjoy fruit much more at any other time of the day, and at any other meal; besides which, I think they are unwholesome from being unnecessary. At any rate, I would have them in great moderation, and confined to a few kinds of ripe fruit. Preserved fruits are in my opinion cloying after dinner, and I believe injurious to the digestion of a substantial meal, and confectionary I think still worse. Desserts are made instruments of show as much or more than dinners, and though, unlike dinners, they cannot well be spoiled by it, yet it makes them a perpetual source of temptation to excess. It is most unphilosophical to set things before people, and to tell them they need not take them unless they please. Contentment and safety mainly depend upon having nothing before us, except what we ought to take.

[*On Invitations*]

. . . I must add a word or two to what I have said respecting the mode of giving invitations, upon which, I think, more depends than at first sight appears. If a formal invitation on a large card requesting the honour, &c., at three weeks' notice, were to be received, and the party should prove to be a small familiar one to a simple dinner, however good, some disappointment would almost unavoidably be felt, partly because the mind would have been made up to something different, and partly on account of the more laboured preparation. It is in general, I think, advisable to give some idea to the invited what it is they are to expect, if there is to be any thing out of the common way, either as to company or repast; at any rate, it is expedient not to mislead, as some people are very much in the habit of doing, and then receiving their company with an apology, which throws a damp over the affair in the very outset. Now, instead of a formal invitation, let us suppose one to such a dinner as the undermentioned, couched in these words—"Can you dine with me to-morrow?—I shall have herrings, hashed mutton, and cranberry tart. My fishmonger sends me word herrings are just in perfection, and I have some delicious mutton, in hashing which I shall direct my cook to exercise all her art. I intend the party not to exceed six, and, observe, we shall sit down to table at half-past seven. I am asking as follows." Now I should greatly prefer such an invitation to a formal one in general terms and I suppose most other people would do the same. It would show an intentness and right understanding on the matter in hand, from which the happiest results might be expected, and the guests would go filled with the most favourable predisposi-tions, which is starting at an advantage; for at parties in general, it requires some time before they can be raised to any thing like the proper tone of fellowship. Such a style puts dinner-giving within almost everybody's reach, and would induce a constant flow of easy hospitality, instead of a system of formal parties, "few and far between." The same mode is equally desirable in invitations to simple dinners of the most costly, or rarest dishes, and in some respects more so, as the anticipations would be more vivid. I have heard it frequently objected to the simple style, that some of the guests, when there is little or no choice, may not be able to make a dinner; but this objection is entirely obviated by particularizing, as above, what the dinner is to consist of, and those whom it does not please, can then decline the invitation. A simple dinner, well served, to a party of a similarity of taste, cannot fail to have peculiar success; it makes perfect the union. These snug little parties, I must confess, have very much the air of being confined to bachelor ones, but I think them equally applicable to a mixture of the sexes. Ladies are very apt to suppose that men enjoy themselves the most when they are not present. They are in a great measure right, but for a wrong reason. It is not that men prefer their own to a mixture of female society, but that females delight in a number of observances, and in forms, upon some of which I have already touched, and upon a certain display and undeviating order, which conspire to destroy that enjoyment, which they seem to think they are debarred from. The fault is their own. If they will study my doctrines, and fall a little into the herring-and-hashed-mutton system, they will soon find a difference in their favour. In their management of dinners, let them think only of what contributes to real enjoyment. Such a system will afford them plenty of scope for the display of their taste in realities, instead of in vanities, which have no charms for men in the article of conviviality.

[*On Fires*]

As the season for fires is approaching, or rather, from the wet weather, is arrived, I must make an observation or two upon that important head. A cheerful fire is our household sun, which I, for one, like to have ever shining upon me, especially in the coming months of November and December, when the contrast between that and the external fogs and mud is most striking and agreeable. A good fire is the next best substitute for a summer sun, and, as our summer sun is none of the brightest, we are wise to make the most of its successor. An Englishman's fireside has, time out of mind, been proverbial; and it shows something of a degenerate spirit not to keep up its glories. There is an unfortunate race, who labour under a constant pyrophobia, or dread of fire, and who cannot bear the sight of it, or even the feel, except from a distance, or through a screen. When we have to do with such, we must compromise as well as we can between comfort and consideration; but I am speaking to the real enjoyers of the goods of life, without any morbid infirmity about them. A bright, lively fire I reckon a most excellent dinner companion, and in proper fire weather I would always have it, if I may so say, one of the party. For instance, two or three at each side of the table, one at the top, and the fire at the bottom, with the lights on the mantelpiece; but then, to have this disposition in perfection, the room should be something after the plan I have recommended in my seventeenth number. Under such circumstances, I think if melancholy herself were one of the guests, she could not but forget her state. A fire is an auxiliary at dinner, which diffuses its genial influence, without causing distraction. As Shakspeare says of beauty, "it is the sun that maketh all things shine;" and as Dryden sings after Horace,

> With well-heap'd logs dissolve the cold,
> And feed the genial hearth with fires;
> Produce the wine that makes us bold,
> And sprightly wit and love inspires.[5]

It might be supposed, from the way in which the fire is ordinarily treated during dinner, that it was a disagreeable object, or a common enemy. One or more persons are made to turn their backs upon it, and in that position screens are obliged to be added to prevent fainting. This is a perverse mode of proceeding, arising partly from the ill adaptation of dining-rooms to their use, partly from the custom of crowding tables, and partly from the risk of oppressiveness, where there are large numbers and overloaded dinners, so that in this, as in most instances, one abuse engenders another, and the expediency of adhering to a rational system is clearly manifested. We are the creatures of habit, and too seldom think of changing according to circumstances; it was but the other day I dined where the top of the table was unoccupied; but though the weather was cold and wet, the master of the house maintained his position at the bottom with his back to the fire, protected by a screen. If I could have wheeled him round, "the winter of my discontent" would have been made "glorious summer," and I should have dined with complete satisfaction.[6]

The conservancy of fires ought principally to fall within the superintendence of the female part of a family, because they are least seldom out of the way, and it is a subject of very great importance in the maintenance of domestic comfort, especially where the males, either from pleasure or business, are exposed to the vicissitudes of weather. Let anyone call to mind the difference between two houses where good and bad fires are kept. To the labouring classes, a good fire at meals is the greatest source of health and enjoyment; and at public-houses a cheerful blaze seen through the windows, is a bait well understood to catch the labourer returning from his work to a comfortless home. If he once gets

—planted unco right,
Fast by an ingle, bleezing finely,[7]

there is no chance of his quitting, till, like Tam O'Shanter, he is compelled by necessity. The essential quality of a fire is to be bright without being too hot, and the best and quickest mode of restoring a neglected fire is to stir out the ashes, and with the tongs to fill up the spaces between the bars with cinders. If carefully done, it is surprising how soon this process will produce an effective and glowing fire. . . .

After my desultory manner I must here mention an instance of barbaric ornament I witnessed a short time since at a dinner which, substantially, was excellent. I had to carve a tongue, and found my operations somewhat impeded by a couple of ranunculuses stuck into it, sculptured, one in turnip, and the other in carrot. It was surrounded by a thin layer of spinach, studded with small stars, also cut in carrot. What have ranunculuses and stars to do with tongue and spinach? To my mind, if they had been on separate and neighbouring dishes, and unadorned, it would have been much more to the purpose.

[*On Wines*]

At length I am come to the consideration of that important accompaniment to dinner—wine, in the management of which there is ordinarily a lamentable want of judgment, or rather a total absence of it. Besides an actual want of judgment, there is frequently a parsimonious calculation on one hand, or an ostentatious profusion and mixture on the other, both destructive, in their different ways, of true enjoyment. The art in using wine is to produce the greatest possible quantity of present gladness, without any future depression. To this end, a certain degree of simplicity is essential, with due attention to seasons and kinds of food, and particularly to the rate of filling the glass. Too many sorts of wines confuse the palate, and derange digestion. The stronger wines, unless very sparingly used, are apt to heat in hot weather, and the smaller kinds are unsatisfactory when it is cold. The rate at which to take wine is a matter of great nicety and importance, and depends upon different circumstances at different times. Care and observation can alone enable any one to succeed in this point. The same quantity of wine, drunk judiciously or injudiciously, will produce the best or the worst effects. Drinking too quick is much more to be avoided than drinking too slow. The former is positively, the latter negatively, evil. Drinking too quick, confuses both the stomach and the brain; drinking too slow, disappoints them. After long fasting, begin slowly and after a solid foundation, and quicken by degrees. After exhaustion from other causes than fasting, reverse this order. Small wines may be drunk with less caution as to rate than the fuller bodied. As soon as the spirits are a little raised, slacken the pace, contrary to the usual practice, which is to quicken it. When the proper point of elevation is attained, so use the glass as just to keep there, whereby enjoyment is prolonged without alloy. The moment the palate begins to pall, leave off. Continuation after that will soon produce a renewed desire, the gratification of which is pernicious. This state is rather an unfitness for leaving off than a fitness for going on. In respect to simplicity, I think four kinds of wine the very utmost ever to be taken at one time, and with observance of what wines go well together; as sherry, champagne, port, and claret, but they should be drunk in uniform order, and not first one and then another, and then back again, which is a senseless and pernicious confusion. For my own part, I rather like one kind of wine at a time, or at most two; and I think more is lost than gained by variety. I should lay down the same rules as to wines, as I have already done as to meats; that is, simplicity on the same day, and variety on different days. [...]

What I have hitherto said has been with a view principally to individual guidance in the use of wine, though much of it may be applied to the management of parties. In the management of parties, so far as relates to wine, judgment, liberality, attention, and courage are necessary; and calculation, inattention, ostentation, profusion, and excess, are the vices to be guarded against. I always take for granted, that whatever wine is produced, it is to be good of its kind. Judgment is necessary in knowing what wines are suitable to the season, the food, and the description of guests; in what order to serve them, at what rate to drink, and when to stop. Liberality is necessary to furnish promptly and cheerfully the requisite supply; attention is necessary to execute what the judgment suggests; and courage is necessary to keep the erring, either from ignorance or refractoriness, in the right path, and to stop at the right point. The master of a feast should be master in deed as well as in name, and on his judicious and confident control depends for the most part real convivial enjoyment; but he should govern rather by imperceptible influence than by any outward demonstration, or appearance of interference. He should set the wine in circulation at the earliest fitting moment, for want of attention to which there is often a flagging at the outset. He should go on rather briskly at first, and should then contrive to regulate its pace according to the spirits of the party. He should cause the wines to be served in their proper order, and should preserve that order as much as in him lies, both by his own example, and by good-humoured recommendation. He should let his guests know what he intends, so that they may have an opportunity of regulating themselves accordingly; as if he thinks proper to produce only a certain quantity of any particular wine, he should say so. Uncertainty is fatal to convivial ease, and the reintroduction of any kind of wine, after other wines have intervened, is specially to be avoided. This error arises either from want of courage in allowing a violation of propriety, or from a calculation that there would be enough, when there turns out not to be enough, and then hesitating to supply the deficiency at the proper moment. He should be liberal as long as liberality is beneficial, and as soon as he perceives that the proper point to stop at is arrived, he should fearlessly act upon his perception. There is a liberal, hearty manner, which prevents suspicion, and enables the possessor to exercise his judgment not only without offence, but with approbation. Calculation, however studiously concealed, sheds a baneful influence over conviviality, which nothing can counteract. Inattention causes things either to go on wrong, or not to go on at all. Ostentation excites disgust or contempt, and destroys enjoyment for the sake of display, by introducing variety without reference to reason. Profusion produces the same effect from ignorance, or mistaken liberality. There may be excess without variety, though it is not so probable. It is much more often the result of want of courage in the master of the feast, than of inclination on the part of the guests, and good government in the beginning is the surest guarantee of a temperate termination. In what I have said, I have supposed the giver of an entertainment to have means at his command, but where it is not so, the plainest wines, provided they are sound, and are heartily and judiciously given according to the rules I have laid down, cannot fail to give satisfaction to the reasonable, and more satisfaction too than the most costly with the many drawbacks which usually accompany them. They are for the most part exposed to the same fate that I have already described to await delicacies in food; that is, they are so mixed up and encumbered with other things, as to be deprived of their relish, and reduced to the level of their inferiors, or even below. It is to be wished that those who are not in the way of giving costly wines, would never attempt it; because they are only putting themselves to inconvenience, and their guests to greater. It is a very serious tax upon one's palate and veracity, to be obliged to drink and pronounce upon compounds, with names to which they have not the most remote pretension. What I have said heretofore about dinners applies equally to wines. Let people keep to their own proper style, and endeavour to excel in what is within their ordinary reach. A little extra attention and a little extra expense are then productive of satisfactory results, and they are sure to please others without any sacrifice of what is due to themselves.

Notes

1. "Cookery Review," *The Foreign Quarterly Review* 33 (1844): 181–212 (203).
2. Felix Summerly, "Preface," *Aristology or the Art of Dining* by Thomas Walker (London: George Bell, 1881), v.
3. In this instance, to fag means to do something wearying; to work hard, labour, strain, or toil.

4. This phrase derives from Alexander Pope's *Essay on Man*, I.99.
5. William Shakespeare, *Love's Labor's Lost* 4.3.242, as printed with slight variation in *The Riverside Shakespeare*, 197; Dryden's lines are a translation of Horace *Ode*, 1.9; see Horatius Flaccus, Quintus, *Carminum Libri IV*, ed. T. E. Page (London: Macmillan, 1959), 10.
6. Quotations from the opening lines of Shakespeare's *Richard III*.
7. Robert Burns, "Tam O'Shanter: A Tale," 38–39, as printed with punctuation variation in *Poems and Songs*, ed. James Kinsley (London: Oxford University Press, 1969), 444.

8
William Makepeace Thackeray
(1811–68)

"Dining-Out Snobs" and "Dinner-Giving Snobs, Further Considered,"
from The Book of Snobs (New York, 1848)

Introduction

The Victorian novelist, William "Snob" Makepeace Thackeray, gave his best portrait of the snobbish high-society life of Regency England in *Vanity Fair*, published serially from 1847 through 1848. Around this time, he also contributed fictional sketches to the popular magazine *Punch*, satirizing a wide assortment of snobs: Royal Snobs, Great City Snobs, Military Snobs, Clerical Snobs, University Snobs, Literary Snobs, Irish Snobs, Party-Giving Snobs, Continental Snobs, Country Snobs, Club Snobs, Political Snobs (including Conservative, Whig, and Radical Snobs), among others. These were collected into his 1848 *The Book of Snobs*. Claiming that both "Stinginess is snobbish" and "Ostentation is snobbish," Thackeray's narrator addresses himself familiarly to "Jones," a hearty, John-Bullish character with no patience for culinary ostentation. Jones also makes a brief appearance in *Vanity Fair*, where he is depicted scribbling at a table in his dining club, "rather flushed with his joint of mutton and half-pint of wine."[1] A fictional reflection of the first-person author of *The Book of Snobs*, he finds Victorian dinner parties, and their middle-class mentality of keeping-up-with-the-Joneses, downright snobbish.

The essays reproduced here are from the fourteenth of twenty-six volumes of *The Works of William Makepeace Thackeray* (1915). Three woodcuts by the contemporary caricaturist George Cruikshank (1792–1878), which Thackeray

Figure 26 Untitled, by George Cruikshank, from William Clarke, *Three Courses and a Dessert* (1830). Courtesy of the author.

considered "some of the best designs of our artist," accompany the text (figs. 26, 27, 28). They were originally published in *Three Courses and a Dessert* (1830) by William Clarke, who modestly claimed that "the *plates* were sure to please even if the dishes failed to do so."[2]

From *The Book of Snobs* (1847)

Dining-Out Snobs

In England Dinner-giving Snobs occupy a very important place in society, and the task of describing them is tremendous. There was a time in my life when the consciousness of having eaten a man's salt rendered me dumb regarding his demerits, I thought it a wicked act and a breach of hospitality to speak ill of him.

But why should a saddle-of-mutton blind you, or a turbot and lobster-sauce shut your mouth for ever? With advancing age, men see their duties more clearly. I am not to be hoodwinked any longer by a slice of venison, be it so fat; and as for being dumb on account of turbot lobster-sauce—of course I am; good manners ordain that I should be so, until I have swallowed the compound—but not afterwards; directly the victuals are discussed, and John takes away the plate, my tongue begins to wag. Does not yours, if you have a pleasant neighbour?—a lovely creature, say, of some five-and-thirty, whose daughters have not yet quite come out—they are the best talkers. As for your young misses, they are only put about the table to look at—like the flowers in the centre-piece. Their blushing youth and natural modesty preclude them from that easy, confidential, conversational *abandon* which forms the delight of the intercourse with their dear mothers. It is to these, if he would prosper in his profession, that the Dining-out Snob should address himself. Suppose you sit next to one of these, how pleasant it is, in the intervals of the banquet, actually to abuse the victuals and the giver of the entertainment! It's twice as *piquant* to make fun of a man under his very nose.

"What *is* a Dinner-giving Snob?" some innocent youth, who is not *repandu* in the world, may ask—or some simple reader who has not the benefits of London experience.

My dear sir, I will show you—not all, for that is impossible—but several kinds of Dinner-giving Snobs. For instance, suppose you, in the middle rank of life, accustomed to Mutton, roast on Tuesday, cold on Wednesday, hashed on Thursday, &c., with small means and a small establishment, choose to waste the former and set the latter topsy-turvy by giving entertainments unnaturally costly—you come into the Dinner-giving Snob class at once. Suppose you get in cheap-made dishes from the pastrycook's, and hire a couple of green-grocers, or carpet-beaters, to figure as footmen, dismissing honest Molly, who waits on common days, and bedizening your table (ordinarily ornamented with willow-pattern crockery) with twopenny-halfpenny Birmingham plate. Suppose you pretend to be richer and grander than you ought to be—you are a Dinner-giving Snob. And oh, I tremble to think how many and many a one will read this!

A man who entertains in this way—and, alas, how few do not!—is like a fellow who would borrow his neighbour's coat to make a show in, or a lady who flaunts in the diamonds from next door—a humbug, in a word, and amongst the Snobs he must be set down.

A man who goes out of his natural sphere of society to ask Lords, Generals, Aldermen, and other persons of fashion, but is niggardly of his hospitality towards his own equals, is a Dinner-giving Snob. My dear friend, Jack Tuft-hunt, for example, knows *one* Lord whom he met at a watering-place: old Lord Mumble, who is as toothless as a three-months-old baby, and as mum as an undertaker, and as dull as—well, we will not particularise. Tufthunt never has a dinner now but you see this solemn old toothless patrician at the right-hand of Mrs. Tufthunt —Tufthunt is a Dinner-giving Snob.

Old Livermore, old Soy, old Chutney, the East Indian Director, old Cutler, the Surgeon, &c.,—that society of old fogies, in fine, who give each other dinners round and round, and dine for the mere purpose of guttling—these, again, are Dinner-giving Snobs.

Again, my friend Lady MacScrew, who has three grenadier flunkeys in lace round the table, and serves up a scrag-of-mutton on silver, and dribbles you out bad sherry and port by thimblefuls, is a Dinner-giving Snob of the other sort; and I confess, for my part, I would rather dine with old Livermore or old Soy than with her Ladyship.

Stinginess is snobbish. Ostentation is snobbish. Too great profusion is snobbish. Tuft-hunting is snobbish. But I own there are people more snobbish than all those whose defects are above mentioned: viz., those individuals who can, and don't give dinners at all. The man without hospitality shall never sit *sub iisdem trabibus* with *me*. Let the sordid wretch go mumble his bone alone!

What, again, is true hospitality? Alas, my dear friends and brother Snobs! how little do we meet of it after all! Are the motives *pure* which induce your friends to ask you to dinner? This has often come across me. Does your entertainer want something from you? For instance, I am not of a suspicious turn; but it *is* a fact that when Hookey is bringing out a new work, he asks the critics all round to dinner; that when Walker has got his picture ready for the Exhibition, he somehow grows exceedingly hospitable, and has his friends of the press to a quiet cutlet and a glass of Sillery.[3] Old Hunks, the miser, who died lately (leaving his money to his housekeeper), lived many years on the fat of the land, by simply taking down, at all his friends', the names and Christian names *of all the children*. But though you may have your own opinion about the hospitality of your acquaintants; and though men who ask you from sordid motives are most decidedly Dinner-giving Snobs, it is best not to inquire into their motives too keenly. Be not too curious about the mouth of a gift-horse. After all, a man does not intend to insult you by asking you to dinner.

Though, for that matter, I know some characters about town who actually consider themselves injured and insulted if the dinner or the company is not to their liking. There is Guttleton, who dines at home off a shilling's-worth of beef from the cookshop, but if he is asked to dine at a house where there are not pease at the end of May, or cucumbers in March along with the turbot, thinks himself insulted by being invited. "Good Ged!" says he, "what the deuce do the Forkers mean by asking *me* to a family dinner? I can get mutton at home"; or "What infernal impertinence it is of the Spooners to get *entrees* from the pastrycook's, and fancy that *I* am to be deceived with their stories about their French cook!" Then, again, there is Jack Puddington—I saw that honest fellow t'other day quite in a rage, because, as chance would have it, Sir John Carver asked him to meet the very same party he had met at Colonel Cramley's the day before, and he had not got up a new set of stories to entertain them. Poor Dinner-giving Snobs! you don't know what small thanks you get for all your pains and money! How we Dining-out Snobs sneer at your cookery, and pooh-pooh your old hock, and are incredulous about your four-and-sixpenny champagne, and know that the side-dishes of to-day are réchauffés from the dinner of yesterday, and mark how certain dishes are whisked off the table untasted, so that they may figure at the banquet to-morrow. Whenever, for my part, I see the head man particularly anxious to *escamoter* a fricandeau or a blanc-mange, I always call out, and insist upon massacring it with a spoon. All this sort of conduct makes one popular with the Dinner-giving Snob. One friend of mine, I know, has made a prodigious sensation in good society, by announcing àpropos of certain dishes when offered to him, that he never eats aspic except at Lord Tittup's, and that Lady Jiminy's *chef* is the only man in London who knows how to dress—Filet en *serpenteau*—or Suprême de *volaille* aux truffes.

Dinner-Giving Snobs Further Considered.

If my friends would but follow the present prevailing fashion, I think they ought to give me a testimonial for the paper on Dinner-giving Snobs, which I am now writing. What do you say now to a handsome comfortable din-ner-service of plate (*not* including plates, for I hold silver plates to be sheer wantonness, and would almost as soon think of silver teacups), a couple of neat teapots, a coffee-pot, trays, &c., with a little inscription to my wife, Mrs.

Figure 27 Untitled, by George Cruikshank, from William Clarke, *Three Courses and a Dessert* (1830). Courtesy of the author.

Snob; and a half-score of silver tankards for the little Snoblings, to glitter on the homely table where they partake of their quotidian mutton?

If I had my way, and my plans could be carried out, dinner-giving would increase as much on the one hand as dinner-giving Snobbishness would diminish: – to my mind the most amiable part of the work lately published by my esteemed friend (if upon a very brief acquaintance he will allow me to call him so), Alexis Soyer, the regenerator—what he (in his noble style) would call: the most succulent, savoury, and elegant passages—are in those which relate, not to the grand banquets and ceremonial dinners, but to his "dinners at home."[4]

The "dinner at home" ought to be the centre of the whole system of dinner-giving. Your usual style of meal—that is, plenteous, comfortable, and in its perfection—should be that to which you welcome your friends, as it is that of which you partake yourself.

For, towards what woman in the world do I entertain a higher regard than towards the beloved partner of my existence, Mrs. Snob? Who should have a greater place in my affections than her six brothers (three or four of whom we are pretty sure will favour us with their company at seven o'clock), or her angelic mother, my own valued mother-in-law?—for whom, finally, would I wish to cater more generously than for your very humble servant, the present writer? Now, nobody supposes that the Birmingham plate is had out, the disguised carpet-beaters introduced to the exclusion of the neat parlour-maid, the miserable *entrées* from the pastrycook's ordered in, and the children packed off (as it is supposed) to the nursery, but really only to the staircase, down which they slide during the dinner-time, waylaying the dishes as they come out, and fingering the round bumps on the jellies, and the forced-meat balls in the soup,—nobody, I say, supposes that a dinner at home is characterized by the horrible ceremony, the foolish makeshifts, the mean pomp and ostentation which distinguish our banquets on grand field-days.

Such a notion is monstrous. I would as soon think of having my dearest Bessy sitting opposite me in a turban and bird of paradise, and showing her jolly mottled arms out of blond sleeves in her famous red satin gown: ay, or of having Mr. Toole every day, in a white waistcoat, at my back, shouting, "Silence *faw* the chair!"

Now, if this be the case; if the Brummagem-plate pomp and the processions of disguised footmen are odious and foolish in everyday life, why not always? Why should Jones and I, who are in the middle rank, alter the modes of our being to assume an éclat which does not belong to us—to entertain our friends, who (if we are worth anything, and honest fellows at bottom,) are men of the middle rank too, who are not in the least deceived by our temporary splendour, and who play off exactly the same absurd trick upon us when they ask us to dine?

If it be pleasant to dine with your friends, as all persons with good stomachs and kindly hearts will, I presume, allow it to be, it is better to dine twice than to dine once. It is impossible for men of small means to be continually spending five-and-twenty or thirty shillings on each friend who sits down to their table. People dine for less. I myself have seen, at my favourite Club (the Senior United Service), His Grace the Duke of Wellington quite contented with the joint, one-and-three, and half-pint of sherry wine, nine; and if his Grace, why not you and I?

This rule I have made, and found the benefit of. Whenever I ask a couple of Dukes and a Marquis or so to dine with me, I set them down to a piece of beef, or a leg-of-mutton and trimmings. The grandees thank you for this simplicity, and appreciate the same. My dear Jones, ask any of those whom you have the honour of knowing, if such be not the case.

I am far from wishing that their Graces should treat me in a similar fashion. Splendour is a part of their station, as decent comfort (let us trust), of yours and mine. Fate has comfortably appointed gold plate for some, and has bidden others contentedly to wear the willow-pattern. And being perfectly contented (indeed humbly thankful—for look around, O Jones, and see the myriads who are not so fortunate,) to wear honest linen, while magnificos of the world are adorned with cambric and point-lace, surely we ought to hold as miserable, envious fools, those wretched Beaux Tibbs's of society, who sport a lace dickey, and nothing besides,—the poor silly jays, who trail a peacock's feather behind them, and think to simulate the gorgeous bird whose nature it is to strut on palace-terraces, and to flaunt his magnificent fan-tail in the sunshine!

The jays with peacocks' feathers are the Snobs of this world: and never, since the days of Aesop, were they more numerous in any land than they are at present in this free country.

How does this most ancient apologue apply to the subject in hand—the Dinner-giving Snob? The imitation of the great is universal in this city, from the palaces of Kensingtonia and Belgravia, even to the remotest corner of Brunswick Square. Peacocks' feathers are stuck in the tails of most families. Scarce one of us domestic birds but imitates the lanky, pavonine strut, and shrill, genteel scream. O you misguided Dinner-giving Snobs, think how much pleasure you lose, and how much mischief you do with your absurd grandeurs and hypocrisies! You stuff each other with unnatural forced-meats, and entertain each other to the ruin of friendship (let alone health) and the destruction of hospitality and good-fellowship—you, who but for peacock's tail might chatter away so much at your ease, and be so jovial and happy!

When a man goes into a great set company of Dinner-giving and Dinner-receiving Snobs, if he has a philosophical turn of mind, he will consider what a huge humbug the whole affair is: the dishes, and the drink, and the servants, and the plate, and the host and hostess, and the conversation, and the company,—the philosopher included.

The host is smiling, and hob-nobbing, and talking up and down the table; but a prey to secret terrors and anxieties, the wines he has brought up from the cellar should prove insufficient; lest a corked bottle should destroy his calculations; or our friend the carpet-beater, making some *bévue*, should disclose his real quality greengrocer, and show that he is not the family butler.

The hostess is smiling resolutely through all the courses, smiling through her agony; though her heart is in the kitchen, and she is speculating with terror lest be any disaster there. If the *soufflé* should collapse, or if Wiggins does not send the ices in time—she feels as if she would commit suicide—that smiling, jolly woman!

The children upstairs are yelling, as their maid is crimping their miserable ringlets with hot tongs, tearing Miss Emmy's hair out by the roots, or scrubbing Miss Polly's dumpy nose with mottled soap till the little wretch screams herself into fits. The young males of the family are employed, as we have stated, in piratical exploits upon the landing-place.

Figure 28   Untitled, by George Cruikshank, from William Clarke, *Three Courses and a Dessert* (1830). Courtesy of the author.

The servants are not servants, but the before-mentioned retail trades-men.

The plate is not plate, but a mere shiny Birmingham lacquer; and so is the hospitality, and everything else.

The talk is Birmingham talk. The wag of the party, with bitterness in his heart, having just quitted his laundress, who is dunning him for her bill, is firing off good stories; and the opposition wag is furious that he cannot get an innings. Jawkins, the great conversationalist, is scornful and indignant with the pair of them, because he is kept out of court. Young Muscadel, that cheap dandy, is talking Fashion, and Almack's out of the *Morning Post*, and disgusting his neighbour, Mrs. Fox, who reflects that she has never been there. The widow is vexed out of patience, because her daughter Maria has got a place beside young Cambric, the penniless curate, and not by Colonel Goldmore, the rich widower from India. The Doctor's wife is sulky, because she has not been led out before the barrister's lady; old Doctor Cork is grumbling at the wine, and Guttleton sneering at the cookery.

And to think that all these people might be so happy, and easy, and friendly, were they brought together in a natural unpretentious way, and but for an unhappy passion for peacocks' feathers in England. Gentle shades of Marat and Robespierre! when I see how all the honesty of society is corrupted among us by the miserable fashion-worship, I feel as angry as Mrs. Fox just mentioned, and ready to order a general *battue* of peacocks.

Notes

1. William Makepeace Thackeray, *The Works of William Makepeace Thackeray*, 26 vols. (New York: C. L. Bowman, 1915), 1: 8–9.
2. Thackeray also considered the text of *Three Courses and a Dessert* to be "some of the most amusing tales in our language." Robert L. Patten, "Introduction," *George Cruikshank: A Revaluation*, ed. Robert L. Patten (Princeton, NJ: Princeton University Press, 1974), 8.
3. A high-class wine produced in and around the village of Sillery in Champagne.
4. Alexis Soyer's *The Gastronomic Regenerator* (1846) is a collection of two thousand elaborate dishes based on the Reform Club's recipes aimed at kitchens of the wealthy. Soyer also wrote *Charitable Cookery, or The Poor Man's Regenerator* (1847); *The Modern Housewife, or Ménagère* (1849); *A Shilling Cookery for the People* (1855). In the mid-nineteenth century, he was the most famous chef of his time in Britain. Born in France in 1809, he left Paris in 1830 and joined service with the Duke of Cambridge; from 1837 to 1850 he cooked at the Reform Club. During the 1847 Irish famine, he took a portable kitchen to Dublin and fed thousands every day. In 1855 he went to Crimea to improve hospital food and introduce his field kitchen.

9

The Alderman (Pseudonym)

The Knife and Fork, Laid By The "Alderman." Founded on the Culinary Principles Advocated by A. Soyer, Ude, Savarin, and Other Celebrated Professors (London, 1849).

Introduction

This strange little volume, illustrated by Joseph Kenny Meadows (1790–1874) who was a close friend of gourmand-writers such as Leigh Hunt, Douglas Jerrold, Charles Dickens, and William Thackeray, is dedicated to the united aldermen or "Corporation of London." These "Enlightened Epicures," as the author (a fellow alderman) calls them, were famous for their annual banquet held in London on the Lord Mayor's Day. They are described as "men of enlarged stomachs" and "discerning palates" who "will greet with warmth any work bearing upon a subject of such deep national import as that of gastronomy." Predicting the downfall of more traditional art forms, the Alderman claims that all "must now succumb to the growing and absorbing demand for a gastronomic era." He predicts that in this new age "a gentleman will not be known by the fashion of his dress, but by the capacity of his stomach." This superannuated author promises to devote the rest of his days "to the dissemination of sound gastronomic principles," counting on the support of his fellow aldermen to safeguard the British Constitution through "the provision of plenty of victuals, and the diffusion of the knowledge of how to cook them in a manner worthy of the age in which we live to eat." The volume also contains the author's "Gastronomic Rambles about London," based on Grimod de la Reynière's "Itinéraire nutritif, ou promenade d'un Gourmand dans divers quartiers de Paris" featured regularly in the *Almanach des gourmands.*

Figure 29 Frontispiece, by Kenny Meadows, from *The Knife and Fork for 1849*.

The material below is from the original London edition.

From *The Knife and Fork* (1849)

The Alderman's Hints to Gastronomic Students: On Taking People as They Are

In the early years of an epicure's life, he has to experience many sore trials—trials which require the most courageous palate to overcome them. It is no easy task to battle against an adverse fate. Every man cannot smile upon a cold shoulder, or swallow a detestable hash without an expression of disgust. It requires a certain degree of moral courage to endure what domestic circles call "a make-shift." Therefore, I shall be at some pains to warn the student against "taking people as they are." I say briefly, do no such thing. If your company be worth having, (and the company of an ordinary epicure is never tedious)—it is worth a decent entertainment. I am fully aware that it requires no ordinary tact to avoid, systematically, invitations to take people as they are; but I am convinced, on the other hand, that experience and study will enable a man to avoid these social nuisances, without giving offence to anybody. Study and observation will accomplish miracles, depend upon it. I give these hints to the rising generation, because I am thoroughly certain that the next generation will be one of epicures. The present tendency of the age goes to prove this. Do not the Ministers already acknowledge the importance of gastronomy, by holding an annual whitebait dinner? Does not the Speaker of the House of Commons, with a sagacity not often to be found in a Government official, give his annual dinner at the beginning of the season? Does not Her Most Gracious Majesty pay graceful tribute to gastronomy, by celebrating still imaginary anniversaries with splendid festivals? Do not the Corporation of London usher in their new Lord Mayors with prodigious feasts? And abroad, do we not hear of the Spanish Isabella's wonderful love of eating? Yes, it cannot be denied, the gastronomic age is dawning upon us; we are on the eve of a glorious future—that will worship Savarin devoutly. Therefore it behoves the youth of the present age to pay strict attention to the elements of gastronomy—to cultivate as far as they are able what has been too long trifled with, or altogether neglected, viz., the palate. I say this emphatically, and as a most necessary preliminary to a sound course of education—avoid taking people as they are.

Intimate friends are the barbarians who will desire you so to take them. They will tell you that they do not look upon you as a stranger—that you will have whatever there may be in the house—in short, that they regard you as one of the family, and will treat you accordingly; that is to say, pay you less attention than any other visitor—make bold to put a knuckle bone before you, and give you the weaker cups of tea. They've known you too long to make any ceremony before you, therefore your host composes himself to sleep after dinner, and your hostess has the baby up (bless it!) and allows it to make various snatches at your hair, nose, watch, seals, &c. Intimate friendship is a delightful thing certainly! Now the purpose of this paper is to urge upon the student the necessity of setting his face against these familiarities. Let him always refuse general invitations; and accept only those when an hour and day are exactly specified. By strictly adhering to this rule, he may avoid taking people as they are; for a host cannot, with any decency, give a friend an invitation for a future day, without preparing some sort of entertainment for him. I think this may be safely taken as a general rule. If a man ask you to "drop in" to dinner, refuse; for you are certain to fare badly—except you are acquainted with a professed and acknowleged epicure—for to such noble individuals these precautions in no way apply. I always mistrust people who ask me "to drop in" to dinner: the very term—dropping—implies, in my opinion, a carelessness of gastronomic refinements.

In days long gone by, but to which I cannot, even now, turn without a shudder; I used to take the Sudds' [sic] as they were—that is to say, in the most uncomfortable and uninviting condition: but I have long since, thank fortune, abandoned the habit, as a dire necessity now no longer existing. I am, at the present moment, one of a happy clique of epicures, and hope to be able to exist without again resorting to my old deplorable shifts.

I might relate divers anecdotes illustrative of my present theme, but I must forbear. The limits to which I must confine my observations will not admit of these digressions. I address my precautions, be it well observed, to those sage young men who have resolutely resolved to make themselves accomplished epicures. I hate those superficial coxcombs, who, as L. E. L. well says, "with mouths never meant but for mutton and mashed potatoes, dilate learnedly on the merits of salmis or santés." Such fellows deserve the contempt of all thinking men, inasmuch as their ignorance tends to bring into contempt that most noble art with which they feign intimacy. I shall live, I trust, to behold the introduction of gastronomy into our Universities. I hope to hail the time when it will be necessary for every gentleman to be versed in the theory of cooking; and I conceive that I am in a measure hastening the advent of this happy era, by bringing before the notice of the public my present work, which M. Soyer has done me the honour to peruse, and upon the tenor of which he has complimented me.

A Geographical Catechism for Gastronomic Students

So deeply do I feel that a gastronomic age is dawning upon us, that the rising generation will need a profound epicurean education, that I cannot forbear printing, for the use of married epicures, the following Catechism, to be studied by the junior branches of their family.[1]

Tutor. Point out to me the town in England celebrated for its bloaters.
Pupil. Yarmouth.
Tutor. Shew me the city, in Europe, renowned for its sausages.
Pupil. Bologna.
Tutor. What town is celebrated for its chocolate ?
Pupil. Florence.
Tutor. Shew me, on the map, the district which is famous, and deservedly so, for producing the finest truffles.
Pupil. Le Perigord, in France.
Tutor. What town, in the same country has won an enviable reputation for its Pâtés de foie gras?
Pupil. Strasbourg.
Tutor. Where would you go to get maccaroni in perfection?
Pupil. To Naples.
Tutor. Where has the gastronomic art been carried nearest to perfection?
Pupil. In France.
Tutor. Name the martyr whose memory epicures should honour.
Pupil. Vatel, the cook of the Great Condé, who, when he found that the fish destined to a banquet his master gave to Louis XIV was missing, refused to survive the dishonour, and died by his own hand.

On the Treatment of Hostesses.

For a woman's soul is by nature a beautiful fresco-painting, painted on rooms, tables, clothes, silver waiters, and upon the whole domestic establishment.—*Richter's Flower, Fruit, and Thorn Pieces.*

I approach this part of my subject with becoming diffidence. I am sensible of very many deficiencies: I feel that I am not the man to do justice to so poetical a theme. Yet I must e'en do my best—must cast aside my scruples—take a goute of some delicious noyeau which I keep by me for my own private enjoyment—and proceed to instruct epicurean youth on the treatment of Hostesses.[2]

A young man cannot attain to any eminence as an epicure, till he has got rid of that bashfulness and trepidation which are the curses of youth. I therefore earnestly beseech all juveniles to shake off, as early as possible, those barricades which inexperience has piled up between them and fortune. Let them ever strive to get rid of bashfulness with their pinafores: let them say good bye to trepidation, when they disown the tyranny of their suburban schoolmaster. I must insist upon confidence as an indispensable element in the epicure's nature: I never saw a bashful gourmand. The opportunities lost by a bashful man are beyond calculation. A bashful man never won an heiress, or became a popular diner out! However, I need not dwell upon the disadvantages of bashfulness, inasmuch as I do not think that disadvantage is spreading among the rising generation: I cannot believe that the young men of the present day are more bashful and retiring than were the youths of my early time; on the contrary, I am perhaps inclined to hold that the youths I notice about me, are not wanting in sufficient confidence, and a certain forwardness, which I, of the old school, am apt to look upon as precocious. Without more ado, then, I will proceed to inform the student on the importance of paying marked and graceful civilities to hostesses. I knew a man who gained a sure footing in a dinner-giving family by telling his wife, on his return from his first visit, that the hostess (a middle-aged lady and a grandmother) was about three-and-twenty years of age; taking care that this opinion should float back to the flattered lady. This is a very fair sample of the diplomacy with which it behoves the student to be acquainted. Let him not, however, prematurely plume himself on his adroitness in this science, or he may find to his cost that he has played a blind game with edged tools. In no matter let him be more careful than in the paying of compliments. A compliment should be implied, never thrust under the nose of the individual complimented. To tell a woman that she is pretty, is equivalent to telling a man that he is honest. So difficult is it to pay a compliment gracefully, that I should warn beginners to refrain from the practice till they have, by continual contact with society, made themselves thorough masters of the art. Meantime they may feel their way by venturing to commend certain qualities of their friends in their absence—this is always a safe venture.

The Alderman to his Mistress
Can you doubt the love I bear you?
Will you wrong a faithful heart?
I'd leave my dinner to be near you
I'd give up truffles—not to part.
Ah! if you could know the anguish
That has thrilled me through and through,
When I've dreamt I'd lost for ever,
Twenty dinner cards and you.

'Tis in vain I seek to smother
Thoughts that turn to you all day;
Except when foie gras calls another
Sentiment—as sweet—in play.
No, I cannot live without you:

You gone; what were creams to me?
Come then, fair, no coy disdaining,
Share my soups and wines with me!

On Mutton

It cannot be concealed, I always feel a strange emotion when the subject of mutton is raised in company. When the haunch is on the tapis, I always feel sheepish. My emotion may be the result of an overweening affection—it may be ascribed to tender reminiscences of Southdown—this I am not prepared to deny, still less am I able to justify the weakness that comes upon me at the sound of those magic syllables—Mutton! Incomparable, and (with caper-sauce) fascinating mutton! He is unworthy of the name of epicure who can calmly contemplate a well-hung haunch, or to whose perverted imagination the saddle does not give a spur. I shall, I trust, be forgiven for lingering thus fondly on a subject so near and dear to my hea—stomach. But I must make an effort to cast aside the blissful reminiscences that float so thickly before my bewildered brain; and, with a prodigious effort, must assume sufficient calmness, to touch upon the subject of mutton in a rational and practical manner.

There are four kinds of mutton in repute at the epicure's table; namely, the Welsh, Dartmoor, Scotch, and, not least in esteem, the Southdown. The Southdown is largest of these four breeds, and, to my mind, the best. It is not often that you find first-rate mutton in London. The graziers do not keep their sheep long enough. Mutton should be from five to six years old; whereas, the mutton generally consumed in England is scarcely three years old. Young mutton is flabby. The flesh of a young leg will separate when the first incision is made by the carver. This may always be taken as a proof of the youth, and consequently, the inferiority and unwholesomeness of the mutton. The flesh of a good leg would rather close over the incision. Let hostesses and hosts attend to this, as the appearance of bad mutton is an indelible disgrace to an epicure's table.

On Toothpicks

I cannot refrain from offering a few remarks on the engrossing subject of Toothpicks. So poetical a theme calls for higher powers, perhaps, than I may modestly lay claim to; however, a matter so weighty cannot be passed by in a work like the present, therefore must I endeavour, holding up a toothpick before the delighted reader, to flirt through the chapter with it.

It is but a third-rate goose-quill that I hold before your mind's eye, reader, yet is it so exquisitely modelled, and of such a delightful texture, that no man who has the least perception of the beautiful can regard it for a moment without experiencing the liveliest emotion. Garner up for closet meditation and enjoyment, the thousand exquisite associations which cling around this pointed quill: it wants but a touch of the penknife, and the guidance of a genius to create a second Hamlet, or to paint to a delighted world another Comus! Pondering on this intently, shall we decide how much of the profuse literature of this age we owe to geese!

Here is Savarin's toothpick! Here is Ude's! Here is Soyer's! They are all three of the costliest metal, presented to their respective owners as grateful mementos of the delightful services these professors conferred upon the human race. Are they not graceful instruments? Do they not recall to the mind that blissful state when the plenitude of the stomach and the coolness of the claret, give to mortal man the most delightful and luxuriant associations? The serenity of soul with which the toothpick is inseparably associated, must ever lend a certain charm to the pointed goose-quill.

He must certainly be a passionless individual who can recur, without emotion, to that blissful period of man's earthly career—after dinner. Who does not feel that he is a better man after a good and ample meal? Who that has a full stomach lacks benevolence? Search the world through, and you will not find an epicure with a bad heart; such a character would be an inexplicable anomaly, since eating, without contradiction, softens and refines the soul. This is why attorneys dine late: after an ample and scientific dinner, I much doubt whether even one of the bum-tribe of Levi could summon the necessary harshness to serve a writ. Therefore does there cling an ineffable charm about the after-dinner toothpick. As a bar of music may recall some dulcet moments long since passed away, so may the toothpick bring back to the epicure the delightful remembrance of feasts of an ancient date. Looking then at the toothpick, in a poetical light, I need scarcely, I trust, apologize for this flirtation with it.

Student, use it secretly and tenderly: it should not be trifled with.

On Tit-bits

A most poetical theme! Tit-bits! The most exquisite morsel of the most exquisite dish! Happy the man who has the taste to enjoy, and the science to pick out, the tit-bits of every dainty—who *does* know which is the best part, and moreover, has the assurance to take it! Such a man has within his grasp happiness of no common order: he may defy the world's vain allurements, while he has the discernment to choose, and the audacity and skill to appropriate to his own enjoyment the tit-bits of his friends' tables. This state of bliss is, however, seldom or ever vouchsafed to the young epicure—it is the reward of experience and persevering study only. There is no royal road to gastronomic learning: he who is ambitious of attaining to excellence in this delightful pursuit must be prepared to suffer his proper apprenticeship; if he covet the reward, he must not shirk the trial that may encumber his path. I am sensible—fully sensible of the sore disappointments and mortifications that too often darken the epicure's early days; but I who have travelled the road, and endured my full share of the mishaps and mortifications, and have reaped, in fact, the delightful harvest of my early ardour, may be allowed to counsel the gastronomic student on his conduct under the discouragements which will probably mark his early career.

As tit-bits are very seldom within the reach of the young (inasmuch as the gastronomic elders take precedence of their juniors in the service of the table), I should advise them to spend their youthful days in studying narrowly, and noting scrupulously, the doings of their seniors. For instance, let students observe the dexterity with which a practised epicure will carve a turkey, reserving for himself—cunningly concealed under the bird—a delightful tit-bit, kept warm and juicy in the gravy; let them note also how judiciously he distributes the several parts, giving the esteemed morsels (always excepting his own) to confirmed epicures, while he carelessly passes the drumsticks to the junior portion of the diners. By making these observations silently and discreetly, the student will be enabled, in a comparatively short space of time, to master the intricacies of the theory; but let him take especial heed, lest he venture in an evil moment, to comment upon his observations before company; let it not fall to his unhappy lot to be the jeering stock of his fellow epicures, by making an untimely allusion to the secretion of a dainty morsel; let him rather, with profound respect for the secretion of the tit-bits, calmly and patiently await that happy period in man's existence, when his age and his experience have enabled him to take that position at his friends' tables which will give him fair scope for the exercise of his talents in the secret abstraction of the choicest morsels before him. And in looking forward to this blissful period in his existence, let him not be troubled by scruples which a few words will shew to be utterly without foundation; I mean scruples with regard to the propriety of taking to himself in a covert manner the best delicacies of the table. He must not imagine that he is acting a mean and undignified part: on the contrary, he may assure himself that he is displaying the profundity of his gastronomic acquirements, by means which custom has sanctioned, and which epicures tacitly acknowledge throughout the world. I would, however, caution the student against making rash ventures in these delicate maneuvres; for he must never lose sight of this fact—that though epicures will feign ignorance of his feat, any gross or palpable blundering in the matter will draw down upon him the everlasting ridicule of the company—in these strange times "that weep with laughing not with weeping."[3]

Lord Mayor's Day. The Alderman to His Brother Aldermen

Brother Alderman,—I have often objected, as an epicure, to the bill of fare provided for our annual banquet on the ninth of November. I object to it as being too substantial—more worthy of a society of butchers than of a corporation famed for its devotion to the kitchen. Now, what I have to propose is, that for the future, the Lord Mayor elect be required to shew the bill of fare of his inauguration banquet before he is allowed to canvass for the dignity of the Mayoralty. Let it be henceforth a rule with us to pay strict and conscientious regard to the elegancies of our banquet, that we may be enabled to take pride in asking to our board all the celebrated foreigners who may visit our shores; let our truffles be from the Perigord, our Stilton direct from Melton Mowbray. Let not our gastronomic affections be exclusively given to turtle, let us cast off the chains that have for so many years bound us to the soup tureen, and consent, with one accord, to divide our affections equally, and with honour to ourselves. Let us study *Soyer's Regenerator*; let us heroically try mutton basted with devil's tears, and on our knees do homage to *foie gras*. Let us resolutely determine to tear ourselves from turtle; let us shew to the world that the Aldermen of London can dine without sickening their guests with the sight of one thousand two hundred and thirty-five pints of "real turtle;" let us give evidence of our gastronomic progress to an admiring country. If we must have forty-six capons on our board, let them be dressed in twenty different ways; if eighty roast turkeys be indispensable, let the delightful bulbs of le Perigord be plentifully provided; in short, let a man of genius—a Soyer—be called to our gastronomic councils, and let this year, 1849, be worthily celebrated—let that famous epicure's axiom—"quality not quantity"—be ever present in our minds; let us in short do our utmost to maintain the high reputation which an indulgent country has magnanimously vouchsafed to us. Let our feasts be in truth "feasts of reason"—let the science of gastronomy yield its choicest gifts to our guests; eschewing forty-six roast capons, let us solemnly proceed to masticate capons scientifically served: let us, in short, be stirring; or we shall one day infallibly sink for ever in the estimation of our countrymen and of the world. Let our maxim be written in our banquetting hall—in letters of gold—

QUALITY NOT QUANTITY.

Notes

1. Cf. Grimod de la Reynière's "Essay on Gourmand Geography" (1806), in this volume, 16–18.
2. A "goute" is a small drop; a "noyeau" is a liqueur with fruits, almonds, citrus peel, and spices.
3. From Shakespeare, *Timon of Athens*, IV.iii.486, as printed in *The Riverside Shakespeare*, 1469.

10
Dining, Considered as a Fine Art (Anonymous)

Harper's New Monthly Magazine (December 1858)

Introduction

Published in New York from 1850 through 1895, this magazine served as the first major forum for American gastronomical writing, revealing the influence of European culinary tradition from the mid-nineteenth century. The following article was published anonymously.

From *Harper's New Monthly Magazine* (December 1858)

Dining, Considered as a Fine Art

A certain philosopher has divided mankind into two great classes: those who cheat, and those who are cheated. Another has partitioned the animated world into those who eat, and those who are eaten. A third—and, to the mind of the present writer, better—classification of mankind, suggests itself, viz., those (who have leisure, money, and taste) who live to eat, and those (who have a good appetite, little money, and no leisure) who eat to live. Now, considering *Dining* strictly as one of the Fine Arts, it appears evident that both these classes are, more or less, artists; for the members of the first make of dining an art, while those of the second—among whom the writer of this is to be counted—have frequently to use every art to get a dinner.

Every Fine Art has its especial literature. If Ruskin has discussed Modern Paintings and Painters, the lamented Soyer—as great an artist in his way, and a more practical man—has done the same office for Modern Dinners and Cooks. If we have histories of painting, sculpture, and poetry, in various times and nations, so we have a "*History of Cookery*, from the earliest period to the present time." And if various of our great men have devoted themselves to the consideration of particular epochs of other arts, have we not been favored with an essay, by an eminent Parisian, "On the Gastronomic Effects of the First French Revolution?"[1] Is there not an energetic remonstrance on the British catalogue, entitled "Thoughts on Roast Pig;" and a critical dissertation on "The Comparative Merits of Male and Female Cooks?" not to speak of various other and more extended works, such as the "Physiologie du Goût," by that great art-critic Brillât-Savarin, who may be called the Ruskin of this department of fine art.

Of 565 Chinese books on Behavior, catalogued by an eminent Chinese scholar, 361 refer directly to the ceremonial of the Celestial dinnertable. The Japanese, Hindoos, and Persians are both luminous and voluminous upon the same point; and to turn to what we are pleased to consider more civilized nations, a French writer assures us that France possesses no less than one hundred and fifty-six works upon Manners—all referring more or less circumstantially to prandial ceremonials, while American, English, Italian, Spanish, German, and even Russian and Dutch writers swell the list of devotees to this the most delightful of the fine arts; which, by-the-way, is dignified by the classical title of "Aristology," the derivation of which the reader may hunt up for himself.

Let us then consider, for a little, some of the peculiarities of Aristology, and the Aristologist, or artistic diner out. First, as to the means necessary for the successful prosecution of the art. Mr. Wellesley Pole used to say that it was impossible to live like a gentleman, in England, under forty thousand pounds a year[2]; and Beau Brummell, when asked by a lady how much she ought to allow her son for *dress*, said that, with *strict economy*, it might be done for eight hundred a year. The art is yet in its infancy in America, and data upon which to form an accurate estimate of the income necessary for an accomplished aristologist are scarce. But we have no doubt that much might be done by a prudent and skillful man with twenty thousand dollars per annum. Of course, the aristologist should, if possible, devote himself entirely to his art. "Generally speaking," says a writer of eminence and authority upon this subject, "a calling of any sort is against a man; for we incline to think that the gentleman *par excellence* (think of this enviable title being monopolized by the Professor of Aristology) should resemble Voltaire's trees, who, when a visitor was complimenting him on their looking so fine, replied, 'They ought, for they have nothing else to do.'"

Good looks are not necessary—happily. Wilkes, a noted and successful diner out, who justly declared that, give him but half an hour's start and he would make a better impression than the handsomest man in the room, was so excessively ugly, that a lottery-office keeper once offered him ten guineas not to pass his window while the tickets were drawing, for fear he would bring ill luck upon the house.

"The finest linen, plenty of it, and country washing," were Brummell's directions to a youthful aspirant to aristological honors. This matter, however, according to a French writer, a member of the Academy, may be carried too far; and he adds that "those who delight in cleanliness change their linen twice a week, and their pocket-handkerchief still oftener if they are obliged to blow their noses frequently—especially those who take snuff." This seems a very moderate estimate, even for a Frenchman, who must be either a cleaner or a dirtier man than his neighbors, as you may choose to interpret the above directions. It reminds one of a remark of Sir Henry Ellis.[3] Johnson confessed to Mr. Langton that he experienced an unusual feeling of elation when (on the occasion of "Irene" being brought upon the stage) he first put on a scarlet waistcoat with rich gold lace, and a gold-laced hat. Sir Henry Ellis declared that he never saw a Frenchman in a clean shirt who did not exhibit symptoms of a similar feeling of elation at the circumstance. In fact, a Parisian exquisite reverses Brummell's maxim, and holds that you are not well dressed if people do *not* stop to stare at you.

As for gloves, the student of aristology will bear in mind that they are strictly for ornament—not use. Let him never fall into the error of the navy captain at a ball, when his partner, a distinguished lady, suggested the propriety of his putting on his gloves before they led off the dance. "Oh, never mind me, madame," said the gallant hero, "I shall wash my hands when I've done dancing!"

"But," the patient or impatient reader will ask, "What has all this matter of clean linen, gloves, etc., to do with the art of dining?"

A great deal, most excellent neophyte! as any proficient in the art will tell you. The sculptor has to carve his image out of marble with a dusty chisel; the painter must daub his on coarse canvas with vulgar oil and filthy paints; the poet is obliged to use ink and paper—and his finger-ends but too often bear witness, in close-bit nails and badly-washed ink-stains, to the partly mechanical nature of his high art. It is reserved for the aristologist—the gentleman *par excellence*, to recur to the words of our before-quoted author—to perfect himself in his art without any of these vulgar adjuncts. He alone combines in his own figure artist, model, and product; he alone develops on his own cherished person all those forms of beauty which vaguely flit through his brain; he alone may be truly said to enjoy what himself creates.

Being prepared to honor the duly received invitation, the artistic diner out proceeds on his way. Among the Sybarites, by-the-way, it was customary to invite ladies to dinner a year beforehand, ostensibly to give them time for beautifying themselves. Those old fellows did not realize how evanescent is true beauty—perhaps they had advanced farther than we in "the mysteries of the toilet." Being arrived at his destination, he is announced. And here is a point: let him be careful to give his name distinctly to the attendant servant. Else may he share the fate of one Mr. Delaflete, of London, who, perhaps supposing that name more generally known than was actually the case, neglected the precaution of distinctness in its utterance, and to his disgust heard himself announced to a crowded drawing-room as *Mr. Hellafloat*.

Being entered, he salutes his host and hostess. Except it be, indeed, that his dinner is in China; where strict etiquette demands that the host leave his house when he has a dinner party.

All writers on aristology agree in terming the salute the touchstone by which any given person's breeding may be instantly and unerringly determined; and the aspirant to prandial benefits and distinctions will, therefore, perfect himself in this important part of his profession. There are, of course, various modes of salutation in different countries. Among the Sandwich Island Kanakas they rub noses; in Timor they pull one another's ears; the Franks plucked out a hair and presented it—an evidence that baldness was, to say the least, unusual among them; the Japanese take off their slippers when they meet. The only salutation permitted to the Carthusian monks of Spain was a slight nod and the lively remark, "We must die;" to which the exhilarating reply was, "We know it." In some of the South Sea Islands they spit in their hands and then rub your face for you; in others, it is the height of politeness to fling a jar of water over your friend. In America, as in England and France, we nod, bow, courtesy, shake hands, and take off our hats. In Germany the men kiss each other. The science consists in knowing on what occasions, and with what persons, these respective modes of salutation are to be used; the art, in attaining perfection in the various genuflexions which, gracefully performed, stamp you an accomplished diner out.

. . .

Dr. Johnson wisely observed that a man who is careless about his table will generally be found careless in other matters. The greatest men in all countries have always been the most perfect aristologists. Louis XVI is said to have been neglectful of his table; and this was, probably, one among the many causes of his fall. Cambacérès, Napoleon's grand chamberlain, was famous for his dinners, regarding dining as *the* business of life; and when his master was especially pleased at the result of a diplomatic conference, he was accustomed to take leave of the plenipotentiaries with, "Go and dine with Cambacérès." Napoleon was himself famous for the nicety of his taste, but, from the hurried manner of his life, he acquired a pernicious habit of eating fast; and this, debilitating his stomach, paralyzed him on two of the most critical occasions of his life—the battles of Borodino and Leipsic. When M. de Suffren was commanding the French in the East Indies, he was one day waited upon by a deputation of natives, who requested an audience just as he was sitting down to dinner.[4] He desired an aid-de-camp to inform them that it was a precept of the Christian religion, from which no earthly consider-ation would induce him to depart, never to attend to business of any sort at dinner-time. The deputation departed, lost in admiration at the piety of the commandant, and returned at the proper time, so predisposed in his favor that he was enabled to conclude an advantageous treaty with them. One of Bolívar's first cares, on becoming President of freed Peru, was to intrust to M. Armand de Bremont the delicate mission of sending him from Paris the best cook he could find. A friend of Mr. Thackeray relates that he was once dining with him in Paris, when a *matelotte* (a fish ragout) of surpassing excel-lence was served up. "My dear fellow," exclaimed the delighted author of "The Virginians," "don't let us speak a word till we have finished this dish!"

Dr. Johnson, though unfortunately extremely coarse in his mode of eat-ing, and not at all orthodox in his tastes, fully realized the importance of the subject. "Women," once observed the sage, "can spin very well, but they can not write a good book of cookery. I could write a better book of cookery than has ever yet been written; it should be a book on *philosophical principles*." What a loss to the world that the great lion of literature forbore! According to Mrs. Piozzi, Johnson's "favorite dainties were, a leg of pork, boiled till it dropped from the bone, a veal pie, with plums and sugar, and the outside cut of a salt buttock of beef." He has been known to call for the butter-boat containing the lobster-sauce during the second course, and pour the whole of its contents over his plum-pudding.

The cardinals have always been noted for their gastronomic skill. Fesch, the uncle of Napoleon the Great, takes especial rank in the annals of aristol-ogy; and there is related of him a story which shows how ingenuity and taste, properly combined, can please the guests, and, at the same time, gain credit for the host.[5] He had invited a select party of clerical magnates to dinner. By a fortunate coincidence, two turbots of singular beauty arrived as pres-ents to his Eminence on the very morning of the feast. To serve them both would have appeared ridiculous; but the Cardinal was most anxious to have the credit of both. He imparted his embarrassment to his *chef*. "Be of good cheer, your Eminence," was the reply; "both shall appear; both shall enjoy the reception which is their due." The dinner was served; one of the turbots relieved the soup. Delight was in every face. The *maître-d'hôtel* advances; two attendants raise the turbot, and carry him off to cut him up. One of them loses his equilibrium: the attendants and the turbot roll together upon the floor. At this sad sight the assembled cardinals became pale as death, and a solemn silence reigned in the conclave. Intense disappointment was expressed on every priestly face. "Bring another turbot," says the *maître-d'hôtel* to the attendant, with the utmost coolness. And now intense delight took the place of disappointment on each cardinal's face; and the host was conscious of another laurel added to his gastronomic crown.

To return from Diners to Dinners. It matters little at what time dinner and diner meet, if only the appetite is prepared and the business of the day over. Henry IV of France ate his at half past eleven; Charlemagne, earlier yet—at half past ten. At present the greatest aristologists dine at half past seven—shrewdly enjoying as long as possible the pleasures of anticipation. Punctuality, however, whatever the hour, is indispensable. Lord Dudley used to say that the most unpunctual persons he ever knew were two distinguished brothers—the elder of whom is now a peer of England, and, it is to be hoped, more regular in his habits—"for," said his lordship, "if you asked Robert for Wednesday at seven, you were sure to get Charles on Thursday at eight." Lord Dudley himself was regular as clock-work—not only in his hours, but also in his habits. He could not dine comfortably without apple-pie, which, properly made, is a proper and excellent dish. Dining, when Foreign Secretary, at Prince Esterhazy's—a grand dinner—he was terribly put out on finding that his favorite delicacy was wanting, and kept on murmuring, pretty audibly, in his absent way, "God bless my soul, no apple-pie!"[6]

The true aristologist wisely considers Dinner as *the* event of the day, toward the proper enjoyment of which all other things are subsidiary or accessory. He regards his cook with veneration, and does not think extravagant the language M. Henrion de Pensey addressed to Messieurs Laplace, Chaptal, and Berthollet, three of the most distinguished men of science of their day.[7] "I regard the discovery of a new dish," said this worthy and ingenuous gentleman, "as a far more interesting event, than the discovery of a star; for we have always stars enough, but we can never have too many dishes; and I shall not regard the sciences as sufficiently honored or adequately represented among us until I see a cook in the first class of the Institute." Genius is to be drawn out only by judicious praise and discriminating criticism. In the days when Paris was most famous for its cooks—days now past—it was the fashion for each guest at a banquet to place a piece of gold in every dish of more than ordinary merit. To facilitate criticism and individualize responsibility, it is even now the custom, at some Russian and German tables—especially at the royal table of Hanover—to print in the *carte*, a copy of which is placed beside the plate of each guest, the name of the cook by whom each dish has been dressed, like the programme of a concert with the names of the performers. In this way only can the highest inspirations of genius be called forth. Is it too much for the enthusiastic aristologist to hope that, at the distinguished tables of even our democratic land, this wise custom may, by-and-by, be introduced? Then may we see reproduced here those now faded glories of the art which once gave renown to the restaurants and private tables of Paris, and inspired master-cooks with that sense of personal ambition and responsibility which made the great Vatel, *maître-d'hôtel* to the Prince de Condè, throw himself upon his sword, because at a royal supper an insignificant dish was wanting at one of the tables—even as a Parisian notary's clerk killed himself, because, having duly calculated and considered the chances, he did not think it possible for him to be so great a man as Napoleon.

And that the great cook is really a genius every philosophic mind will readily perceive. Dugald Stewart—admirable philosopher!—was struck by the analogy between cookery, poetry, and the other fine arts.[8] He says, in one of his Philosophical Essays, "*Sweet* may be said to be *intrinsically* pleasing, and *bitter* to be *relatively* pleasing; while both are, in many cases, equally essential to those effects which, in the *art of cookery*, correspond to that *composite beauty* which it is the object of the poet and the painter to create!" So Robert, the inventor of the sauce, Rechaud, and Merillion, have been characterized as the Raphael, Michael Angelo, and Rubens of cookery; while Beauvillier was placed by acclamation at the head of the classical school—so called by way of contradistinction to the romantic school, of which the famous Carême used to be considered the chief. And although as of the poet it is said, *Poeta nascitur, non fit*, so it is true of the cook that he is born, not made: yet both poet and cook must go through a long course of training for the proper development of their genius. Thus Carême tells us of himself that he began his studies by attending a regular course of roasting, under some of the leading roasters of the day (how many blockheads have gone through a course of scholastic roasting, without becoming either poets or cooks!); next placed himself under M. Richant, the famous "*saucier de la maison de Condé*," to learn the mystery of sauces; then under M. Asne, with a peculiar view to the preparation of cold dishes; and took his finishing degree under Robert l'Aine, a professor of *l'elegance moderne*. How thorough this course! and how did industry and perseverance here come to the aid of genius!

Your true cook, like your poet, is an erratic being. Restless and inconstant, he wanders from place to place and depends upon the lucky moment for the grand inspirations of his life. His comfort is one of the chief cares of an appreciative master. The late Marquis of Hertford had a cook who, in his master's opinion, was inimitable in a *suprème*. Dining one day with an intimate friend, a distinguished privy councilor of England, who had frequently contested the point, his lordship declared the *suprème*, which he was with difficulty persuaded to taste, detestable.

"Now I have you!" exclaimed the Right Honorable. "That dish was dressed by your own *chef*, who is at this moment in my house."

"Then all I can say," replied the Marquis, "is, that you must have spoiled his palate by drinking beer with him."

Colonel Damer, happening to enter Crockford's one evening to dine early, found Ude—Louis Eustache Ude, one of the great cooks of the day—walking up and down in a towering passion, and naturally inquired what was the matter.[9]

"The matter, Monsieur le Colonel! Did you see that man who has just gone out? Well, he ordered a red mullet for his dinner! I made him a delicious little sauce with my own hands. The price of the mullet, marked on the *carte*, was two shillings; I added sixpence for the sauce. That *imbécile* apparently believes that the red mullets come out of the sea with *my* sauce in their pockets!"

Ude's sauce was no better appreciated than some canvas-back ducks once sent by our historian, Prescott, to an English friend. It is related that they were forwarded accidentally to Melton,[10] and eaten by a select party as common ducks—to their intense disappointment when made aware of the facts. And ducks bring to mind a rule to be observed of birds in general: no bird worth eating should be inundated with gravy. The peculiar flavor is washed away. Sydney Smith, who knew a thing or two in the aristological way, on once hearing a lady at table exclaim, "No gravy, if you please!" turned to her and proposed to swear eternal friendship on the instant, saying that he had been looking all his life for a person who on principle rejected gravy.[11]

But enough of the cook. Let us say that with him, as with the poet, simplicity is the acme of perfection. His labors are not to be valued by their cost, but by their intrinsic excellence. We think with disgust of those barbarous Roman banquets, or medieval feasts, which were certainly more remarkable for profusion and costliness than for taste. The sole merit of a dish composed of the brains of five hundred peacocks, or the tongues of five hundred nightingales, must have been its dearness. The Prime Minister of England's first James kept no less than five hundred servants in his town-house; and yet his royal master owned but a single pair of silk stockings, which he was sufficiently generous to lend his noble minister upon occasion when that worthy had to grant audience to a French Embassador. The Duke of Medina-Coeli, contemporary with the famous and cruel Duke of Alba,[12] paid no less than twenty thousand pounds per month as servants' hire alone, yet had not in his spacious palace a room fit to dine in. It somewhat diminishes our admiration of Anne Boleyn's fabled beauty to know that that lady breakfasted each morning on boiled pork and beer. If a mode of swallowing most money in a given time be thought a desideratum, surely Cleopatra, with her pearl,[13] will take the prize; although even she was fairly beaten, in originality and neatness of conception, by a frail fair one, the famous Mrs. Sawbridge, who, to show her contempt for an elderly adorer, sandwiched the hundred pound note which he had laid upon her dressing table between two slices of bread and butter, and ate it in his presence.

And now, having discussed the Diner and the *Cook,* let us come—at last, the impatient reader will say—to the *Dinner;* about which we have been hovering for some pages. Unfortunately—or the reverse—the editor of this Magazine is inexorable in the matter of space, and we are compelled by the sternest of fates to cut short the delightful thoughts which crowd to every right-minded man's heart when he contemplates that greatest object of life—a well-served dinner. M. Anthelme Brillat-Savarin, Judge of the Court of Cassation, member of the Legion of Honor, and of most of the scientific and literary societies of France, from whose famous before-mentioned treatise on the "Physiology of Taste" we are about to quote reverently a few rules for the dinner-table, was—to the mind of a true aristologist—one of the most notable men France ever produced. Like all true epicures he was of a sober, moderate, and easily-satisfied disposition; like all men of genius, he was an enthusiast. It is related of him, in confirmation of the latter trait, that during his residence in America (he was compelled to emigrate by the Reign of Terror) he was one day shooting in the Virginia woods. Having had the good fortune to kill a wild turkey, he was returning, when he fell in with Jefferson, who knew him, and who presently began relating some interesting anecdotes of Washington and the war then but just over. Observing the distracted air of M. Savarin he stopped, and was about to take offense at the lack of attention.

"My dear Sir," said the gastronomer, recovering himself with a strong effort, "I beg a thousand pardons—but I was thinking how I should dress my wild turkey."

It is this gentleman—whom, as Democritus was called the Laughing Philosopher, we may call the Dining Philosopher—to whom we are indebted for a short and comprehensive set of aphorisms on dining, by following which he proposes to unite "all things requisite to the highest pleasures of the table." A good cook is, of course, premised. Without him your table enjoyments will be as the apples of Sodom, fair without, in anticipation—but ashes within, in the realization. As was proven by Byron, who, being compelled to celebrate his birthday in Italy, determined on nothing less than a plum-pudding, by aid of which to eat himself a happy return of the day. Plum-puddings are, or were, not so familiar to Italian gastronomes as macaroni, and the noble poet busied himself a whole morning in giving directions for the proper compounding of the British luxury. One can fancy his disgust when, after all his pains and anxious cares, the pudding appeared in a tureen, and about the consistency of soup.

A capable cook being then presupposed, M. Savarin recommends:

That the number of the party do not exceed twelve, that the conversation may be constantly general;

That the eating-room be luxuriously lighted, the cloth remarkably white, and the atmosphere at the temperature of from thirteen to sixteen degrees Reaumur;[14]

That the dishes be exceedingly choice, but limited in number, the order of progression, in fluids as in solids, being from the most substantial to the lightest;

That the act of consumption be deliberate, the dinner being the last business of the day; and that the guests consider themselves as travelers who are to arrive *together* at the same place of destination;

That the party be detained by the charms of society;

That the retreat be not begun before eleven, but

That every body be in bed by twelve.

These recommendations seem to us unexceptionable. We will only add to them three dinner rules given by John Bulwer, a quaint but sensible writer of the seventeenth century: *"Stridor dentium—Altum silentium—Rumor gentium;"* which, being rendered into the vernacular, signifies; Work for the jaws—A silent pause—Frequent ha-has.

Notes

1. Abraham Hayward, *The Art of Dining* (New York: G. P. Putnam's Sons, 1899), 23.
2. Lord Wellesley Pole distinguished himself by giving sumptuous dinners at his luxurious mansion at Wanstead, following the opera at midnight, the drive from London being an apperative. He married Miss Tylney Pole, an heiress of fifty thousand a-year, but he died a beggar largely thanks to his dinatory extravagance.
3. Sir Henry Ellis (1777–1869) was Keeper of Printed Books and later, Principal Librarian, at the British Museum.
4. Admiral Suffren is known for his campaign in the Indian Ocean, where he fought the British led by Vice-Admiral Sir Edward Hughes.
5. Cardinal Joseph Fesch (1763–1839), was the uncle of Napoleon and a noted patron of the arts.
6. Probably a reference to Lord Dudley Coutts Stuart (1803–54), a British diplomat, and Prince Pal Antal (Paul Anton) Esterhazy (1786–1866), an Austrian prince reknowned for his extravagance.
7. M. Henrion de Pensey was a prominent lawyer; the Marquis de Pierre Simon Laplace (1749–1827) was a French astronomer, mathematician, and mathematical physicist; Jean Antoine Chaptal, (1756–1832) was a French chemist, industrialist, and statesman who later became minister of the interior (1801–09) and director-general of commerce and manufactures (1815) under Napoleon I; Count Claude Louis Berthollet (1748–1822) was a French chemist who collaborated with Antoine Lavoisier in his researches and in reforming chemical nomenclature.
8. Dugald Stewart (1753–1828) was a Scottish philosopher and mathematician at the University. of Edinburgh, whose work included *Outlines of Moral Philosophy* (1793), *Elements of the Philosophy of the Human Mind* (1792–1827), and *Philosophical Essays* (1810).
9. George Lionel Dawson Damer (1788–1856), younger son of the Earl of Portarlington, was a cavalry officer and Regency dandy who frequented White's [club]; William Crockford built a luxurious gambling house in London in 1827, which was all the rage amongst high society.
10. Melton Mowbray is located in the heart of the East Midlands in the county of Leicestershire, best known for its pork pies and Stilton cheese.

11. Sydney Smith (1771–1845) was an English clergyman, writer, wit, and one of the original founders of the *Edinburgh Review* (1802).
12. The Duke of Medina-Coeli was a seventeenth-century Spanish governor; the Duke of Alba (1507–82), a ruthless soldier and military leader during Hapsburg rule of sixteenth-century Spain.
13. A reference to the legendary banquet at which Cleopatra, in order to impress Marc Antony, swallowed a pearl.
14. The *Réaumur* temperature scale, so named after the French scientist René-Antoine Ferchault de Réaumur (1683–1757), was first proposed in 1731 and is no longer in use.

11
William Blanchard Jerrold (1826–84)

The Epicure's Year Book and Table Companion (London, 1868)

Introduction

A favorite of Charles Dickens who owned two copies, this serial published from 1868–69 was authored by the playwright and journalist W. Blanchard Jerrold who claims to have "dug into the gastronomic literature of my country, in search of something to the advantage of the living generation of gourmets." With the exception of Thomas Walker's essays on Aristology, however, he claims to have come up empty. Despite the continental prejudice against British food, he is determined to do justice to his nation's cuisine: "We have half-a-dozen clubs in London wherein a dinner equal to anything done in Paris may be eaten. And yet—albeit a knowledge of eating is spreading fast—we have no gastronomic literature, no organ of gastronomy." *The Epicure's Year Book and Table Companion* is therefore his heroic effort to fill in the gap, "a first endeavour to create a centre for English gastronomy." Although Benson E. Hill's *Epicure's Almanac* made a brief, unsuccessful appearance in 1842, the excerpts published here from the 1868 *Epicure's Year Book* represent a more successful attempt to replicate Grimod de la Reynière's *Almanach des gourmands* for English readers.

Like Grimod's gastronomical *amateur*, Jerrold incorporates materials appropriate to the almanac genre, including menus from the best feasts of the year and an epicure's calendar. Each month of the calendar highlights dates of interest to connoisseurs, including in January, for example, the day on which codfish spawn, the Literary Society's Annual Dinner, and the last day of Partridge Shooting in Ireland. Also contained are accounts of memorable dinners of 1867 and seasonal menus for each month. Miscellaneous morsels, such as a meditation on "The Water Chestnut" and "A Frenchman's Idea of an English Dinner," are followed by a bibliography for English epicures and contemporary reviews of cookery books. The selections below, taken from the first London edition, are characteristic of the spirit of the Year Book.

From *The Epicure's Year Book and Table Companion* (1868)

Art of Laying the Table

The revolution which has been effected in the art of laying a dinner table has been complete. The massive silver that encumbered the tables of our grandfathers, so that the diner could not see his opposite neighbour, and the host was screened,—as it has been happily said in a recent French criticism on the British plate which was introduced into France with the return of the Bourbons after Waterloo—by so many ingots of silver run into the most substantial mould he could afford; has been put aside for light and graceful stands in silver, glass, and porcelain, which hold flowers, and leave to every guest a full command of the table. The guest sits before a dainty array of flowers and fruit, so artfully disposed as to keep the guests the chief objects at the banquet. It has been said by a classical authority, that you may know whether you are going to have a good dinner by the soup which opens it. I think we may go further, and say that you may safely guess by the manner in which the table is laid;—by no means by the costliness of the service: but assuredly by the grace cast about, it may be, the homeliest ware and *couvert*. You can tell, on entering an empty drawing-room, the degree and tastes of the ladies who are its habitual queens; in like manner you may prophesy of a host's gastronomy by his dining-room.

It should be a cheerful room. The candelabra should hold the light well above the heads of the guests. The curtains should be rich and ample. The table should be a picture of bright well-adjusted colours, as Desgoffes understands colour, and refined grouping. The glass should be light as bubbles. The use of glass and flowers in the decoration of the table is a happy change. It is impossible to conceive more delightful ornaments than are to be found in Mr. Dobson's pretty room of crystal flower-stands, in St. James's Street. Salviati's Venetian glass is also worth a visit.

It has been laid down that there should invariably be four glasses to the right of each diner: the madeira glass nearest to the table's edge, then the bordeaux glass to the right, the water glass to the left, with the champagne glass for the crown of the array. Special glasses appear, of course, with particular wines. *Bols* are handed by the servants after the prawns or crayfish. The *rince-bouche* has, happily, disappeared.

There are two, and only two, modes of serving a dinner, viz., in the pure French style, or *à la Russe*.

The French style is, to the gourmand, the best, when the guests are few, and are close friends. The dishes to be consumed appear in three services, or relays, upon the table. This method entails vast responsibility on the host; let him be a poor carver, and the dinner (cooked though it be by a Francatelli or a Gouffé) is spoiled. For example, a pheasant (the bird, that according to Brillat-Savarin, is an enigma of which only complete adepts have the key), unskilfully carved, distresses the sight and deadens the taste.[1] But the host who is worthy of his *chef*, delights his guests at a service *à la Française*, by the learned skill with which he distributes the recondite treasures of his kitchen to them. It is given to few, however, to carve perfectly—that is daintily, learnedly, and expeditiously. In the ancient days there was a carving-master as well as a dancing-master. Dinner served in the French method is parted into three categories or services. The first service comprehends the soup, hors d'œuvres, relevés, and entrées; the second comprises the rôts, vegetables, and sweet dishes; the third is the dessert. All the dishes appear upon the table.

À la Russe

À la Russe, means a table tastefully adorned with flowers and fruits, and the triumphs of the confectioner's art; indeed, all the cold dishes. The hot dishes are served, carved apart, to the guests.

The French regime is the more comfortable, under the foregoing conditions, when the party is a small friendly one; but *à la Russe* is the regime when a banquet or state of ceremony is to be served. Some gallant hosts crown the lady's couvert with a little bunch of flowers;[2] but surely the manner of Lady Granville, who caused a bouquet to be handed to each lady as she entered the room, at the banquet given to the Imperial Commissioners by the Foreign Commissioners last October, is the more graceful mode.

Many writers have descanted on the duties of the host, and the proper manner of discharging them; but guide-books will never make ladies or gentlemen. A manual of etiquette in the possession of a diner out, is almost a *pièce de conviction*. Here is a gourmet's dictum: "The host who has compelled a guest to ask him for anything, is almost a dishonoured man."

Is it needful now-a-days to say that the guest should arrive to the minute; or that the host should not keep those who are punctual waiting for those who are not? Guests can wait a few minutes, when the *chef* has miscalculated his time, but the *chef* can never wait. A delay of ten minutes may destroy the triumphs of his gastronomic genius. The master on whose punctuality the cook cannot rely, is never well served.

The Order of Service

1. The soups.
2. The hors d'œuvres.
3. Relevés of fish.
4. Relevés of meat.
5. Hot entrées, of meat, fowl, and game.
6. Cold entrées.

The punch, or *sorbet Romain*, is invariably served immediately before the Rôts.

7. The roasts of fowl and game.
8. Salad.
9. Entremets of vegetables.
10. Sweet entremets.

After the confectionary, the table is swept clear, and the dessert follows, and is served in the following order: 1. Cheeses. 2. Fruits. 3. Cakes. 4. Sweetmeats. 5. Ices.

Coffee and Liqueurs

And now we pass to the marshalling of the wines; it being observed, by the way, that champagne may appear at intervals throughout the banquet, as a sweet air rises again and again throughout an opera.

1. After the soup: Madeira, sherry, Vermouth (with the oysters, if they open the gastronomic march, Chablis), Sauteme, accompanying the hors d'œuvres.
2. Bordeaux and Burgundies with the relevés and hot and cold entrées.
3. Between the cold entrées, and when the moment for serving the sorbets—Château d'Yquem, and very lightly iced Rhenish wines.
4. With the roasts, and thenceforth to the disappearance of the vegetables, Burgundies (Romanée-Conti, Chambertin, &c.), and Bordeaux, (Laffitte, Margaux, Haut-Brion, &c.).
5. With the sweets: sherry.
6. With the dessert: white and red Muscat, Constantia, Tokay, &c. These wines should be carried round in glasses.

There has been progress at table, as well as in other departments of polite life. It was only in 1805, a distinguished gourmet maintained that a well-bred host would press his guest to partake of a dish three several and distinct times. There were "very valiant trenchermen," too, in those days, who were at table some time before they required the least pressing.

The Point of the Knife

"Sir, the man who would mangle a capon would kill a child," was lately observed in a company of gastronomic dignitaries. "Your chef has sent you up a bird cooked *à point*. He has spent some anxious moments over that dish. There is a boor in the company (the creature turns up at times in all societies), and the bird is placed before him. You might as well set the first butcher-boy round the corner to chisel a head of Venus. The boy would decline, and inquire who Wenus was; but your boor at table is an animal of infinite confidence. In a few moments the work of art is a ruin, and the remains are spread round the table to a company of angry guests."

Whereupon a learned conversation ensued on the art of carving. And the oracle of the company spoke as follows: "Carving is one of the polite arts; an essential accomplishment, as much as riding is. Consider the wrongs and torments a bad carver—all elbows and splashes—inflicts upon his fellow creatures in the course of his life. His clumsy knife proceeds on a blind pursuit of the tendon. He cuts through the bone at last, and gets a jagged morsel, neither leg, nor wing, nor breast, upon a plate. You can see that he has started without a plan, and that he depends upon the sharpness of his blade to get through everything; and not upon the point of his knife and the skilful direction of it. Sometimes, while he is destroying the chief dish of an admirable dinner, he will chatter away to the company with the air of a man who is making a good figure in society. If you were not a witness of his disgraceful exploit, you would, from the sprightliness of his discourse, imagine that he not only knew that ten delicate and acceptable pieces can be carved from a fowl for as many guests, by a good carver; but that he was master of the art of turning a fowl to this equal advantage, for all the guests. He would attack a hare at the legs with unruffled equanimity. This creature is the terror of diners, and the scorn of cooks. He is at times amusing, because of his profound belief in himself, while he is blundering over even a bird that has been subjected to Soyer's admirable tendon separator. You may cut the tendons so that the knife, intelligently handled, would glide between the joints; but Dunderhead doesn't know where the joints lie. There is no more intolerable nuisance at the table, however, than confident Dunderhead."

"No, no!" cried the company.

"Gentlemen, bear with me a moment, while I present you the nervous—the bashful carver. It may be that he has a fair stock of science. But observe his hand tremble, directly there is a pause in the conversation, or that an authoritative eye falls upon his proceedings. He tries to mend his pace, and only stumbles into mistakes. His plan of action fades out of his brain; and the hesitating point of his knife wanders, purposeless, over the dish. In vain you try to encourage him by diverting the attention of the company; he never gains that complete and cheerful composure, lacking which I here deliberately assert, as the experience of a long life, no man can carve."

This solemn assertion was received by the company with expressions of approval, not only because the speaker had been a wise and thoughtful minister to his mouth for the better part of half a century, but also because truth was the basis and substance of it.

The venerable speaker's eye now brightened, as it played benignly round the table; and, after a pause, he broke gently into speech:

"I shall take leave now to submit to your minds a picture, that grows wonderfully upon me, as I contemplate the many claims it has on our regard and on our gratitude. I have before me the figure of the perfect carver. He is the most gracious of guests, the most loveable of hosts; he is—he must be—a man of happily balanced mind; a just and impartial man, too, or he cannot righteously distribute the dish that lies before him. How lightly, and with what grace of movement, he lifts the knife and fork! Have you seen Sivori take up his fiddle? Has it been vouchsafed to you to behold Landseer adjust the palette upon his thumb? The model carver I have in my mind's eye, drops his instruments upon the bird, and it falls apart with a few gentle turns of his wrists. He is in the conversation the while; can give a *mot* delicately as you hand a peach to your bride on a summer morning—while he removes a wing; and he can laugh with you while he disengages the legs. Observe him with a saddle of mutton; how he lifts the long clean slices away, and is mindful of the wealth of juice in the cutting. It is a treat to him to be entrusted with a haunch, or wild-fowl. He knows exactly the number of slices the hare's back will yield; and when his labour of love is over, how gently he deposits the scarce soiled knife upon the dish! To be so accomplished is, to my old-fashioned mind, to be a benefactor to your species. You delight them whenever you meet them at a dinner-table. You are the cook's best friend."

The art of carving is not to be easily got by the study of diagrams. You will not get much out of directions to cut from B to C. But the advice of Gouffé, Françatelli, Soyer, and Périgord is useful to the beginner. He cannot be far beyond the rudiments which instruct you how to keep the bird under treatment out of your neighbour's lap, who does not know that the fillets from the back of the roast hare are the only morsels offered to the company: and that the best part of the duck is the breast, cut obliquely, in delicate slices. But before the above picture of the consummate master of the carving-knife can be realised, the beginner has years of study to pass through. The triumph is worth all the trial.

The Scrap Book

Francatelli's Literary Dishes
  Imitation Soufflé iced à la Walter Scott
Ingredients: 1 pint of syrup of 32 degrees strength, 15 yolks of eggs, a gill of
curaçoa, half a gill of orange-flower water, half a gill of juice of oranges, half
a pint of double cream whipped.
  Imitation Soufflé iced à la Byron
Ingredients: 1 pint of syrup of 32 degrees strength, half a pint of noyeau,
half a pint of juice of cherries, 2 ounces of bruised macaroons, half a pint of
double cream whipped.
  Imitation Soufflé iced à la Charles Kean
Ingredients: 1 pint of syrup of 32 degrees strength, 3 gills of filtered raspberry juice, the juice of one lemon, a gill of maraschino, 15 yolks, 2 ounces
of chocolate drops, and half a pint of double cream whipped.

Mix the syrup and yolks of eggs, and strain this into the warmed egg
bowl, then add the raspberry and lemon juices and the liqueur; whisk the
composition till it creams substantially, then whisk it off the hot water for
ten minutes longer, add the chocolate drops and the whipped cream; lightly
fill the case, set it in the cave placed in a tub well buried in pounded rough
ice with salt, and two hours after take it out, remove the band of paper from
round the case, cover the surface of the *soufflé* with powdered baked savoy
biscuit, and serve immediately.
  Iced Biscuits, à la Charles Dickens
Ingredients: 1 pint of syrup of 32 degrees strength, 15 yolks of eggs, 3 gills
of peach pulp pinked with carmine, 1 gill of noyeau, half a pint of double
cream whipped, and a small quantity of chocolate water ice, made with half
a pint of syrup, with 4 ounces of best chocolate very smoothly dissolved in
it, and frozen ready to be used as hereinafter indicated.

Mix the syrup and yolks of eggs (strained) with the peach pulp and the
noyeau and a few drops of essence of vanilla, and whisk the composition as
previously directed; when ready for freezing pour this into brick moulds, and
set these imbedded in rough ice with salt to be re-frozen for an hour and
a half; at the end of that time they are to be unmoulded, cut up into slices
an inch thick, coated all over, or at all events on the upper surface and side,
with the ready frozen chocolate ice, smoothed with a knife dipped in cold
water, placed in an ice cave; as soon as the cave is filled with the biscuits,
let it be entirely buried in rough ice with salt; an hour and a half afterwards
they will be ready for table.

These biscuits may be dished up with leaf-shaped pieces of green preserved angelica, or placed in small oblong-shaped white paper cases made
to their size.

Iced Biscuits à la Thackeray

Ingredients: 1 pint of syrup of 32 degrees strength, 1 pint of strawberry pulp, 15 yolks of eggs, 1 ounce of vanilla sugar, half a pint of double cream whipped.

Mix the syrup and yolks, strain, then add the strawberry pulp and vanilla sugar, set the composition as above directed; incorporate the whipped cream lightly, and fill the paper cases (either plaited and irregular, or square); these must be surrounded each with a band of stiff paper, of sufficient width to reach half an inch above the edges of the cases, the bands to be pinched thick, or pinned together at one corner, so as to render them secure. The biscuits filled, place them in the ice cave, and imbed them in ice in the usual way.

When about to send these biscuits to table, after having first removed the bands of paper, cover their surfaces with brown coloured ratafias bruised to a fine powder, and sifted upon them. It will be obvious that the bands of paper to be placed round the cases are intended to give the biscuits the appearance of the composition having risen out of the cases while the biscuits are supposed to have been baked.

Notes

1. What refined intricacies are there in the *rôt*! It is much worse than a minuet.—*Almanach des gourmands*, 1805. [Jerrold]
2. "Couvert" is equivalent to "cover" or place setting: the utensils, plate, napkin, etc., set for each individual's use at table.

12
Alexandre Dumas (1802–70)

Le Grand Dictionnaire de Cuisine [Dictionary of Cuisine] (1873)

Introduction

One of the most celebrated French writers of the nineteenth century, Alexandre Dumas, formed a Romantic triumvirate with Victor Hugo and Alfred de Vigny. Readers familiar with his historical novels, *The Three Musketeers* and *The Count of Monte Cristo* (1844–45) will recognize the degree to which his gastronomical interests infiltrate his dialogue. Descended from a French nobleman who had settled in Santo Domingo and a black slave from the colony, Dumas (whose father left his family in poverty after his death in 1806) claims to have written all of his novels for the sake of money. His *Grand dictionnaire de cuisine*, published posthumously in 1873, was reputedly the only book he wrote for pleasure. Nicknamed the "King of Paris," Dumas himself lived as adventurously as the heroes in his novels, earning fortunes and spending them in the finest restaurants of the city, where he could be found devouring scores of oysters.

Dumas also threw his own costly entertainments, for in addition to being an omnivorous reader and writer, he was himself a gourmet chef with a professionally equipped kitchen. Gastronomical literature since the 1870s is replete with references to Dumas's culinary skill as well as his *Dictionary*, just as he himself acknowledged a debt to Grimod de la Reynière and Brillat-Savarin. Visitors tell of his rushing, upon a sudden burst of inspiration, from the saucepan to his desk to polish off a scene or a chapter. Like his fiction, his *Grand Dictionary of Cuisine* was formidable in length, running roughly 600,000 words in the manuscript form that he left it at his death. When he died of a stroke on December 5, 1870, his last words expressed regret for his

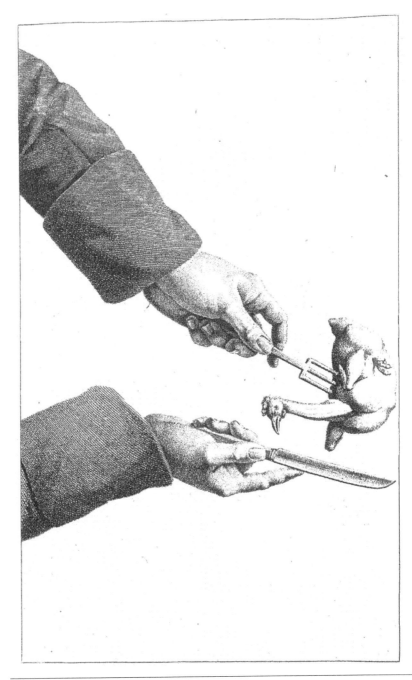

Figure 30 "Position de la main, du couteau, et de la fourchette à découper" [Position of the hand, knife, and carving fork]; from Grimond de la Reynière, *The Host's Manual* (1808). Courtesy of Special Collections, Stanford University Libraries.

unfinished dictionary as if it were one of own favorite novels: "I shall never know how it all comes out now."

The text below is from the 1958 edition, edited and translated by Louis Colman.

From *Dictionary of Cuisine* (1873)

A Few Words to the Reader

...Rome, most privileged of cities, has had two civilizations, both brilliant: its warrior history and its Christian history. After the luxury of its generals and emperors, it had the luxury of its cardinals and popes.

Through its commerce Italy regained the riches it once had conquered with its arms. As it had had its heathen gourmands, its Lucullus, Hortensius, Apicius, Antony and Pollio, it had also its Christian gourmands, its Leonardo da Vinci, Tintoretto, Titian, Paolo Veronese, Raphael, Boccio Bandinelli, Guido Reni. Until finally this new civilization could no longer be contained. It overflowed into France.

France was very backward in its cuisine. Only our excellent wines, though they had not attained the degree of perfection they have today, were superior to those of old Rome and new Italy. But by a happy chance, in the midst of the dispersion of peoples and the inundation of barbarians, the convents had remained places of refuge in which the sciences, arts, and tradition of cookery lay hidden. But cookery had turned from pagan to Christian and suffered a division into meat and meatless.

The luxury of the table that we find in the paintings of Paolo Veronese, especially in his Marriage at Cana, came to France with Catherine de Medici, and continued to grow during the reigns of Francis II, Charles IX, and Henry III.

Linen, especially fine linen, made its appearance late in France. Cleanliness does not presage civilization. It results from it. Our lovely ladies of the thirteenth and fourteenth centuries, at whose feet Galaor, Amadis, and Lancelot of the Lake knelt, not only did not wear undergarments but, it must be admitted, did not even know about them. Tablecloths, already in use at the time of Augustus, had disappeared, and their white surfaces were not seen on our tables until the close of the thirteenth century, and then only for kings and princes.

Napkins did not come into use until forty years later, under the reign that followed.

Our first ancestors, the Celts, wiped their hands on the bales of hay that served them for seats. The Spartans put a piece of soft bread beside each guest for the same purpose. In Rheims, before the first table napkins came into use, hands were wiped on hanks of wool that were neither new nor newly washed.

In 1792, at the time of Lord Macartney's voyages, the Chinese still used nothing but two little pieces of wood to bring their food to their mouths. The fork and spoon were just about absent from France until the sixteenth century, and their use was not widespread until the last century.

St. Peter Damian relates with horror that the sister of Romain Archile, who had married one of the sons of Pietro Orseolo, Doge of Venice, instead of eating with her fingers used golden forks and spoons to lift food to her mouth—which he regards as an effect of insensate luxury that must call down divine wrath upon her head and her husband's head. Both, in fact, died of the plague.

Knives had been in use long before forks, because they were necessary to cut meats that could not be torn apart with the fingers.

As for glasses, they were known to the Romans, as the story I have told about Pollio shows. Today, the curious traveller who visits Pompeii can see for himself that the use of glass was common among them. But after the barbarian invasion glasses were known only by tradition.

From the days of Phaedrus to Aristotle, about four centuries before Christ, wine was kept in earthenware amphorae, which held about twenty quarts, or in goatskins, from which it evaporated so much that it was necessary to scrape the skins and dissolve the coagulated liquid before it could be imbibed. In Spain it is still kept in goatskins, which give it an abominable flavour. The Spaniards, however, consider this as appetizing as the flavour of our Burgundy and Bordeaux. And in France there was no such thing as a bottle before the fourteenth century.

As for spices, which today provide the major condiments for all our sauces, they began to be a little commoner in France when Christopher Columbus discovered America and Vasco da Gama the passage of the Cape of Good Hope. But in 1163 they were still so rare and precious that the Abbé of Saint-Gilles in Languedoc, having a great favour to ask of Louis the Young, could think of no better way to propitiate him than to send bags of spices with his plea. Presents given to judges were called spices [épices], and this expression still survives.

In countries almost surrounded by the sea, like France, salt was used in the most ancient times as a seasoning for meat and vegetables. Pepper, on the other hand, has been known for no more than a hundred and fifteen or twenty years. M. Poivre, a native of Lyons, brought it from the Île de France, in Cochin China. Before that, it sold for its weight in gold. Spice dealers who were so fortunate as to have a few ounces proclaimed themselves "Spice and Pepper Merchants" on their shop signs. Apparently, pepper was not that rare among the ancient Romans, for three thousand pounds of it were included in the tribute levied upon Rome by Alaric.

The intellectual faculties seem to have soared in an enduring exaltation under the influence of spices. Is it to spices that we owe Ariosto, Tasso, and Boccaccio? Is it to spices that we owe Titian's masterpieces? I am tempted to believe it.

It was especially under Henry III that the elegant delicacies of the Florentine and Roman tables flourished in France. The tablecloth was folded and curled like a lady's collar from the time of Francis I. Already silver-plated luxury had passed all bounds, and it took an ordinance of Philip the Fair to curb it. Under his successors further ordinances unsuccessfully attempted to impose further limits on it.

In the early sixteenth century, under Louis XII and Francis I, dinner was at ten o'clock in the morning and supper at four. In the seventeenth century, dinner was at noon, supper at seven. If anyone, in this connection, wants to see something quite curious, and learn of great numbers of dishes that have been lost and forgotten, let him read the Memoirs of Héroard the physician, whose task it was to record the lunches and dinners of Louis XIII.

In those days pages, and sometimes the mistress of the house and her daughters, brought silver basins to the guests to wash their hands. This done, everyone sat at table, and after eating each went to an adjoining room to wash his hands again. If the master wished to show special honour to a guest, he sent his own full glass to him. In Spain today, when the mistress of the house wishes to indicate her favour, she touches her lips to the glass and sends it to you to drink her health. Our forefathers said that to live in health it was necessary to get drunk once a month.

Commerce, establishing itself along the shores from the Bay of Bengal to Dunkirk, completely changed the routing of the spices that came to us from India, while those that came from America crossed the Atlantic. Italian commerce languished then, and bit by bit disappeared. Scientific, and especially culinary, discoveries no longer came to us from the Venetians, Genoese, and Florentines, but from the Portuguese, the Germans, and the Spaniards. Bayonne, Mainz, and Frankfurt sent us their hams; Strasbourg smoked its sausages and bacon for us; Amsterdam sent us its little herrings, and Hamburg its beef.

At this point coffee made its appearance in France. A Moslem priest had noticed that the goats in Yemen which ate the berries of a certain plant growing in that country were happier, gayer, and livelier than the others. He roasted the berries, ground them, made an infusion from them, and discovered coffee as we know it.

Despite Mme de Sévigné's prophecy, coffee continued to be the high spot of every dessert in the reign of Louis XIV.[1]

Cabarets or taverns, prototypes of the cafes, had long been in existence, and began to soften our ways. Eating in the same room, often at the same table, Frenchmen learned to live like brothers and friends.

In the reign of Louis XIV the cuisine was elaborate, sumptuous, and fairly subtle. At the Condé table one began to surmise how delicate it could become.[2]

To the suppers of the Regent Philip of Orleans, to the cooks he developed and treated and paid so royally, we are indebted for the excellent cuisine of the eighteenth century. This simple and at the same time knowledgeable cuisine, which we have today in a complete and perfected form, moved forward in a tremendous, rapid, unhoped-for fashion. Full of verve, far from obscuring wit, it whipped it into life. French conversation, a model for all Europe, found its perfection at table, from midnight to one in the morning, between the pear and the cheese.

The conversation ranged from the great questions of the day to those of preceding centuries, and was developed at table with profundity, reason, and light by Montesquieu, Voltaire, Diderot, Helvetius, d'Alembert, and others like them, the while refinements of cookery spread from the Condés, the Soubises, the Richelieus, and the Talleyrands, and—what enormous progress!—one could dine as well in a restaurant for twelve francs as in Talleyrand's home and better than at Cambacérès'.

Dedication: A Letter to Jules Janin

You and I were born at the meeting of two centuries, two years apart, I believe—I in 1802 and you in 1804 or 1805. As a result, neither of us ever knew—except by reputation—the most famous gastronomes of the last century.

The most famous table of those days was kept by Talleyrand.

Bouché, or Bouche-sèche, who was trained in the Condé household and whose good food was renowned for tastiness and impressiveness, was given full charge of the Prince's kitchens. It was he who created those large diplomatic dinner parties which have become classic and will always be imitated. The Prince had complete confidence in him, left him completely free in his expenditures, and accepted everything he did as good. Bouché died in the Prince's service. Carême dedicated the *Pâtissier royal*, one of his finest books, to him. Much has been said about Talleyrand's table, but many of the things said do not have the virtue of being exactly true.

Talleyrand was one of the first to realize that a wholesome, well-thought-out cuisine would improve the health and prevent serious diseases. In fact, his health during the last forty years of his life is a powerful argument in favour of this opinion.

All of Europe that was illustrious in politics, learning, and art, great generals, ministers, diplomats, and poets, sat at Talleyrand's table, and not one failed to recognize that it was here that the finest hospitality was dispensed. The Revolution had killed all the great lords, the great tables, the great manners. Talleyrand re-established all that. Thanks to him France's reputation for magnificence and hospitality went around the world once more.

At eight o'clock every morning, Talleyrand spent an hour with his cook, discussing the dishes for dinner. This was the only meal he ate, for in the morning all he had before getting to work was three or four cups of camomile tea.

Here is the illustrious cook Carême's opinion of Cambacérès' cuisine, which, it seems, has often been mistakenly praised:

"I have written several times that Cambacérès kitchens never merited their great reputation. I shall repeat certain details, and cite a few more, to clarify the picture of that villainous house. M. Grand Manche, chef of the kitchens of the archchancellor, was a learned practitioner and an honourable man, whom we all esteem. Having been called in by him for the great affairs at the Prince's house, I was able to appreciate his work, and I can consequently say a little about it. The Prince occupied himself with his table every morning, expending minute care—but only to discuss and decrease its expense. He showed, in the highest degree, that worry and concern over details which marks the miser. At every service, he took note of the dishes that had not been eaten, or only partly eaten. Next day he composed his dinner from these vile leftovers. Heavens! What a dinner! I do not mean that leftovers cannot be used. I do mean they cannot yield the dinner of a prince and an eminent gastronome. This is a delicate point. The master has nothing to say about it, nothing to see. Only the ability and probity of the cook are concerned. Leftovers must be employed only with caution, ability, and, above all, silence.

"The household of the Prince de Talleyrand, which is the first in Europe, in the world, and in history, operates according to those principles. They are principles of taste. They were the principles of every great gentleman I ever served: Lord Castlereagh, George IV, the Emperor Alexander, etc.

"The archchancellor [Cambacérès] received innumerable presents in the form of food from the departments, especially the finest birds. All these were stuffed into a vast larder of which the Prince himself had the key. He took note of the provisions and the day of their arrival, and he alone gave orders for their use. Frequently, by the time he gave the order, the provisions were spoiled. Food never appeared at his table until it was at least stale.

"Cambacérès was never a gourmand in the true, learned sense of the word. He was born a big, even a voracious, eater. Can it be believed that his favourite dish was hot meat-ball pie, a heavy, insipid, stupid dish? One day, when the good Grand Manche wanted to replace the meat balls with quenelles of poultry, cockscombs and cock's kidneys, will you believe it, the Prince turned red with anger and demanded his old-fashioned meat balls that were tough enough to break one's teeth. He found them delicious. For hors d'oeuvres, he was often served a bit of warmed-over pastry crust, and the butt of a ham that had seen service all week appeared on his table. And his able cook, who never had the great sauces! Not even that cook's assistant a bottle of Bordeaux! What parsimony! What a pity! What a house!

"How different was the great, dignified dwelling of the Prince de Benevent [Talleyrand]! Complete confidence, completely justified, in the chef, one of the most illustrious practitioners of our day, M. Bouché. Only the most sanitary and the finest products were employed. Everything was ability, order, splendour. Talent was happy there, and highly placed. The chef governed the stomach. Who knows but what he influenced the charming, active, or great thoughts of the minister. Forty-eight-course dinners were given in the halls on the Rue de Varenne. I have designed them and I have seen them served. What a man was M. Bouché! What great tableaux he created! Who has not seen them has seen nothing!

"Neither Cambacérès nor Brillat-Savarin ever knew how to eat. Both of them loved strong, vulgar foods. They simply filled their stomachs. That is letter-perfect truth. Savarin was a big eater and it seems to me he talked very little and with difficulty. He had a heavy air, and looked like a parish priest. At the end of his meal, he was absorbed with his digestion. I have seen him sleep."

Let's finish the picture. Brillat-Savarin was neither a gastronome nor a gourmet. He was just a vigorous eater. He was tall, and because of his heavy bearing, his vulgar manners, and his clothing, which was always ten to twelve years behind the fashion, he was called the drum major of the Court of Cassation.

Suddenly, twelve years after his death, we inherited one of the most charming books on gastronomy one could dream of, his *Physiology of Taste*.

Grimod de la Reynière was one of the heroes of that period. An accident when he was very young deprived him of his hands. By dint of ingenuity and perseverance, he made of the remaining stumps organs nearly as supple as hands themselves. As a youth he was very elegant. His health was sound, his stomach stanch. He died at the age of eighty. His nephew, the Count d'Orsay, presented me to him. He kept us to dinner, and gave us one of the best I ever ate. That was about 1834 or 1835.

It was said that at Louis XVIII's dinners, even when he dined tête-a-tête with M. d'Avray, the King exhausted the mysteries of the most recherché luxury. Chops were not merely grilled. They were grilled between two other chops. The diner himself opened this marvellous censer, which poured forth its juices and most delicate perfumes. Ortolans stuffed with truffles were cooked in the stomachs of partridges, so that His Majesty sometimes hesitated for moments between the delicate bird and the perfumed vegetable.

There was a tasting jury for the fruits that were to be served at the royal table, and M. Petit-Radel, librarian of the Institute, was peach taster. One day a gardener from Montreuil, having by artful grafts obtained the most beautiful variety of peaches, wished to offer them in homage to Louis XVIII. But first he had to pass the tasting jury. He presented himself, therefore, at the library of the Institute, bearing a plate with four magnificent peaches, and asked for M. Petit-Radel.

He had some difficulty getting in. The librarian was engaged in some pressing work. The gardener insisted, asking only that he be permitted to pass the plate, the peaches, and his forearm through the door.

At the sound of this operation, M. Petit-Radel reopened his eyes, which had closed beatifically over a Gothic manuscript. At sight of the peaches, which seemed to advance on him of their own volition, he uttered a cry of joy, and cried out twice: "Come in! Come in!"

The gardener announced the purpose of his visit, and the jubilation of a gastronome spread itself over the savant's face. Lounging in his armchair with legs crossed and hands joined, he prepared himself with a gentle adjustment, a sensual movement of the shoulders, for the important judgment required of him.

The gardener asked for a silver knife. He picked up one of the peaches and cut it in quarters, put one on the point of the knife, and gaily presented it to M. Petit-Radel, saying: "Taste the juice."

Eyes closed, forehead impassive, full of the importance of his function, M. Petit-Radel silently tasted the juice.

Anxiety was already appearing in the gardener's eyes when, after two or three minutes, the judge's half opened.

"Good! Very good, my friend," were the only words he could say.

Immediately the second slice was offered, but the gardener said, with slightly more assurance: "Taste the flesh!"

Same silence, same serious mien of the learned gourmand. But this time the movements of his mouth were more evident, for he was chewing. Finally, he nodded.

"Ah! Very good! Very good!" said he.

Perhaps you think the superiority of the peach was established and everything was said? No.

"Taste the aroma!" said the gardener.

The aroma was found worthy of the flesh and the juice. Then the gardener, who had progressed little by little from a supplicant to a triumphant attitude, presented the last piece and, with a pride and satisfaction that he did not seek to hide, said: "Now. Taste the whole!"

It is superfluous to say that this last slice had the same success as its predecessors. M. Petit-Radel, his eyes moist with emotion, a smile on his lips, took the gardener's hands in his own as effusively as he would an artist's.

"Ah, my friend," he said, "it is perfect. Allow me to express my sincere compliments. Beginning tomorrow your peaches will be served at the King's table."

Louis XVIII had no illusions. He saw gourmandism fading away, and it saddened him.

"Doctor," he said one day to Corvisart, "gastronomy is disappearing, and with it the last of the old civilization. It is the organized professions—the physicians, for example—who should put forth every effort to prevent the dissolution of society. At one time France was full of gastronomes, because it was full of groups whose members have now been annihilated or dispersed. There are no more farmers-general, no more abbés, no more white monks. All that is left of gastronomy resides in you, the physicians, who are predestined gourmands. You should uphold more firmly the burden with which destiny has charged you. You should attempt to emulate the Spartans at Thermopylae."

Louis XVII, a delicate eater, had profound contempt for his brother, Louis XVI, a gross one who when he ate did not accomplish an intellectual, reasoned action, but a completely brutal one. When Louis XVI was hungry he had to eat. On August 10th, when he went to the Convention to ask asylum, he was put in a box—I won't say the stenographer's box, because there were no stenographers at that time, but at least the box of the man responsible for an account of the proceedings. Scarcely was he seated when hunger overtook him, and he demanded food on the instant!

The Queen argued with him, trying to avoid such an exhibition of gluttony and thoughtlessness. He would not listen to reason. He was brought a roast chicken, into which he bit immediately, apparently indifferent to the grave discussions of life and death around him. What did it matter? He was eating, therefore he was alive. And he continued to eat until not a shred of chicken nor a crumb of bread remained.

This tendency of his towards insatiable hunger was so well known that Camille Desmoulins was able to spread the story, an odious calumny at such a moment, that he was arrested because he would not pass through Sainte-Menehould without eating the famous pigs' feet of that town. But everyone knows that Louis XVI was not arrested at Sainte-Menehould but at Varennes, and that pigs' feet had nothing to do with this arrest.

...

A word on those useful establishments, whose chefs sometimes vied with men like Beauvilliers and Carême.[3] In Paris they have existed no longer than eighty to a hundred years. They cannot, therefore, credit their nobility to their antiquity. Restaurants are directly descended from the cabaret-taverns. At all times there were shops where wine was sold and shops where food was served. Those which sold wine were called cabarets. Those which sold food were called taverns.

The profession of wine merchant is one of the oldest that survives in the capital. Boileau cites statutes for them from 1264, but the merchants were not organized into corporate bodies for another three hundred and fifty years. At that time they were divided into four classes, hostelers, cabaretkeepers, taverners, and sellers of wine by the pot. These last sold wine retail but did not keep taverns. The wine they sold could not be consumed on the premises. There was an opening in the grille before their establishments through which the customer passed his empty pot and withdrew it after it had been filled. Of this custom all that remains today is the grille that constitutes part of the wine merchant's storefront.

The cabaretkeepers were permitted to serve drinks in their own establishments, and food as well, but they were expressly forbidden to sell wine in bottles. They were obliged to use standard pint pots. In the eleventh century, lords, monks, and kings did not consider it beneath their dignity to sell by the pot or at retail the wine produced on their estates. To make a quick profit they abused their absolute authority by ordering the cabarets of the city closed down until all their own wine was sold.

It was towards the middle of the last century that one Boulanger established the first restaurant in Paris, on the Rue des Poules. Over his door was the legend: Venite omnes, qui stomacho laboris, et ego restaurabo vos—"Come, all ye that labour on your stomach, and I shall restore you."

The establishment of restaurants in Paris marked great progress indeed. Before they were invented, strangers were at the mercy of the cooking of the innkeepers, which was generally bad. There were some hotels serving a table d'hôte, but with few exceptions they offered only the barest essentials. Of course there were the cookshops, but they served only whole cuts, and if one wished to dine with a friend, one had to buy a whole leg of lamb, a whole turkey, or a whole chine of beef.

Finally, a genius came along who understood that if one diner asked for a chicken wing, another could not fail to appear who wanted the drumstick. Variety of dishes, definite prices, care given to service would bring success to the first who established all three qualities.

The Revolution, which destroyed so many things, created new restaurantkeepers. The stewards and chefs of the great lords, left without employment by the immigration of their masters, turned philanthropic and bethought themselves to share the fruits of their culinary science with the public.

At the time of the first Bourbon restoration, in 1814, the restaurant-keeper took a great step. Beauvilliers appeared in his dining rooms dressed like a gentleman, sword at side.

Among the restaurant-keepers who wielded the sceptre in the kitchen we must mention one Méot. He sold consommé, fresh eggs, and chicken au gros sel, serving them on little marble tables like those in the cafés today. In my youth I still heard talk of the succulent dinners Méot served, and of the brisk, engaging air of his wife at the cashier's desk. Méot had been chef to the Prince de Condé—that is to say, Vatel's successor.

After Paris, the city with the most restaurants is San Francisco. It has restaurants from every country, even China.

Today there is little difference between the cookshops and the restaurants, and it was long the custom, at the end of the last century and the beginning of this, to go to a cookshop for oysters and fish soup. And this made sense, for often one dines better at Maire's, Philippe's, or Magny's than at the finest restaurants in Paris.

Here are some of the restaurant-keepers whose names the gourmands of the last century and the beginning of this one have remembered with gratitude: Beauvilliers, Méot, Robert, Rose, Borel, Legacque, the Véry Brothers, Neveux, and Baleine.

Those of today are Verdier of the Maison d'Or, Bignon, Brebant, Riche, the Cafe Anglais, Peter's, Véfour, the Frères Provençaux.

If I omit any celebrities, may they forgive me. It is an oversight.

Notes

1. According to Voltaire, Mme. de Sévigné predicted that coffee would be in fashion for only a short time, like Racine. This appears to be anecdotal; her letters do not mention the prophecy.
2. During the reign of Louis XIV (1643–1715) a new "French" cuisine emerged. No new book of recipes had appeared in more than a century; then, in 1651, François Pierre, called La Varenne, cook for the Marquis of Uxelles, published *Le cuisiner françois* (The French Cook), the first in a series of twelve titles, or about seventy-five, counting new editions, representing about 100,000 volumes, published up until 1791, the date of the publication of the well-known *Cuisinier royal et bourgeois* (Royal and Middle-Class Cook) by Français Massialot. Jean-Robert Pitte, *French Gastronomy: The History and Geography of a Passion,* trans. Jody Gladding (New York: Columbia University Press, 2002), 93.
3. This final section is from Dumas's "A Few Words to the Reader."

Joseph Berchoux (1762–1838)

La Gastronomie; ou l'homme des champs à table, Poëme didactique in IV chants (1801); trans. Gastronomy, or the Bon-Vivant's Guide: A Poem, in IV Cantos (1810)

Introduction

The first recorded instance of the term *gastronomy* occurs in this didactic poem by Joseph de Berchoux, an antirevolutionary émigré. His poem, subtitled "l'Homme des Champs à table," responds to "l'Homme des Champs," by the French litterateur, Abbé Jacques Delille (1738–1813) in four culinary cantos: (1) "Historie de la cuisine" (a verse essay on the cookery of ancient Greece and Rome); (2) "Le premier service" (instructions for the successful conduct of a meal, including advice on household organization, food presentation, invitations, and the maintenance of one's appetite); (3) "Le second service" (containing advice for the host on orchestrating conversation during a meal, with a description of the events surrounding the unfortunate suicide of Vatel, chef to the Prince de Condé); and (4) "Le dessert" (treating dessert, wines, spirits, and conversation, concluding in praise of dining as superior to poetry).

While the first through third (1801–04) editions of the poem were signed Joseph B***, the fourth (1805) and subsequent editions acknowledged his surname. The second edition included an engraving by Edme Bovinet (1767–1837), titled *Le sénat mit aux voix cette affaire importante, et le turbot fut mis à la sauce piqunte* and a *Prière du soir d'un poëte*, both of which were copied without attribution by Dick Humelbergius Secundus in *Apician Morsels*.

Reprinted here is the fourth canto of Berchoux's poem, translated into English in 1810 with a slightly more elaborate and ironic tone than the original French.

From *Gastronomy, or the Bon-Vivant's Guide* (1801)

Canto IV: *The Dessert*

His Grace, my Lord Duke, whom no cares have oppress'd,
Served by Hebe's fair hands, and by Plutus caress'd;
Neither hunger nor want, knowing, more than by name,
With pleasure, but little acquaintance can claim.
In luxury nurtured, his breast will ne'er glow
With the raptures that contrast alone can bestow.
But, when absent from home, where enjoyment e'en palls,
If some trifling disaster his Lordship befalls,
And delay'd, he must stoop to the farmer's rough fare,
Or a scanty repast with the cottager share;
'Tis then, if kind chance or good fortune should grant
A neatly-dress'd meal, in the moment of want,
O'er and o'er he surveys it, scarce trusting his eyes,
So increased his delight by the pleasing surprise. —
Doubly bright are the sun-beams emerging from rain,
And sweetest the pleasure preceded by pain.
   In a neighbouring country, some seasons ago,
When such horrors prevail'd, as may we never know,
By a barbarous tyrant expell'd from my home,
For a time, in disguise, I was fated to roam;
In the national ranks then enlisted, through fear,
Becoming, like others, a *forced volunteer.*
Though, thank Heav'n, I ne'er fired it, a musket I bore,
And a knapsack, containing the whole of my store.
Thus equipp'd, I set off; — who'd not pity my plight?
O'erwhelm'd with regret, and half dying with fright.
Farewell, lively dinners, where flow'd wit and wine,
And gay parties embellish'd by beauty divine!
Adieu, *fricandeaux*, and dear *perdrix aux choux*,[1]
With all the nice cooking, at home that I knew!
   As I slowly moved on, at each step near me lagg'd
Some poor wretch, to the armies inhumanly dragg'd.

When a town we approach'd, the alarm became great,
The poultry was watch'd, closely barr'd was each gate;
Whilst, at night, the best supper we found at our inn,
Was black bread and *soupe maigre*, with wine rough and thin;
And the comforts, our billets procured us, were these,
Fire, water, and beds where the soldiers must squeeze.

    Before we reach'd Lyons, for there were we bound,[2]
On our route, a fair friend, by good fortune I found;
Who, from plunder exempt, still lived snugly at home,
Awaiting her turn, which was certain to come:
For her house's defence, the measures contrived,
Then enjoy'd the time present, — 'Twas here I arrived. —
My musket and knapsack were scarcely deposed,
When each cheering relief from fatigue she proposed;
Whilst supper, preparing, oft' scented the gale
With an odour; I greatly rejoiced to inhale.
'Midst the elegant plenty, which there was display'd,
To a fowl, stuff'd with truffles, attention I paid;
With frequency, too, I the quality tried
Of a bottle of excellent wine, by my side.
All hardships forgotten, my spirits were raised,
My friend and her bounty were toasted and praised;
No longer a soldier, who tyrants arraign'd,
A monarch myself, in idea, I reign'd!

    'Tis time now, my muse, to our guests to return. —
How their lively eyes sparkle — their rosy cheeks burn!
The moment's at hand, to your Cook to declare
That you highly approve of his delicate fare;
To-morrow, at table, the vantage you'll feel
Of a public eulogium, in praise of his zeal.
With a smile of complacency, thus, may you say —
"I'm pleased, as I ought, with my dinner, to-day.
Proceed, soon a happy occasion I'll take,
A wreath for your brow, from the garnish to make
Of some favourite dish, which my friends greatly praise;
May you think the reward your bright merit repays!"

    Now arrives the Dessert: – to its splendid display,
The dairy's rich produce, alas! must give way;
For, though lovers the smell may deride, if they please,
I the relish esteem of a good Chesire-cheese.

    Let an elegant service, in order exact,
Of your exquisite dinner, adorn the last act.

Of numerous artists the talents combine,
But chief the confectioner's labours will shine;
Gay palaces, temples, pagodas, appear,
And their miniature turrets and cupolas rear;
Gibraltar, in biscuit, the Spaniards defy,
Or sugarplumb-pyramids totter on high.
On such fairy productions, your strength don't essay:
Let these castles aërial live through the day.
Abundance of objects, around will you meet,
Though they less please the eye, to the palate as sweet.
By the apricot, more is your notice deserved,
Which art has, in nature's full beauty, preserved;
By the peach or the quince; or, what many think best,
By the citron or ginger, which come from the West.

Of your tasty arrangement, complete the delight,
And gay Flora's rich tints, with Pomona, unite;
Let the jasmine, the violet, lilly and rose,
Your fruits, in the charms of the parterre, enclose.
Here, too, let the lovers of botany find
The flow'rs that delight them, in sugar enshrin'd.

When each varied delight of the appetite's o'er,
Still, Bacchus reserves us a pleasure, in store.
Approach, rosy God! by thy presence I'm fired,
And more, than by all the nine Muses, inspired;
Wit and harmony spring from thy liquor divine,
While spirit and ease guide the smooth-flowing line.

With a pleasing anxiety, now, we survey
Decanters and glasses, in brilliant array.
How eager each eye! with what ardour we burn
To commence the attack, when it comes to our turn!
Nor long do we wait; — see the column advance!
In the van, are the delicate natives of France,
Purple hermitage, burgundy, sparkling champaign.
Old-hock forms the center, with sherry from Spain.
Constantia, rich mountain, imperial tokay,
As skirmishers act, — fire a shot and away;
Leaving claret, madeira, and generous port,
In the rear, well prepared the chief shock to support.[3]

At times, you may fairly attention engage
By the growth of your Bordeaux, your Malaga's age;
But dwell not too long on such topics as these,
Lest the story should tire those your dinners may please.

And here, though the caution may needless appear
To all who pretend e'en to value good cheer,
I fain, for your cellar, would claim ev'ry care;
Neither money nor pains, in the filling it, spare:[4]
Since, the juice of choice vintages, mellow'd by time,
Alone will condition and flavour combine.
    Drink now, 'tis the time, but your hurry refrain;
And from bumpers, too often repeated, abstain.
Thus, pleasure prolong'd, you insensibly rise
To the exquisite glee, which description defies;
Taste the unalloy'd bliss, the oblivion of care,
Which Bacchus's votaries only can share.
Ye, who gravely address us, with visage demure,
On the means which our happiness serve to secure;
Enforce your advice in the best way ye can,
It ne'er will be follow'd: — the bottle's my plan. —
Has the reason ye boast of, with so much parade,
By its precepts, a change in your destiny made?
What good, by obeying it, e'er did ye get?
Believe me, if lost, it deserves no regret!
    In an evening's walk, did you ne'er meet a clown
Returning, well primed, from the next market town?
Head-foremost, and reeling about, though he go,
He, by instinct, appears the way homeward to know.
His tripping and stumbling need give no alarm,
For the god he is full of will shield him from harm.
With a pipe in his mouth, he defies ev'ry sorrow,
And cares not a whiff, what may happen to-morrow.
After strolling around, to his cottage restored,
As great he's become, if as drunk as a Lord.
With happy delusions his liquor inspires,
His sons acquire riches, his daughters wed 'squires;
At his wife in a coach, all the neighbourhood stare;
And he, pleased with the joke, falls asleep in his chair. —
Why not triumph like him? — the famed Galen, I think,
Once a week, for our health, recommends us to drink.
    At your table, encourage convivial glee,
Give, to wit, a free scope, and invite repartee.
Banish personal jokes, which too often annoy;
The laugh, with your friends, but not at them, enjoy.
Abstaining from slander, of satire beware;
And debates, on religion or politics, spare:

More by actions, than words, you may either support.
Prove your orthodox faith, by your orthodox port;
And, to baffle invasion, you claret should drink,
Leave the French without wine, and their courage must sink.
      To toasts I object not; — but hate party-cant.
Drink no minister's health; nor exclaim with a rant,
"Be liberty welcome! equality, hail!
May the sovereign-will of the people prevail!"
By sentiments, oft' you some guest may displease;
I'd fain, in their stead, drink such wishes as these —
"May we, fifty years hence, stout and hearty remain,
And a hundred times meet, at this table, again!
May no change of season endanger the vine,
Nor war or taxation deprive us of wine!" —
Your spleen 'gainst your foes, is most strongly express'd,
By wishing "their dinners may ne'er be well dress'd;
"That, out of condition, their wines may be found,
Their port chill'd and muddy, their claret unsound;
That no friends, at their table, may sociably meet,
But, stupid and sulky, alone they may eat!"
Let this be the only revenge they've to fear;
For if Jove grant your pray'r, they'll do penance severe.
      The prevalent follies amusement afford;
When he spars with a porter, we laugh at my Lord.
On the shock-headed boys, grooms and coachmen by trade,
A good-humour'd joke may, with freedom, be made.
We smile, too, at ladies, when dashers or nudes;
At their blue-stocking clubs, and their conclaves of prudes.
But touch these points lightly, avoiding complaints;
View the bright side of things, leave the dark to the saints:
For with me 'tis a maxim, whose comfort I feel,
To perceive nothing wrong, when I've made a good meal.[5]
      Though Bacchus, with Orpheus, no rivalship hold,
Yet, to sing with their wine, was a custom of old.
Adopt the gay plan; by true glee when inspired,
No exquisite science or taste is required.
At table, we seek not perfection ideal,
The notes may be false, yet the pleasure prove real.
How joyous the accents which echo around!
How loudly and long does the chorus resound!
Where our rapturous praises of Venus divine,
Give her myrtle's perfume to each goblet of wine.

But allow me, my friends! on your prudence to call,
You either see double, or see not at all;
Most dissonant topics you jumble and blend,
And all are more ready to speak than attend.
E'en I, to the pleasing delirium a prey,
Partake the confusion I wish to portray.
'Tis enough: — at the dictate of reason, abstain;
After pausing awhile, you may lose it again:
Whene'er you are able, its presence reject,
Too often, alas! are we forced to reflect.

     Farewell, lively Comus! — gay Bacchus! adieu —
Forgive, if preferring libations to you,
To courting the Muses at Helicon's stream,
My verse prove unworthy so noble a theme.

     To the public I offer this banquet of mine;
Though my cooking displease; if they buy, I shall dine.
From the friends of the table, protection I claim,
Whilst, with sorrow I own, I fall short of my aim;
And to censure exposed, how I long for the pow'r
Of *shutting the mouths* of the critics so sour!
But their mercy I crave, of this truth well aware —
"That a *poem* can ne'er with a *dinner* compare."

Notes

1. The opening stanzas are close to the original French, though strangely enough neither of these two French phrases occur in Berchoux, who lists instead *friands apprêts* [pastries], *gibier* (venison) and *pâtés dores* (golden pâtés).
2. They are heading toward Italy in the French version.
3. This military metaphor is not developed in the original. The following discussion of wine departs in an enthusiastic English recollection of French wine.
4. Berchoux's verse suggests that one avoid reminiscing about negative aspects of history and claims that ambition destroys health and appetite; he adds several lines to suggest that one particularly avoid speaking of France's troubles.
5. This stanza does not occur in the original, which refers instead to the Terror and the hopes that France will avoid famine in the future.

Subjects of the Frontispieces

ENGLISH TRANSLATION BY MICHAEL GARVAL

From *The Gourmand's Almanac* (1803–12)

Figure 1 The Library of a Nineteenth-Century Gourmand (1803)

(Bibliothèque d'un Gourmand du XIXᵉ Siècle)

At the far end of a study decorated in the most modern taste—that is to say with furniture in the most ancient style—stands a bookcase with, upon its shelves, not books, but rather all manner of foodstuffs, among which one can see a suckling pig, various sorts of pâtés, enormous saveloys, and other such delicacies, along with a good number of bottles of wine and liquor, jars of fruit either crystallized or preserved in brandy, etc.

From the ceiling, in place of a lantern, there hangs a monstrous Bayonne ham.

In the foreground a table is laden with refined fare, enough for fifteen people, yet one sees only two place settings.

A sideboard which already holds the second course, and a serving table placed between the two chairs, signify that no servants shall disturb this solitary dinner.

At the bottom of the Print the legend reads:

The Library of a 19th-century Gourmand.

Figure 2 A Gourmand's Audiences (1805)

(Les audiences d'un Gourmand)

In a study, where all the shelves are filled with the most refined foodstuffs, and where several sorts of large and small game, like hare, wild boar, venison, wild goose, and rock partridge, as well as sugar loaves, bundles of coffee, etc., all hang from the ceiling, a Gourmand can be seen in the foreground, seated at his desk, busy meeting with several persons bearing provisions, who have come seeking to be acknowledged and legitimated. He takes note of these various *legitimations*, which line the walls of his study and even spill over onto the floor.

At the moment, he is receiving a letter of credit—a gigantic pâté—from one of the purveyors. The others, who also bring fine things, rush to meet him so that they too might figure honorably upon the list of those who have been legitimated.

A sentinel cat at the Gourmand's feet indicates that no rodent shall come near this larder.

Several works concerning culinary art, and placed upon the top shelves, are the only books to be found in this library, whose volumes have, over time, been supplanted by the foodstuffs which can be seen there.

At the bottom of the Print the legend reads: *A Gourmand's Audiences.*

Figure 3 A Jury of Gourmand Tasters in Session (1806)

(Séance d'un Jury de Gourmands dégustateurs)

This Print continues the one in Volume Two, where a Gourmand is seen busy receiving and recording various foodstuffs, brought to him as so-called *Legitimations*, to be submitted to his censure, and to that of the professors in the art of Gourmandise who make up the Tasting Jury.

Here one sees these professors holding their session at the dining table, busy tasting different foodstuffs which their creators have an interest in making known, having accredited, and having appear with favorable mention in the *Gourmand's Almanac.*

At this moment they are tasting the Pâté that was seen in volume two's print; on their faces one can observe the depth of reflection that is the hallmark of a Gourmand carrying out his duties.

At a separate table sits a scribe who writes up the results of their judgments, as these are conveyed to him by the Secretary of the Society, who turns around to dictate them to him. Opposite the Secretary sits the President, who has just tallied the votes.

Upon a sideboard several other foodstuffs await such consideration.

A ringer placed near the vice-president to facilitate service signifies that domestic help shall only enter these chambers when called, so that the judges may deliberate without distraction and with complete independence.

Several paintings whose subjects are drawn from the history of cooking are the only form of decoration in this hearing room.

At the bottom of the Print the legend reads, *A Jury of Gourmand Tasters in Session*.

Figure 4 A Gourmand's Meditations (1807)

(Les méditations d'un Gourmand)

In a Study decorated in the modern style, one sees in the foreground a Gourmand in his dressing gown, seated at his desk; he is in the middle of writing, but has just interrupted his work to reflect upon the material he is considering at the moment. The various objects of his reflections are placed around him upon several separate pedestal tables. One holds a stuffed Calf's Head from the *Puits-Certain*; another a Capon seasoned with coarse salt, from the *Marmite perpétuelle*; yet another a Foie gras Pâté from Strasbourg, sent via the *Hôtel des Américains*; still another holds Abbeville Biscuits from Mademoiselle Rose DesJardins, etc. At this instant, the Gourmand's attention is focused entirely on the first of these: the Calf's head seems to preoccupy his own.

Various Treatises on culinary art, such as The Learned Cook, Healthful Pastry-making, Comus's Gifts, The Modern Confectioner, are at his feet or spread out around him. These various works are taken from the library seen in Volume Two's Frontispiece.

The whole rear wall of this Study is taken up by a trapezoidal sideboard, its shelves displaying in no particular order a large number of *Legitimations*, which await consideration. One can see a wild boar's head from Troyes and a timbale of truffled red partridge, from M. Rouget; a sponge cake from M. Benaud; a truffled turkey from M. Chevet; a mortadella from Lyon, courtesy of M. Jean; an Italian cheese and some sausages, from M. Corps; a Bayonne ham from M. Pelletier-Petit; various small fowl from Madame Biennait; a Périgueux pâté from M. Corcellet; several loaves of crystallized sugar, from M. Martignon; various provisions from Provence, some fruit preserves from Montpellier, and apple jelly from Rouen, all courtesy of the Hôtel des Américains; several types of liqueurs and syrups from the workshops of MM. Sauvel, Tanrade, Le Moine and Noël Laserre; dessert and fortified wines from M. Taillieur, M. Le Moine, and M. Labour, etc., etc. All these items must be considered one after another by the Gourmand, since this is the goal of his undertaking, yet they shall doubtless obtain his approval, since they have come from the finest establishments in each category.

No other artwork decorates this Study, for nothing must distract the observer.

At the bottom of the Print the legend reads, *A Gourmand's Meditations.*

Figure 5 A Host's First Duty (1807)

(Le premier devoir d'un Amphitryon)

In the middle of a huge, beautiful Kitchen, equipped with all the tools and furniture needed to function properly, as well as a fireplace surmounted by three Bayonne Hams from the workshop of M. Pouillan and M. de la Bouille, and holding spits laden with Loins from Mme. Simon, Sirloins from M. de Launey, Legs of Lamb from M. Darras, Venison from Madame Chevet, and Fowl from Madame Biennait, etc., etc.; one observes a Host in his dressing gown, receiving from his Chef's hands the day's dinner menu. Saucepans upon the stove, Pâtés in the oven, cauldrons over the fire, soup pots upon the hearth, Appetizers on the table ready to be garnished, a young kitchen hand dressing a Chicken, etc., etc., all indicates that a great Feast is being prepared, and that these preparations are characterized by a level of activity that contrasts felicitously with the Chef's calm demeanor, and the Host's peaceful and contented air.

The small format of this Volume has allowed us only enough space to sketch this touching scene, and forced us to leave out the most interesting and salient details. Gourmands' minds shall make up for whatever lacks, recalling that the largest painting that exists, Veronese's Marriage at Cana, barely sufficed for this immortal artist to depict some Gourmands dining. What if, for example, he had needed to represent an Arch-Chancellor's kitchen?

At the bottom of the Print the legend reads, *A Host's first duty.*

Figure 6 A Gourmand's Dreams (1808)

(Les rêves d'un gourmand)

In the middle of a richly-decorated bedroom, upon a voluptuous bed in the classical style, a Gourmand lies in deep sleep, though at this instant his dreams, in harmony with his proclivities, are making him the happiest of men.

He dreams of being seated at a splendidly-appointed Table, like that of the *Tasting Jury* in full session. Calves' heads from the Puits Certain, Monsters from the seas, streams, and ponds; Salt-meadow mutton, Bayonne and Westphalian Hams, Capons from the Maine and La Flèche, etc., appear there in all their glory, and are complemented by admirable pastries from MM. Rouget, Le Blanc, Le Sage, George, Bouchon, Bégnaud, etc.; by Divine *Charcuterie* [cooked meats] from MM. Corps, Caillot, Jean, Hervet, Malherbe, Véro and Masson (from Saint-Germain-en-Laye); by terrestrial Monsters from

Madame Chevet; marine Monsters, native items, or exotic ones, from M. Balaine as well as from MM. Labour, Corcellet, Catheux, etc.; finally by lovely delicacies from the stores of MM. Duval, Berthellemot, Oudard (Madame La Motte's successor), etc., etc., etc., all accompanied by the best wines and most delicious liqueurs, from M. Taillieur and M. Le Moine, respectively.

All these good things can be seen upon a huge, luxurious sideboard, the idea of which delights our Gourmand, giving rise to the sweet mirth one can observe on his round, ruddy face, which recalls that of the famed M. d'Aigrefeuille.

Beneath this table, which floats on clouds, LEGITIMATIONS can be seen upon the floor, guarded by the AUTHOR's friendly, watchful cat—a superb white angora, which is the very least one can say about her.

At the bottom of the print the legend reads, *A Gourmand's Dreams*.

Figure 7 A Gourmand Rising (1810)

(Le lever d'un gourmand)

This Vignette offers a sequel to the one entitled A Gourmand's Dreams, which we published in our sixth Volume.

Here these dreams are in a sense realized. Upon awaking, the Gourmand sees his chef—big and fat like the one at the Rocher de Cancale—who has come to show him the Menu (almost as long as an Andouille de Vire [chitterling sausage]) for the dinner he is preparing. In order to receive this, he forsakes the cup of digestive tea he was about to drink, yet all his attention is directed at a crowd of Legitimations hurrying toward him.

Mane salutantum totis vomit œdibus undam[1]

Among the Acolytes sagging beneath the weight of their offerings, one can see the Ambassador of M. Boudeau, the renowned Pastry-Maker from Périgueux, carrying a Truffled red Partridge Pâté, the worthy precursor of a Turkey from the same Workshop; M. Taillieur's envoy, carrying on his head a basket filled with the best Wine from his famed cellars; one of M. Le Moine's salesclerks, carrying two bottles of the excellent liqueurs from his workshop; Madame Chevet's head Clerk, bearing veritable manna from heaven including, notably, a Terrine from Nérac and another made of Duck Liver, from Toulouse; Madame Des Noeuds's trusted salesgirl, carrying in her hand a superb Pike from Rouen, etc., etc.

Upon the floor one can see some other Legitimations that arrived the day before, such as an oyster basket from the Rocher de Cancale; fattened chickens from Le Mans; a Pâté from Strasbourg, Plover Pâté from Chartres, made by the famed Le Moine; a Boar's Head from Troyes, sent by M. Corcellet; preserved Sardines from Nantes, courtesy of M. Sellier, etc.; all under the watchful eye of the most adorable of Cats, who has never bitten nor scratched anyone, and has a very keen sense of hearing, even though she's an Angora.

This bedroom's luxurious furnishings, which come from the superb Stores at the Hôtel de Choiseul, and were donated by M. Baudouin, contrast with the collection of foodstuffs filling the space.

At the bottom of the print the legend reads: *A Gourmand Rising*.

Figure 8 Dinner's Most Mortal Enemy (1812)

(Le plus mortel enemi du dîner)

This Print is a sequel to the one in Volume seven, in which a Gourmand can be seen receiving his Cook, and various Legitimators. Here he is shown embarking upon a Lunch that, while proper, is so substantial that unless he has an extraordinary stomach, he shall have to eat lightly for the rest of the day.

How could it be otherwise, since the table before him and the serving tables at his side are overloaded with such an abundance of dishes, one more nutritive than the other? One can see several plates laden with Cancale Oysters, Kidneys from Madame Hardy, little Pâtés *au jus* from M. Rouget; Sausages from M. Corps; some *Boudin noir* [black pudding] from M. Masson; Cutlets from M. de Lanney; a Ham Pâté from M. Le Blanc; a Bayonne Ham from M. de Rouille; excellent Burgundy Wines from MM. Joyet and Vilcoq of Autun; superior Liqueurs from MM. Noël Lasserre and Le Moine of Paris, from Marie-Brizard and Roger of Bordeaux, and from M. Bouscarat of Clermont-Ferrand, etc., etc., etc.

The Gourmand is depicted eating Oysters, the obligatory prelude to all *Déjeûners à la fourchette* [Fork-breakfasts].

The Tasting Jury's regular Cat—posted near the door of the stove placed beneath the table to facilitate the Gourmand's digestion—is the latter's faithful companion, and looks at him, as well as at the meal, with a mix of tenderness and appetite.

A megaphone device placed at the Gourmand's right allows him to communicate with his kitchen, and convey his orders without resorting to intermediaries.

All these things, rendered with such wit and grace in the drawing by M. Ch. F., certainly deserved better engraving. How unfortunate that M. Mariage contributed only his name to this Plate, and left the job to the least worthy of his pupils.

At the bottom of the Print the legend reads: *Dinner's most mortal enemy*.

Notes

1. Virgil, *Georgics*, ii. 461: "His lordship's palace view, whose portals proud / Each morning vomit forth a cringing crowd"; trans. Joseph Warton.

Index

relinquishment, 26–27
response, 95
semi-general, 16
silent acceptance, 26
vague, 16
women, 188–189
written, 15–16, 69, 95
written answer, 69
Italy, 182, 265

J

Janin, Jules, 268
Jerrold, William Blanchard, 255–262
Johnson, Dr. Samuel, xxi, 63-64, 66, 246, 247
Journal des gourmands et des belles (Grimod de la Reynière), 2
Jury des Dégustateurs, *see* Tasting Jury

K

Kean, Charles, 261
Keats, John, xiii
Kilgour, Maggie, xv
"King's Kitchen" at Brighton Pavilion, xxx
King, William, 177, 181, 202n11
Kitchen, as "source of all the arts," xxiii
Kitchen measures, 64–65
Kitchiner, William, xxiii, xxxiii, 57–73
The Knife and Fork (The Alderman), 233, *234*, 235–242
Knives, xxxvii, 8–10, 259–260, 266, *see also* Cutlery
carving, 10, 41–42
table-setting, 10

L

La Varenne (François Pierre), 274n2
Lamb, Charles, xxii, xxxvi, 58, 81, 127–139
choosing friends for gastronomical acumen, 128
praise of pig, 127, 128, 129–134
pseudonymous identity, 81–82
trip to France, 127
Le Gacque, 110–111, 274
Legitimations, 82, 284, 287
Lerer, Seth, xxxix, xliin61, xliiin70
Linens, 77n36, 245, 265
Liqueurs, 107–108, 145, 187, 203n18, 258
Lister, Martin, 177
Literature
anthologistic, xxxix
antiquarian nature, xxxix, xxxvi
Chinese, 244

dining, 244
English gastronomical tradition, 58
generic fragmentation, xxxix
literary genre of gastronomy, xvii
literary hodgepodge, 175–176
philosophico-literary genre of writing, 58
picaresque, xxxix
poetry, 249
satiric, self-mocking style, xxxiv
writerly modes, xxxiii
London, xvii
architecture, 97
Lord Mayor's Day banquet, 84, 123n13, 233, 242
Louis XIV (King of France), 120, 267–268, 274n2
Louis XVI (King of France), 246, 272
Louis XVII (King of France), 272
Louis XVIII (King of France), xxviii, 143, 270–272
Luncheon clubs, xxvi

M

Macdonough, Giles, 4, 144
Macquin, Ange Denis, xix, 177
Manners, 52–53, 90–93
comic, 90–93
Man of Taste, xix
eighteenth-century, xx
modern, xxiv
nineteenth-century, xx
postrevolutionary, xxi
revitalized, xxi
Manuel des Amphitryons (The Host's Manual) (Grimod de la Reynière), 40–53
Mastication, xxiii, 11–12, 72–73, 113, 198
Matelotte, xxxvii, 173n8
May, Robert, 116
Meadows, Kenny, 233, 234
Meats, carving, *43–49*
importance, 40
principles, 40–50
Mennell, Stephen, xxxviii
Menus, xvii, xviii, xxix, 50–52, 55n37
Méot, M., 274
Methodists, grace at meals, 138–139
Military spirit, 119–120
Milton, John, xxxiv, xv, 58, 134, 136–137
quoted, 61, 62, 107, 108, 136–137
Missionary Society, 118
Mnemonics, 116–118
Moderation, xxi, xxxviii, 106

Made in the USA
Middletown, DE
20 July 2023

35474982R00190